W9-CRJ-192

THE ENCYCLOPEDIA OF
AMAZONS

THE ENCYCLOPEDIA OF

AMAZONS

Women Warriors from Antiquity to the Modern Era

JESSICA AMANDA SALMONSON

PARAGON HOUSE

NEW YORK

First edition, 1991

Published in the United States by

Paragon House
90 Fifth Avenue
New York, NY 10011

Copyright © 1991 by Jessica Amanda Salmonson

All rights reserved. No part of this book may be
reproduced, in any form, without written permission
from the publishers, unless by a reviewer who wishes
to quote brief passages.

Library of Congress Cataloging-in-Publication Data
Salmonson, Jessica Amanda.
The encyclopedia of Amazons : women warriors from antiquity to the
modern era / Jessica Amanda Salmonson. — 1st ed.
p.   cm.
Includes bibliographical references.
ISBN 1-55778-420-5 : $21.95
1. Women soldiers—Biography.   I. Title.
U51.S34   1991
355'.0082—dc20
[B]   90-46258
CIP

Manufactured in the United States of America

The paper used in this publication meets the minimum requirements of
American National Standard for Information Sciences—Permanence of Paper
for Printed Library Materials, ANSI Z39.48–1984.

3 3309 00220 1016

To Susan Lee Cohen
for aiding and abetting.

She climbs the mountains of the Moon
Hot on the trail of the milk-white boar.
The fields are laced with fallen spears
of gold-bright hoar.

MARGARET TOD RITTER,
describing Artemis

ACKNOWLEDGMENTS

❖❖❖❖❖❖❖❖❖❖❖❖❖

I have been assisted in large and small ways by so many individuals that I despair of remembering them all, and I apologize to any I might inadvertently slight. The following good people have provided material or solid clues to follow: Dr. Mary Jane Engh, Phyllis Ann Karr, Rosemary Pardoe, Valerie Eads of *Fighting Woman News*, Valerie A. Olson, Wendy Wees, Claudia Peck, Dr. Sydney Harth, Trina Robbins, Gordon Derry, Charles R. Saunders, Eileen Berkun, K. L. Cobbe, Lumchuan Salmonson, Elizabeth A. Lynn, Carolyn Clarke, Jan Sherrell Gephardt, Dr. Jane Yolen, Nina Romberg Anderson, C. J. Cherryh, Grania Davis, Elissa L. A. Hamilton, Gordon Linzner, Sandra Segal, Roger Daggs, Lillian Stewart Carl, Nikki Smith, Laurine White, Susan Wood, Milton Shiro Takei, Chris Minard Smith, Robbie Sturm, Andrea Schlect, Sherri File, Eileen Gunn, Warren G. Burrus, Sharon Frey, Dr. Doranne Jacobson of Columbia University, Dr. A. K. B. Pillai, Zacharias P. Thundy of North Michigan University, the University of Washington Suzallo Library, the Seattle Public Library, Elaine Katz, Joanna Russ, and Susan Ribner. Jules Faye aided in editing as well as offering insights and providing that scarcest commodity, emotional support.

I would be glad to hear from anyone who wishes to forward to me information overlooked in the present compilation.

Jessica Amanda Salmonson
P.O. Box 20610
Seattle, Washington 98102

INTRODUCTION

❖❖❖❖❖❖❖❖❖❖❖❖❖❖❖

The archetype of the Amazon has always been with us and appeals as easily to the dreams as to the dislikes of women, and to the desires as well as the fears of men. After I published my first book relating to the subject of Amazons in 1979 and edited a series of newsletters about women warriors, I received in excess of two thousand pieces of correspondence, chiefly but not exclusively from women. It was surprising to see just how many varied responses the world has to the subject.

One woman wrote with the assumption that I would like to start a dominatrix studio like her own, which catered to masochistic men and which, she assured me, was a highly lucrative business. She included several articles about her services published in underground magazines and offered to visit my city and help me get set up. I was amused that she never for a moment questioned whether or not this would interest me. By contrast, a young man wrote me about his all-Amazon set of war-game miniatures, and about the numerous imaginary battles he had won with them; but when he found another essay of mine, on the topic of gay rights, he wrote to me again, quoting the Bible and assuring me I would perish in flames. I was fascinated that here was someone who adored Amazons but who was totally closed minded about lesbians. In both cases, it was clear that the Amazon archetype meant something very narrow and specific to each individual, and it never occurred to either that it could mean something altogether different to someone else!

ix

Less extreme responses were nevertheless slanted to one or another assumption on the part of my correspondents, and also on the part of reviewers of my books. Young lesbians wrote to me, often from such sad and lonesome places as Arkansas or Oklahoma, to say my novels and anthologies about Amazons had given them new hope, or had changed their philosophy of life, or had given them goals and role models to strive toward. Heterosexual women wrote to me with equal passion about their relief in discovering evidence that they were not anomalies or psychopaths for their warrior dreams, and about their sense of disorientation when asked to relate to the usual romantic heroine encountered in the majority of books. Women wrote from prisons saying that their main crime was a failure to be weak and submissive in the face of judges who disapproved more of their manner than their breach of law. Women in the armed services let me know how the Amazon signified a proper and patriotic devotion to flag and country, whereas feminists and Marxists wrote with the opposite sentiment, that the Amazon represented rebellion against a sexist status quo. Contrary feminists maintained the Amazon was only a male masochist's daydream (and a few men wrote letters that lent a partial agreement with this sentiment). Disapproving "male feminists" wrote that the Amazon was nothing but reverse sexism, and one man published a "liberal" review of my work in which he compared the Amazons to Nazis.

The most coolheaded merely wanted to share clippings and articles about martial women. Students wrote begging for a bibliography in order to pursue their interest in ancient Amazons. In several cases, academicians and amateur scholars dashed off letters asking whether or not I already knew about this or that Amazon of one or another medieval or antique era. It was this latter type of correspondence that inspired ten issues of the woman warrior newsletter called *Naginata*, after the halberd used chiefly by Japanese women.

The Amazon archetype appears to be highly mutable, and easily interpreted according to the whims of subjective taste. The Amazon was an antisexual man hater, or she was an aggressive, demanding sex object. She served the system by emulating men, or she was a rebel expanding the meaning of femininity, a threat to patriarchy. She was a demeaning, impossible fabrication, or she was an uprising, revelatory reality. She was objectified as fearful and repellent, glamorous and appealing; a destructive and negative role model, or one that was ideal and suitable for all young girls. For many, the Amazon was a fascination, a fixation, a flirtation, to hate or to admire.

As I see it, there must be a reason why the typical textbook overlooks the woman warrior ninety-nine percent of the time, and creates instead a corrupt history, whether of samurai society or castle life in medieval Europe, that is grotesquely false in its portrait of absent or subservient women. This oversight indicates that the Amazon is indeed perceived as dangerous to the status quo, or her history would not be shunted aside so completely. But if even feminists are divided for and against her, it may well be that the Amazon thrives in a shadowy area that neither serves nor entirely destroys the patriarchal order. She exists apart from the conventionality of humdrum politics and theories. Whatever her meaning, purpose, or effect, the Amazon's history should be more easily accessible, whether theorists choose, according to their own prejudices and personalities, to use her as proof of women's infamy or valor and greatness.

The Encyclopedia of Amazons is arranged primarily by women's names and attempts to be exhaustive in the area of the Amazons of antiquity and swordswomen of recorded history. In order to convey historical continuity, I have added a broad sampling of twentieth-century combatants and armed revolutionaries. The Amazon of ancient and medieval times—whether warrior queen, castle defender or besieger, pirate, or street duelist—has been treated in greater depth than today's female soldier who fights with gun; to this extent, the encyclopedia favors the romance of the sword, the ax, and the bow over the romance of the firearm.

For the purposes of this encyclopedia, an Amazon is taken to mean a woman who is a duelist or soldier, by design or circumstance, whether chivalrous or cruel, and who engages others in direct combat, preferably with some semblance of skill and honorability. Excluded are many fascinating individuals who do not achieve the specific ideal of the swordswoman or Amazon; the adventures of undercover spies, assassins, modern frontline technicians, women forced only once into a single heroic act, famous criminals and murderesses, modern athletes, explorers, orators, big-game hunters, mothers saving their children from wild beasts (as a typical motif), and so on. These have all been deemed to fit into a category other than "Amazon" in the sense intended here. It may well be that the thousands of women who have worked under fire as nurses to save lives rather than take them are the braver Amazons, but heroic nurturing is beyond the scope of the present overview.

I have assumed that an Amazon is best exemplified by *the* Amazons of Greek mythology. She is martial by nature, skilled with weapons and/or hand-to-hand combat. Every century down to our own has produced more Amazons comparable to the ancient ideal than can be crowded into any single compilation, so the scope had to be whittled somewhat.

Perhaps more stringent definitions were used for inclusion than is altogether fair. Many of the greatest *male* generals of history have been old men who, from a safe distance, sent young men to die, and military historians rarely question the validity of these old men's soldierliness. Nonetheless, I have excluded women commanders who avoided direct engagement—such as President Lincoln's tactician Anna Ella Carroll—out of the sentiment that the Amazon must be skilled with weapons whether as a huntress, warrior, duelist, or signal athlete.

I have given special consideration to active defenders of castles. Many writers have addressed them as special cases, implying they weren't really in the thick of battle if they were behind walls, "merely" holding against siege. Actual siege conditions were otherwise, as women were not passively hoping the gates and the water supplies held out until siege forces got tired and went home. The noblewomen who captained, and the maids cum soldiers who fought along the battlements, took wounds or died while struggling to kill many of their foe. An active siege involved direct conflict, as the many examples throughout this encyclopedia definitively convey. Male generals have not been subject to a proviso that "*defense* doesn't count." It is, in fact, nobler and no less dangerous than offense, even if I must confess that I find the several instances of women setting out to *take* castles especially thrilling moments in history.

I have included War-goddesses selectively, to indicate the religious underpinnings that spawned actual and mythic Amazons. I have also included them out of the sentiment that many of these War-goddesses were deified mortals from prehistory. The combination of War-goddesses, "legendary" women of Amazonia, warring queens of ancient and medieval history, and modern-day guerrilla fighters reveals the historical continuity of fighting women, and lays bare the lie that such women were, or are, rare or nonexistent.

The present compilation touches only the peak of a buried mountain. Most heroines of a chivalrous or warlike nature have not been recorded and are lost to history. Others remain to be discovered in works so rare as to have gone unnoticed by the present writer. Time and again, I have seen finite lists of warring women that ended with the lament "and these appear to be all that ever were," though no two of these lists were exactly the same, and their compilers should have realized that the handful of popularly remembered examples indicated a much, much larger hidden history. It is important, therefore, to make it clear that although the present encyclopedia is many times the largest compilation on women warriors ever attempted, it is nonetheless random and incomplete, and, like the numerous short lists in a variety of texts, still indicates only a far larger subject awaiting investigation.

"Many heroes worthy of renown," said Horace, "have existed, acted, and been forgotten." More so the heroines. I have collected their histories for about fifteen years, and what I've come to realize is that there remains a great deal more to be uncovered.

A

❖❖❖❖❖❖❖❖❖❖❖❖❖

Aba: (fl. 55 B.C.) Warrior daughter of Xenophanes, Aba ruled from the city of Olbê in the country of Tencer, supported in her campaigns by **Cleopatra VII** and Marc Antony. She was eventually overthrown, but the country remained in the control of her descendants. [Strabo]

Abra: According to medieval Spanish romance, Abra was the warrior queen of Babylon. She was joined by Queen **Florelle** and fifty thousand female archers to fight the invading hero Lisuart of Greece. [Kleinbaum]

Acca: "She Who Is a Maker." Closest friend and companion-in-arms to **Camilla.** In Camilla's final battle, Acca held her as she died on the battlefield and heard her last words. She is named for the ancestral goddess of Akkad. [Virgil]

Achillia and **Amazon:** A relief in the British Museum, from Halicarnassus, portrays two women gladiators fighting, and, according to Michael Grant, "inscriptions from the same era record female combatants named Achillia and Amazon." See under **gladiatorial women.**

Ada: A warrior-queen and sister of **Artemisia.** In 344 B.C. she was helped by Alexander to regain her throne from a usurping brother. She personally handled the siege of the capital's acropolis, ultimately regaining the whole of her city, "the siege having become a matter of anger and personal enmity." [Strabo]

Adadimo: An officer of the **Dahomey Amazons** met by traveler John Duncanin in the 1850s. "In each of the last two annual military campaigns she had taken a male prisoner, and the king awarded her with promotions and two female slaves." She was tall, slim, pretty, quiet, unassuming, and about twenty-two years old. [Loth]

Adea: See **Eurydice, Queen of Macedonia.**

Adelaide of Susa: (A.D. c. 931–999) Tenth-century Italian princess, Adelaide of Susa donned armor and fought in defense of the lands she was to inherit from her father, the Marquis Olderic of Turin and Susa. She married Otto of Savoy and was coruler during his life, and sole ruler as regent through her son when widowed. [Schmidt]

Adelita: Celebrated in Zapata's revolutionary song "Adelita," she was not merely a songwriter's romance, but an actual fighter in the revolutionary forces circa 1900. She was a "guacha," typical of the armed women in Zapata's (and, ten years later, Poncho Villa's) peasant armies, also called "soldaderas." At first, these women provided the water, fuel, and clothing for the men, some traveling alongside the men, others staying to the rear as camp followers, depending on rank. They formed their own internal organization, carried rifles and pistols, and very soon evolved into "warriors as fierce as the men."

Admete: "Untamed." In a battle with Heracles, Admete subdued the giant and indentured him into the service of **Hera,** the goddess who despised him. Robert Graves, however, thinks that this was a war of transformation, that Admete tried to defeat Heracles by taking the forms of a mare, the Hydra, a crab, a hind, and a cloud, but that finally he raped her. This seems less likely given that Heracles is afterward Admete's retainer and invaded Amazonia at her behest to obtain **Hippolyte's** girdle. The girdle was possibly a symbol of the priestess of **Tauropolos,** and Admete desired it for her own temple to Hera.

In an earlier battle against aborigines, Admete was driven out of Argos, and took refuge on the isle of Samos. Hera appeared to her in an epiphany and appointed her her priestess on the island. It may have been for this sanctuary that Admete sought the fabulous girdle as an important relic. She later spread the Argosian cult of Hera far and wide. [Kerényi]

Aëllo: "Whirlwind." An Amazon brave during the reign of **Hippolyte,** Aëllo was the first to attack Heracles, but because he had been awarded invulnerability from Olympus, her ax broke on his chest, and he cut her down.

Aëllopus: "Storm Foot," one of the **Harpies** battled by the Argonauts.

Aethelburg: British warrior-queen of Ine. She raised the stronghold of Taunton in A.D. 722. [Damico]

Aethelflaed: (A.D. 870–918) Having disliked her only experience of child-birth, Aethelflaed swore herself to chastity and took to the sword. She "retained a cordial friendship" with her husband, and they accompanied each other into battle until his death in 912. She continued on her own to assist Alfred the Great, whose eldest daughter she was, against the Danes.

Aethelflaed became the chief tactician of her time; she united fragmented Mercia and conquered Wales; she restored her nation's defenses against the Danes; and finally became de facto ruler of the Danes and Mercians. She fell in battle in June 918 at Tammorth in Statfordshire.

Her daughter, Aelfwyn, inherited the throne directly from her mother, but it was taken from her by force the following year by Aethelflaed's brother, who stepped in to become the "mightiest" English ruler of a land tamed and fortressed by a woman allowed by the historians only an occa-sional footnote. Had Aethelflaed not been the daughter of Alfred the Great, *we might not have any knowledge whatsoever* of the greatest military commander in medieval England! [Geis, Macksey, Hale]

Afra' Bint Ghifar al-Humayriah: An Arabian woman warrior who in the seventh century A.D. assisted **Khawlah** in the famous "tent-pole battle," which consisted of women fighting their Greek captors armed only with tent poles. [Miles]

Agave: "High born," a **Maenad** named for a Sea-goddess. At the height of revelry, Agave wrenched off the head of her grown son, Pentheus, thinking she was wrestling a lion. She strutted afterward, with the head held aloft, "in a victory of tears." She was said also to have slain her husband during another bacchanalia. Agave was also a Moon-goddess, presiding over the beer revelries predating the Dionysus wine cult.

In Euripides' *Bacchae,* Agave calls the *thyrsus* (Maenad staff tipped with a pine cone) both a "mystic wand" and a "weapon." Her captains were her sisters **Ino** and **Autonoë.** The soldiers who sought the Maenads fled them in terror, informing King Pentheus, "We by flight hardly escaped tearing to pieces at their hands," and described how the women ripped even fierce young bulls apart with the strength of "their knifeless fingers." Pentheus was killed for attempting to spy on the Maenads in transvestite disguise. He was fallen upon "by the mystic huntresses and torn to pieces, his mother being the first to begin the sacred slaughter."

The idea that the Maenads were "mad" and thought they were killing a lion seems to be a later rationalism or, conversely, the Maenads' own religious affectation. The lion was associated with the Great Goddess, and was considered as suitable a sacrifice as a bull or man. Pentheus was the declared foe of the Maenad cult, thus the calculatedly chosen victim. [Tyrell, Graves]

Agnes de Chastillon: Dark Agnes was created by Robert E. Howard in his two historical tales "Sword Woman" and "Blades for France," published posthumously as *Sword Woman* (1977) but written in the 1930s. Her great speech, leveled against a man who insulted her, was:

> Ever the man in men! Let a woman know her place: let her milk and spin and sew and bake and bear children, not look beyond her threshold or the command of her lord and master! Bah! I spit on you all! There is no man alive who can face me with weapons and live, and before I die, I'll prove it to the world. Women! Cows! Slaves! Whimpering, cringing serfs, crouching to blows, avenging themselves by—taking their own lives, as my sister urged me to do. Ha! You deny me a place among men? By God, I'll live as I please and die as God wills, but if I'm not fit to be a man's comrade, at least I'll be no man's mistress. So go ye to hell, and may the devil tear your heart!

Agostina: See Augustina, the Maid of Saragossa.

Agrath: "Beating." Also called Agrat bat Mahlat. She and her mother Queen **Makhlath** were rivals of Queen **Lilith** for rule of the night. All three are dark avatars of **Ishtar** or **Astarte.** Agrath commands hosts of evil spirits and demons and rides a war chariot. [Rappaport]

Agrippina the Elder: (d. A.D. 33) Granddaughter of Augustus and mother of Caligula. In youth, she accompanied Germanicus into the Syrian war and gave birth to a daughter "amidst the excitement of war, in a Roman camp, on the shores of the Rhine." Horace has only praise for her: "You shall be described as a brave subduer of your enemies, on ship board and on horseback." [Hale]

Agrippina the Younger: (d. A.D. 60) Daughter of Agrippina and Germanicus. She was born in a Roman camp on the shores of the Rhine. As empress and wife of Claudius, she sat at the head of the Roman legions, though not all wives of Caesars were so public in their command. When

Celtic captives were brought to Rome to give obeisance to the emperor, the defeated warriors of Britain (both male and female) automatically assumed Agrippina was the martial head of state and, ignoring the emperor, placed themselves directly in front of her throne. In their own land, **Cartimandua** was the warrior-queen.

Agrippina had sought to "rule the world," first through her husband Claudius, then through her son Nero. Therefore, in A.D. 59, Nero had her killed, not, however, before she had an opportunity to write her autobiography. [Assa, King]

Agrotera: Goddess of battle, an avatar of non-Olympian **Artemis.** She received sacrifices from the Spartans before the beginning of new campaigns.

Ahilyabai Holkar: (d. A.D. 1795) A fighting queen of Maratha in Indore State of India. [Rothery]

Ahotep: (fl. 1790 B.C.) Queen-regent of Egypt in the 17th Dynasty, ruling in behalf of her young son Kamose until his majority. After her husband fell in war, she continued the struggle against the Hyksos, occupational rulers from Palestine. An 18th Dynasty inscription says of her: "She assembled her fugitives. She brought together her deserters. She pacified her Upper Egyptians. She subdued her rebels." Ahotep and other famous Egyptian women, including **Cleopatra VII,** were descendants of the royal houses of Kush, and thus are part of the history of powerful black women. [Sertima]

Aife: Pronounced "EE-fah." Queen of Alba, today Scotland, said to be the most famous woman warrior of the Celtic heroic age, although **Mebd** of Ireland was her contemporary and is better remembered today. Aife led a troop of women warriors and was often in conflict with her sister, **Scáthach** of Skye, for they ran rival military academies. Cû Chulainn, the Celtic national hero, gained his military expertise from Aife and Scáthach.

There remain a few historians who habitually deny the likelihood of such women having existed outside of epics and fairy tales, though it requires lead-lined blinders to hold to such a belief in light of the evidence. There were fighting women among the Christian Celts as well as among the pagans, warring beside men with "as much gusto as any of the clansmen," according to Douglas Hyde. The first effort to exempt women from military service was in A.D. 590, through the influence of Columicille at the synod of Druim Ceat. The law proved useless. Women continued to fight when it served their purposes and that of their clans, for they had many rights over their personal property, including the right to defend it. A century later,

Adamnam, who thought little of women, tried to enforce the law passed by the synod of Druim Ceat, perhaps with slightly greater success. [Chadwick, Goodrich]

Ainia: "Swiftness," an Amazon portrayed in a terra-cotta **Amazonomachy** as an enemy of Achilles, therefore a companion to **Penthesilea.** No literary source identifies her further. [Bothmer]

Ainippe: "Swift mare," an Amazon brave. She participated in the battle to avenge **Hippolyte's** murder, defeating Heracles' generals along the beach. She, or another Ainippe, also engaged Telamon in single combat during Heracles' war against **Andromache.** [Sobol, Bothmer]

Alcibie: One of **Penthesilea's** companions during the liberation of Troy. [Sobol]

Alcinoë: "Mighty Wisdom." One of **Andromache's** braves in the war against Heracles and Telamon. [Bothmer]

Alcippe: "Powerful Mare," an Amazon brave who lived during the reign of **Hippolyte.** She perished with others in the suicide-challenges against Heracles. [Sobol]

Alcithoë: "Impetuous Might," a **Maenad.** See **Leucippe.**

Alecto: "The Unresting," one of the **Furies.** In the *Anaeid*, **Hera** summoned Alecto and had her unleash war in Italy. See **Tisiphone.**

Aleksandrovna, Major Tamara: Commanded a Russian all-female airborne regiment on more than four thousand sorties and 125 combats, destroying thirty-eight enemy aircraft in World War II.

There were many similar heroines of World War II: Captain Budanova, air ace, downed eight aircraft in combat flights; Nancy Wake, a New Zealander, led combat raids into France in 1944; and Ludmilla Pavlichenko, a sniper, was credited with killing 309 Germans. [Macksey]

Alfhild: Daughter of Siward, king of the Goths. Alfhild dressed in male attire and went on viking raids against several nations' coasts, accompanied by her shieldmaiden **Groa.** With a band of like-willed women, Alfhild became a notorious "rover captain" and "performed deeds beyond the valor of women." [Saxo]

Alkaia: "Mighty One." Judging by her placement in certain **Amazonomachies** on black-figure vases, she was one of **Andromache's** most important generals in the war against Heracles and Telamon. In one portrait, she wears a highly unusual cap with bull's ears and tail attached. The white bull was one of the emblems of the Mother-goddess, but this unusual cap appears nowhere else in mythology or art. Alkaia may have been a Thracian bull dancer who immigrated to Amazonia with her *torera's* prizes made into a hat.

Allen, Alma: A Danish Resistance fighter in the early 1940s. She personally led men and women on a dozen missions against the Nazis, surviving many German traps. She joined British intelligence at war's end. Another Dane, Ruth Weber, was a machine gunner on a merchant vessel that ran the Nazi blockade. [Truby]

Allen, Eliza: In 1851, she self-published a remarkable memoir, *The Female Volunteer; Or the Life, and Wonderful Adventures of Miss Eliza Allen, A Young Lady of Eastport, Maine.* Such books were a veritable genre of the time. Born in Eastport in January 1826, she was refused permission as a teenager to marry a young man with whom she was in love. Her response was to disguise herself as a man and set off to wild adventures, including fighting and taking wounds in the war against Mexico. It was typical of young men of that era, upon experiencing some disappointment, to set off to the wars in Mexico and South America. Eliza Allen's memoir, which she called "An Authentic and Thrilling Narrative," shows that some women pursued the same route!

Alrude, Countess of Bertinoro: When Aucona was held siege by imperial troops in 1172, the Italian countess led an army to deliver the city. Her terrified foe was instantly broken and scattered. On her return route, she engaged the fragmented enemy at several points, defeating the ambushers each time. [Hale]

Alwilda: A medieval Swedish captain of a pirate vessel that terrorized ships in the Baltic Sea. [Truby]

Amage: Ruling as regent to a dissolute husband, this Sarmatian queen determined causes, stationed garrisons, and repulsed invaders. She sent a letter to a Scythian prince warning him against further incursions into one of her protectorates. He contemptuously continued his policies. Amage then rode with only 120 well-chosen men to Scythia, attacking the prince's guard and slaying them. Rushing into the palace, Amage engaged her foe and slew him while her soldiers killed his friends and family, saving only the life of his son, whom Amage allowed to rule in obeisance to her edicts. [Polyaenus]

Amastris: (fl. 299 B.C.) Warrior-wife of Dionysius the tyrant of Heracleia. She forged a new city-state, named for herself, by conquering four settlements. One of these forcibly united settlements later revolted and regained independence, but the other three remained under Queen Amastris.

There was also an Amestris, Queen of Persia, wife of Xerxes. Little survives of her history except for a cruel episode in which she mistreated the mother of Artiante, her husband's mistress, by cutting off her nose, ears, lips, breast, tongue, and eyebrows. [Strabo]

Amazonaeum: A temple in Athens commemorating the treaties between Theseus and the Amazons. Although the Attic War battle is generally given as Theseus' victory, the full story suggests that the death of **Antiope** (in some versions, **Hippolyte**) is what ended four months of battles. She had been queen of the Amazons before Theseus attacked their capital, but in Athens she became the mother of Theseus' son; therefore, she might be considered all but neutral, or at least severely torn, as regarded the battle. Her death ended both the Amazon invasion and the need for Theseus' defense. In shared grief, the treaties were signed and the Amazons returned to their capital with a bittersweet sense of vengeance achieved (see **Orithia**). In other versions, Antiope effects a mutual treaty, which the Amazonaeum commemorated, and she was only much later betrayed by Theseus and slain fighting for her position in Athens.

Amazonia: The Bronze Age nation of the Amazons situated on a plain by the River **Thermodon** and founded by **Lysippe. Themiscrya** was its capital, and served as the Amazons' Rome during the age of expansion and conquest. Their nation is sometimes called Amazones or Amazonides. The best evidence places Amazonia in an area of Anatolia on the Black Sea, with influences in Sarmatia (the Russian steppes) and the Tauric Mountains. This "nation" very likely existed as a city-state or a series of religiously fanatic ashrams. The best evidence suggests an area of special Amazon dominion to be a port in northern Anatolia, from whence the cult spread throughout the world, leaving its stamp everywhere from China to Africa to Scandinavia.

Amazonium: Cities founded by the Amazons on the Island of Patmos, and in Pontus bore this name. A very high number of ancient cities of Europe, Asia Minor, and the isles of the Aegean Sea claimed to have been founded, in their own antiquity, by the Amazons. Smyrna was the longest surviving of such cities, Ephesus among the most influential. Many cities stamped coins in honor of their foundresses, and honored the women in temples, showing that the historicity of the Amazons was taken for granted in virtually all regions. Cities continued to be founded by women even after the collapse of **Amazonia** (for examples, see **Messene, Amastris,** and **Dido**).

The Amazon of Letters: Remy de Gourmont's name for the American expatriot poet and lesbian socialite Natalie Barney (1876–1972). "A horse riding enthusiast, Barney was agile and graceful." Radclyffe Hall's *The Well of Loneliness* fictionalizes her as Valérie Seymore. [Wickes, Jay]

Amazonomachies: In art, representations of battles between Greeks and Amazons. By extension, portrayals of any war between the sexes. A few Amazonomachies portray scenes of "everyday life," such as preparing arms, setting out for battle, returning with the dead, leading horses, riding, dismounting, harnessing chariots, driving chariots, resting, and exercising. As inscriptions are common, the names of many Amazons who would otherwise be unknown to us are preserved on them. [Bothmer, La Rocca]

Amazons: In generalized terms, an Amazon is any physically and/or intellectually powerful or superior woman, or, more specifically, any woman skilled at battle. In Greek mythology, the Amazons were exceedingly warlike and worshipped the Moon-goddess and Earth-mother in their most violent aspects (see, for example, **Tauropolos**). Several Greek myths deal with encounters between Grecian warriors and the Amazons, with the apparent intent of glorifying bittersweet male victories over brave, noble, beautiful, but squashed females. The symbolic power of these stories has never been adequately interpreted, as one would think the ability of invulnerable supermen like Achilles or immortals like Heracles to kill and mutilate mortal female cult warriors would be poor evidence of valor. However, the ancient world still lived in the emotional and cultural shadow of a far earlier age of government structures approaching **matriarchy,** so that the actual ramification and impact of stories of Amazon defeat was that these myths upheld the propriety of patriarchal ascendancy.

The greater body of Amazon tales do *not* regard Greek victories, as in the case of those tales that recount wars between factions of **Gorgons;** the founding of **Amazonia** by the lawgiver **Lysippe;** the slaying of the king of Troy by **Egee;** the numerous conquests of **Marpesia** among the **Thermodontines;** tales of the sister-conquistadoras **Myrene** and **Mitylenê** among the Gorgons; and the founding of innumerable cities, such as **Clete's** Italian colony. Many superficial texts are even today fond of repeating the false statement that all Amazon myths are about Greek victories, for today only the tales of **Hippolyte's** stolen girdle, the kidnapping of **Antiope,** and the death of **Penthesilea** are popularly retold. Yet the great majority of Amazon tales regard the successes of their champions, and the expansion of Amazon influence generally. After a period of no less than three hundred years, the empire began decay, and only then were Greek incursions effective.

The Greeks were keenly aware of several Amazon cult centers, notably in North Africa and the Mideast. Awareness of these women was by no means limited to the Greeks, as they earlier influenced the Hittites; the *hieroduli* were notoriously warlike priestesses among them. Graves of priestesses in Sarmatian cemeteries have been found to include their armor and weapons, marked, quite uniquely, with even more ancient symbols of the Scythians, indicating the far greater antiquity of their warring faith. In Indic myths, they were called rhackshasis, ruled by the Rani **Paraminta,** worshipping the warlike Moon-goddess **Uma.** Chinese myth tells of "the Woman's Kingdom," their rich and unapproachable capital existing near a distant sea, possibly referring to the same Themiscrya in Amazonia, located on the Euxine. The **Valkyries** represent the northern branch of the cult.

Africa, Europe, and Asia were each aware of the Amazons. There is good reason to suppose their cult did actually exist, and that a rough outline of their history may be deduced from various surviving mythological tales. See also **Andromache, Hippo, Melanippe, Orithia,** and **Otrera.**

Ambika: The most violent aspect of **Parvati,** All-mother of India worshipped since the Neolithic period. Ambika slew the buffalo demon Mahishasura. Her worship survives in the form of **Durga.** The *Devi-Mahatmyam* says of her: "The sighs of Ambika, breathed in battle, become at once her battalions." Her sighs killed "with axes, javelins, swords and halberds."

Ambree, Mary: The Spanish captured Ghent in 1584. Dutch and English volunteers set out to liberate the city, among them a captain named Mary Ambree, who gave rise to one of Ben Jonson's favorite ballads of the English Renaissance, which goes in part:

> Then Captain Courageous, whom death could not daunt,
> Had roundly besiegéd the city of Gaunt,
> And manly they marched by two and by three,
> And foremost in battle was Mary Ambree.

Then brave Sergeant Major was slain in the fight,
Who was her own true love, her joy and delight,
She swore unrevenged his blood should not be;
Was not this a brave bonny lass, Mary Ambree?

Then took she her sword and her target in hand,
And called all those that would be of her band,
To wait on her person there came thousands three;
Was not this a brave bonny lass, Mary Ambree?

The drums and the trumpets did sound out alarm,
And many a hundred did lose leg and arm,
And many a thousand she brought to their knee;
Was not this a brave bonny lass, Mary Ambree?

In this woman's praises I'll here end my song,
Whose heart was approved in valor most strong;
Let all sorts of people, whatever they be,
Sing forth the brave valors of Mary Ambree.

P. C. Wren, author of *Beau Geste,* wrote *Sowing Glory* in 1931, regarding a woman French Legionnaire. Her identity was protected under the name of Mary Ambree, but Wren swore she was based on an actual woman.

Améliane du Puget: *née* de Glandèves. In 1524, the Constable de Bourbon warred with his king and held Marseilles siege. When the battle was its roughest, a reinforcement arrived: a troop of women led by the governor's daughter, Améliane. She and her force drove the assailants back. When the enemy laid mines, these women laid countermines, "digging a trench that was long known as the Tranchée des Dames," and in modern days became the Boulevard des Dames. Améliane later married Guillaume du Puget, who added her name to his, becoming Puget-Glaudèves. [Gribble]

Amina or **Aminatu:** (fl. sixteenth century A.D.) Warrior-queen of the Songhai in mid-Niger who ruled the whole of the Hausa empire of west and central Africa. She ruled in succession to her mother, being the eldest daughter of Queen **Turunku.** She ruled without interruption from about 1536 to 1573, expanding her nation's boundaries to the Atlantic coast, founding cities, receiving tributes, and spreading cola nut cultivation. The ruins of some of her fortifications still stand today. She personally led her army of twenty thousand soldiers, annexed surrounding states, and established long-lasting trade routes into North Africa. Her capital was in Zazzau, later renamed Zaire after her youngest daughter. In Lagos, Nigeria, on the grounds of the National Theater, is an equestrian statue of Queen Amina with sword in hand. A Nigerian creation myth tells how the world began when a woman set forth to found a nation. Queen Amina seems to have taken the story to heart. [Miles, Loth, Qunta]

Amphitrite: Queen of the sea in Greek myth. She was armed, like her husband Poseidon, with a three-tined fork. She turned **Scylla** into the famed sea monster. See **Eurynome.**

Amynomene: "Blameless Defender." Amazon brave in the Attic War led by **Orithia.**

Ana: See **Anan.**

Anaea: According to Ephoros, Anaea was a conqueror among the **Thermodontine** Amazons. She founded a city named for herself. Her tomb in the city of Anaea was opposite that of Samos and was a site of pilgrimage even into the classical Greek age. Similar Amazon tombs were recorded for **Orithia** in Megara, **Myrene** near Troy, and **Antiope** in Athens. [Bennett, Bothmer]

Anahita: A Zoroastrian goddess of war and agriculture, worshipped in ancient Iran. She wore otter skins and gold. Her full name, Aredvi Sura Anahita, translates "water-born powerful virgin." A religious text calls her "Goddess of sacred water, dwelling in the sky. She advances in a four-horse chariot, crushing demons and tyrants. All the gods invoke her." [Kramer]

Anan or **Ana:** Sometimes given in lieu of **Nemain,** as one-third of the Great Queen **Morrigane's** warring trinity, the other two-thirds being **Bodb** and **Macha.** A number of Celtic **hags** are related to Anan, such as Black Annis of Leicester, who devoured children, but who becomes a beautiful nymph in the pagan Easter and hare hunt. She was originally Danu, the great Mother-goddess of the Celts.

Anas: The name of St. Anne, mother of the **Virgin Mary,** when transformed into a heavenly angel. A twelfth-century manuscript in the British Museum tells that Anas and her consort Sahail came to Earth to war against twelve demonesses of fever, on behalf of humanity.

Anath: "To Answer," or perhaps "To Rape." When her twin brother Baal was slain by Mot, Anath set out to revenge him; she seized Mot and "with sword cleaved him, with fan winnowed him, with fire burned him, with millstone ground him, and in the field planted him," suggesting a regicidal fertility rite. Anath and Baal lend better understanding regarding the nature of pre-Classical **Artemis** and Apollo.

Anath was the Canaanite virgin of the hunt and battle. According to one story, she returned from the hunt and while the scent of game was still fresh upon her doorstep, her palace was surrounded by troops.

> And lo Anath fights valiantly
> She slays the sons of two cities
> She fights the people of the seashore
> Annihilates mankind of the sunrise.

She exulted as her foes' heads and hands were lopped off by her sword and flung into the air. This indicates an affinity for **Kali,** with her girdle of human hands and necklace of heads. A similar War-goddess, **Qedeshet,** is known from Syrian seal cylinders. Anath "plunged knee-deep in blood, neck-high in gore," fought also with club and bow. At the end of the skirmish, she was not yet sated, and pursued the soldiers of the two kings into the palace where they had taken refuge and tried to keep her out.

> Much she battles, and looks;
>   Much she slays, and views.
> Her heart is filled with joy
>   For in the hand of Anath is victory.

She afterward washed her hands in the blood of dead soldiers. In the wake of her violent deeds came her blessings for the fertility of the land and of humanity, for in the typical manner, the War-goddess is also a Fertility-goddess. [Kramer, Friedrich]

Anaxilea: Amazon brave. Her shield's insignia was a white bird. Her name suggests royalty. [Bothmer]

Andate: British Victory-goddess, Adraste to the Iceni, Ardarta to the Gauls. **Boudicca** prayed to her on the eve of her revolt against Rome, saying, "I address thee as a woman speaking to a woman." [Fraser]

Androdameia: "Subduer of Men." Amazon brave in the Attic War.

Andromache: "Man Fighter." Queen of the Amazons. In the earliest preserved depiction of Heracles' war against the Amazons, **Hippolyte** and her girdle are not included and the Amazon Heracles meets in single combat is Andromache (not Hector's widow of the same name). The evidence is in the form of vase paintings and other **Amazonomachies;** there is no surviving written tradition to explain this episode further, though many conclusions may be drawn from the preserved portraits.

Andromache could well have been a **Gorgon** of Ethiopia, but other pictorial evidence places her among the **Thermodontines.** The two traditions of Amazons—of Africa and of Asia Minor—may have been linked through Andromache's rule.

A recurrent episode shows Heracles pulling off Andromache's helmet, revealing her long, flowing hair (whereas other Amazons bind their hair back with cords), implying an attitude similar to that of Achilles, who felt that **Penthesilea** could have been a lover. Her hair is a very striking feature in another Amazonomachy, where she fights without shield or helmet— proof of mightiness—her hair flowing about her. She holds a Greek by his hair and stabs him in the throat with her spear.

Andromache is also encountered as a minor figure in the Attic War, entering into single combat with Perithous. [Tyrrell, Bothmer]

Andromeda: "Ruler of Men." One of **Andromache's** braves in the battle against Heracles and Telamon, not to be confused with the famous Ethiopian princess molested by the Krakon. [Bothmer]

Androphonos: "Slayer of Men." A black **Aphrodite** of Greek myth. She castrated and eviscerated her lovers. Perhaps a remembrance of the **Gorgon** conquistodoras of North Africa, who may have been Meroitic.

Angela: *The Faerie Queene* calls her "no whit lesse faire, then terrible in fight," dreaded more than any other Saxon warrior. She was the Saxon queen and in battle defeated Ulfin, a knight of the Round Table. She wielded a magic spear and provided **Britomart** her armor. Spenser implies that England took its name from her.

Anna Perenna: Sister of **Dido,** deified by the Romans as goddess of the first moon of the year. She accompanied her sister into exile, helped establish the new city of Carthage, and fought against the armies of their ungallant brother. She ruled Carthage after her sister's death. [Hale]

Anne, Queen of England: (A.D. 1665–1714) In her youth, Queen Anne was an accomplished huntress with hound and falcon, and an exemplary equestrian. Jonathan Swift described her on a typical hunt, clad in dark robe and hood, "furious like Jebu, mighty as Nimrod." On her state visit to Bath, she was surrounded by an honor guard of women archers attired as

Amazons. In her later years, she had gained too much weight to remain athletic, but still delighted in the warrior image, riding in a sizable chariot. [Fraser]

Antandre: "Preceding Men." One of **Penthesilea's** elite corps of Amazons who fought for Troy.

Antianara: Queen of the Amazons of the **Thermodon** in their Decadent Era, sometime after **Penthesilea** fell at Troy and before Alexander the Great met **Thalestris.** According to the twelfth-century scholar Eustathius, the Amazons continued to cripple their male children even into this period of isolation, peace, and decadence, but no longer to domesticate them more easily. Rather, they believed strength denied an arm or a leg would be transferred to the penis. When reproached by a Scythian prince for her slaves' limping gait, Queen Antianara explained, "The lame are superior in the art of love."

Antianeira: Amazon brave in the Attic War. She dueled Theseus in single combat. Her name is also a Homeric adjective for Amazons. [Bothmer]

Antibrote: One of **Penthesilea's** twelve companions who helped her temporarily liberate Troy.

Antimache: "Confronting Warrior." A foe of Heracles in a lost epic set in the time of the rule of Queen **Andromache.** [Bothmer]

Antimachos: Amazon brave in the Attic War led by **Orithia.** [Bothmer]

Antiope: "Confronting Moon." Queen of the Amazons when Theseus attacked their nation. After valorous efforts, she was defeated, resulting in an alliance by marriage. According to this version, she is the mother of Theseus' son Hippolytus, named for another Amazon queen, **Hippolyte.** Hippolytus followed his mother's rather than his father's religion (a remarkable and crucial point in understanding Antiope's authority in Athens), and he ultimately died for his vows to **Artemis.**

By some tellings, Antiope survived the battle between the Amazons and the Atheneans only to be betrayed by Theseus, who required a new marriage alliance elsewhere. Antiope in full armor interrupted the wedding, together with the Amazon retainers she had with her even before the Attic War. With her two-headed ax drawn, she strove to massacre Theseus' guests for his infidelity. It took the combined effort of Theseus and his companions, including invincible Heracles, to slay her. See also the **Amazonaeum** and **Molpadia.** [Graves]

Antiope, Queen of Thebes: In a war waged against her by King Lycus and Antiope's aunt, Queen **Dirce,** she was at last defeated and imprisoned. Her twin sons by Zeus (i.e., conceived in an orgiastic fertility rite) rushed to her defense, killing Lycus and dragging Dirce to death, by her hair, behind a bull. [Graves]

Antiopeia: Archer in the Attic War led by **Orithia.** [Bothmer]

Antonini, Louise: A privateer on the high seas during the French Revolution. [Croix]

Anukis: Egyptian Cataract-goddess of the Lower Nile. She was called "the Embracer," for she embraced either as a suckler of pharaohs or as their strangler. [Hart]

Apa-kura: A warrior-queen of Mauri legend, whose symbol was a spider's web. A warrior chant has Apa-kura singing:

> My arms and hands and feet
> Shall wage a lasting war.

In another Mauri legend, a female chief dons a dogskin cloak—symbol of war—and sets out to avenge a tribal insult. Mauri myth, and myths throughout Polynesia, include Death-goddesses, War-goddesses, and Earth-goddesses indistinguishable from such Mediterranean goddesses as **Hecate** and **Cybele.**

Aphrodite: "Foam-born." Virtually every goddess of antiquity had a warlike nature at times, and the goddess of love was no exception, there being localized worship of Warrior Aphrodite in Sparta and Corinth. As Aphrodite Urania, she destroyed the sacred king annually by mating with him and tearing out his organs; she was worshipped in this form especially in Laconia at Sparta. As the daughter and/or consort of the war god Ares, she was called Wolfish Aphrodite and wore a **Gorgon** mask during cattle sacrifices. She was Aphrodite Victorious in times of conflict. At the battle of Troy, she was wounded by Diomedes. She approved the **Maenads'** slaughter of Orpheus and his followers when no other deity would do so. As Venus Apatura, she demanded human sacrifice. Myrto is one of her warlike aspects, a destroying Sea-goddess. When Aphrodite fell in love with Adonis, she became goddess of the hunt in order to stay with him even during the chase, and her relationship with him parallels that of Attis and warlike **Cybele.** See **Harmonia.** [Friedrich, Graves]

Apollonia: An alternative name for the huntress **Cyrene,** consort of Apollo. Many cities of the ancient world were named for her, under both her names. The matrilinear Milesians, for example, founded a city named for Apollonia in Thrace on the shores of the Euxine, an area notorious for Amazon activity.

Arachidamia: Spartan princess and captain of women soldiers who fought against Pyrrhus' siege of Lacedemon in the third century B.C.

Araphenia: In Charlotte Perkins Gilman's unpublished "A Fairy Tale," the Amazon fairy **Emandine** appoints Princess Araphenia commander of the troops. The princess led the troops into war, restoring her father's kingdom. The manuscript is housed at the Arthur and Elizabeth Schlesinger Library.

Areia: A nymph of the War-goddess **Artemis.** Her name means "warlike." Such nymphs echo a remembrance of warring queens and violent moon cultists.

Arethusa: "The Waterer," an agricultural/fertility reference. As described by Ovid, Arethusa was a huntress and swift runner of Sicily who followed the tenants of **Artemis.** Artemis transformed her into a river to escape a god's attempted rape.

Areto: "Unspeakable." One of the Amazon braves who followed **Pantariste** onto the beach to slay soldiers and captains during Heracles' attack on the Amazons' capital. Her shield's emblem was the white snake, symbolic of the Mother-goddess. The contest on the beach was won by the Amazons, amidst much blood and death, but it was Heracles who decided the day elsewhere in the capital. Donald Sobol has this battle take place concurrent with the larger battle elsewhere in **Themiscrya,** when **Antiope** is taken hostage. The evidence of **Amazonomachies** places Areto, Pantariste, and others of Sobol's reconstruction in a separate war of Telamon and Heracles against Queen **Andromache.** [Sobol, Bothmer]

Areximacha: A Phrygian Amazon brave who fought for Queen **Andromache** in the war waged by Heracles and Telamon. [Bothmer]

Argante: In *The Faerie Queene,* Argante is the daughter of the Titans, and a female rapist, of a kind exemplified by **Eos** of Greek mythology.

Argea: "Bright One," a moon reference. Daughter of King Adrastus of Argos. Hers is among the most beautiful, grotesque, and tragic of all heroic tales. Word came to her that her husband had fallen in battle and that King Creon had decreed the corpses of his enemies would be left to rot all in a heap, under penalty of death to whoever disobeyed. Argea clad herself for battle and, engaging ambushes along the way, reached the field of dead after a long journey. She searched all day among the putrescent corpses and, at night, continued by the light of a flickering torch to seek her beloved. At last, she recognized him, though his armor was corroded and his face half eaten away and filled with pus. "Neither the infection of his body nor the filth covering his face could keep her from kissing his mouth and embracing him tightly." She built a pyre and afterward placed his ashes in a golden vessel. And last of all, with her small band of valorous and heartstricken soldiers, she attacked the citadel of King Creon with such vengeful and suicidal ferocity that his city was taken and all within put to death. [Pizan]

Aristoclea of Larisa: Daughter of Megacles, victrix of a two-horse chariot race in the early second century B.C. [Lefkowitz]

Aristomache: "Best of Warriors." Amazon brave who fought Mounichos in the Attic War. [Bothmer]

Armida: A magician-queen in Tasso's *Jerusalem Delivered,* whom Tasso shows us on the battlefields, piloting a war chariot, firing arrows, and commanding knights.

Arno, Madame: An artist who, in 1915, organized a Parisian regiment of women to fight Germans.

Arrhippe: "Best of Mares." A huntress and chaste attendant of **Artemis** who was raped by Tmolus, husband of Queen **Omphale.** Arrhippe invoked Artemis as she hung herself from a beam in the goddess's sanctuary. Artemis sent a bull that ripped into Tmolus, throwing him into the air. He came down on sharp stakes, where he died in agony.

Arsinoë: Sister of the last **Cleopatra,** and much hated by her. Arsinoë plotted wars of self-defense, but Cleopatra's ally, Caesar, sent armies against her. She was captured and placed on public display in Rome, weighted down with chains. She was said to have been so beautiful and sad that the citizens of Rome were seized with regret that she had been defeated. [Mahaffy]

Arsinoë II Philadelphus: (d. c. 269 B.C.) Daughter of Ptolemy I and **Berenice I.** Arsinoë's name, traditional among Hellenic queens, means "The Male-Minded." She was a **Maenad,** like **Olympias** who married Philip II, and, also like Olympias, she was constantly plotting and battling her way to personal glory.

She had originally been given in marriage, at age eighteen, to the elderly

Lysimachus, for political purposes, and soon controlled his policy, and participated in sundry plots. Widowed, she garrisoned herself at Cassandreia, but in 280 B.C. was very quickly cornered into marrying Keraunos, King of Thrace, but he perfidiously killed her children as threats to his throne, and banished her to Samothrace. Keraunos subsequently fell in battle. Arsinoë founded a temple in Samothrace, later introducing her cult into Egypt. In 275 B.C., she was in Syria, and took the lead in battles her brother, Ptolemy II Philadelphus, was losing. She reversed his losses with her own decisive victories. She married her brother about 278 B.C. and was recognized thereafter as the real authority in Egypt. Ptolemy Philadelphus never carried that name in his life—only Arsinoë was called Philadelphus—but such was her influence that historians grafted her name onto his, and, unfortunately, grafted some of her successes onto his as well.

She soon wielded more power than any Ptolemy queen until the last **Cleopatra.** At Mendes and in Fayyum, where she kept a standing army, she was deified in her own lifetime. Temples were built in her honor in Thebes, and in Sais, where she was called Isis Arsinoë. Her temples were centers of agriculture, their only crop being grapes, and, as befits a Maenad, their only product was wine. Her income from temples' tithes, taxes, and wine manufacture was considerable.

She built dikes, extended canals and farmland, always spreading her rule outward from Fayyum. She came into conflict with priests who held sway before her deification, thus rode often at the head of her army to settle revolts. She founded numerous new cities including Konope, and cities named for herself in Aetolia, Crete, Cyrene, two in Cilicia, and two in Cyprus, besides those in Egypt.

Legends grew up around Arsinoë, including an interesting demise. Preferring battle to lovemaking, she rejected a suitor, who committed suicide as a result. **Aphrodite,** to punish her for her lack of a soft heart, turned her into stone. The legend may have concerned a lifelike statue of Arsinoë, for several were erected during and after her life. At Athens stood the statues of several Egyptian rulers, Arsinoë the only queen among them, and Pausaneas saw at Helicon a statue of her riding an ostrich, done in bronze. The temples in which she was worshipped were called Arsinoeions, and each bore her image. When she died, Pliny states that her grief-stricken husband planned, but was unable to carry out, an especially large Arsinoëion with a lodestone roof, above which a statue of her was to float in perpetuity. [Hale, Mahaffy]

Arsinoë III Cleopatra: Wife and sister of Ptolemy IV Philopater, mother of Ptolemy V. According to *The Third Book of Maccabees,* she was a **Maenad** and rode at the head of infantry and cavalry to fight Antiochus the Great at Raphia near Gaza in Palestine in 217 B.C., Philopater's most famous battle. [Cook, Macurdy]

Arsippe: "She Who Raises Her Foot," also called Aristippe, "Best of Mares." One of the three daughters of Minyas who were turned into bats for their criminal behavior in the cult of the **Maenads.** See **Leucippe.** [Graves]

Artakama: Warrior daughter of Artabazus, satrap of Bactria. She became the wife of Ptolemy I Soter, the "great marriage of Europe and Asia." [Mahaffy]

Artemis: Greek goddess of midwifery and the hunt, **Diana** to the Romans, Laodicea in Syria, Anaiitis in Lydia, Eleuthera in Lycia. She was the Lady of Wild Things, or the Huntress, associated with the forest and the chase. Although capable of great cruelty, she was not in essence a War-goddess, and is seen only with bow and arrow, not with sword or ax.

Warlike versions of Artemis were common enough, but were related to the Olympian Artemis in name only, **Artemis of Ephesus** being the much more ancient, warlike, and powerful goddess with differing origin, associated with knives, swords, axes, and bees.

A Pastoral-goddess to a degree, the Olympian Artemis was worshipped by groups of young women living wildly in the forests. Maidens would honor Artemis by living as huntress-virgins for a season, or for several years. Such service was believed to ensure her protection later in life, during marriage, and especially during pregnancy and childbirth, for Artemis was simultaneously the goddess of midwives. [Farnell, Tyrrell, Bennett, Vermaseren]

Artemis of Ephesus: The Amazons worshipped many warring goddesses, but most especially the Thracian Artemis (or Tauric Virgin), and the Artemis of Ephesus, derived from the Phrygian and Cretan Great Mothers, **Cybele** and **Rhea,** of Scythian and Anatolian origin. She was worshipped also at Rhodes in Sicily, in Pontus and Galatia, and, in her later period, in North Africa and elsewhere. She was paid homage by Alexander the Great, who saw her temple restored in his lifetime, which more than any other single act of his career made the people love him. The Ephesian Artemis is mentioned in the Bible as "worshipped throughout the world," and the Apostle Paul sought especially to suppress her temples. The Artemisium where she was worshipped at Ephesus was the most fabulous temple of antiquity, its site chosen by the Amazons themselves (see **Hippo**).

She was unrelated to the Greek Artemis, predating the gods of Olympus by millennia, although often the independent origins cross and converge. In her various aspects, she was more apt to be associated with cities than was the Lady of Wild Things, and more overtly a War-goddess as opposed to a huntress. Cytherea, worshipped in Cythera, was a War-goddess derived from the Oriental Artemis, but also incorporated aspects of the Huntress-goddess and **Aphrodite.**

Of similarly Oriental derivation are such seemingly diverse goddesses as **Ma** of Cappadocia and Caria, the Magnesian Artemis, Hipta of Lydia, Agdestis, Artemis Brauronia, the Spartan **Orthia,** Lemnian **Bendis,** and the Indic **Uma.** (See also **Ninmah, Mami,** and **Aruru.**) The idol of Artemis Brauron had an obsidian knife hidden in her crown, which priestesses used to cut the throats of sacrifices. Young girls were brought to her sanctuary for confirmation ceremonies, part of which consisted of "playing at little she-bears."

Artemis Apaturos, according to Strabo, killed her lovers after copulating, reflecting the earliest Mother-goddess cults, in which the young sacred king is sacrificed in the spring. Her most savage cult was that of the Thracians and the Taurians of Cimmeria, where priestesses of Artemis Taurica brutally sacrificed male victims (see **Iphigenia**). The Amazons knew this Tauric Virgin as **Tauropolos.** [Farnell, Seltman, Graves]

Artemisia: Queen of Caria and one of Xerxes' leading military advisers. She led a sea battle against the Greeks in 480 B.C. and was afterward commended as the best tactician on any of the ships. A Restoration play of 1676 refers to her as:

> The Noble Carian Queen whose fame flies far
> for aiding Xerxes in the Persian War,
> She, whose renown through the East speeds
> For Godlike virtues, and heroick deeds.

In *Stratagems of War,* Polyaenus describes several of her tactics. Among the tributes she received in acknowledgment of her gallantry was a suit of Grecian armor, while a less successful sea captain found himself awarded a distaff. As she had an adult son, there was no pressing reason for this monarch personally to lead her famous army and navy; she did so "out of courage and the spirit of adventure." [Herodotus, Diner, Pizan, Starling, Hale]

Artemisia II: Often confused with the **Artemisia** who aided Xerxes in the battle of Salamis, there was a second Queen Artemisia of Caria who lived about 350 B.C. She, too, was a noted warrior, having subdued Rhodes and put to the sword many notable princes who thought her nation would be easily taken after the death of her brother/husband, King Mausolus. She is indirectly remembered in our language, for she built a fabulous crypt for her husband, the Mausoleum, one of the Seven Wonders of the World. Its name remains part of the common vocabulary. The British Museum today houses relief carvings of Amazons taken from this very Mausoleum.

Aruru: Also known as **Mami,** a Mother-goddess of love and war, and mother of Gilgamesh. To the Akkadians, she was **Ninmah.** [Kramer]

Asia: Warrior-queen and wife of Prometheus, for whom we name the continent. She was exiled to India after the war with the Titans. Shelley uses her as a symbol of love and nature as it existed in the pre-Jovian (hence prepatriarchal) epoch when culture flourished. [Davis]

Aslog: Or Aslaug. Last of the Volsungs, daughter of the Valkyrie **Brynhild,** and an avatar of **Freya.** Her totem beasts were the goat, the hound, and the raven, and she is sometimes called Krake ("the Raven"), a goddess of magic, mightiness, and prophesy. In *Ragnar's Saga,* she is a shield maiden to Ragnar and daughter of Sigurd, taking the name Randalin during her warring years. [Saxo]

Aso: Warrior-queen of ancient Ethiopia, ally of Typhon. [Plutarch]

Astarte: Ashertu to the Hittites, Tanit to the Carthaginians, also known as Ashtart, Ashtaroth, **Ishtar,** etc. Judges in the Bible describes the tensions between the worship of "Ashtaroth" and the new patriarchal god, leading to war. Astarte was the Great Goddess of ancient Semitic peoples, notably the Canaanites. The Amazons worshipped a huntress Moon-goddess, which is occasionally identified both as "savage Astarte and her Hellenized counterpart, Artemis." The Amazons built a shrine in Pyrrhichus, a town in southern Greece, to honor Artemis Astrateia, which some scholars believe to be a corruption of Astarte.

In the Book of Jeremiah (44:15–20), the women revolt against the new patriarchal faith, preferring the original Semitic goddess. A priestess, surrounded by a crowd of women, addresses the patriarch Jeremiah boldly: "We will burn sacrifices to the Queen of Heaven as we used to do in the cities of Judah and in the streets of Jerusalem. Our husbands knew full well that we made crescent-cakes marked with Her image and poured drink-offerings to Her."

She had many aspects, some of them kindly, but as a War-goddess ranked among the most bloodthirsty. [Rothery, Bennett, Kramer, Farnell]

Asteria: "Of the Sky." One of the Amazon braves slain by Heracles during his ninth labor. Though understanding he was blessed with Olympian invulnerability, the Amazons for honor's sake insisted on challenging him one by one. She was named for the Titan mother of Hecate, who was transformed into the Island of Quails (Ortygia) forbidden to men. Asteria was also one of the Amazons in Heinrich von Kleist's play *Penthesilea*. [Sobol]

Asynjor: Guardians and attendants of **Freya** and **Frigga** of Norse mythology. Among them, **Gudur** and **Rota** were **Valkyries,** and many others have Valkyrielike traits. They included **Skadi,** a giantess and mother of Freya; Fimila, an aspect of the goddess Frimla; Fjorgyn, a giantess and mother of Frigga and Thor, originally an Earth-mother; Horn, Mardoll, Menglad, **Gefjon,** and Vandanlis (avatars of Freya); Fulla, a very ancient goddess and guardian of Frigga's magic casket, inheritor of Nanna's ring; Nanna, Baldar's grandmother; Sif ("kindred"), giantess and wife of Thor; Hnossa, most beautiful of the Asynjor and daughter of Freya; Gerda, a giantess; Jord, another giantess, originally an Earth-mother; Gna, messenger of the Asynjor and whose horse was called Hofvarpnir; Siguna or Sin, the wife of Loki and guardian of truth; Saga, a giantess and seer; plus others.

Atalanta of Arcadia: "Unswaying," a famous huntress, daughter of Zeus and **Clymene,** elsewhere given as daughter of Iasius, of the race of **Callisto** and a mortal aspect of **Artemis.** She survived her father's attempt at infanticide and was suckled by a wild she-bear. In the famous hunt for the Calydonian Boar, she was first to wound the beast, slowing it down for Maleager, who awarded her the skin. As a wrestler, she was unequaled and even defeated young Peleus, later the father of Achilles. She was the only woman with the Argonauts. [Seltman, Evans]

Atalanta of Boeotia: Daughter of Schoeneus of Boeotia, she refused to marry any man who could not outrun her in a footrace. Her suitors were given a head start, then "armed with weapons she pursues her naked suitor. If she catches him, he dies." She was finally won by Hippomenes, who dropped golden apples along the route, slowing Atalanta down as she stooped to collect them. The couple were later turned into lions for violating a shrine to **Aphrodite** or some other deity with their lust. Atalanta is sometimes identified as the lioness who, with her lover, flanks **Cybele** or pulls her war chariot. Rather than a punishment, this would have been an honor. [Seltman, Tyrrell, Evans]

Atargatis: Semitic Moon-goddess, sometimes given as the mother of **Semiramis.** She was capable of taking the form of a fish, for which reason the Syrians would not eat fish. Her warlike manifestations resemble **Lamia.** She was also known as **Derceto,** goddess of the hunt, and was Dea Syria to the Romans.

Até: Goddess of ruin and destruction, sister of the **Furies.** According to Homer, "Eldest daughter of Zeus is Até, who blinds all, a power of bane; delicate are her feet, for not upon the earth she goes, but over the heads of men, making them fall. Yea even Zeus was blinded one time, he who they say is greatest among gods." She was later considered an avenger similar to **Nemesis.**

Athaliah: (d. 878 B.C.) Queen of Jerusalem, daughter of Queen **Jezebel.** She flourished about 840 B.C. When her son fell in battle, "the fierce Athaliah cast aside feminine pity and did not mourn her son but drew sword against all descendants of David. She persecuted them until no male member of that family was left alive." She ruled seven years, restoring the shrines of **Astarte** or **Anath,** before she was overthrown. [Boccaccio]

Athena: Goddess of war and wisdom, her name may translate as "Queen of Heaven," although her name is not of Greek origin, and it is feasible she originated in Ethiopia and was carried from North African trade ports to Crete and the Aegean region. She was widely known when Zeus was still a minor vegetation spirit of Crete, thus the myth of her birth from his brow is a very late-occurring attempt of men's religions to usurp women's mysteries. Her mother was Metis (Counsel), who conceived her parthenogenetically; the grafted myth of Zeus swallowing pregnant Metis does not adequately rationalize Zeus' claim of birthing Athena.

She became the guardian of Athens and a spokeswoman for patriarchal values in the Greek plays. The Athenians would naturally make their patroness a strong figure, but she is also a dominant presence in the Homeric poems, where Athens is not an important city. She is portrayed on a hydria now in the Louvre, personally battling the Amazons. In a few black-figure **Amazonomachies,** she assists Heracles in his and Telamon's war against **Andromache.** Her siding against Troy was an additional blow against matristic standards. Furthermore, she helped Perseus destroy **Medusa** and assisted Bellerophon's capture of Pegasus, which he rode in his battle against the Amazons.

Athena is the one War-goddess often, even generally, considered to be the Amazons' foe. Yet she must have been quite different in her earliest manifestations, and the **Gorgon's** head that forms her coat-of-arms (see **gorgoneum**) may originally have referred to something other than Perseus' slaughter of Medusa, variants of her myth showing that she went forth to do personal battle with Medusa. She was sometimes positively associated with the Libyan Amazons, who were also called Gorgons, who predated the **Thermodontines,** and who purportedly found Athena worthy of their worship (see **Net**).

Audata: Illyrian warrior-princess, first wife of Philip II. Out of political expediency in Macedonia, she changed her foreign name to the Greek **Eurydice** (see that entry).

Augusta Geraldine Almeda: Amazon heroine of Emily Brontë's poetic cycle *Gondal's Queen.*

Augustina, the Maid of Saragossa: (A.D. 1788–1857) In 1808, twelve thousand soldiers besieged the pitifully inadequate, ancient walls of Saragossa, Spain. One brave woman among the main ranks has been immortalized as "the Maid of Saragossa" in verse by Byron and Southey and in art by Wilkie and Goya, for, when Spanish men were ready to desert, she placed match to gun and cried, "For so long as French are near, Saragossa has one defender!" Byron wrote of her:

> Her lover sinks—she sheds no ill-timed tear;
> Her chief is slain—she fills his fatal post;
> Her fellows flee—she checks their base career;
> The foe retires—she heads the sallying host.

She was later offered military honors but asked only that she retain the rank of artillery captain, along with an artilleryman's pay and pension. She also retained the right to dress as a soldier and bear arms. [Starling, C. Morris]

Aurinia: According to Tacitus, she was the War-goddess of the ancient Germans. Her priestesses stood on ladders in the midst of battle, cutting off the heads of fallen foe, draining the blood into cups, and giving it to the Teutonic warriors to drink. Plutarch described the Germanic women "with swords and axes, falling upon their opponents uttering hideous outcries." Teutonic women warriors were documented by Flavius Vopiscus, Dio Cassius, Paulus Diaconus, Saxo Grammaticus, and others.

Autonoë: "With a Mind of Her Own." One of the leaders of the Theban **Maenads** who warred against Pentheus when he attempted to suppress their cult. Her sisters were **Ino** and **Agave.** The entire female population of their city joined the revolt. In the battles, Autonoë seized the Lydian rebel, who turned out to be Dionysus himself. Autonoë's son was Actaeon, whom **Artemis** transformed into a stag and, with a college of nymphs, hunted to the ground, letting his own dogs tear him to pieces. Actaeon's sacrifice to Artemis and Pentheus' to Dionysus suggests a link between these violent women's cults. [Tyrell]

Avemanay, Lorenza: South American Indian who in 1803 led a revolt against the Spanish in Ecuador.

Awashonks: Native American woman warrior. In 1671, she agreed to end her long-standing war against English settlements. But in 1675 she allied herself with "King Philip," an Indian chief of a confederacy of tribes, in an attempt to repulse whites from Indian lands. Awashonks and her warriors fought for one year before it became clear that the cause was lost, at which time she met with an Englishman friend and agreed to return to peace in exchange for amnesty for herself and her followers, unlike another woman chief of the day, **Weetamoo,** who would not relent. The English were glad enough to accept Awashonks's bargain. [Josephy]

Ayesha or **'A'ishah:** (A.D. 614?–678?) Favorite of Muhammad's wives, she argued religion with him even in the presence of his captains, so that he told his people, "Take half your faith from this woman." She especially resisted the idea of the subordination of Islamic wives. When widowed at the age of eighteen, she raised an army at Mecca, which she led against Caliph Othman. She met the army of Bassora and drove it into the city, where the citizens braced themselves against siege. She refused all pacifistic offers and a long battle began along the city walls. Mounted on a camel, Ayesha rode amidst the carnage. She was eventually captured but released on condition that she lead no further battles. She continued, however, to exert authority in affairs of state, with the title "Mother of the Faithful." [Hale, Miles, Fraser, Beard]

Az: In the myths of Zarathustra, Az was a female demon, comparable to **Lilith** and probably of like origin. Many of the Iranian demon-goddesses, or *druxsan,* were "cruel, strong and wicked," but elsewhere called "charming and pleasant." [Kramer]

Azurduy, Juana: A guerrilla leader in Bolivia in the early 1800s.

B

◈◈◈◈◈◈◈◈◈◈◈◈◈

Baba Yaga: A Slavic witch-goddess who helps or hinders heroes according to their merit. With her mortar and pestle, she crushes her foes. She becomes the fair maiden Vasilisa the Wise in her positive aspect, and this maid aspect is in turn sometimes **Vasilisa Vasily,** a beautiful androgynous warrior. [Preston]

Baide, Maria: A scout in Crimea during World War II. Surrounded by enemy submachine gunners, she shot it out with the Germans, killing fifteen, wounding several more, and routing the rest. She escaped with wounds and received Russia's highest award, Hero of the Soviet Union. [Laffin]

Baktscharow, Lieutenant Marie: Leader of the first Russian women's battalion of 1917, organized by Aleksandr Kerensky. Her battalion of 250 young working-class women already had combat experience while serving as nurses on the front. They went to the northern front with official recognition as warriors, although many of them were only seventeen years old. Other women's "suicide battalions" were to follow, and similar groups and individual heroines appeared in World War II.

A peasant girl in Lieutenant Baktscharow's battalion described her experience: "I found myself next to a German and ran him through with my bayonet, shot him, and took his helmet for a memento." Another said they were all scared and excited; bombs were falling all around them; but on the

27

order to charge, "Over the top came our mob of bellowing girls." An Austrian who encountered this battalion lived to tell of it: "They were brave and frequently bloodthirsty. We felt no knightly sentiments for these **Penthesileas.** They did not wear trousers, but blue smocks, with the knees bare."

Another women's battalion, fighting in Austria, called itself "the League of Death." [Hirshfeld]

Barbara, Saint: The antique Amazons, their presumed virginity, and their knightly honor, shifted from classical heroism to Christian martyrdom in the early Middle Ages, retaining many of the adornments of the original myths. St. Barbara entered into Christian myth no later than A.D. 800, and is said to have lived in the third century, but incorporates Pallas **Athena** and **Bellona** of antiquity. She is patron of armorers and gunsmiths, of firearms and fortifications, and is invoked at the moment of death. When she was beheaded, thunder and lightning repeatedly struck the executioner, her father, until he was completely consumed; she is thus worshipped with fireworks displays. In art, she is depicted with sword and palm leaf, and is likely to be ornamented with shield and armor. She sometimes carries firearms instead of sword. Her feast occurs in December, for many of Christianity's holdovers from the War-goddesses are associated with winter.

Similar warlike saints include St. **Ursula,** St. **Margaret of Antioch,** and St. **Catherine.** The patriarchal nature of Catholicism disdains warrior strength in these women and subverts artists' visions by insisting saintly resistance was passive, their possession of weapons notwithstanding. Such powerful acts as subduing or protecting, we are told, are strictly allegoric. But Catholicism is a schizophrenic faith, patriarchal yet in many ways preserving goddess worship in the form of the **Virgin Mary** and innumerable female saints. The images of armed women in hagiographic art are the understandable result of millennia of pagan and Christian histories of warring queens, Amazons, and violent goddesses, plus the fact that early convents, as landlords to peasants prone to rebellion, often had to take up arms to defend their properties, as in the cases of the abbess **Leubevére** and Philothéy **Benizélos.** The female saints, far from being the passive resisters supposed, were, in the words of Mary Ritter Beard, "active, energetic, highly individualized women who were taking a forceful role in the world," and the artists capture this accurately. [Kleinbaum, Weigle]

Barbara of Erecourt: Also known as the Lady of St. Belmont, born in 1609 near Verdun. From childhood, she studied military arts and swordplay "and all knightly virtues." The Lord of Belmont saw her out hunting when she was still very young, and instantly sued for marriage. They were much attached to each other thereafter, often hunting together. During the Thirty Years War, she frequently defended her castle and "on several occasions made sorties against her foes." [Hale]

Barkida: An Amazon brave during the reign of **Hippolyte.** While Heracles decimated the Amazons in one battle, a secondary skirmish was headed successfully by the heroic **Pantariste,** in which success Barkida also participated. She is also encountered, by evidence of the **Amazonomachies,** at the Telamon and Heracles battle against **Andromache.** [Sobol, Bothmer]

Barnes, Dame Juliana: "An ingenious virago whose personal and mental endowments were of the highest character." Dame Juliana was prioress of Sopewell Nunnery, near St. Albans, Hertfordshire. As was common for medieval women, she was a devoted and consummate huntress, and we may picture her in the common manner of riding upon her hunting expeditions with either her hounds or hawk. She published, in 1486, rhymed treatises on hunting, falconry, coat armor, and angle fishing, making her, as well, the first Englishwoman to whom has been ascribed any English rhyme. [Bethune, Hale]

Barrau, Liberté: Praised in *Recueil des actions héroïques,* Liberté Barrau fought at her husband's side in the war with Spain in 1794.

Basilea: "The Queenly One." A warrior-queen of the nation of Atlas of North Africa (today Egypt), and daughter of the Earth-mother **Gaia.** She was purported by Diodorus to have ruled fifty thousand years ago. Out of the chaos of those protohistorical times, Queen Basilea brought order by use of force. Hers may have been the first government on a grand scale, military or otherwise, as well as the first Amazonian nation. [Davis]

Bastet: See **Ubastet.**

Bastidas, Micaela: Fought alongside her husband Tupac Amaru in a Peruvian rebellion in 1780. She led troops of men and women into battle.

Battistati, Louisa: Italian patriot. In the Revolution of 1848, she defended Milan for five days, and afterward was defender of Bettabia, a nearby town.

battle-ax: Used in a derogatory way to describe any contentious woman, especially in her later life, as in "the old battle-ax." The reference to a lybrys seems certain, and it may originally have indicated a respectable, retired soldier, equivalent to the manner in which "old warhorse" indicates a male veteran.

Bat Zuge: Tenth of ten divinities that flank the left side of God's throne. The *Zohar* says these ten angels were evil and that, as a fallen angel, Bat Zuge became known as **Lilith.**

Baudihille: Her name means "Ruler of Battle." She was a war divinity of northern England during Roman times, an Alaisiagi associated with Mars and equivalent to a **Valkyrie.** Other Alaisiagae, whose names are known from a votive stone discovered on Hadrian's Wall and an altar to the Alaisiagae at the same fort, were **Bede, Fimmilene,** and **Friagabi.** [Davidson]

Baumes, Louise Houssaye de: French infantrywoman who served from 1792 to 1795 and fought at Quiberon. [Laffin]

Bazao-Turunku: Queen of a warrior tribe south of Zaria in fifteenth-century Nigeria. [Fraser]

Beam, Beebe: An American who fought in the Spanish-American War. She said, "I saw war and I lived it." To reach the Philippines, she disguised herself as a cabin boy. In Manila, in male guise, she fought as a soldier for twelve months. [Gribble]

Bearskin-woman or **Grizzly-woman:** A heroine of Blackfoot folklore. She married a grizzly bear, which so enraged her father that he set out to slay her lover, whom Bearskin-woman defended. She transformed herself into a grizzly bear and killed many of her father's people. See **Sinopa.** [Spence]

Beauglie, Madame de: In the eighteenth century, attired as an Amazon and commanding thirty cavaliers, she defended the coast near La Vendée. [Kavanagh]

Bebhionn: Daughter of Teon of Celtic legend's Land of Maidens. She was a powerful maiden-giantess who warred against Aedh, to whom she had been unwillingly betrothed. He was a cruel, beautiful, effeminate giant who fought with spear. She routed his troops and expelled him from her nation, but died afterward of wounds. Her burial site was long known as the Mound of the Dead Maiden. [Ellis]

Bec and **Lithben:** In *The Life of St. Mochua of Balla,* they are referred to as companion-warriors of the Celts, probably of a violent lesbian cult. [Ellis]

Bede: Name of one of the Alaisiagae ("the strongly storming ones"), warlike goddesses of ancient northern England, associated with Mars much as the **Valkyries** were associated with Odin. It is likely no coincidence that in Danish legend, one of the **Asynjor** is named Beda. [Davidson, Damico]

Beiko, Alexandra: She and her husband Ivan bought their own tank so they could go into World War II together, with Stalin's permission. Alexandra was awarded the Order of the Patriotic War, Ivan the Order of the Red Banner. [Laffin]

Bel-Anna: Ben Jonson's "Queen of the Ocean" based on Anne of Denmark, in *The Masque of Queens*. She leads a group of women who signify family allegiance, bravery in battle, and good rule.

Belisama: "Most Warlike Goddess." A War-goddess of the British Celts. [Edwardes]

Belit: A Babylonian War- and Sex-goddess, a cult name for **Ishtar.** Pulp author Robert E. Howard of the 1930s named one of his swordswomen after her, and Conan the Barbarian sat at her feet like a doting puppy.

Belletz, Louise: Parisian daughter of a fringe maker. Of her, the following story was told to Mme. de Staël at one of her salons, by Marshal Masséna:

> I perceived a young soldier belonging to the light artillery, whose horse had just been wounded by a lance. The young man, who appeared quite a child, defended himself desperately, as several dead bodies of the enemy lying around him could testify. I immediately despatched an officer with some men to his assistance, but they arrived too late. This artilleryman had alone withstood the attack of a small troop of Cossacks and Bavarians. His body was covered with wounds, inflicted with shots, lances and swords. There were at least thirty. And do you, madame, know what this man was? A woman! And a handsome woman, too, although she was so covered with blood that it was difficult to judge her beauty. She had followed her lover to the army. The latter was a Captain of Artillery; she never left him; and when he was killed, defended like a lioness the remains of his body. [Laffin]

Bellona: Said variously to be the wife, daughter, and mother of Mars. Bellona was a Roman War-goddess. In Greece, she was **Enyo.**

Belphoebe: A javelin-wielding huntress of Spenser's *The Faerie Queene* who puts Braggadocio to flight. She sets herself especially against the wealthy and the pompous, prefers the wilderness to court life, and is Spenser's idealized concept of **Cynthia.**

Beltran, Manuela: In Columbia in 1780, she organized a peasant revolt against excess taxation.

Bendis: The Great Goddess of gynocratic **Lemnos** and of Thrace, where, Plato noted in his *Laws,* women worked the land and tended sheep and cattle. Bendis was the fierce Huntress of the Two Spears and required human sacrifice. She provided the religious underpinning for the Lemnosian women's revolt in which all the men of the island were slain (see **Hypsipyle**). To the Greeks, Bendis was the same Thracian **Artemis** worshipped by the Amazons as **Tauropolos** and closely aligned with **Cybele** and **Hecate.** [Bennett]

Benincasa, Caterina: A fourteenth-century Italian mystic who, like **Joan of Arc,** was inspired by visions. She waged war against the Muslims, but tried to deliver peace to her homeland. She is the patron saint of Italy.

Benizélos, Philothéy: In the 1650s, she founded a convent college of women in Greece, and drew so many women to her tutelage that local government feared her growing political base. Peasants who lived on clerical lands often found their religious landlords no better than any others, and commonly rose in arms against convents and monasteries. Benizélos was typical of abbesses who found themselves warring against peasants seeking possession of convent lands. The secular government ultimately imprisoned her and tortured her to death. [Schmidt]

berdache: Today, this term designates lesbian or gay American Indians; anthropologically, a berdache was a native American man who adapted the ways of women, or a woman who adapted the ways of men. Among the Cocopa Indians, according to a 1933 study, lesbians were known as "warhameh" and "fought in battle like men." Another author in 1841 reported a widow of the Snake tribe who, because of a dream, adapted her late husband's habits; the mystical touch was expected of the berdache, who often became shamans. This Snake tribal woman "went on hunts and on the war-path. By fearless action she obtained the title of 'brave' and the privilege of admittance to the council of chiefs."

Women pursued men's occupations in the Kaska tribes, sometimes emulating men in other ways and sometimes not. A Kaska huntress would break the bow and arrows of any man who made advances, believing that a heterosexual affair would ruin her luck in hunting. Mohave and Klamath women warriors were usually lesbians and called themselves men, despite the fact they did not necessarily dress like men or try in any manner whatsoever to appear mannish. Women warriors and lesbians of the Yuma were called kwe'rheme and did cross-dress and talk with deeper voices, as did the berdache minorities of the Kamia, Navaho, Zuñi and other tribes.

Berengaria of Navarre: (A.D. 1172?–1230?) Daughter of Sancho the Wise, King of Naples. She married Richard the Lionheart in 1191 and accompanied him to the Mideast, participating in the Crusade against Saladin. After the death of Richard, she founded an abbey and ruled its vast estates. [Hale, King]

Berenice I: Half-sister, mistress, then wife (316 B.C.) of Ptolemy I and mother of **Arsinoë II.** She fought beside Ptolemy on the battlefield, was of fine character and intellect, and exerted influence in all matters of state. In her widowhood, she saw her sons fall in war, and afterward took up arms and led an army against her brother-in-law, the slayer of her children. She killed him with her own hands, then drove her war chariot back and forth across his body. [Mahaffy, Pizan, Boccaccio, Macurdy]

Berenice II of Cyrene: (273–245? B.C.) She "rode in battle, killed many enemies, and routed the rest." Like her namesake, she was beautiful, greatly beloved, and brave in battle. She was victrix of a chariot race held in Nemia, after she had already become famous for honors in the games of Olympia. Early in her career, she raised an army in rebellion against her betrothed, whom she found repellent. She married her cousin, Ptolemy III Euregetes, in 247 B.C. The astronomer Conon of Samos reported that Berenice's hair, after it was dedicated to the temple of **Arsinoë II,** was transformed into a constellation, *Coma Berenices.* [Pomeroy, Cook]

Bersilat: The Malayan national art of self-defense is silat, with many schools and forms, and a belt-ranking system similar to karate. According to popular legend, the fighting system of silat was created in A.D. 1511 by a Sumatran woman named Bersilat, after learning it herself from a dream. [Winderbaum]

Bhairavi: "The Terrible Female," a fierce goddess of the Hindus, an incarnation of **Kali.** Bhairavi takes unusual delight in destruction.

Bilistiche of Magnesia: (third century B.C.) Hetaera of Ptolemy Philadelphus and a horse breeder. Her steeds were famous in the Olympiad. After the success of **Cynisca,** first female victrix of the chariot races, many women became active participants. Bilistiche from Ionia appears to have been one of those early victrices, winning the four-horse chariot race in 268 B.C. and in 264 B.C. A few scholars wonder if the several names of female charioteers weren't merely breeders whose horses were raced by men, yet there is ample evidence of women typically racing chariots under a variety of circumstances—at festivals to Hera, for example—and it is ridiculously cautious to assume such women as Bilistche only *watched* their horses win. She was made a goddess upon her death as Aphrodite Bilistiche. [Lefkowitz]

Bint-Anat: (fl. c. 1280 B.C.) Daughter of Ramses II. Her specific history is lost, but her recorded name translates "Daughter of the Syrian War-goddess" (see **Anath**). It would appear her character resembled that of other Egyptians such as the **Cleopatras** and **Arsinoës.** [Hart]

Black Agnes: Lady Agnes Randolph (A.D. 1300?–1369?), wife of Patrick the fourth earl of Dunbar and the second earl of March. In her youth, she fought for the Bruce, but is better remembered for the later defense of her castle.

In 1334, Black Agnes, daughter of the great Randolf, earl of Moray, successfully held her castle at Dunbar against the besieging forces of England's earl of Salisbury for over five months, despite the unusual number of engineers and elaborate equipment brought against her. After each assault on her fortress, her maids dusted the merlins and crenels, treating her foes and the dreadful siege as a tiresome jest. She is celebrated in a folk song attributed to Salisbury:

> She kept a stir in tower and trench,
> That brawling, boisterous Scottish wench;
> Came I early, came I late
> I found Agnes at the gate.

Sir Walter Scott said, "From the record of Scottish heroes, none can presume to erase her." [Marshall, King, Fittis, Crawford]

Black Mary: There are numerous European Black Marys, generally with North African and Indic influences, and most are occasionally warlike. Our Lady of the Arch, worshipped in Naples, is a goddess of punishment. Her worship dates to the seventh century and she is believed to be the last vestige of **Cybele.** She is a devil fighter, "a terror to demons," and performs violent exorcisms, reminiscent of **Durga.** Black Mary is also found in the Americas. The Virgin of Guadalupe, a Mexican Black Mary, incorporates elements of the Aztec Defender-goddess **Tanantsi.** When Tanantsi was suppressed by conquistadores, the natives immediately embraced the **Virgin Mary** as the same goddess under a new name. [Preston]

The Black Virgin: (fl. A.D. 1855) A Kurdish chieftainess of Constantinople who at the opening of the Crimean War led a body of one thousand horse. She also fought under Omar Pasha against the Russians on the Danube. [Rothery]

Blanche, Lady Arundel: (A.D. 1583–1649) Defended Wardour Castle in her husband's absence. For nine days, she fought the parliamentary forces of Sir Edward Hungerford, Edmund Lodlow, and Colonel Strode, who united against her in May of 1643. There were only twenty-five men to aid in the defense. There were more than sixty casualties. [Starling, Hale]

Blanche of Rossi: Italian heroine. In 1237, during the war between the Ghibellines and Guelfs, Blanche of Rossi aided in the defense of Ezzelino. She "fought beside her husband in various skirmishes and upon the walls of the city." When her husband, Battista of Padua, fell in battle, a hero's tomb was built for him, but the conqueror demanded Blanche as part of the victory award. Deciding on heroic suicide, she threw herself upon her husband's tomb, causing the stone door to collapse upon her. [Hale, Starling]

Boadicea: See **Boudicca.**

Bocanegra, Gertrudis: During the Mexican War of Independence (1810), Gertrudis raised an army of fighting women and led them into war. She died in 1817 after arrest and torture. [Miles]

Bodb or **Badb:** With **Morrigane** and **Macha,** the Gaelic trinity of War-goddesses, although sometimes Bodh is said to be the whole of Morrigane, Macha, and **Nemain,** thus mightier than the three. Elsewhere, she is shown to be subservient to Morrigane, who leads her two sisters into battle. The *Book of Conquests* mentions them as daughters of Emmas, hinting at their origin as mortal fighting women. She is sometimes given as "the Washer by the Ford," a **hag** who cleanses the entrails, limbs, and weapons of those who have fallen in battle. Her name probably means "crow," but has also been translated "boiling," as of a witch's cauldron, or "fury." [Markale, Davidson, Ellis]

Bonilla, Amalia: The following historic passage was quoted from Louis Delapree's *The Martyrdom of Madrid* (1937) in Virginia Woolf's *Three Guineas* (1943), regarding the Spanish War:

> The eyes deeply sunk into the sockets, the features acute, the amazon keeps herself very straight in the stirrups at the head of her squadron. Five English

parliamentaries look at this woman with the respectful and a bit restless admiration one feels for a "fauve" of an unknown species.

"Come nearer, Amalia," orders the commandant. She pushes her horse towards us and salutes her chief with the sword.

"Sergeant Amalia Bonilla," continues the chief of the squadron, "how old are you?"

"Thirty-six."

"Where were you born?"

"In Granada."

"Why have you joined the army?"

"My two daughters were military-women. The younger was killed in Alto de Leon. I thought I had to supersede her and to avenge her."

"And how many enemies have you killed to avenge her?"

"You know it, commandant, five. The sixth is not sure."

"No, but you have taken his horse."

The amazon Amalia rides in fact a magnificent dapple-grey horse, with glossy hair, which flatters like a parade horse. This woman who has killed five men, but who feels not sure about the sixth, was for the envoys of the House of Commons an excellent introducer to the Spanish War.

Bonney, Anne: (A.D. 1700–1722?) The most famous of all women pirates. Of Anne's various activities and proclivities, the one thing reporters are loathe to tell about is her lesbianism, citing instead her long association with Calico Jack, although Jack's lover was known as Pierre the Pansy Pirate, originally a dressmaker. Pierre had a passion for silk and velvet, of which there was too little in New Providence of the early 1700s. When Anne told him there'd be fine bolts of cloth to be taken on the high seas, he joined her crew. Pierre designed Anne's black velvet pants and Jack's famous calico coat.

Anne's actual lover was, of course, Mary **Read.** The four of them attempted at one point to retire from piracy and live peacefully inland as an extended family, but they were too notorious and pirate hunters were heavily rewarded in those days, forcing Anne and her chums to see it through to a dismal end. Another story to "prove" Anne's heterosexuality is that when she, Mary, and their crew came to trial and were condemned to die, they claimed to be pregnant, as pregnant women could not be hung. Few commentators question the peculiar coincidence of both of them being pregnant at the exact same handy moment, though all-round whorishness is generally implied. A wiser investigator discovered that the doctor who checked to see if they were indeed pregnant was, in fact, a long-standing associate of Anne's. Another myth quickly dispelled is that Jack introduced

Anne into piracy. The fact is that he had never pirated until after he met her. She required a front man so that she could rule a pirate crew as regent.

She made a brave and crafty pirate. After boarding and looting a ship that included a trunk of fancy dresses destined for a bordello, her men could not resist a most absurd costume dance in celebration. Suddenly, there appeared on the horizon yet another ship worthy of attack. Anne had her cross-dressed men smear blood or red paint upon themselves and arrange themselves about the ship like corpses. Sailors are notoriously superstitious, and Anne took her next prize without resistance, as she was perceived as not a pirate but a ghost ship.

Her end is not really known. It is believed Mary died in prison of pneumonia while awaiting the phantom birth, but that Anne escaped and lived quietly thereafter, or may later have been hanged with a group of fanatical nuns over whom she held sway. Of her and Mary's capture, there is ample record, and they were by far the fiercest of their crew. Anne is reported to have quipped during the final fray, "Dogs! If instead of these weakings I only had some women with me!" It is doubtful she meant to be ironic. [Carlova, Myron, Croix, Snow]

Bordeau, Renée: (A.D. 1770–1828) French patriot in the army of La Vendée.

Bordereau, Joanne: See **L'Angevine.**

Borginis, Sarah: In 1836, she fought at Fort Brown, Texas, against the Mexicans. Years later, she served under General Taylor against eighteen thousand Mexicans led by the heroic Santa Ana. In 1866, she received a military burial. [Laffin]

Botaichu Kodaiso: Warrior heroine of the medieval novel *Suikoden,* subject of many *ukiyoe* block prints. Other heroines from the story include **Boyasha Sonjiro** and **Kosanjo Ichijosei.**

Botchkareva, Maria: After a difficult life as a prostitute, this serf's daughter became radicalized and joined the Bolsheviks. Known as "Yashka," she became a much-decorated frontline warrior during World War I, famed for rescuing wounded comrades even in the face of machine-gun fire. She proposed and ultimately commanded the Russian women's Battalion of Death, and many other battalions of this nature followed the example. When she found herself in the cross fire of Bolshevik politics, rather than enemy Germans, she found it expedient to flee Russia in 1918. In the

United States, she stayed with suffragist and socialist Sylvia Pankhurst and helped in the promotion of the radical Women's Party.

Her autobiography is written in a highly pitched, operatic style, filled with thrilling and tragic moments. A group of antigovernment activists once blocked the march of Yashka's Battalion of Death, chanting, "Down with war! Down with war!" Though ordered not to argue, one of Yashka's women could not restrain herself. "When you say that, you mean the destruction of Free Russia!" At which point the chant turned to "Kill her! Kill her!" Yashka found herself standing amidst a rioting mob, a pistol in each hand, but never once firing, for she still considered them "my own people." She was shot and carried unconscious from the demonstrators' reach. [Botchkareva, Mitchell]

Botssi, Despo: (late eighteenth century A.D.) With her eleven daughters and granddaughters, Despo Botssi aided in the defense of the Greek town of Souli in Albany. When the battle was going against them, the dozen women vowed to die rather than be taken, then set themselves and the powder rooms of the Castle of Dimoula afire. The flames spread and not a soldier survived. [Schmidt]

Boubalina, Lascarina: (A.D. 1783–1825) A Greek naval captain "born to be a warrior," known in the early 1800s as "Capitanissa." She had a small fleet of four warships, which she used to besiege coast towns and liberate them from Turks, and to pursue Turkish vessels at sea. In one battle, her men came ashore to set fire to a fortress and in the chaos they began to set upon the women with the intent to rape them, although their Capitanissa forbade such activity. Aroused to anger, she "rushed sword in hand to rescue the women." Her career ended in 1825 with her assassination in her house at Spetsai. [Schmidt]

Boudicca: Or Boadicea, derived from a Celtic word for "Victorious." Warrior-queen of the Iceni of Norfolk. She led a rebellion in A.D. 61, sacking numerous Roman settlements and setting fire to Londinium (London) and sacking Verulamium (St. Albans) and numerous settlements. The death of seventy thousand Romans and Romanized Brits temporarily liberated her people from the Roman yoke. The earliest sources described her as "tall of person, of a comely countenance, apparelled in a loose gown of many colors. About her neck she wore a chain of gold and in her hand she bore a spear. She stood a while surveying her army and, being regarded with a reverential silence, she addressed them an eloquent and impassioned speech."

Her victories were reversed the following year. According to varying traditions, she either died upon the battlefield, survived the final battle but took poison rather than be taken prisoner, or died of illness shortly afterward. One tradition, which has nothing of history about it, held that Stonehenge was her burial place.

Boudicca was by no means the only woman on that famous battlefield. The Roman army was urged on with the observation that the Celtic queen's forces included "more women than warriors." For all such disparaging feelings toward an army consisting largely of women, the Romans were routed. Celtic warriors were so accustomed to women rulers that a group of prisoners brought before Emperor Claudius in Rome ignored him completely, and went straight to the throne of Empress **Agrippa,** to the chagrin of Roman society. [Tacitus, Diner, Davis]

Bowdash: A woman of the Kutenai (or Kootenay), a Montana tribe, Bowdash traveled extensively, sometimes in the company of one or another wife. She was a guide for whites in the early to middle 1800s. A sort of folk hero in oral tradition, she is described variously as a prophet, messenger, peace mediator, and warrior, traditional roles for the female **berdache.** Her death, after a long and successful career, is remembered in Indian legend as bloody and magical. Each time her enemy slashed her with knives, she continued to make war hollers, and her wounds closed up. After several times, however, she couldn't holler anymore, and the wounds healed more slowly. Finally, a foe cut out her heart and that wound couldn't heal. This rather extreme story no doubt exaggerates the simpler fact that she was very hard to kill. [Hungry Wolf]

Boyasha Sonjiro: Warrior heroine of the thirteenth-century novel *Suikoden.*

Braceti, Mariana: Puerto Rican mountain fighter, known as "the Golden Arm," revolutionary junta leader in the late 1860s. [Schmidt]

Bradamante: Bradamante of the House of Clermont was sister to Rinaldo in the Charlemagne cycle of tales. Ariosto and other poets often place her name before that of Orlando in order of importance. She fought at the side of the pagan Rogero, eventually converting him to her faith. As a Christian knight she was "equal to the best." She defeated Sacripant, king of Circassia, in one-to-one combat, disgracing him before Princess Angelica of Cathay, but not killing him. When Sacripant demanded to know what knight it had been who proved superior, he was informed by an interested party that it was the "fair and illustrious Bradamante who has won from you the honors of victory."

In another of her adventures, Bradamante was called upon by a distraught woman to save her husband from the Moorish King Rodomont, who held many knights prisoner and demanded tribute for a tomb. Bradamante hastened to the bridge leading to the tomb, where an armored King Rodomont demanded tribute. Bradamante shouted that her offering would be "your life and your armor," assuring him that she alone was fit enough champion to deliver them. Two horses, two warriors, and two lances raced to the height of the bridge, and Bradamante's golden lance unseated the Moorish king. "Silent and sad, he unbound his helm and mail and flung them against the tomb." As is the case with many of Bradamante's victories, she spares her adversary. [Bulfinch, Ariosto]

Breese, Mary: (A.D. 1721–1799) A huntress of Norfolk, England, and a capital markswoman. Upon her death, her hunting hounds and favorite mare were killed and buried with her. [Hale]

Bremusa: "Raging Female," one of **Penthesilea's** twelve companions-at-arms at Troy, killed with a wound through the breast.

Breshkovskaya, Ekatrina: Member of the Russian women's Battalion of Death in World War I. A contemporary article noted that such women as Ekatrina became "symbols of unselfish love and everything big and noble."

Brigit or **Brigantia:** Eponymous Mother-goddess of the Brigantes, an "elusive cult-figure whose very name may be far older than the Celts," harking back to the Stone Age. The Romans, who co-opted local religions wherever they went, associated the English goddess Brigit with their own War-goddess **Minerva.** Lady Gregory says that her name means "fiery arrow" and that half her face was comely, half horrible, a goddess of war and poetry. She fought under the Great Mother Danu (**Ana**), as did the daughters of Dagda, heroines Eire, Fodla, Banba, Eodon, the tripartite of **Morrigane,** and many others.

Brigit was patroness of all arts, including arts of war, presiding over swordsmiths, and was a guardian of wells. She was Christianized as St. Brigit or St. Bride, and lost her warlike aspects.

Brilliana, Lady Harley: (A.D. 1598?–1643) Defender of Brampton Castle near Hereford. In 1642 and 1643, she held out valiantly with a great public show of defiance, having promised her husband to defend his holdings in his long absence. Ill health and pregnancy did not temper her militancy.

Seven hundred foe stormed her walls, but she was able to hold them in check for weeks at a time, though sadly "diverse women were killed by soldiers in the tumult." When the siege was lifted, her fame spread through England, for "a mere woman" had jeered at the king's army. [Fraser, Blashfield]

Britomart: Woman warrior of Spenser's *Faerie Queene.* She is the "good" Amazon contrasted to **Radigunde's** "evil" Amazon nature, possibly analogous to the patriarchal "good" **Athena** and the feminist man-slayer **Artemis.** In their climactic battle together, they fought "like a tiger and a lioness," and Radigunde fell under Britomart's sword of goodness.

Britomartis of Gortyna: Companion of **Artemis,** keeper of her hounds. Her name means "Good Maiden." She was a daughter of Leto and inventor of the hunting net. Upon her death, Artemis deified her as **Dictynna.** She was worshipped by the Spartans as "Artemis, the Lady of the Lake," and by other warlike or hunting peoples, especially in Crete. The Philistines and Syrians knew her as **Derceto,** whom Diodorus identifies as a warrior-queen who killed her lovers, spider-fashion, after copulating.

Brownell, Kate: (b. A.D. 1842) Served with the Rhode Island Volunteers as a markswoman in the American Civil War, fighting in several battles alongside her husband. She was the standard bearer at Bull Run. A stunning photograph of her survives, with trousers under her knee-length dress, a tasseled sash about her waist, standing at attention with her sword. [Moore]

Brûlon, Angélique: Served from A.D. 1792 to 1799 in the defense of Corsica. She fought first in male guise, and by the time she was found out, had already shown such courage that she remained in service, known popularly as Liberté the Fusilier. She was in seven campaigns and displayed particular courage at Calvi and at the attack on Fort Gesco. The men she commanded drew up a testimony: "We the garrison at Calvi certify that Marie-Angélique Josephine Duchemin *veuve* Brûlon, acting sergeant, commanding the attack of Fort Gesco, fought with us with the courage of a heroine." Their testimony prided her on her skill with sword in hand-to-hand fighting. When a sword cut injured her right arm, she continued to fight with dagger in her left. In 1822, at the age of fifty-one, she was promoted to the rank of lieutenant and retired. Napoleon III pinned upon her the red ribbon of the French Legion of Honor. Even as an octogenarian, she continued to "swagger innocently about in her lieutenant's uniform." [Gribble, Laffin]

Bruna: One of the **Valkyrie,** and the shield maiden to the hero of *Hálf-danar Saga.*

Brunhilde: "Mailed Woman." The German national epic *Nibelungenlied* features the virtual archetype of the Amazon as viewed in the West: Brunhilde, general of a women's army, queen of a matriarchal country (Iceland), defeated not by superior strength but by magic and male treachery.

Like **Atalanta,** Brunhilde slays all courters who cannot defeat her in physical tests. Helen M. Mustard, one of the more unreliable translators of the epic, unfortunately considers Brunhilde's strength a "vulgar display of muscularity and contempt for men." But it is obvious that Brunhilde only preferred to remain a ruler in Iceland rather than a king's wife in a foreign land.

The queen is "fierce" and "arrogant" according to Siegfried. She rules a country dominated by women "with a noble air" in Gunther's words. The ferocious Hagard stands downcast and feels threatened by the strong, comely Brunhilde. "We're as good as dead," he says, for it takes three men to lift Brunhilde's spear, and she can throw a boulder that "twelve men could not carry." When Brunhilde is knocked down by Gunther, she springs up to congratulate him, not knowing he is aided by Siegfried's magic. That magic was needed to defeat her hints that she was more formidable than Fafner the dragon, snuffed by Siegfried without aid of magic, at a time when he was not yet invulnerable.

Brunhilde "stepped forth, full of anger, and raised the stone high, flinging it a long distance from her. Then, with her armor ringing, she sprang forth." Gunther could never have outdone this performance except by cheating and by magic. If Brunhilde is later a vindictive wife, it is perhaps justified by the fact that she traded freedom and supreme rule for the company of liars and cheats. Had her honor not been so much greater than theirs, she could have turned her soldiers on them and not gone away into wedlock, for she had reasons to suspect Gunther's trickery.

The idea that she killed herself for love of the murdered Siegfried (in which treason she conspired) is a late addition. More properly, her revenge seeking should be viewed akin to the Japanese system of a revenge sought for honor, followed by expiation suicide since the act was illegal though just.

Brunhild of Austrasia: She was "patriotic and devoted to her country" and "did so much for her country that her name as a public benefactor was long afterward remembered." She is described as having a noble soul and "strong in all those qualities which go to make a vigorous queen." She was queen by rights, as she was widow of a king, yet found it expedient to rule her East Frankish nation as regent through successive male heirs, her son and grandsons, until her death in A.D. 613. She was a military tactician as well, and once faced a troop of Frankish warriors alone, winning the day by means of her orative powers.

She was despised by greedy landlords, who preferred their own terrible feudal control to the centralized government she established. There were foes outside her country, too, and she needed to see to defense especially against Neustria, which today is also part of France, and which was ruled by Queen **Fredegonde,** who herself rode at the head of her forces, carrying her tiny son, through whom she ruled. Fredegonde was by far the more barbarous. Brunhild was a patron of the arts; a poet contemporary to her age, Fortunatus, dedicated verse to her.

In A.D. 614, Queen Fredegonde's son saw to the dragging of Austrasia's elderly monarch. Brunhild may have been more tyrannical before her downfall, as long rules often corrupt politicians, and several historians describe her in very negative terms. Her armies abandoned her near the end, but that, too, is the fate of many an aging general. It may be that, like Richard III, who contrary to Shakespeare's version was a progressive king, Queen Brunhild, too, was so despised by her usurpers and adversaries that they strove to see her history rewritten negatively. [C. Morris]

Brynhild: Sometimes interchangeable with **Brunhilde** of the *Nibelungenlied,* she is, in the *Volsung Saga,* a **Valkyrie** who challenged the Norns (Fates) and as a result was placed into a magic sleep from which she was doomed to wake a mortal. Like her German counterpart, she is tricked into marriage, but avenges herself before taking her own life.

Búanann: "The Lasting One." The Celtic Mother of Heroes who operated a martial arts school akin to those of the sister warriors **Aife** and **Scáthach.** She is treated as an incarnation of **Ana** (Danu).

Budeia of Boeotia: Princess Budeia (whose name means "Goddess of Oxen"), also called Buzyge ("Ox Yoker"), raised an army to march against Thebes. She was victorious. [Graves]

bulldyke: A derogatory term for a powerfully built lesbian; also "diesel dyke." The shortened form "dyke" has been reclaimed by some lesbians as a term of endearment, though not all like it. Poet Judy Grahn, in what Antonia Fraser termed "a leap of creative imagination," believes "bulldyke" to be a corruption of **Boudicca,** the Iceni warrior-queen. Among African Americans, the term "bulldagger" is preferred, an even more amazingly coincidental term that could refer to the Cretan bull sacrifices, during which the priestess bled the bull to death by means of a dagger. The confusion over the term's origin may stem from the tendency to seek the root of all things in Europe. Much American slang comes in great part from black culture, and a direct connection with the North African **Gorgons** might be imagined through the importation of black slaves to the American South.

Bunduca: Spenser's warrior-queen, ancestress of **Britomart,** overtly derived from **Boudicca.**

Burita, Countess: In A.D. 1808, among the heroes of Saragossa during the French war on Spain, there was **Augustina, the Maid of Saragossa,** and the women's organizer, Countess Burita. She arranged noblewomen as captains and low-born women in the main ranks, and a grueling record was set for the annals of war: No city before or after ever held out so long with its walls utterly destroyed. The French were beaten back and would have to try another time, but with thirty-five thousand soldiers. As with the first onslaught, companies of women and their general, the Countess Burita, fought side by side with men, though inevitably to a tragic end. [C. Morris]

Butcharev, Vera: Captain of the women's Battalion of Death of Russia in World War I. She was noted for heroic conduct on the front. She continued to fight Germans when male soldiers were in retreat.

◆◇◆◇◆◇◆◇◆◇◆◇◆◇◆

Cabigayan, Nelida: In the early 1970s, "Commander Lina" of the Philippine's New People's Army fought the Marcos dictatorship for two years. She became a folk hero whose 1974 surrender was considered a major coup for the corrupt government. [Truby]

Caenis: "Renewed," a nymph whom the Sea-god Poseidon turned into an invulnerable male warrior, at her request, "because I am tired of being a woman," but who was later turned back into a woman and continued to live out her life as a warrior. In another legend, she had been a male in her youth, by the name of Caeneus, and was turned back into one at some later time, only to die in a battle with the Centaurs. Caenis was also goddess of the new moon. As Caeneus of Lapith, he was among the Argonauts. [Virgil, Evans, Graves]

Caeria: Queen of the Illyrians, a foe of **Cynane.** The two martial women met in battle, with Cynane's forces defeating the Illyrians "with great slaughter." Caeria met Philip's daughter in hand-to-hand combat and in that encounter met her end. [Polyaenus]

Cahina: See **Dhabba the Cahina.**

Cailleach: Scottish War-goddess, as bloodthirsty as **Sekhmet** of Egypt and **Kali** of India.

45

Caitlín of Kilcummin: A tall, strong Irish maiden of fairy lore. When her mother died, Caitlín O'Faherty set off on adventures. She sharpened the spear of Lugh, which was so heavy even gods could not lift it, though she handled it deftly. With a breath, she brought tides to a sea that had been stilled a thousand years. She sailed for Ternanog, where she learned she was the long-lost queen of the fairies.

Calamity Jane: Mule skinner, stage driver, range rider, gambler, sharp-shooter, midwife, scout, and railroad woman—the life of Martha Jane Canary, better known as Calamity Jane, was not as unusual for a woman as some would prefer to believe.

A gentle healer and samaritan on the one hand, who cured the sick and "couldn't eat a mouthful if I saw some poor little brat hungry," Calamity would nevertheless shoot off the hat of any man who couldn't watch his manners. In 1880, she wrote in a diary for her daughter, Jane Junior, of an adventure with Wild Bill Hickok:

> Everyone blamed the Indians but they were white men who did the killing and murdering and robbed the boys of gold dust. Your father dared me to drive the stage that trip after the killing. I did and found it was myself in one hell of a fix, Janey. The outlaws were back of me. It was getting dark and I knew something had to be done, so I jumped off the driver's seat on the nearest horse then on my saddle-horse which was tied to the side and joined up in the dark with the outlaws. Your father was bringing up the rear but I couldn't see it in the darkness but after they got the coach stopped and found no passengers but heaps of gold they got careless. Your father and I got the whole bunch. There were eight of them and of course they had to be shot for they wouldn't give up.

She died in poverty in 1903, her age unknown, and was buried beside Wild Bill. [Hickok, Myron, Rogers]

Califia or **Calafre:** A black Amazon queen of Ordonez de Montalvo's romance *Las Sergas de Esplandian* (Madrid, 1510). "The things that this Queen did in arms, like slaying knights, or throwing them wounded from their horses, as she pressed audaciously forward among her enemies, were such that it cannot be told nor believed that any woman has ever shown such prowess." Queen Calafre ruled an island named California in the Indies; in Columbus's day and in that of his son, common belief moved Califia's empire of gold-armored women to the Caribbean. It was from this Spanish romance, and this fictional Amazon, that the state of California took its name. [Kleinbaum, Sobol]

Callisto: A huntress and companion to **Artemis,** seduced by Zeus despite her vow of maidenhood. Artemis turned her into a she-bear and hunted her to the ground. By another account, Zeus turned her into a bear, and Artemis killed her unknowingly. [Godolphin, Graves]

Calpendre: Amazon queen of medieval Spanish literature. She and her daughter **Penthasilée,** with their armies of women, included in their forces rhinoceros-drawn chariots and war unicorns.

Camilla: Daughter of the king of Volsci, gloriously romanticized by Virgil. The *Aeneid* chiefly regards the exploits of the Trojan hero Aeneas, mythical ancestor of the Romans. When Troy fell, he led his followers to Italy, where they had to fight for the right to settle, opposed by Latin tribes led by Turnus. One of Turnus' allies was the warrior-maiden Camilla: "All the young men, rushing from houses and fields, and a crowd of mothers, wondered and watched her pass, gaping with awe in their hearts at the royal cloak that covered her slender shoulders with purple, at the clasp that bound her hair with gold, at the way she bore a Lycian quiver and a shepherd's myrtle-wood shaft tipped with a spear-head." As Turnus prepared for battle, "Camilla met him, standing in his way, with her armed host of Volscians, and under the very gates the Queen leapt from her horse; her whole troop, following her example, slipped from their horses to the ground. Then she said, 'Turnus, if a brave person may rightly feel self-confident, I dare; and I offer to attack Aeneas' cavalry, and go alone to face the Tyrrhenian horse.' "

The goddess **Diana** meanwhile told the nymph Opis that Camilla was destined to be killed. She explains Camilla's history: Her father, a tyrannical king, was driven from his throne, fleeing with his infant daughter. His way was barred by the River Amasenus. He could not swim carrying the baby, thus he tied her to a spear and threw her over the water, praying to Diana and dedicating the girl to her. The spear carried the child safely over the river; the father swam to rejoin her; and he raised her in the wilderness, having her suckled by a wild mare. Faithful to his bargain, he brought her up as a devotee of Diana, trained with weapons, and she learned to eschew marriage.

The Etruscan and Trojan cavalry met the Latin forces on the plains. Camilla was accompanied by her lieutenants, all women. "Camilla raged in the midst of the slaughter. She hurled the supple javelins, scattering them from her hand; now, unwearying, she grasps with her right hand the strong two-edged ax; the gilded bow sounded from her shoulder. And whenever she retreated, driven back, even while fleeing she turned her bow and sent back arrows. Who was the first, who was the last, to fall to your weapon, fierce virgin? How many dying bodies did you scatter on the ground?"

She killed several of the enemy, and stalked after a gloriously clad priest of **Cybele,** not knowing she was likewise stalked by Arruns, who was destined to kill her. "When the spear sent from his hand made its sound through the air, all the Volscians turned their attention and fixed their eyes on their Queen. She herself was not aware of the rush of air or the sound, or of the weapon coming through the sky; until the spear, striking home, was fixed below her bare breast, driven in, and drank deeply of the virgin's blood." Her companions, alarmed, rushed together and caught their mistress as she fell. The dying woman pulled at the weapon with her hand, but the iron point stayed fixed in a deep wound among the bones of the ribs. Then, dying, she spoke to **Acca,** one of her friends, the one truest to Camilla, who knew all her cares, and said, "So far I have succeeded, Acca my sister, but now a terrible wound has ended it. Run from here, and take this last message to Turnus: let him take up the fight, and keep the Trojans from the city. And now farewell."

For Diana's revenge against Arruns, see **Opis.** Other key literary Amazons include **Brunhilde, Bradamante, Califia,** and **Clorinda.**

Camilla: In Maude Meagher's *The Green Scamander* (1933), Camilla is a contemporary of **Penthesilea,** and her lover.

camp followers: Behind every army the world has sent marching over land, and with a good many of the naval forces as well, there were always camp followers, who might be the wives of soldiers following from the start, or women who joined the "baggage" along the way. They cooked, carried the baggage, served as nurses and as sanitation officers who buried the dead, served as scouts and spies, and suffered the same rigors as the soldiers. In antiquity, such women were apt to worship **Venus Victrix.** Camp followers followed in the wake of the Roman armies everywhere in the empire.

Not only were there camp followers in the American Revolution, but the wives of soldiers, such as the famous **Molly Pitcher,** were semiofficial conscripts who stayed close to their husbands and were habitually on the field of battle, rather than traveling with the baggage. Some were afterward granted soldiers' pensions. Camp followers of the Napoleonic era often entered the campaigns already seasoned veterans, having gained warring experience in the streets of Paris during the early days of the revolution, despite that the Napoleonic Code attempted to suppress women's soldierliness. Consuelo Dubois was a sutler who accompanied her husband for twenty years in the Napoleonic wars, "sharing victory and defeat," and was finally murdered in a famous sea disaster. The women in the armies of Attila the Hun were notoriously warlike and were integrated into the main ranks rather than relegated to the rear guard, as was true in the armies of Genghis Khan.

Virtually all of history's conquerors, whether Napoleon, the Khans, the Romans, or the Spanish conquistadors, sustained a large population of camp followers, many of whom were as a matter of course provided with uniforms (or who presumptuously designed their own) and held imitative officer ranks. Exceptions are noteworthy: Alexander the Great was said to despise camp followers, mainly because he encouraged homosexuality in his armies' ranks. By and large, without camp followers, the day-to-day needs and business of camp life simply would not have functioned. Often, one or another camp follower of especially warlike temperament would edge her way by degrees into the main ranks, slowly accepted as a regular combatant.

Canabee: An Amazon island of Spanish medieval romance, ruled by Queen **Florelle.** Columbus believed a similar island, Mantino, would be found in the Caribbean. See **Lemnos** and **Tritonia** for some idea of the origins of the recurrent myth of the Amazons' Island, bearing in mind that island nations, such as Crete and Lesbos, or in more recent history Japan, tend to preserve far older norms of government and society, by right of their relative seclusion.

Candace: Also called "Black Queen Candace" (pronounced "CAN-duh-see") was "one of the greatest generals of the ancient world," a Kushite warrior "world famous as a tactician and field commander." Bachofen states she was from India, but others identify her more credibly as Meroitic.

When Alexander marched on Old Ethiopia in 332 B.C., the fighting empress waited with war elephants at the head of her army. Alexander was stopped at the border and, as a wise general not wishing to fracture his "unbroken chain of victory," gazed upon Candace's readied host, then turned his own forces around, settling for Egypt's obeisance. Not until Ptolemy I inherited Egypt was Kushite Ethiopia in peril. [C. Williams]

Candace Amanirenas: About 30 B.C., Amanirenas was challenged by Patronius, the Roman governor of Egypt, who wished to extend Roman control into Ethiopia. She waged successful campaigns against his designs.

In 22 B.C. Amanirenas' Kushites sacked Cyrene and sent the Roman legions packing. She spread her nation's influence into Roman territories for several years before Patronius returned to his governing post to "punish" the Kushites. Yet Rome could not actually assume control of Kush while Amanirenas lived, just as Rome's hold on Egypt was feeble while **Cleopatra** lived.

A wall painting in a pyramid chapel of Meroë portrays Amanirenas with bow, arrows, and spear, holding by one hand a tethered group of seven captives. Other Candaces left monuments, including famous ones at Nagaa built during the reign of Candace Amanishakhete, and others built by Candace Nawidemak and Candace Malequereabar. The bas-reliefs at Nagaa show various Candaces armed with one or two swords, keeping pet lions that go with them into battle to help kill the foe, and subduing large numbers of enemy generals. The biblical Acts mentions a Candace who ruled about A.D. 38. [Sertima, Vlahos, Beard]

Candace Shenakdahkete: (fl. 170 B.C.) Meroitic queen who ruled as sole sovereign of Ethiopia. She is portrayed in a wall painting in a chapel in Meroë as wearing a helmet and spearing military enemies. Meroitic script has not yet been deciphered, so only a little is presently known of the histories of the "Kentakes" or, as the Greek historians called them, Candaces, warlike queen-mothers, regents, and sovereigns. [Sertima]

Canidia: A Roman sorceress criticized by Horace for her various activities, including the capture and mutilation of youths. She and her college of witches worshipped **Hecate, Tisiphone, Nemesis,** and **Diana,** and performed secret rituals by night. Canidia had "woven into her uncombed hair little vipers." She promised, "I will attack your faces with my hooked talons and deprive you of repose by terror." Her elder instructress was **Sagana,** and Horace claimed they could conjure serpents and infernal bitches. Horace also implies theirs was a lesbian cult, and satirically invites homosexual men to pee on him if he made any of it up.

Cartimandua: British warrior-queen of Brigantia in the middle of the first century. She aligned herself with Rome as a client state, in part to placate Rome and thereby aid her people, but more in order to oppose her husband, whom she had divorced in favor of his squire, and with whom she was consequently at war. Her name means "Sleek Pony," referring to a specific breed that drew chariots; this type of name was typical, as well, of the Bronze Age Amazons.

In A.D. 51, Cartimandua delivered to the Romans a powerful rebel lord in chains. She does not seem to have liked Rome, however. It was Tacitus' opinion that the yoke of Roman rule would have been thrown off had she remained in power. By some accounts, she stepped down from rule apparently of her own volition about A.D. 69. Elsewhere, it is stated that she was defeated in the year A.D. 57 by the Scottish King Corbred, who buried her alive. [Hale, Markale]

Castora: One of the innumerable Amazon queens encountered in Spanish romance. Any man who came to her nation was forced to remain for two years, on pain of death. The children of their union belonged to the state. [Kleinbaum]

Catchpole, Margaret: (A.D. 1762–1819) A British **virago,** daughter of a laborer, whose exploits began by the age of thirteen, when she was already noted for swiftness on horse. In 1797, she disguised herself as a sailor and, when discovered, was sentenced to be hanged. This was commuted to seven years' imprisonment, but she escaped to continue her career. In 1801, she was in custody again, and transported to Australia with other women prisoners. Even there, she refused ever to marry, and lived out her life as a storekeeper, midwife, and nurse. [Crawford]

Catherine, Saint: Alexandrian Christian martyr whose symbols are the sword (warrior strength), crown (virginity, defense), wheel (torment), and palm (death), and who, like the Death-goddesses of old, was associated with winter, her feast being on November 25.

Because their worship arose simultaneously and both are associated with knightly courage, St. **Barbara** and St. Catherine are often portrayed together. St. Catherine became a special favorite of women soldiers (see under **Catherine the Great**). She was tied between four wheels with turning swords, but the wheels broke asunder in an explosion of such violence that "the executioners and three thousand spectators perished," suggesting not so much a true miracle as a religious riot led by Catherine. She was later beheaded. Her worship has been suppressed from time to time, and she was stricken from the liturgical calendar in 1969, but she remains the most popular saint in the Western world, after Mary Magdalene, honored as the patron of philosophy and science because of her extraordinary intellect.

Catherine de Clermont: In the sixteenth century, this French heroine valiantly defended her estates and compelled her soldiers to acknowledge Henry IV.

Catherine the Great: (A.D. 1729–1796) A German princess who became queen of Russia. The fame of aristocratic women at arms is reflected in Arthur Quiller-Couch's fairy tale "The Czarina's Violet." The story says, "In the days when the Czarina was a bride, court ladies used to be famous for archery, and she most of all." Voltaire considered Catherine the Great to be "a Northern Semiramis," and certainly at the height of her career her ability as a commander in chief was noteworthy. One tale has it that she appeared personally on the battlements during siege, and instructed additional cannons be made from the winter's ice, but these cannons blew to pieces upon their attempted use (it seems more likely that such dummy cannons were intended to mislead a besieging foe as to the number of cannons available).

In June of 1762, Catherine, then grand duchess, appeared in military uniform at the head of rebel regiments. Her lady-in-waiting, the Princess Dashkova (1744–1810), was also in uniform. Both claimed association with the warlike Order of St. Catherine. Catherine's bold appearance inspired a young officer—Grigory Potemkin—to rush forth with a pennant for her naked sword. [Fraser]

Cathuboduae: A Gallic War-goddess known from a Gallo-Roman inscription discovered at Savoy. Perhaps an incarnation of **Bodb.**

Cattle Kate: Born Ella Watson (A.D. 1862?–1888), she was a Wyoming outlaw of the Old West. She was hanged for cattle rustling. Local legend had it that she was an Indian fighter before she became a bandit. [Horan, Aikman]

Cavanagh, Kit: (A.D. 1667–1739) She was among the women who became dragoons, fighting in the 1690s with the British Army and taking wounds. At first she went disguised as a man, but later fought openly as a woman. Between campaigns, she twice owned and operated public houses. She was also known as Christian Davies, but her best known sobriquet was "Mother Ross." She survived to a natural death and received a military burial. [Defoe]

Celaeno: "Obscurity," one of the **Harpies.** Also, an Amazon spearwoman who lived during the reign of **Hippolyte.** She hunted together with **Eurybe** and **Phoebe,** and they always stood shoulder to shoulder in combat. Their last battle was against invulnerable Heracles, who "with one obscene swipe of the sword disposed of the gallant threesome."

Centaurs: That the Centaurs were originally Amazons, the first race to ride astride horses, and mistaken for composite monsters by the first peoples they conquered, is a theory presently in disfavor, though unconvincingly debunked. The numerous horse-headed goddesses, goddesses who can take the form of mares, and female creatures like the **Empusaë** that can take a form part horse, part woman, suggest an antiquity for the female centaur greater than for the male. See **Nephele.**

Ceto: In Greek mythology, mother of the **Gorgons** and Echidna, daughter of **Gaia.**

Cezelli, Constance de: In 1590, after her husband's capture, she was entrusted with the defense of Leucates in Languedoc. She showed herself at the town's walls with pike in hand, repulsing the besieging Spanish wherever they tried a breach. She attempted to ransom her husband with her own possessions, but would not give up the town, having received her husband's explicit instructions never to do so. When she learned that he had been tortured and killed, she was grief stricken, but continued the defense coolheadedly and was successful. Henry IV, hearing of her valor, commissioned her to continue as governor of Leucates, which position she held for twenty-seven years, after which it passed to her son. [Starling, Hale, Montez]

Chamunda: Demon-quelling goddess of ancient India, related to **Durga, Kali,** and **Parvati.** [Kramer]

Chand Bibi: A Moslem queen of Central India in the late sixteenth century who fought for her people against the Monguls. She united the feuding factions of Ahmednager. [Hale]

Chandika or **Chandi:** "The Fierce," a Hindu Moon- and War-goddess, one of **Kali's** incarnations, an aspect of the **Devi.** Bana, a seventeenth-century author, states that Chandika was worshipped in the Vindhya Mountains of central India, where she was given offerings of blood and flesh gouged from the worshippers' own bodies. He says she was worshipped by the aristocracy of western India as well. Her temples were "filled with demonesses sacred to the Mother." For centuries, she was the patron of robbers of the Vindhyas. As a Robber-goddess, she was said personally to waylay travelers and relieve them of possessions. As Chandi, she was the defender of rajas. Her worship continues in India today.

Charlotte, Countess of Derby: Charlotte Stanley became the famed countess of Derby and was said to have "stolen her husband's breeches" by being the better soldier. She defended the house of Lathom against parliamentarian troops for two years in the mid-1640s. A French Hugenot, granddaughter of William the Silent (of Orange), she was raised in the splendor of court life. In 1643, her husband, the earl of Derby, was on the Isle of Man seeing after various affairs, while the countess remained in Lathom House, an impregnable fortress with good supplies and its own water source.

By the rules of siege, with a quick surrender no one would be killed, meaning that the enemy would not slaughter all the women and children defenders after all. Without surrender, the enemy gave no quarter. The countess sent word to the besieging captain that, given her higher social status, he should submit to her, not she to him. Various other summons were rebuffed in similarly ladylike, highborn manner. She said, "I will preserve my liberty by my arms, rather than to buy a piece of slavery."

Mortar fire pounded the walls and flaming grenades were unleashed upon the towers, where women scorched their hands putting out fires. For his final, self-assured assault, the captain invited the public to witness his last attack, but to his humiliation the countess's motley army rushed forth, took possession of the mortars, and drew them into the fortress.

The "Heroick Countess" lived another twenty years. In her old age, she delighted in telling her war stories to neighbors. [Fraser, Starling]

Charope: "Brilliant Confrontation," an Amazon brave of the Attic War, known from a lecythos now housed in the Museum of the City of New York.

Charybdis: See **Scylla.**

Chauteau-Gay, Madame de: In the writings of Tallemant de Reaux (*Historiette 460: Femmes vaillantes*), several swashbuckling women of the French age of duelists are mentioned, among them two sisters, one married to a M. de Chauteau-Gay of Murat. The married sister "was both gallant and handsome; she was generally to be seen on horseback, wearing huge top-boots, kilted skirts and a man's wide-brimmed hat with steel trimmings and feathers to crown all, sword by side and pistols at saddle-bow."

She had an affair with a man other than her husband. This fellow was subsequently arrested and ill treated by a captain of a private company of Light-Horse. This so angered Mme. de Chauteau-Gay that she felt compelled to challenge the captain of the Light-Horse in a duel. The captain, aware of Madame's ability with the sword, made his appearance at the appointed hour with two other swordsmen of his company.

The squire of the gallant lady of Murat begged her to give up her cause, for her enemy was too coarse to duel in fairness. But she replied, "It shall never be said that I encountered them without attacking them." The fight was engaged, and the lady put up an excellent fight. Despite "every possible resistance," the trio surrounded her and "they were cowardly enough to kill her."

Whether Mme. de Chauteau-Gay's boisterous sister ever sought revenge is not told, but we can hope such was the case. For it was this sister's delight, we are told, "to pass her leisure time in snuffing candles with an arquebus." [Beaumont]

Chelidonis: A princess of Sparta. In 280 B.C., the city was preparing for siege, and planned to send the royal wives and daughters to a farther town for their safety. Chelidonis appeared unexpectedly in the Senate, sword in hand, swearing that the women of the city would fight. She not only captained the Spartan women atop the city wall, but kept a rope tied about her neck, so that if any foe succeeded in dragging her over the side, they would not have her alive. [Hale]

Chernova, Tanja: Red Army gunner in World War II. In one raid on a German headquarters, she set explosives and killed guards with silenced rifle fire. She killed an SS agent in hand-to-hand combat. [Truby]

Chesnières, Virginie: A sergeant of the 17th Infantry Regiment who fought throughout the Peninsular War, serving Napoleon. She remained in the rear guard to fight off British during the retreat over the Pyrenees. She lived until 1873. [Laffin]

Chess queen: The queen in the game of chess acquired her ascendency over the king in the late fifteenth century, due in great part to the exploits of the militant queen Caterina **Sforza.** Many queens were warriors in the medieval world, and in many cases they were their kings' superiors; hence, it was only natural that the queen became the most powerful piece on the chessboard.

Chiang Ch'ing: (b. A.D. 1914) Wife of Chairman Mao. In 1937, she was a student radical who fled Shanghai and the Japanese invasion. In Yenan, she met women who were survivors of Mao's "Long Walk." She underwent rigorous military training and Marxist indoctrination. In the 1940s, she participated in "the military drama" of the liberation wars. She later played the pivotal role in the politicizing of all cultural activity in China. She virtually ruled China after Mao's death, not altogether wisely. [Wolf]

Chicomecoatl: The Terrible Mother, Great Goddess of the aborigines of Mexico, before Christianization. She created the world and was a benefactress, but was also a violent Death-goddess clad in snakes, armed with flint knife, and having claws like a jaguar. The skull is her symbol. [Lederer]

Chief Earth Woman: (nineteenth century) One of many fighting women of the Objibwa Indians, she claimed to have gained magic powers from a dream, justifying her accompanying braves on the warpath. [Niethammer]

Ch'iu Chin: See **Qin Jin.**

Ching, Hsi Kai: In 1804, a man named Ching Yih led a pirate fleet of six or seven hundred junks. He died in 1807 in a typhoon, and his widow immediately became leader. With the help of Chang Pao, who had been one of her husband's lieutenants, the widow Ching built the largest pirate fleet the world has ever seen, ruling a veritable floating nation of seventy thousand men, women, and children upon more than two thousand vessels. She harried the Chinese coast for three years and so controlled the seas that she alone could offer safe passage through her ships' waters, guaranteeing, for a fee, protection from herself.

It was the famine of 1799 that drove so many Chinese to become buccaneers. Sympathetic to peasants, Madame Ching encouraged her mighty fleet to prey on Portuguese, English, and Mandarin ships, and insisted the coastal peasants not be molested, under penalty of death. Because her imposing navy had family ties along the coast, villagers actually benefited from the existence of Madame Ching's industry.

When it came to military tactics, Ching was brilliant, defeating the Mandarin navy in all attempts to exterminate the "wasps of the sea." One such fleet retreated at the mere sight of her ships. In 1808, she met the warships of the Chinese Empire with only a few ships of her own, but she had cunningly placed many more of her ships behind a headland; during the battle, these hidden ships were able to achieve a rear attack. Twenty-eight war junks surrendered to her that day.

The Chinese government eventually forbade all ships to enter her waters, hoping to starve the pirates out of business. Ching's followers perforce laid aside their high principles in the treatment of peasants and poured into the coastal regions, plundering and murdering up the rivers. At this point, her fortunes began to turn, and even foreign ships began to hunt her down, although a joint Chinese and Portuguese blockade failed to destroy even one of her ships.

Chang Pao, Hsi Kai Ching's able lieutenant, began to have ambitions to take over Ching's sea empire. About this time, a strong offensive by the

Chinese government crippled one of her squadrons. The government offered amnesty and even paid pirates to surrender. One entire squadron took advantage of the offer. A second amnesty, offered in 1810, was accepted by Madame Ching and her lieutenant. They received pardons, money, and commissions. Hence, Madame Ching was able to spend the rest of her days in prosperity and at the landlubberly job of smuggling. [Snow, Glasspoole, Day]

Ch'in Liang-yü: (d. A.D. 1668) Ming loyalist famed for political and military exploits. One of her most important captains was **Ma Feng-i,** her daughter-in-law. When the Ming government collapsed, Ch'in Liang-yü managed to preserve her personal political base, her authority in Szechwan being recognized until her death. [Wolf]

Chiomaca: A martial princess of the Gauls captured during the war between the Galatians and the Romans in 186 B.C. When the call for retreat was sounded, she refused to leave the battlefield, but raged on with her few companions. When captured, she was raped by a centurion. She subsequently killed the centurion and chopped off his head, which she delivered to her husband. [Hale, Starling, Goodrich]

Chloris: The **Heraean** Games were a woman-oriented Olympics founded in Hera's honor by Queen **Hippodameia.** The women contested with right breast exposed, hair flowing free, in knee-length tunics. Chloris, Niobe's only surviving daughter, also named Meliboëa, was the first victrix of these games, which occurred every fourth year.

A Roman Chloris is mentioned by Horace as the wife of Ibycus. She abandoned her husband to "sport with damsels," in a lesbian-oriented bacchanalia.

Christian, Lady Bruce: Sister of Robert I. During the Wars of Independence and the reign of Edward I, Lady Bruce defended Kildrummy Castle when it was besieged by David the Strathbogie, who served English interests. Strathbogie fell in battle, and it was left to his widow to defend (for seven months) the island fortress of Lochindorb against three thousand vengeful Scots. Christian's sisters Marjory Bruce and Mary Bruce were also warlike, as was that grotesquely punished Bruce supporter **Isobel, Countess of Buchan.** [Marshall, Fittis]

Christina, Queen of Sweden: (A.D. 1626–1689) Christina cut off her hair, wore pants, abdicated the throne, and became a notorious adventurer throughout Europe in the seventeenth century. Her autobiography is circumspect; had she been capable of honesty to the last, we might have been left a chronicle to rival the autobiography of Benvenuto Cellini. She went with sword at her side, a holster on her belt, and a riding crop in hand. Her contemporary, Madame de Motteville, described her thus: "Her boots are like a man's and so are her voice and almost all her features. She affected to be a man in all her actions. She laughed immoderately when anything pleased her. She put her legs up on seats," and once she was spied by King Louis's mother "with two hideously ugly women who wallowed in her bed." Many of her biographers (and there are easily a score) have overlooked her lesbianism while making much foolish todo about her liaisons with men. A few, such as Georgina Watson, acknowledge her "lesbian tendencies" but homophobically attempt to explain it as tied to her "tainted heritage" of "insanity on both sides of her family." In actuality, she was fearlessly eccentric in days when it was not easy for a woman to be so. Whether as commander in chief campaigning against Naples or as a sensualist arranging festivities for the citizens of Hamburg (several of whom she had to kill when the mob became rowdy), she was to her very core a swashbuckler born, a Don Juan among women, and a thoroughly misunderstood Amazon par excellence. [Mackenzie, Taylor, Masson, Myron]

Chrodielde: A martial nun of the convent of Poitiers. Her bid to usurp **Leubevére,** abbess of Cheribert, in A.D. 590, began with political maneuvering and escalated to battle. Repulsed from the convent along with her partisans, Chrodielde withdrew to the fortified cathedral of St. Hilary and there raised an army of criminals and outcasts, who fought against the bishops seeking Chrodielde's arrest. At the heart of Chrodielde's popularity with the peasants was the greed of the landholding church authority, who were frankly no better than any other landlords then or now. It seems evident that nuns and midwives commonly filled the void of sympathetic leadership among the peasants of the medieval world, which is but one of the reasons for the massive witch burnings.

Childebert, King of France, sent his troops to put down the war between Chrodielde and Leubevére, "but Chrodielde and her banditti made such a valiant resistance that it was with difficulty the king's orders were executed." Chrodielde was ultimately excommunicated for leading peasants to rebellion. [Hale, King]

Chuiza, Baltazara: Led a revolt against the Spanish in Ecuador in 1778.

The Cimbrian Women: In the year 102 B.C., Caius Marius was recalled from Africa to organize the Roman legions against invading barbarians, the Cimbrians, whose violently nomadic ways threatened Gaul and northern Italy. Among the moving hosts were enormous mobile dwellings with thick wooden wheels. These were called wagon-castles, in which the children were protected. During skirmishes, women came forth from the wagon-castles to defend them with swords, or fired arrows from above, while the men ranged farther throughout the battles.

In 101 B.C., on the plain of Vercellae, frightful carnage ensued. Marius wrote that when the Cimbrian men were driven back, they were greeted by their women with swords, ready to kill their own husbands if they failed against the Romans. Thus, the northern barbarians fought to the last, retreat being impossible. The women were sole defenders of their camp, and they continued to resist even when the men were annihilated by the combined forces of Marius and Catulus. When all was lost, these women fell upon their children, slaying them, rather than have them become slaves, then sought their own deaths, "either by the hands of friends or by nooses twisted of their own hair."

Cintrón, Conchita: Born of a Puerto Rican father and Irish-American mother in Chile, Conchita was raised in Peru. When she began bullfighting in Mexico, she was an instant success for her physical beauty, grace, and bravery. In the 1940s, she was the only woman worthy of the title "*torera.*" Most women of the bullring were limited to fighting "Portuguese style" from horseback; Conchita was the first modern *torera* to fight bulls on foot. She retired in the early 1950s to the busy life of fame, motherhood, and newspaper reporting on bullfights. See also Doña Ana Lezama de **Urinza** and Patricia **McCormick.** [Cintrón, Conrad, Campbell]

Clara: The heroine of *Love's Cure; The Martial Maid* (1621). She fights in war, alongside her father, in the guise of a young man. It is later decided she must be cured of her inappropriate behavior, but nothing overcomes her sense of valor, honor, and her need to fight for a just cause, until she falls in love and utterly caves in.

Claridiana: Amazon of Ortunez de Calahorra's epic *Mirror of Knighthood.*

Claudia Quintas: (fl. 143 B.C.) A Roman matron and strongwoman who had a grounded ship tied to her girdle by means of a long rope. After praying to the Magna Mater (**Cybele**), she dragged the ship out of the shallows, though scores of young men working together had been unable to do it. [Boccaccio]

Clelia: The exact history of this Roman heroine has been obscured by romance. As an equestrian statue was erected in her honor, the Romans evidently considered her a soldier. She was the leader of ten virgins sent as hostages to Porseuna, an offering to stay his march on Rome. They escaped and made their way to the Tiber River, pursued by their enemies. Clelia encouraged the other nine to leap with her into the river, and, despite the rough currents, all swam to the further bank and to safety. The Senate, fearing reprisals, returned them to captivity, but Porseuna, admiring their valor, gave them their liberty.

Cleopatra: Daughter of **Olympias** and Philip II, one of innumerable vigorous Hellenistic women of this name. Like her mother, she was warlike, and traveled freely about Macedonia and nearby nations, performing Olympias' will. After the death of Olympias, Cleopatra fell into a state of semicaptivity at Sardis, due to the machinations of Antipater and Antigonus. In 308 B.C., she attempted to flee from Sardis, planning a marriage-alliance with Ptolemy in Egypt, who was amenable to her proposal. An armed group of women was sent from Sardis to waylay her, and she was killed. Antigonus perfidiously had the assassins put to death, rather than rewarded, lest he suffer repercussions for Cleopatra's murder. "Like Philip's other daughters," writes Grace Macurdy, "Cleopatra was murdered by men who feared her power."

Cleopatra I: Called "Thea the Assyrian," and Goddess Manifest, she flourished in the second century B.C. Only a little is known of her history, but sufficient to surmise that she set the tone of rule for dynastic Cleopatras to follow. She was the daughter of Antiochus the Great and mother of **Cleopatra II.** She coruled Egypt with her husband, then ruled as regent to her son, and stabilized Egypt at a time when every surrounding country was in turmoil. It is a good guess that she established the tradition among the Cleopatras of giving high military office to Jewish soldiers, ensuring a militant base of support for her interests.

Cleopatra II: Daughter of **Cleopatra I.** She was an energetic queen and actual ruler of Egypt until her death in 173 B.C. Her son was murdered by Physkon of Alexandria after he was expelled from rule due to cruel excesses. Cleopatra was established in Physkon's place as sole sovereign in 130 B.C. In vengeful anger, he chopped her son into small pieces and sent them to her on her birthday in a box. Diodorus reports only the mother's grief. Justin tells more of her history: that she warred against Euergetes who invaded Egypt, but, losing his bid for the throne because of Cleopatra's strength, was forced back into Syria. She remained queen for fifty-seven years, and not until her death was another Syrian-Egyptian war declared.

For two centuries, the Ptolemies of Macedonia kept Egypt independent by force of arms. Seven Ptolemy queens (together with numerous of their daughters, sisters, or mothers) were called Cleopatra, and while only the seventh and last is well known today, many of the others were very notably warlike and the actual rulers of Egypt during their lives.

Cleopatra III: (second century B.C.) Elder daughter of Ptolemy VI Philometer and **Cleopatra II,** she was "a very strong and remarkable woman" and "the most domineering of the Macedonian-Hellenistic queens." She ruled as regent to Philometer II. Her uncle, Euergetes Physkon, married her in order to legitimize his own claim to the throne. But he later divorced her and married *her* daughter (his niece), also named Cleopatra. Philometer I's elder daughter immediately raised a rebel army and forced her power-grabbing, faithless husband into exile in Cyprus, the family's traditional wound-licking retirement camp. Three years later, Philometer II was allowed to return to his throne, chastised, subservient, and devoted thereafter only to art and literature.

During Philometer's exile, Cleopatra placed her son Lathyrus on the throne, but he had delusions of actually ruling Egypt himself. "Partly by intrigue, partly by actual force," she caused his exile as well, having led an army against him in Gaza. Lathyrus' army was noted for its strength and cruelty, yet Cleopatra crushed him. She hadn't been certain she could overcome the odds, for "upon opening the campaign in Palestine, she felt the situation so grave that she sent her grandchildren with treasure and her will to safekeeping in Kos." But the campaign was so successful that she was tempted to continue to subdue cities and obtain sovereignty over Palestine. She did not do so because Rome was a threat and because the Jews, whom she always favored, were a large part of her power base, and there was no certainty they would want to help her conquer other nations. So, settling for a decisive victory over Lathyrus, she withdrew, having first married her own daughter to the Syrian king, ensuring no further quarrels over the throne of Antioch. She ruled thereafter, "an energetic despot," with only minor molestation, and was worshipped as **Isis** incarnate. Upon her death in 81 B.C., at about the age of sixty, power passed to another of her sons, Ptolemy IX Alexander. [Macurdy]

Cleopatra V Selene: (129?–69 B.C.) Second wife and younger sister of Ptolemy X Soter II, and possibly the mother of **Berenice II.** Sir John Mahaffy observes, "It must have been the personal wealth of these Egyptian princesses Arsinoë, Cleopatra Tryphaena and by and by Selene, which gave them the power of assembling armies, waging wars, and marrying royal claimants." Grace Macurdy refers to Selene's "adventurous life" and compares her to the notably warlike **Cleopatra III.** Of her exact exploits, little specific information survives.

Cleopatra VI Tryphaena: Until her death in about 50 or 57 B.C., Tryphaena ("Luxurious") was the actual ruler of Egypt, as sister-wife of Ptolemy XI Auletes. "She observed no restraint," says Sir John Mahaffy, who believes that the Cleopatras, Arsinoës, Selene, and other of the Ptolemy queens were able to wage their wars due to independent wealth and the attendant ability to sustain their own armies. Grace Macurdy, on the other hand, believes of Tryphaena that too little survives to judge her character, although she was "apparently a lady of no spirit," whose only claim to excellence is the likelihood that she was the mother of **Cleopatra VII,** last and most famed of the dynastic Cleopatras.

Cleopatra VII, Queen of Egypt: (69–30 B.C.) "The Romans feared her as they had feared only Hannibal." Cleopatra first came to the rule of Egypt at the age of seventeen. She was tall and athletic, with exquisite mental gifts, uncommonly fond of science and philosophy, studying, besides art and history, metallurgy, chemistry, and astronomy. She was clever, cruel, and ambitious, considered by her people to be the incarnation of the goddess **Isis.** When she was temporarily forced from the throne, she went to Palestine and Syria to raise an army. While she may also have been a sensualist, the popular image of her is not just. She should be remembered as history's second female admiral, after **Artemisia.** She dreamed of a multilingual Eastern Empire with herself at its head, for which purpose she allied herself with Mark Antony's cause, their "love affair" being in great part a battle of charisma to see who could use the other's ambition to his and her respective best interests. Their joint sea battle at Actium was a disaster, but had it fallen otherwise, she and Antony need not have committed suicide, but would have ruled from their respective capitals as master and mistress of the world. [Shepherd, Pomeroy, Hale, Jameson]

Clete or **Cleite:** "The Invoked." The Amazon who raised **Penthesilea.** On hearing Penthesilea had gone to liberate Troy, Clete set sail to join her, but was blown off course to Italy, where she founded the city Clete. The successive Amazon queens who ruled this city were called the Cleitae. The city was eventually destroyed by the Crotonians. [Graves]

Clonie: One of **Penthesilea's** hand-selected companions-at-arms during the liberation of Troy. She slew Menippus, splitting him in two, and was afterward killed by Podarces, and he in turn was killed by Penthesilea.

Clorinda: Heroine from Tasso's epic poem *Jerusalem Delivered*. She is introduced to the story as she charges onto the scene of injustice to save the lives of a young couple. She fought on the Moslem side during the Crusades, yet is treated with complete dignity by the Catholic author.

Clymene: "Famous Might." Given sometimes as the mother of **Atalanta.** Another Clymene was in the Attic War, engaging both Theseus and Phaleros in single combat. [Bothmer]

Coatlicue: "Serpent-Skirt." Malevolent goddess of skulls and serpents, worshipped by the Indians of Mexico, of Aztec origin. The benevolent protectress **Tanantsi** went to war with Coatlicue, defeating her. [Preston]

Cochrane, Grizel: A seventeenth-century Scottish heroine. In 1685, she heard that a warrant had been issued for the death of her father, who had been imprisoned by political foes. She immediately saddled her horse and set forth to waylay the messenger, take the document by force, and destroy it. The nobleman was pardoned before a second warrant could be issued. [Fittis, Hale]

Coinchend: In Irish myth, she was a monstrous warrior and wife of Morgan of the Land of Wonder. She was slain by Art, High King of Ireland. [Ellis]

Colestah: (fl. A.D. 1877) Warrior-wife of the famous chief Kamiakin, American Indian of the Pacific Northwest. At the Battle of Spokane Plain, "Kamiakin was accompanied by his youngest wife, Colestah, who was known as a medicine woman, psychic, and warrior. Armed with a stone war club, Colestah vowed to fight to the death by her husband's side. For this reason she went into battle wearing her finest buckskin dress with her hair tightly braided around her head. When Kamiakin was wounded, Colestah carried him off and used her skill as an Indian doctor to nurse him back to health." [Trafzer]

concubator: The masculine of concubine. The concubators of the **Macouda,** highest ranking officer of the **Dahomey Amazons,** were expected to remain faithful, under penalty of death. **Nzingha** of Angola had fifty or more concubators, dressed and named like women. Heracles became the concubator of **Omphale.**

Connie Ann: In American Negro folklore, Connie Ann (a variant of Polly Ann) was John Henry's wife. He was the mightiest of steel-driving men for the railroads. Once when John fell ill, Connie took his place. In the race with an automatic steam hammer, John died defeating the machine, and Connie carried on his work afterward.

> John Henry had a wife
> Name of Connie Ann
> John got sick and couldn't get well
> Connie drove steel like a man.

A mighty man needed a mighty woman! [C. Williams]

Corbin, Margaret Cochran: (A.D. 1751–1800) "Captain Molly," one of many heroines of the American Revolution. Margaret was a cannoneer who fought against the Hessians (German mercenaries) and bloody-backs (British redcoats) alongside her husband. When he was killed at the Battle of Monmouth, and her own body was torn with grapeshot, she continued to fight. So brave were her actions that she was afterward awarded a commission. [Evans, Logan]

Cornelia: Daughter of Scribonia. Cornelia was a young woman who in the first century B.C. took up arms to defend her honor against Caesar. She took flight in one of her fastest ships, and the jilted Caesar set out after her. Hers was the faster ship and she could have outpaced him, but, perceiving that she was ruined in Rome in any case, she resolved upon a glorious death. She halted her ship, and faced Caesar's men, sword in hand, and was killed. [Assa]

Coyolxauhqui: "The One Whose Face Was Tattooed with Rattlesnakes," Aztec patroness of war. Her last battle was against her mother **Coatlicue**, mother of a Warrior-god. When Coatlicue's son was born in the midst of battle, he immediately took up arms to defend his mother. He beheaded the Rattlesnake-goddess and killed her armies. [Kramer]

Cratesipolis, Queen of Sicyon: (fl. 300 B.C.) She fought alongside her husband, Alexander, and continued to be embroiled in warfare after his death, commanding important Greek cities and maintaining a vast army of mercenaries. She conquered Corinth on behalf of Ptolemy I, and expected, in reward, to achieve a marriage-alliance with him. He considered the alliance, but it never came about. [Hale, Macurdy]

Creidne: In the Celtic heroic age, Creidne was the female champion of the Fenians. She had three sons by an incestuous relationship, but escaped from her wicked father in order to take up arms and distinguish herself mightily. [Ellis]

Crocale: The most skillful of **Artemis'** huntress nymphs. With **Nephele** and **Hyale,** she attended Artemis the day Actaeon spied them naked, for which he was transformed into a stag and torn apart by his own hounds. [Bulfinch]

Cuhtahlatah: A Cherokee **Molly Pitcher,** her name means "Wild Hemp." When her husband was killed in an enemy attack, she took up his toma-hawk and screamed "Kill! Kill!," attacking the enemy. Her people had been in retreat, but her bravery caused them to rally and they gained victory. [Niethammer]

Cunningham, Ann: (d. A.D. 1647) In 1639, the Calvinist militant Lady Ann Cunningham was "a notable Virago" who struck terror in the hearts of the English. At Berwick on June 5, 1639, she rode with pistols at saddle, daggers at girdle, leading a troop of horse. Her attendant women were also soldiers and expert markswomen. [Fraser]

Cushman, Pauline: (A.D. 1835–1893) A darkly beautiful gypsy who earned the honorary rank of major for her part in the Civil War behind enemy lines in Tennessee. She lectured in the West in full uniform and became a well-known actress specializing in Amazonian roles. She ran a hotel in a rough Arizona town and, packing a .45, helped maintain law and order. In San Francisco, she publicly bullwhipped a man who had spread rumors about her. [Horan]

Custer, Elizabeth: (A.D. 1842–1933) When Major General George A. Custer came to Indian country in the Western territories after the Civil War, he was accompanied by his wife, Libbie. She often rode with the 7th Cavalry when they were out on patrol, covering as many as forty miles a day at the head of the regimental column, beside her husband or with such scouts as Wild Bill Hickok and Medicine Bill Comstock. Custer, aware that his regiment might one day be overrun by Indians, had given orders to his men to shoot Libbie rather than let her fall into the hands of the Indians, of which plan Libbie did not approve. She only barely missed being at the Battle of Little Big Horn. She and her sister-in-law had ridden out the night before with the 7th Cavalry, but the next morning they rode back to the fort. In old age, she traveled to India and rode horseback through the Kyber Pass to Afghanistan. She died at the age of ninety-two and was laid to rest near her husband at West Point.

Cwoenthryth: (early ninth century) Mercian princess and abbess who inherited property and authority from King Coenwulf of Mercia. Her authority was challenged by Archbishop Wulfed, and bitter wars were waged for control of the abbey estates. [Crawford]

Cybele: "She of the Ax," the Phrygian Mother-goddess, worshipped by the Amazons of the Thermodon as **Tauropolos** and by the Cretans as **Rhea.** As Kubala-Cybele, she was Mother of Gods, Men, Mountains, and Lions. The Great Mother was worshipped everywhere in Europe, North Africa, and Asia Minor, preferably in caves, sometimes in the form of meteoric stones, her worship apparently dating to the early Stone Age, before the advent of anthropomorphized deities. A hymn to Cybele survives from the second century A.D., which goes in part: "She prepares the fast-riding chariot, drawn by bull-killing lions." Bulls were slaughtered for her, symbolic of sacrificing men. Her lover was the castrate youth Attis. Though repeatedly absorbed regionally into various other goddesses, her worship survived into Roman times when, as Magna Mater, her fiercest attributes were preserved (see also **Black Mary**). [Tyrrell, Farnell, Vermaseren]

Cymê: Commander of one thousand cavalry and ten thousand footsoldiers of the Libyan Amazons or **Gorgons,** serving under **Mitylenê,** sister of the Amazon queen **Myrene.** Equal numbers were headed by other of Myrene's captains, **Pitana** and **Priénê.** She founded a city in her name, from which coins bearing her image survive.

Cymothoe: In Greek myth, an immortal Nereid who fought the storms of Aeolus in defense of the Trojan fleet. She served **Hera.**

Cynane: Famed for military knowledge, Cynane conducted armies and "in the field charged at the head of them." She was the widow of Amnytas, son of Perdiccas, and never took another husband after his death. By him, she had birthed **Eurydice, Queen of Macedonia,** destined to be a foe of **Olympias.**

As the daughter of Philip and half sister of Alexander, Cynane was rightful heir to Alexander's empire, but, upon his death, the generals divided the empire among themselves. Cynane set out to right this injustice to her line. Beyond the Hellespont, she was met by the Macedonian army's superior numbers. The generals did not think well of themselves for their treasonous self-interest and, no doubt, knew that even though they outnumbered Cynane's forces, she would yet wreak havoc among them. Thus, they offered her a respectable retirement. She thought this unworthy of the daughter of Philip and, reviling her foes for their ingratitude, "resolved upon a glorious death," and pressed the battle to the end. [Polyaenus, Pomeroy, Macurdy]

Cynethryth: (late eighth century) Queen of Mercia, wife of King Offa. When widowed, she received vast estates to rule as lady-abbess. These she staunchly defended, by violence when necessary. She is the only Anglo-Saxon queen who struck coins bearing her own image. [Crawford]

Cynisca: The daughter of Spartan nobility, she won the chariot race at Olympia in the fourth century B.C., the first woman victrix at the games. Women of Sparta, under the laws of Lycurgus (seventh century B.C.), were encouraged in the arts of the javelin toss, running, and wrestling. Cynisca's brother had dared her to enter the games, believing her victory would undermine the games' importance to the Greeks. [Hale, Starling, Pomeroy]

Cynthia: Alternate name for **Artemis,** Moon-goddess of the hunt, after Mt. Cynthus in Delos, where she was born.

Cyrene: "Sovereign Mistress of the Bridle." At Pelias' funeral games, she defeated the swiftest runners, winning two hunting dogs. Her son by Ares was King Diomedes, who owned the four savage man-eating mares roped by Heracles as one of his labors. These horses imply a link to the horse-headed Moon-goddess of the Amazons.

Cyrene was the daughter of the Naiad Chlidanope and King Hyseus of the Lapiths. Apollo spied her wrestling a lion, and fell in love with her. She birthed him two sons. She founded a city in Libya named for herself, and indulged her passion for hunting in the surrounding hills, accompanied by a circle of archer-nymphs. [Graves]

Cythna: A female knight in Shelley's *Revolt of Islam* (1818).

D

◇◆◇◆◇◆◇◆◇◆◇◆◇◆◇

Dahomey Amazons: The most famed of numerous African tribal Amazons, whose traditions survived into the twentieth century. See **Nausica, Adadimo, Seh-Dong-Hong-Beh,** and **Macouda.**

Dakini: A War-goddess of northern India. She feasted on the flesh and blood of defeated warriors.

Dana: Same as Danu or **Anan.**

Daphne: "Laurel." She was a huntress nymph of **Artemis,** but Apollo desired and pursued the unwilling, fleet-footed virgin. When nearly captured, she called for the assistance of her father, a River-God, who transformed her into a laurel tree. Thereafter, the laurel wreath, symbol of victory, youthfulness, and purity, was worn by Apollo, and also by the Caesars. Another account says she was saved by her mother **Rhea,** who whisked her away to Crete, where she was known as Pasiphaë, mother of the Minotaur.

In yet another of Daphne's legends, she was seen amidst her college of huntresses by Leucippus, who fell in love with her, but knew the huntresses were lesbians. He disguised himself as a girl in order to win Daphne's heart, but, during a lustration ceremony, his sex was discovered, and he was torn limb from limb. [Graves]

Daphoene: "The Bloody One." A violent Moon-goddess worshipped at

68

Tempe "by a college of orgiastic laurel-chewing **Maenads.**" Bay laurel is a hallucinogen that incited the women to riot. Daphoene had the head of a horse, and in her honor the sacred king was torn to pieces in an annual celebration by the wildwomen who were her devotees, similar to rites practiced in Crete and by Druidic priestesses of Britain. [Plutarch, Graves]

David, Julienne: A privateer during the French Revolution. She also spent time in the belly of an English prison ship. [Croix]

Davies, Christian: Best known as "Mother Ross," her real name was Kit **Cavanaugh.**

Deborah: "The Bee," a typical goddess reference. Deborah was a biblical heroine, prophetess, and eventually monarch over an age of peace. She led an army against the enemies of Israel in 1296 B.C. Her song of triumph is the oldest Hebrew verse that survives: "The people were oppressed in Israel, until you arose, Deborah, as the mother of Israel."

Deianeira: "Strings Together Spoils," one of the Amazon braves slain by Heracles as they challenged him one by one.

Deidameia: "Taker of Spoils," she attacked and took Ambracia to revenge the death of Ptolemy. Sadly, Deidameia, daughter of Pyrrhus, did not live long enough to appreciate her victory. Through treachery, she was slain by a villain while she was worshipping in the temple of **Diana** Hegemone. [Polynaesus]

Deinomache: "Terrible Warrior," cavalry brave of the Attic War led by **Orithia.** [Bothmer]

Delaye, Marguerite: At the siege of Montélimar laid by Admiral Coligny in A.D. 1569, Marguerite Delaye lost an arm in the fighting. In consequence, a one-armed statue of her was erected. [Gribble]

Demeter of the Furies: Also called Demeter Melaina, or Black Demeter of Phigalia, a fierce aspect of the famed Barley Mother still worshipped by Catholics as St. Demetra, patron saint of grain.

Black Demeter was associated with the sea as well as the underworld. She had a horse's head, and was patronized by sorceresses. Celtic **Macha** and Scandinavian **Freya** had similar aspects. **Medusa** may well be connected with Black Demeter, the winged Pegasus being born from her death. In the Eleusinian mysteries, women bore torches through the night and sacrificed pregnant sows by throwing them into pits, to placate Black Demeter. **Hecate,** queen of death, is her ally. Demeter, even in her more familiar form, is a goddess of fecundity and destruction, her winter aspect being a **hag;** so the punishing Black Demeter, though a separate goddess, is not a far step from the seasonal Barley Mother. [Farnell, Friedrich]

Dennis, Mary: A member of the 1st Minnesota Regiment, Stillwater Company. At six-foot-two, she was one of several women who we know fought in the front lines of the American Civil War. [Macksey, Laffin]

Deone: "Queen of Spoil." A warlike nymph of **Artemis.**

Derceto: The Philistine name for the same War-goddess known to the Cretans as **Dictynna.** Said by the Greeks to be the mother of **Semiramis,** who was herself worshipped after her death as an avatar of **Astarte** or **Ishtar.**

Derimacheia: One of **Penthesilea's** twelve hand-selected companions-at-arms. Together, they temporarily liberated Troy.

Derinoë: One of the elite circle of Amazons to follow **Penthesilea** to Troy. She slew Laogonus in hand-to-hand combat.

d'Est, Isabella and **Beatrice:** Sisters who put on public displays of fist-icuffs, mentioned in the 1613 treatise *The Excellency of Good Women.*

d'Estrada, Marie: She accompanied her husband, Hernándo Cortés, to Mexico in A.D. 1519. She rode in battle at his side, "accomplishing extraordinary exploits of valor, to the astonishment of all who beheld her." [Hale]

Detzliffin, Anna Sophia: (A.D. 1738–1776) A German who at the age of nineteen fought in male guise in the Seven Years War, in Prince Frederick's regiment of cuirrasiers. In two battles, she took saber wounds, the second bad enough that she had to be abandoned in a hospital by her regiment. On recovering, she joined the Grenadiers and was severely wounded and captured by Austrians. She escaped, and in 1761 was with Colonel Col-ignon's volunteers when she was falsely charged of some petty crime, which accusations stemmed from a rivalry in the troops she had attempted to ignore. Outraged that anyone with her exemplary record could be subjected to such indignity, she revealed her sex and offered to resign her commission, but was given, instead, an honorable discharge. [Schmidt, Laffin]

Devi: Also called Mahdevi, the Great Goddess, whose worship reaches back into the prehistory of India. She is the female principle of the universe, and embodies the traits of all other goddesses, which are her avatars, and is also invested with the powers of all male gods. In her warlike aspects, she is best known as **Durga** and **Kali,** protector and destroyer respectively. She is thousand-armed and carries a different weapon in each hand: sword, trident, spear, the staff of death, thunderbolt, elephant bell, noose, shield, ax; she rides a mystic tiger and wears a serpent for a necklace. By some tales, the Devi took the name Durga after her first great victory, but she seems to have continued to exist separately as the Devi as well.

The *Devi-Mahatmyam* is a religious text upholding the complete supremacy of the Devi, and praises her most in her manifestations of Durga, **Ambika,** and **Chandika:** "Ornamented with weapons, the Devi gave out a roar of defiant laughter. The world shook, the sea trembled. Making the earth bend with her footstep, scraping the sky with her diadem, shaking the netherworld with the twang of her bowstring, pervading the cosmos with her thousand arms, then began a battle between the Devi and the enemies." [Ions]

Dhabba the Cahina: Or Dahia-al Kahina, queen of Carthage, ruler of the Berbers and Mauritanians. Cahina means "Sorceress." In A.D. 698 she rallied forces against Arab invaders and drove them from her city. She was a black Jew attempting to stand against Moslem incursions. She sent the Moslems howling back to Egypt, where they prepared for a new attack. Part of Dhabba's tactics included laying waste to her own country so the Moslems could not survive on the land and would find nothing worthy of pillage. The tactic impoverished her own people so that when the Moslems came again, led by Hossan Ibn Annoman, his conquest was effected. In A.D. 705 the Cahina either died in battle or was beheaded. [Sertima, Rothery]

Dho Minde: South Vietnamese soldier from the region of Min Top, where three generations carried Swedish blood from a European mining operation. Min Top women were much taller than average, and exceedingly strong. Dho Minde could run forty-five miles nonstop. She once shot a limb off a tree, causing a Viet Cong guerrilla to fall at her feet. She then dispatched him with a knife. [Laffin]

Diana: A Roman trinity goddess who in the sky is Phoebe (the moon), beneath the earth is **Hecate,** queen of darkness, and upon the earth is Diana, the huntress-maiden. She is for all intents and purposes interchangeable with the Olympian **Artemis** but bares no resemblance to **Artemis of Ephesus.**

The youth Actaeon spied Diana bathing in a river and so incensed the goddess of the chase that she turned him into a stag and hunted him to the ground. That Actaeon's mother was a **Maenad** tells us of a connection between Maenads and the nymphs of Artemis, and also that Actaeon wasn't a chance victim, given that Maenads commonly sacrificed their sons.

Dictynna: "She of the Hunting-Nets." A very ancient Sea- and Moon-goddess of the hunt, worshipped in western Crete as Dictynna and in eastern Crete as **Britomartis,** though originally they were probably separate huntresses, and possibly comrade-lovers in the Dorian manner of homosexual initiation ritual.

Her cult spread to the Peloponessus, where she was honored particularly in Sparta. In Aegina, she was called Aphaea, "the Vanisher." To the Philistines, she was **Derceto,** and on Cephalloura she was Laphria. She invented the hunting net used for both mammals and fish and was said to participate in the murderous chase of the sacred king when he was ritually sacrificed in early, matriarchal Crete. [Graves, Bennett]

Dido: Known in her youth as Elissa, Dido was a Phoenician princess, founder and queen of Carthage, and defended the young city against the greed of her rival brother.

She purportedly died for love, not valor, and thus has been remembered in a somewhat unfavorable light, though even Aeneas, for whom she died, remembered her "with sword in hand." She actually lived about 980 B.C. and was not a contemporary of Aeneas, hence the unfavorable legend is a late addition.

Christine de Pizan translates Dido's name as "The Woman with the Strength and Force of a Man," while others translate it "Most Valiant Woman." [Hale]

Digby, Lettice: (d. A.D. 1658) Baroness of Offale, of the house of Fitzgerald, married Lord Digby of Coleshill, creating a powerful alliance of families. She was a woman of vast political and economic influence, drawing therefore enemies upon herself in the English Civil War. "Insurgents often assaulted her in her castle, which she defended with great resolution." [Hale]

Ding Le Tunn: She was a half-French Vietnamese who fought the Viet Cong in 1962. She was a leader of Min Top markswomen. Their system was to wound a soldier with a single bullet, then run forth and club him to death with their rifle butt, thereby preserving ammunition. [Laffin]

Dionysia: Victrix of Roman games circa A.D. 45. Her equally athletic sisters were **Tryphosa** and **Hedea.** They were the daughters of Hermesianax of Corinth. [Lefkowitz]

Dionysiades: Spartan **Maenads,** usually eleven in number, who in association with the **Leucippides** held athletic games and arranged violent rites for **Orthia,** Dionysus, and Apollo.

Diotima: Leader of a band of **Artemis** huntresses in Helena Cross's 1935 novel *Artemis, Fare Thee Well.* Her chief companions were her lover Laodike and Timandra. In the course of the story, a young man named Philip disguises himself as a huntress in order to win Diotima's heart, and succeeds. This is based on the legend of **Daphne** and Leucippus, except that in the legend when Leucippus is discovered not to be a girl, the outraged huntress-nymphs tear him limb from limb. When they are married, Diotima becomes active in **Maenad** rites. Later still, she becomes a priestess of **Demeter.** The fictional character was named for the Grecian teacher of Socrates.

Dirce: "Double," perhaps referring to the horned moon, or the horns of a bull. She was "the savage aunt" of **Antiope, Queen of Thebes,** against whom she warred. These two queens fought in hand-to-hand combat, although Robert Graves interprets their battle as merely a bacchic dance, Dirce being a **Maenad.** After a long period of cruelty to Antiope, the Theban queen was saved, and Dirce, tied by her hair, was dragged behind a bull. Dionysus avenged the death of his devotee by driving Antiope insane. She wandered the mountains wildly, but this appears to be a conventional manner in mythology of recording guerrilla leaders as madwomen killing in the mountains (see, for example, **Ino**).

Dixon, Mary: A British soldier of the Napoleonic era. Her sixteen-year career ended at Waterloo. [Laffin]

Djaa: An Amazon in Virgil Burnett's *Towers at the Edge of a World: Tales of a Medieval Town,* published in 1980.

> She hewed down the people of the cities,
> She smote the folk of the sea-coast,
> She slew the men of the sunrise.

This excellent fictional creation appears to have been influenced by the Canaanite virgin huntress **Anath,** who "annihilates mankind of the sunrise."

Dolgorunaya, Princess Sophie Alexandrovna: She obtained her pilot's license in 1914 at the Aero Club's flying school at St. Petersburg. She volunteered for the Air Service in 1917, when Kerensky gave permission for women to join the Russian army. She flew missions with the 26th Corps Air Squadron for nine months. She was demobilized after the October Revolution, and her ultimate fate is unknown. [Robertson]

Dolope: "Snare." A brave of the Attic War led by **Orithia.** [Bothmer]

dominatrix: A prostitute of the Victorian era and twentieth century who, posing as an Amazon, binds and whips men who pay for the privilege. See **Wanda von Dunayer** and **Evoë.**

Doris: "Bountiful." Amazon spearwoman in the Attic War, named for a Sea-goddess, mother of the immortal Neriads, and alluding to the original city of the predominantly homosexual Dorians. [Bothmer]

Dosa, Anna: During the Coronis campaign of the Greek Civil War (1943–1947), Anna Dossa was a twenty-five-year-old commander of thirty-three montagnards. There was no real cover when a machine-gunning aircraft dove out of the sky. Soldiers flattened themselves to the ground, trying to cast no shadows, but Anna stood tall and emptied a magazine from the Bren braced against her hip. The aircraft circled and dove again. Anna emptied another magazine. When the craft came in for a third strafing, smoke trailed from its engine and it could not pull out of its dive. About twenty percent of the civil war troops were women. [Eudes]

Dourova, Alexandra: A Russian heroine who fought in the 4th Hussars as a cornet in 1812, in the war against Napoleon. In World War I, this same regiment included Olga Serguievna Schidlowskaia in its ranks. [Gribble]

Duessa: A malevolent duelist in Spenser's *The Faerie Queene,* unjustly representing Mary, Queen of Scots.

Dularkukht: Warrior-queen in the twelfth-century Georgian epic *The Knight in the Lion's Skin* by Sht'ha Rust'hveli. "Even her fighting men cannot excell her in feats of arms."

Durga: The most impressive of India's several War-goddesses is Durga, a serene warrior of great beauty and prone to taking on enemies of Shiva that he cannot defeat. Her many names include Kalyani, Sulini, Bhadrakali, **Ambika,** and Vindhyavasini. She battled armies of elephant-drawn chariots and billions of soldiers. When a mountain was thrown at her, she cleaved it asunder with her sword. In some of her battles, she fought alone;

in others, she led armies of enslaved demons; in still others, her armies consisted of goddesses only slightly less mighty than herself who were her many daughters.

Durga was born with ten arms, although in some pictures she has more. Her most famous battle was with Mashihasura, the buffalo demon who threatened the safety of all the other gods. In each of her many hands, she carried a different weapon, gifts of the various deities who proved incompetent to use them themselves. Durga's mount is commonly a giant tiger, occasionally a lion, which also fights fiercely.

A typical statue of Durga carved in sandstone was displayed in the National Gallery of Canada. It showed her armed with a *khadga* sword among other weapons, but her lowest hand is weaponless, making the *abhaya mudra,* or gesture of assuring protection. Another representation, which is kept in the Victoria and Albert Museum, shows her battling Mahisha by tearing off his head. Durga is the beautiful, wise, strong, defending mother-warrior, in sharp contrast to the frightening, headstrong destroyer **Kali** of the same Brahman pantheon. See **Parvati, Uma,** and the Chinese **Kuan Yin.** [Ions, Berkson, Sen]

Durgautti: Or Durgawati. Warrior-queen of Gurrah in Hindustan. Her wealthy nation was set upon by Asaph Khan's army of six thousand horse and twelve thousand infantry. Queen Durgautti met him with fifteen hundred elephant and six thousand horse. "Like a bold heroine, mounted within her elephant's howdar, armed with lance and bow and arrow," she rode against the khan, crushing his forces beneath the feet of elephants.

The Mongol Asaph Khan later returned, bolstered by fine artillery. Durgautti met him again, and her son fell in battle, causing panic and retreat, though the queen pressed onward with her elephants. She took an arrow in the eye and, endeavoring to remove it, broke off the shaft, leaving the point within. Another arrow pierced her shoulder. She shouted to her elephant handler, "We are overcome! But shall we be vanquished also in honor? Haste! Let your dagger save me from the crime of self-immolation!" The handler wept for sorrow, and could not bring himself to kill his injured queen, so she grabbed his dagger and plunged it into her breast. [Starling]

Durieux, Mademoiselle: Saint-Foix in his *Essais sur Paris* tells of a Mlle. Durieux who took up sword and "fought in the open street with a certain Antinotti, her lover." In 1742, a young lady of Versailles did the same.

Duston, Hannah: (A.D. 1657?–1736?) A Massachusetts Bay colonist captured in 1697 by Indians, who killed her newborn baby. She succeeded in killing nine of her captors with a tomahawk and returned home with their scalps, earning a bounty of twenty-five pounds. [Macksey, Blashfield]

Dutreux, Hélène: World War I flying ace of France, known in the army as "the Eagle." She was the first of many women the French officially permitted to become a military aviatrix. [Hirshfeld]

Dymoke, Anne: In 1657, with Cromwell occupying Scotland, Anne Dymoke, the bastard daughter of minor gentry from Lincolnshire, fought originally in male disguise, later with the knowledge of her commander, who felt there to be "nothing but modesty in her carriage since she has been with us." [Fraser]

Dynamis, Queen of Bosphorus: (first century B.C.) Her name means "She Who Must Be Obeyed." She overthrew her aging husband's rule and assumed control of the Cimmerian kingdom, opposing even Rome. She was defeated by King Polemo, a Roman pawn of neighboring Pontus, but retained a portion of her authority by marrying him. She soon after raised a new army and with her Sarmatian allies revolted against Polemo. After a series of campaigns, she was successful in regaining sovereignty. To circumvent further interference from Rome, she offered fidelity to the empire and was duly observed to be "A Friend to the Roman People," and ruled happily until A.D. 7 or 8, when she died of old age. [Fraser]

◆◇◆◇◆◇◆◇◆◇◆◇◆◇◆

Éabha Ruadh Mac Murchú: Thirteenth-century Welsh warrior who before battles wound iron bars into her long red braids. [Ellis]

Eberhardt, Isabelle: (A.D. 1877–1904) Nineteenth-century European who in her teens ran away to the Mideast and converted to Islam. She became an esoteric mystic, rebel, author, drunkard, and profligate who lived the life of an Arab nomad. She dressed always in nomadic costume, carried swords, and underwent incredible hardship in the desert. When in the cities, "at night she could be found lying on the floor of some native café smoking kif or arm wrestling with the soldiers from the barracks." She died young in a flash flood in the Sahara, and only fragments of her manuscripts survived, as she kept them always with her. [Eberhardt, Mackworth]

Echephyle: "Chief Defender," an Amazon brave who fought Eudoros in single combat, armed with a wicker shield, in the Attic War.

Echidne: "She Viper." In Greek myth, a beautiful maiden whose lower half was a speckled serpent (see **Lilith, Eurynome,** and **Tiamat**). Echidne ate men raw, but never wanted for lovers. Her "dreadful brood" included the hell-hound Cerberus, water-serpent Hydra, Prometheus' eagle, the Cromyon sow, Sphinx, Nemean lion, dragon of Hesperides, and the fire-breathing Chimaera.

Edmonds, Sarah: (A.D. 1841–1898) In the American Civil War, she took part in the battles of Blackburn's Ford and Bull Run, disguising herself as a man for a full year. In Texas of the 1890s, she became the first female regular in the Grand Army of the Republic.

Edwards, Sarah Emma: Inspired by the 1844 novel *Fanny Campbell, the Female Pirate Captain,* she left home at the age of fifteen disguised as a boy, partially to avoid being "married off" by her father. She lived in Nova Scotia as a bookseller for a few years before the Civil War, and fell in love with another woman, and "came near to marrying the pretty little girl who I found that I could not leave Nova Scotia without." Sarah later joined the Union Army in male guise, fighting for two years undetected. From her autobiography, *Nurse and Spy in the American Civil War* (1866), and from an interview published several years afterward, Sarah makes it clear she by no means wished to be a man, for in fact she had "a natural antagonism toward men" and felt that society had wronged her mother. "I probably drew from her breast with my daily food my love of independence and hatred of male tyranny." [Katz]

Egee: Ancient African Amazon queen, she led a women's army into Libya and Asia and warred against Troy. After slaying King Laomedon, she exacted heavy tribute against the city, then set out by sea for Africa. It is believed her navy perished in a storm before it reached home.

Egeria: "Of the Black Poplars," indicating an association with a Death-goddess of a dark grove. She was a warrior-nymph and a queen in Italy. After the tragic death of Hippolytus, son of **Antiope,** the virgin goddess **Artemis** restored him to life and placed him under the protection of Egeria. Egeria was also the lawgiver and right-hand counsel of King Numa of Rome, as **Themis** was counsel to Zeus. Upon Numa's death, Egeria pined away and was transformed into a fountain. [Bulfinch, Graves]

Ehyophsta: She is recorded as having fought with the Shoshoni Indians in 1869. She was a member of an exclusive secret society of Cheyenne women warriors who held private council. The Cherokee had a similar society and so might have other tribes, although the evidence may not have survived. The full importance of these societies and the decisions made in closed meetings have been seriously underestimated by modern scholars. [Niet-hammer]

Eleanor of Aquitaine: (A.D. 1122?–1204) Romancers have placed her in the Second Crusade, clad in polished armor, plume dancing in the sun, dashing over the hillsides and killing Moors. The reality is hardly less impressive. On Easter Day, A.D. 1146, she offered the Abbé Bernard of Clairvaux, at Vézelay, her thousands of vassals, who formed the core of the Second Crusade. She intended to lead her legion personally and opinions vary as to how far she actually succeeded, although contemporary legend assumes the most. On the day of her army's departure, Eleanor appeared in Vézelay riding a white horse, clad in armor, "with gilded buskins on her feet and plumes in her hair," surrounded by other armored women, including Sybelle, Countess of Flanders, Mamille of Roucy, Florine of Bourgogne, Torqueri of Bouilon, and Faydide of Toulouse, all splendidly appointed. If it was a charade, she kept it up all along the route to the Holy Land. She met the Byzantine Emperor Manuel Komnenos and went from his court, by sea, to Syria, where her uncle, Raymond of Poitiers, one of the most brilliant knights of the age, was ruler. She went thence to Jerusalem, where she was greeted by Queen Melisande, ruler of Christians during the Crusades. Melisande not only fought Moslems, but also her own son, refusing to give up her rule when he came of age.

Independent evidence from the Greek historian Nicetas describes European women in the Crusades, and names especially "the Lady of the Golden Boot," whom we can reasonably assume to be the same Eleanor with gilded buskins who started out from Vézelay, though some historians believe Nicetas referred to a troop of women in the employ of the German Conrad. The Greek historian describes her elegant and martial bearing, and describes, as well, her armored ladies with spears and axes, mounted on fine chargers.

Eleanor had been inspired by Tasso's *Jerusalem Delivered* and the character of **Clorinda** when she had armor specially made for herself and her ladies-in-waiting. Many historians today dismiss this event, and suggest that, at the first sign of trouble, she and her women turned around and headed home. Nicetas' report strongly suggests otherwise. The Bull of the Third Crusade (1189) expressly forbade women to join the expeditions, although the First Crusade included equal numbers of men, women, and children, and the Second seems to have included numerous noblewomen inspired by Queen Eleanor after her spectacle at Vézelay, where she had ridden about the countryside calling for crusaders. Whether the Bull of the Third Crusade was obeyed seems unlikely, as too many of the warrior-monks were of denominations that included nun auxiliaries, and a great many mendicant-nuns were free to roam at will. [Kelly, Bloss, Harksen]

Eleanor of Castile: (A.D. 1240?–1290) Daughter of Ferdinand III and wife of Edward I of England. In 1270, she accompanied Edward on the Seventh Crusade. She was a consummate huntress and loved music and literature.

Eleanor of Provence: (A.D. 1220?–1293?) Queen of Henry III of England, she accompanied him into battle. During the Baron's War of 1264, she raised her own army of mercenaries. She was cannonized after her death, but is greatly to be faulted for her persecution of the Jews.

Elene: Called "the splendid battle-queen, adorned in gold," she had also the power of wisdom. She was a legendary Judeo-Christian heroine who set out at the head of a band of hand-chosen soldiers "to seek treasure across the sea." [Damico]

Eleonora d'Arborea: (A.D. 1347–1404) She reconquered Sardinia, sustaining a two years' war against the Aragonese, and distinguished herself as a legislator.

Eleonora typifies the valor of Italian women. In 1352, thirty women of Mugello kept numerous armed men at bay. In 1554, in Siena, three women's battalions formed, with uniforms of red and violet taffeta, to defend the city walls. At the siege of Pavia by Francis I of France, and again when Maniago clashed with Padua, medieval Italian women played pivotal roles in the defense. [Boulting]

Eleonore of Toledo: In 1543, she married Cosmos I, a young Medici prince who was constantly embattled by his hereditary foe, the house of Strozzi. Eleonore fought beside him in several ghastly battles, and led skirmishes of her own. "One day while riding with an escort of only fifteen horse, she met the leader of the hostile force, Philip Strozzi, who had with him forty-five horse. Without a moment's hesitation, she threw herself upon them, cut them to pieces, and made Strozzi prisoner." In a later campaign, the valiant prince and princess fought side by side in the war between Charles V and Francis I, and took the city of Sienna. [Hale]

Elissa: See **Dido.**

Elizabeth I: (A.D. 1533–1603) Named the Virgin Queen of England and Ireland. In August of 1588, to encourage her troops to repulse the Spanish armada, Elizabeth went to Tilbury clad as an Amazon: "Buskined and plumed, having a golden Truncheon, Gauntlet, and Gorget; Armes sufficient to express her high and magnimous spirit." The actual military exploits of the famous English queen were limited, for she never headed battles. But as the figurative protector of her nation, her warrior ability was still expected, as it had been of the medieval queens before her. She was accordingly a consummate huntress, her arrows tipped with silver and fletched with peacock feathers. She relished the hunt even in her old age. [Fraser, Shepherd]

Emandine: Warrior-fairy of Charlotte Perkins Gilman's unpublished juvenilia "A Fairy Tale." She saves damsels in distress, in one scene defeating twelve men who were harassing a maiden. She invited Princess **Araphenia** into her bed, and the princess was delighted.

Emma, Countess of Norfolk: In A.D. 1075, she held Norwich against siege, after her husband, the rebel Earl of Norfolk, had fled across the sea. Her defense could not be broken, so she was offered safe conduct to join her husband in exchange for her castle, which she found acceptable. [Fraser]

Emma, Queen of France: In A.D. 948, King Lothaire left his queen, daughter of the German Emperor Otto, to guard Verdun, which they had conquered together, and he continued onward. The city was soon attacked by a large army, which Emma repulsed. Lothaire returned just prior to the enemy's second drive and together with Emma was able to crush them. [Hale]

Emma of Normandy: (d. A.D. 1052) Queen of Ethelred the Unready, King of England. In 1035, she warred against Harold so that she might become regent through her son. She fled to Flanders in defeat, but continued her intrigues for many years.

Empusaë: Demonic daughters of **Hecate,** akin to the children of **Lamia** and **Lilith.** Of Persian origin, they are sometimes said to have the haunches of asses, the **Centaurs** being their masculine counterpart (see **Nephele**). They symbolized cruelty and lust. They could appear as beautiful women, cows, or snarling bitches.

Enepsisgos: A three-headed, many-armed prophetess who warred against King Solomon. She came from a mysterious demon land to liberate other monsters Solomon had sealed in jars. She succeeded against him, and caused her race to be disseminated throughout the world. [Lacks]

Enheduanna: A priestess of the War-goddess **Inanna** and daughter of Sargon I. She is the world's first named poet, flourishing about 2300 B.C. Her surviving hymn to Inanna praises the goddess as a devastator of land, killer of vegetation, destroyer by fire and flood, "raging, malevolent, smiting, and devouring." [Friedrich]

Enju: Swordswoman-avenger, daughter of Numada Shoji, fictionalized in the kabuki play *Ume no Hana Aioi Hachinoki* of the mid-1700s.

Enyo: Greek goddess of war, companion to Ares, **Bellona** to the Romans. She was also one of the **Graeae,** guardians of the **Gorgons.**

Eos or **Aurora:** The Dawn-goddess. She is the best-remembered aspect of a once widely known Sun-goddess of very ancient times, her cults stretching from the Baltic nations to India. She is all but unique as a female rapist, having physically captured the beautiful youth Orion, whom she had blinded for better submission. She similarly kidnapped Cephalus, whose name is a genital reference and implies an Attislike castrate lover (see **Procris**). Her association with war is indicated in the Scandinavian belief that the Aurora Borealis was evidence of the **Valkyries** riding. The Baltic Sun-goddess Saule and the Vedic Sun Maiden (or Dawn Maiden) Ushas were exceedingly sexual, sometimes violently so. Savatri, another Vedic Sun-goddess, was dual sexed. **Selene** the Moon-goddess may once have been a Dawn-goddess as well. [Friedrich]

Eppia: (fl. c. A.D. 100) Juvenal says she was the wife of a senator and a notorious glatiatrix who ran off from her children and husband to pursue her affair with a fellow gladiator. She traveled with him to Pharos and along the Nile. "She eats dinner with the sailors, walks the quarter deck, and enjoys hauling enough rope."

Erauso, Doña Catalina de: (c. A.D. 1592–1650) Called La Monja Alferez, "the Nun Ensign," Catalina was a veritable Robin Hood of Latin America. At a young age, she ran off from a Spanish convent, asking bitterly of her family, "Why have you made me manly and strong like my brothers, only to compel me now that I am fifteen to do nothing but mumble a lot of interminable prayers?" Earning her way to Central America in the early seventeenth century, she became a soldier of fortune of great sword skill and renown throughout Mexico and Peru, and, in Chile, served under her brother's command against the Araucanian Indians. "Her career was one of singular adventure, of wild passions, of unsparing cruelty, of heroic bravery." Her stirring autobiography suggests that she spent her early adventures in South America in the guise of a man, although this seems to have been partly a novelistic device, since such women as Catalina were not uncommon in her day, and her own brother was one of her patrons. She was already famous when she returned briefly to Europe, clad as a cavalier ("filling the hearts of girls with love, of their gallants with terror") and Pope Urban VIII granted her special permission to wear men's garb. King Philip awarded her a pension for defending the Spanish territory and flag, despite that such defense consisted largely of "gambling, stabbing, robbing" and the seduction of beautiful ladies.

At one stage, she was condemned to the gallows. When the hangman had trouble getting the rope around her neck, she snapped at him, "Do it right or let me alone! This priest will do it better than you!" A twelfth-hour reprieve came in the delay, her fame and gallantry providing her many protectors. She remains today an important folk hero of the Latin American romantic age. [Myron, Shepherd, De Quincey, Hale]

Ereskigal: The Sumerian version of **Hecate.** She took the husband of **Inanna** into death, much as Persephone stole **Aphrodite's** Adonis. The result was war between the sister-goddesses. Inanna, "ambitious and aggressive," intended to extend her rule of sky and earth into the netherworld, but was defeated by Ereskigal. Later in Ereskigal's reign, she was warred against by the god Nergal, who entered the netherworld with many allies. She lost this war and, to avoid beheading, agreed to marry her foe and serve as his queen. This is but one of many myths that show the supplanting of goddesses by gods the world over. [Kramer]

Erinyes: See the **Furies.**

Eriobea: An Amazon brave during the reign of **Hippolyte,** slain by Heracles.

Eris: "Discord." Sister of Ares. She and **Enyo** accompanied Ares into battle.

Erni: A warrior-maiden in the service of **Medb** of Connacht, guardian of the queen's treasure, and captain of the queen's handmaids. [Ellis]

Error: In Spenser's *The Faerie Queene,* Error is a monster, half woman and half serpent, suggestive of **Lamia.** In combat with the Red Cross Knight, she was slain.

Erythra: "Crimson." Daughter of Porphyrion. She is shown in one surviving Gigantomachy, on an amphora now in Boston, *aiding* Heracles in battle. She was probably a priestess of **Athena,** Heracles' ally on this mission. [Bothmer]

Euclea: A War-goddess worshipped in Athens when commemorating the battle of Marathon. [Farnell]

Eucrateia: A princess of Argos and victrix of the four-horse chariot races at

Olympia circa 194 B.C. Her mother **Zeuxo** was also a breeder of horses and charioteer.

Eumache: "Good Fighter." Amazon brave in the Attic War led by **Orithia.** When her arrows were expended and she was disarmed, she fought with a stone. [Bothmer]

Eumenides: See the **Furies.**

Europa: "Full Moon." Warrior-queen and ancestress of the Cretans, from whom Europe takes its name. [Davis]

Euryale: One of the snake-haired **Gorgons.**

Eurybe: "Grand Strength," an Amazon spearwoman who always fought alongside **Phoebe** and **Celaeno** in an undefeatable pattern—undefeated until they faced the invulnerable Heracles. Their spears broke against his lion's skin, and he slew all three with one sword stroke. [Sobol]

Eurydice: (fl. 360 B.C.) "Justice." First wife of Philip II. Her name was originally Audata, but she took the Greek name upon marriage, for in Macedonia it was a political disadvantage to have a foreign name. She was an Illyrian warrior princess and never adopted the quieter manner of Greek women.

She passed the Illyrian tradition of fighting women on to her daughter **Cynane** and her granddaughter, who took the name Eurydice after her. That her traditions were kept and honored even in Philip's land indicates the authority that women were able to maintain in marriage. [Pomeroy, Mahaffy, Macurdy]

Eurydice, Queen of Macedonia: Granddaughter of Philip, Alexander's niece, daughter of **Cynane.** Her mother gave her a military education. Cynane married her to Philip III Arrhidaeus, ensuring that the throne followed Cynane's family line instead of the lines of Philip's other wives. Eurydice became de facto ruler since Arrhidaeus was feebleminded.

She was originally named Adea but changed her name for political reasons, to remind the Macedonians of her warrior grandmother of the same name, and to do away with the Illyrian name alien in Macedonia. The name Eurydice was somewhat dynastic in nature, and merely to take the name was an announcement of intent to rule. In 319 B.C., she waged a defensive war against **Olympias,** who considered her a pretender to the throne. The historian Duris of Samos considered this the first war waged between two queens (but see **Dirce** and **Antiope, Queen of Thebes**).

Olympias sent Eurydice a knife, a vial of poison, and a rope, suggesting she choose her own manner of death before Olympias came for her. Eurydice hanged herself with her own girdle, which was considered an act of bravery akin to the Japanese code of self-immolation. [Polyaenus, Pomeroy, Macurdy]

Eurydice of Egypt: (fl. c. 286 B.C.) When repudiated by Ptolemy I and supplanted by **Berenice,** Eurydice refused to give up power, but entrenched herself in Cassandreia, ruling the region with a fair hand, defending her position by means of mercenary troops. Polyaenus says she restored liberty to Cassandreia and was greatly loved. After her death, a festival was established in her name. [Macurdy]

Euryleia: "Woman Wanderer." A hoplite in the Attic War led by **Orithia.** Her name reflects the immigrant status of many of the women of Amazonia. [Bothmer]

Euryleonis: A Spartan princess and horse breeder. Her horses were reliably the winners of chariot races at Olympia, and by some accounts she became a charioteer after the success of **Cynisca,** making her one of the earliest woman victrices of the races. [Pomeroy]

Eurynome: "Wide-wandering" or "Wide-ruling." She was a Titan ruler of the underworld and the sea. **Echidne's** death at the hand of Argus probably refers to the suppression of her worship. She (or her brother Ladon) may have been the serpent of Eden (see **Lilith** and **Leviathon**). She ruled the whole world until deposed by **Rhea.**

In her earliest myths, she was the goddess of all things, the original Creatrix and Egg-mother. In Sumer, she was Iahu, "the Exalted Dove," who laid the Universal Egg.

Eurynome rose naked from Chaos and was cold, so that she danced erotically to warm herself. Dancing thus, she was aroused, and so created for herself a gigantic snake-consort from the wind of her whirling body. Mating with this serpent Orphion, she birthed the Sun, Moon, Planets, Stars, and Earth, with all its creatures and herbs. Orphion later claimed he created the world, so Eurynome crushed his head with her heel, kicked out his teeth, and exiled him to the underworld. [Graves]

Eurypyle: Commander of a women's expedition against Babylonia. In 1760 B.C., she captured the Amorite capital. [Diner]

Eurytion: "Widely Honored." One of **Andromache's** braves, slain by Telamon. She was named for a **Centaur.** [Bothmer]

Evandre: One of the elite corps of twelve to follow **Penthesilea** to Troy.

Evoë: A Roman bacchante praised by Horace: "My mind trembles with recent dread, my soul tumultuous with joy. Spare me, thou who art formidable for thy fearful thyrsi." The thyrus was a **Maenad** staff used to beat men into submission. Drooling Horace has only praise for such activity (though he despised the same practices when men were not invited; see **Chloris**). He says to Evoë, "Ornamented with your golden horn, even the hellhound Cerberus gently wags his tail; his triple-tongue licking your feet and legs."

F

◆◇◆◇◆◇◆◇◆◇◆◇◆◇◆

Fan, Madam, the Bow Maker's Wife: During the reign of Duke P'ing (551–531 B.C.) a bow maker of Chin was commissioned to make the duke a bow. It took three years. But when the duke missed his target, he blamed the bow maker and condemned him to death. Madam Fan went to the duke's court and chastised him for his behavior, described the high morals of rulers before him, described the love, skill, and labor that had gone into the creation of so fine a bow, and finally instructed him in archery. "I have learned the art! The left hand is placed out strongly as if to resist. The right hand sends forth the arrow without resistance. This is the method of archery." After attending her lessons, the duke was able to hit his target every time. He pardoned the bow maker and awarded Madam Fan. [Chuan]

Farzana Somru: Daughter of an Arabian nobleman, Farzana fell in love with the handsome Walter Reinhard, a German soldier-of-fortune known in India as "the Sombre" due to his melancholy nature, the name becoming corrupted by dialect into Somru. He fought for India against the British, accompanied by his mistress, Farzana, whom he eventually wed. The two fought valiantly in the service of Najaf Khan, the Wazir of Sah Alam, emperor of Delhi. In consequence, the German freelance and his fighting wife received an estate at Sarahana, which they defended with their private army.

When her husband died in A.D. 1778, Farzana was only twenty-eight.

She became sole head of the troops. In 1780, the Begum Somru led her forces against rebels who had hoped to unseat the Moghul Shah Alam. Again in 1787, the Moghul emperor was besieged and the Begum rushed to his aid, once more preserving his rule.

The people believed the Begum Somru had supernatural powers and, in battle, need only spread her scarf to destroy enemies. "Fearless in battle, upright in her dealings, generous to friends, and feared by those who offended her. She led her troops in person, and displayed in the midst of the most frightful carnage the greatest intrepidity and presence of mind." She lived to the age of eighty-six. [Masud-ul-Hasan]

Fates: See the **Moirae.**

Fatima: Daughter of the prophet Momammed, identified by the Gnostics as an incarnation of the **Virgin Mary**: mother, wife, sister, and daughter of God. She appears at the Last Judgment with hair flying wild and sword in hand, a merciless figure of divine retribution.

Fea: "Hateful." A Celtic Battle-goddess and wife of Nuada. Perhaps interchangeable with **Macha,** who was also a warrior-wife of Nuada and died with him in battle against Balor of the Evil Eye. [Ellis]

Feigner, Vera: A member of the Russian women's Battalion of Death in World War I. This battalion became world-famous. The women shaved their heads and wore men's uniforms. Later women's battalions had special uniforms designed for them.

Féithlinn or **Fedelm:** Amazon fairy of Celtic myth, she foresaw the battles between Cu Chulainn and **Medb.** [Hyde, Goodrich]

Femilsema: Shepherdess of the seventeenth-century Spanish romance *Diana*. She rescued several nymphs from savages and was declared to be the daughter of Mars and **Minerva.**

Feminie: A medieval Amazon island purported to exist off the coast of Africa, and elsewhere.

Fernig, Félicité and **Théophile:** (late 1700s A.D.) "The Amazons of Jemmapes," celebrated by Lamartine in *Histoires de Girondins.* They were aged twenty-two and seventeen respectively. Félicité was a distinguished member of an archery society, and both were skilled with firearms. They joined in the battles with the invading Austrians on the village borders, armed with rusty sabers and antique blunderbusses. Félicité rode in a charge by the side of the Duc de Chartres, afterward Louise-Philippe.

Théophile captured a Hungarian major. "The Fernig girls," General Beuronville reported, "were very capable of killing the enemy." [Gribble]

Ferrers, Lady Maude: (fl. seventeenth century A.D.) A British highway robber of St. Albans, Lady Ferrers had a secret passage from her room to the stables. By night, she roamed the countryside "in her suit of Lincoln green." She was wounded on her final midnight sortie and made it back to her doorstep to die. Legend has it that her ghost is still seen. [Briggs]

Fery-Bognar, Corporal Marie von: Fought in the Austria-Hungarian army as a volunteer, receiving for her valor a special medal, engraved with her name, from Emperor Franz Josef. [Hershfeld]

Fief, Madame de: In the eighteenth century, she distinguished herself in the army of Charretel. [Kavanagh]

Fields, Mary: Born a slave in Tennessee, this belligerently self-reliant woman—six feet tall and two hundred pounds, she allegedly could whip any man her size—spent the last thirty years of her life in Cascade, Montana. "Black Mary" was the second woman to drive a U.S. Mail coach, and the first woman in Cascade to be granted the official privilege of drinking in the town's saloons, normally off limits to women.

Mary had been a fighter all her life and was already in her fifties when she moved to Cascade in 1884, where she was hired by the Catholic mission twenty miles out of town. Her job for the next eight years was to haul freight and perform heavy chores. With a cigar clamped in her teeth and a jug of whiskey at her side, usually armed with rifle and revolver, she drove eight horses pulling two wagons in tandem.

As she was driving back to the mission one night, wolves attacked her wagon and the horses bolted, spilling Mary and the supplies. She spent several hours fending off the wolves. Other adventures included her shoot-out with a man who insulted her; the establishing of a restaurant that went broke because she always fed penniless travelers; and the debtor she knocked flat in the streets when in her seventies. In time, she had come to be so revered that Cascade's public schools closed on Mary's birthday, sometimes—because she wasn't sure when she was born—twice a year. [J. Reiter]

Figueredo, Candelaria: Cuban patriot. In 1868, at the age of sixteen, she joined revolutionary forces, becoming "the first woman to fight in the ranks in the defense of Cuba." [Schmidt]

Figueur, Thérèsa: (A.D. 1774–1839) She was called Mademoiselle

Sans-Gêne, and an unflattering play on that name was popular during World War I.

Active in the Napoleonic era, this young woman of Lyon served under Dugommier at the siege of Toulon. She took part in battles at Ulm and Austerlitz. She was famous for spurring her horse into the thickest of battle, and at one time or another had four horses shot out from under her. She briefly served Empress Josephine. She was involved in romantic scandals and was occasionally rumored not to be a woman at all, or else actually to be one. She ultimately married happily, and France marveled that an ex-dragoon should wed a gendarme. [Gribble]

Fimmilene: One of the Alaisiagae ("the strongly storming ones"), warrior goddesses of northern England, roughly equivalent to the **Valkyries.** In Danish legend, a Valkyrie is similarly named Fimila. The Alaisiagae are known from the archaeological site of Hadrian's Wall dating to the first century B.C.

Findmor: Warrior-queen of ancient Ireland and a foe of Queen **Medb.** Queen Findmor kept a standing army of women, fifty of whom were captured or slain by Medb. [Miles]

Fine-Weather-Woman: Goddess of storms in Haida myth. The more she opened her garments, the more powerful was the storm. Snowstorms were her shedding feathers. [Spencer]

Flannery, Kate: An Amazon gang member of old New York, who worked as a bouncer at the Hole-in-the-Wall tavern. She was One-Armed Charley Monell's most trusted lieutenant, along with **Gallus Mag.**

The Flemish knight: In Scotland in the time of Robert the Bruce, the warrior Richard Shaw met in battle a Flemish knight conspicuous in valor. They charged each other and each was fixed to the other's lance, and fell together from their saddles. It was afterward found that the Flemish knight was a woman, whose identity was never discovered.

Florelle: In medieval Spanish romance, queen of the Amazon island of **Canabee.** The episode parallels the Argonauts' adventure with the Lemnosian women. [Kleinbaum]

Florine: Betrothed to the king of Denmark, she accompanied him in A.D. 1097 on the ill-fated First Crusade, and died with him in battle. [Hale]

Foot, Adeline: Many areas of the American West count among their local heroes pioneer women who became Indian killers of necessity, for the native race was not about to leap happily into the Pacific, and the whites had no intention of going back from whence they came. In a letter from Gayle N. Netzer of Helena, Montana, the history of her great-grandmother Adeline Foot, a heroine of Minnesota history, is recorded for the first time. The story is typical of scores that have been handed down to us, but only this example need be given.

On August 19, 1862, the Indians, mostly Decotah Sioux, took advantage of the Civil War, which had drawn off many of the younger white men, and made a bid for the repossession of the Minnesota Territory. After killing the whites at the nearby Acton Indian Agency, they swept out to attack the scattered homesteads. Adeline Foot and her husband Solomon ended up on the Erickson stead along with several children, the windows barricaded, peepholes at each. Indians camped in the woods outside, maintaining that they were "good Indians" not involved with the Acton killings. For a while things looked bright, since a Swede who spoke little English was allowed through the Indian camp that night without trouble, and came into the Erickson cabin assuring the two families that the Indians meant no harm. Next day, he was first to die, killed when he went to the potato patch, scalped and mutilated in sight of the terror-stricken Foots and Ericksons. Solomon Foot and Mr. Erickson were wounded in short order, the first unconscious for a while and the other so scared mad that he tried to kill himself. Adeline was eventually wounded, too, but kept up the fight until they were out of ammunition and all seemed lost. Remarkable luck was with them. The Indians gave up before realizing the people in the cabin were helpless.

The women took the youngest children with them, since the men were too badly wounded to watch the two infants, and went in search of aid. The trip was grueling, as they were carrying infants and Adeline was wounded. After they left, the husbands were found, doctored, and saved by another heroine, Guri Endreson. Although Adeline's wound never healed well, she lived several more years, birthed two more sons, and eventually died, probably from bone fragments in her always-painful injury.

The site of the Erickson cabin is now a golf course in Willman, Minnesota, near Foot Lake. A plaque tells duffers that on that spot Solomon and "a companion" fought off fifteen Indians, and that he received wounds from which he never recovered. Adeline is not mentioned. But Solomon, who lived into his eighties, said that the Decotahs told the story under the name of "Brave Woman Who Defended Her House with Her Gun."

Frances Mary Jacqueline of La Tour: (A.D. 1600–1645) Born in France, she traveled to Nova Scotia and in 1625 married Charles La Tour and helped him establish Fort La Tour. She was a huntress, skilled with firearms, and "her soldier husband admired his soldier wife." An acid wit called her "a remarkable woman or an uncommon man." She traveled in the New World throughout Nova Scotia, New Brunswick, Maine, and as far as Boston serving her husband's trading business. Their life was prosperous until the ambitious Jesuit Seigneur D'Aulnay Charnisé became aggressive in his designs on Fort La Tour.

In the first of the ensuing battles, Madame La Tour commanded a portion of the fleet of three ships and numerous small craft, chasing Charnisé from the bay. In the 1640s, she valiantly defended the fort with cannons, blowing Charnisé's ships out of the water, and throwing his soldiers from their scaling ropes and ladders.

Her husband had meanwhile gone into hiding as Charnisé's machinations had resulted in Charles's becoming outlawed. But Madame La Tour's defense had been so successful, Charnisé's hatred transferred to her with increasing venom. She awaited four months for his next attack, knowing there was no chance of Charles arriving to help her. Charnisé's bitter enmity knew revenge, for he won his renewed attack and had Madame La Tour forced into a halter that held her head rigid, so that she could not turn away as her soldiers were hanged one by one. She died a few weeks later, a captive at Port Royal. Charnisé, at least, accidentally drowned himself, at the height of his villainous success. [Brooks]

Fredegonde of Neustria: (A.D. 545–597) She rode at the head of her army, fighting the Austro-Burgundians with babe in arms. Her lifelong foe was **Brunhild of Austrasia,** but she was unable to defeat her until Brunhild's old age, when she was dragged to death after, by some accounts, Fredegonde had brutally tortured her for three days. [Miles, C. Morris]

Freya: The Nordic version of **Cybele.** She was earlier known as **Frigg** and had dual-sexed forms. The worship of Freya, in whose honor we still name Friday, may account for the numbers of women warriors among the Danes and Swedes. In *Grímnismal,* a Nordic saga, it is stated that Freya receives half the dead of battle, the War-god Odin the other half. Although many modern texts maintain that Freya was a relatively innocuous deity of sexual joy and fertility, she was actually very much a goddess of war and of magic, both good and evil. According to the eleventh-century Icelandic historian Snorri Sturluson, Freya was worshipped into relatively modern times, until his own century at least, although the other Norse gods had long been forsaken for Christianity. Many ancient place names survive into our century incorporating Freya's name, so, unlike other Norse gods, her importance went far beyond the imagination of poets. Since her cult survived into the twelfth century or later, the great witch burnings doubtless provided terrible demises to Freya's priestesses.

Women of the Freya cult were noted seers, wandering through Nordic and Gothic nations, a famous example being **Gambara.** Freya was known in Iceland, Greenland, Sweden, Norway, and in Germany and Denmark, by such names as Gefion, Godo, and Ostara. Her abilities included the power to change into a falcon, a symbol of warfare, and she was said to look like a falcon. She could change into a horse, an ability usually symbolic of black magic, in common with **Macha** and sundry witchcraft goddesses. Her warlike aspect gave rise to the Scandinavian proverb, preserved in *Frithiof's Saga,* "Freya's sword is short," meaning "Much can be done even if your sword is a short one," which is a variation of the saying, "Thor's hammer is short." She was the guiding counsel of the **Valkyries** and about her was a college of women called the **Asynjor.**

Freydis: *Greenlanders' Saga* and *Icelanders' Saga* tell of the Viking efforts to settle North America nearly five hundred years before Columbus. Among the women of the voyages was the swords woman Freydis Eriksdattir, who rebelled against women's traditional role, preferring to lead rather than serve men. She fought the American Indians in defense of her colony. Her final battle, after the colony had failed, is sometimes cited as evidence of a cruel nature. But Elizabeth Boyer's reconstruction in *Freydis and Gudrid* (1976) is probably closer to the reality, Freydis electing to kill four women whose actions would otherwise keep them all from getting back to Greenland alive. Boyer makes the point that if it had been a man against four male enemies, he would be considered a great hero.

Friagabi: "Giver of Freedom." She was an Alaisiagi, or War-goddess resembling a **Valkyrie,** of ancient northern England during Roman times, associated with Mars. [Davidson, Damico]

Frigg or **Frigga:** War-goddess of Scandinavia, displaced by **Freya.** She is shown in ancient carvings carrying a short sword and is occasionally hermaphroditic, an image that for the ancients symbolized the idea that a goddess could be sole progenitrix.

Frija: War-goddess and wife of Odin, protectress of the Lombards. In Scandinavia, she was **Frigg.** In time, her worship was absorbed into that of **Freya.**

Frith, Mary: (A.D. 1584?–1659) Alias Moll Cutpurse. Mary customarily dressed in doublet and breeches, smoked a pipe, and "challenged the field of diverse gallants." An especially bold example of the roaring girls of the age, she was the first woman to appear on the Elizabethan stage (when boys still played women's roles). She appeared at the Fortune Theatre dressed as a lascivious cavalier, singing bawdy songs and playing the lute.

During the English Civil War, she sided against the Parliamentarians, and on one occasion wounded and robbed the commander in chief of Parliamentary forces, General Fairfax, despite the fact that he was guarded by armed servants and was himself a famous fighter. She killed several of his servants, as well as all his horses so that no one could follow her. Eventually, she was captured, imprisoned, and sentenced to hang, but bribed her way to freedom for two thousand pounds.

Mary once appeared at Paul's Cross as a weeping penitent, but like Falstaff was only "maudlin drunk" and was soon back at highway robbery when the hangover wore off. She died wealthy, in her seventies. [Solgado, Vincent]

Fujinoye: (twelfth century A.D.) Warrior-wife of Kajiwara Genda Kagesuya in the wars between the Minamoto and the Taira. She defended Takadachi Castle in 1189. In direct combat on the castle stairs, she defeated Yemeto Juro and Nagasawa Uyemen-taro, armed with sword and **naginata.** She afterward sat by the shore and wrote a poem about her feelings.

Fuld, Bracha: (d. 1946) At age eighteen, she was already an officer training Jewish women soldiers. She led her own platoons, captained military detachments, and fought at the Battle of Sarona, Palestine, in World War II. In a night battle against British tanks, she was fatally wounded. A street is named for her in Tel Aviv. [Laffin]

Fulvia: (d. 40 B.C.) Plutarch said Fulvia was not content to rule a husband but must rule an army. Clad in armor and armed with sword, she led her knights against Octavius and led the Perusian war. She assisted Marc Antony during the massacres of the triumvirate. But Antony eventually turned against her, so that she fled to Greece and died there of grief. [Assa]

The Furies: Also called the Eumenides, a euphemism meaning "Kindly Ones," or, more pointedly, the Erinyes, "Angry Ones." They were three fierce demigoddesses, **Megaera, Tisiphone,** and **Alecto,** who sprang from **Gaia** the Earth Mother as the blood of mutilated Uranus fell upon the earth; they were therefore called the Daughters of Earth and Night. As they are older than the Olympian gods, in them can be seen some echo of an earlier time of goddess worship and matriarchies; they are in no way answerable to Zeus. In a play by Aeschylus, the Furies pursue the matricidal Orestes to punish his actions. They call themselves "Slayers of men, we hurtle from their homes."

They are most often represented as hideous old women (see **hags**), wearing long robes with scorpions for fasteners. Sometimes they have snakes for hair, as do the **Gorgons.** They punished with daggers and scorpion whips. Surprisingly, Grecian artists frequently portrayed them as beautiful. Their temple at Athens was one of the wealthiest, their worship nearly universal. They may have much the same origin as the **Valkyries,** who, before becoming mythologized, were priestesses to a goddess of death and battle. The very sight of the Furies was sufficient to drive men mad with fear.

G

◈◈◈◈◈◈◈◈◈◈◈◈◈

Gaboimilla, and the South American tribal Amazons: Queen of the Amazons of Chile, according to Augustin Zarate, secretary of the Royal Council in Spain, writing in 1543. In the Indian tongue, her name meant "Heaven of Gold." Reports of Amazons in South America were so common, from Columbus's discovery of the New World onward, that the sheer weight of rumor was convincing in itself, until later "scientific" tracts debunked them. It is now known conclusively that the early reports were accurate, though such a body of denial literature has accumulated through much of this century that recent ethnologists' and anthropologists' findings during field investigations have had trouble surfacing in the pile.

Gonzalo Pizarro saw "some ten or twelve Amazons fighting in the front ranks of the Indians," killing many of Pizarro's soldiers. In the sixteenth century, Francisco de Orellana explored South America. He reported being set upon by a women's army on the Marañon River, later called the River Amazon, near the Venezuelan coast. Many tribal legends recount an earlier era of women's domination. Violent goddesses occur among the aborigines, as in the Orinoco Valley, where Huiio, goddess of the river, is a monstrous anaconda. Her army of Mawadi are supernatural anacondas that cause floods and upturn canoes. The rainbow is her crown and therefore an evil omen. Another Serpent-goddess is Ñono, mistress of snakes, devourer of souls. Poisonous snakes are her minions. Orinoco tribal people told early explorers of the Aikeambenanoes ("Women Living Alone"). A 1745 explorer was told that these women fought with poison darts and were not interfered with by other natives.

A group of Peruvian women fled the conquistodores to establish an Amazon tribe on the puna, nearly inaccessible tablelands high in the mountains. The priestesses claimed knowledge of pre-Incan culture and arranged the society in accordance with older norms. Today in Andean culture, the puna is still considered "women's territory."

Father Cristobal de Acuña gave a very credible account of warrior women in the early monograph *New Discovery of the Great River of the Amazons,* and Sir Walter Raleigh was among the explorers convinced of their existence. But whether legends, hearsay, or eyewitness accounts, no amount of evidence convinced the nontraveling scholars of the twentieth century that such women ever lived in South America—until startling discoveries of modern field researchers.

The anthropologists Yolanda and Robert Murphy found that even today Brazilian tribal women live apart from men "in convivial sisterhood." Their authority exceeds that of men in all practical matters. In 1970, Jesco von Puttkamer, a German ethnologist, gradually befriended a tribe of warring women, who maintained a small arsenal of firearms. His exploration turned up cave drawings and artifacts clearly showing the legendary Amazons of the region were real. Among the artifacts were ancient helmets and guns that had belonged to early Spaniards killed by these Amazons— relics of Pizarro.

In retrospect, it was always fairly obvious that these warring tribal women had to have existed. Robert Southey said it best—that he would have found the accounts credible had he not heard of the classical Amazons who were so often described as living just barely beyond the boundaries of the maps, implying a universal myth rather than a universal reality. Amazons were a cliché of Spanish-Portuguese romantic literature, fantasies read as though they were history, and Columbus's vain quest for an Amazon island in the Caribbean was predicated as much on those romances as on anything real. Modern nay-sayers felt secure disbelieving in what broader knowledge would reveal a common rather than improbable worldwide phenomenon of fighting women. At the heart of such disbelief is nothing more than a simple refusal to accept that women are ever mighty. [Shepherd, Etienne, Truby, Rothery, Kleinbaum]

Gaia: Or Gaea, the Great Earth Mother, among the very earliest of humanity's deities. She invented the sickle, used to reap harvests, but also in battle, as in the myth of the castration of Uranus. Such Earth-goddesses were invariably double-natured, nurturing like the "barley mother" **Demeter,** and warlike (both protective and destructive), as were **Artemis** and **Cybele.**

The association of death with fecundity meant that when the blood of Uranus the Sky was spilled upon Gaia the Earth, she gave birth to the **Moirae,** the **Melic Nymphs,** and other beings. Similarly, the death of **Medusa** created Pegasus and other creatures that sprang from the stump of her neck; in all myths wherein a goddess kills or is killed (and by extension, when her priestesses kill on her behalf), miraculous births are the reaction.

These beliefs help us understand why goddess-worshipping women were so easily and extraordinarily violent. What cannot be known with any certainty is whether such violence occurred as a response to the rise of patriarchal standards, which threatened the matristic status quo, or whether patriarchal standards erupted from the standards of violence and warfare inherent in matristic culture. Many romantics, feminist and otherwise, despise the latter possibility, their belief system demanding a more wholesome and peaceable Great Earth Mother than is likely to have existed.

Gaidinliu, Rani: She joined Indian freedom fighters in the 1920s, when she was only thirteen years old. By the age of sixteen, she held the leadership of guerrilla forces fighting the British. Captured, she was imprisoned for fourteen years, until freed by Nehru in 1947.

Galatea: "Milk White," a goddess or warlike nymph who led a band of nymphs against "the ungentle race of men." She and her huntresses were pursued by the lustful Cyclops, and driven into the sea. Her consort was Acis, akin to **Cybele's** Attis. Acis was a wounded youth whom Galatea transformed into a River-god, whose water was tinged purple with his blood. She was worshipped in dark grottoes and shared attributes of both **Artemis** and **Aphrodite.** A country was named for her, overlapping Syrian and Phrygian peoples, and Strabo states that people from this region migrated into Tauric regions associated with Amazonia. A marble image of Galatea was the probable origin of the story of Pygmalion. [Bulfinch]

Gallus Mag: In New York City of the mid–nineteenth century, there was a Water Street tavern called the Hole-in-the-Wall, run by a gangster called One-Armed Charley Monell, and his two most trusted lieutenants, Gallus Mag and Kate **Flannery.** Gallus Mag was a giant Englishwoman, over six feet tall. She gained her name from her use of suspenders, or galluses, to hold up her skirt. She was a bouncer and stalked about the Hole-in-the-Wall with a pistol in her belt and bludgeon strapped to her wrist. Whenever she was forced to prove her might to some troublesome fellow, she would catch his ear between her teeth, then trudge toward the door, the blighter yelling all the way. If he protested too much, she bit the ear off, afterward depositing it in a jar of alcohol with other pickled trophies. Police of the day described her as the most savage female they had ever encountered. [Asbury]

Gambara: The Teutonic tribe called "Lombards" or Long Beards (perhaps "Helm" or "Long Hair" originally) were so named, by some accounts, for the long beards of Gambara's two sons, who led the migration of Danes into Italy. Gambara was a noted wisewoman of the age, a matrilinear queen-mother and priestess of **Frija,** often called the goddess of fruitfulness, but this included the fruits of war. Some scholars believe the image of the **Valkyries** was derived from the earthly behavior of Freya's priestesses. It was due to Gambara's prophecy that the Lombard migration began, much as among the Germans it was Veleda, a first-century prophetess, who incited her people to revolt against Rome. When the Romans finally captured her, they installed her in a temple in Ardea, where she continued her military prophecies, but in Rome's behalf.

A separate legend explaining the origin of the title "Long Beards" has to do with the front rank of a Danish army that came against the Vandals. This front rank consisted exclusively of women, whose victory rendered unnecessary the following host of Danish men. Odin himself appeared before the Amazons of Frija and asked, "Who are these *longobardi*?," for the hair of the women had looked like beards to Odin. [C. Morris]

Gefjon or **Gefn:** "To Give" and "Earth." Protector of girls who died unwed, and an avatar of **Freya.** She became one of the **Asynjor** and is sometimes given as a **Valkyrie.** She was a giantess who won land from the king of Sweden and dragged it with her ox to Denmark. [Davidson, Dumézil]

Geiravor: "Spear-goddess." Other **Valkyries** with similar names include Geirahoo ("Spear of Battle"), Geironul ("Spear-fierce"), and Geirskogul ("Spear-mountain"), conveying that the spear was the chief weapon of the Valkyries. [Davidson]

Gelman, Polina: Russian bomber pilot in World War II, she flew eighteen sorties and was decorated five times. She was not a rarity. Thirty Russian airwomen received the Gold Star of a Hero of the Soviet Union. Over 100,000 women were decorated for defending their country against Germany. [Macksey]

Geneviève, Saint: (A.D. 423–501) A warrior-nun, patron of Paris. She battled Attila the Hun in 451.

Gerberge: Wife of Louis IV, daughter of Henry, King of Germany. In A.D. 954, Louis died and Gerberge became regent through her young son, Lothaire. She already had her own army, as defender of Rheims, and used it to ensure her regency. With her young son at her side, she set out to besiege Poitiers. In 960, she led her army against a traitor who held the fortress of Dijon and, retaking the city, had him drawn forth and beheaded in the presence of the army. [Hale, King]

Ghesquière, Virginie: In the late 1700s, she substituted in the French army for her brother, who had no taste for battle. She distinguished herself under Junot in Portugal, received the red ribbon of the French Legion of Honor, and was praised in a popular song of the day. [Gribble]

Giesela, Countess of Eltz: A semilegendary figure of medieval Germany. She was betrothed at birth but, when old enough to rebel, broke the betrothal with the Lord of Braunsberg in the Rhineland. Spurned by the Countess Giesela during a feast, he took revenge for his public humiliation by setting upon Eltz Castle one dark autumn night. In the ensuing battle, an unknown nobleman appeared amidst the fray, clad in full armor, distinguishing himself above all others. The Lord of Braunsberg sought him especially, and fired a crossbow bolt at close range, piercing the armor. The knight fell dead and was afterward discovered to be the Countess Giesela. [Antz]

gladiatorial women: The Roman circus very typically included the gladiatrix. Tacitus in *Annals,* running through the "disgraceful" goings-on under Nero, says that in the year A.D. 63 there were "a number of gladiatorial shows, equal in magnificence to their predecessors, though more women of rank and senators disgraced themselves in the arena," leaving the clear impression that women and senators had already been disgracing themselves in this manner. In Petronius' *Satyricon,* set again in the time of Nero, there is idle chat about the forthcoming circus entertainment, which is to include a *mulier essedaria,* "essadarius" being the usual term for a gladiator who fought from a British-style chariot. Since only one "woman chariot-fighter" is mentioned, she was apparently to be pitted against a man. Statius, in one of his poems praising Emperor Domitian, describes the delightful gladiatorial show given in A.D. 88, which included Moors, women, and pygmies.

Novelty was essential. In addition to gladiators, there were the venatores ("hunters"), who fought wild animals in the arena. An epigram by Martial, also in the time of Domitian, tells of a lion in one of the emperor's shows "killed by a feminine hand." Female venatores also appeared in the animal fights given by Emperor Titus at the dedication of the Colosseum in A.D. 80. Cassius Dio reported that nine thousand animals were killed "and women—not those of any prominence, however—took part in despatching them." He also mentions women gladiators in Domitian's shows and in shows under Alexander Severus, before he issued an edict in the year A.D. 200 prohibiting women from entering the arena. This edict may or may not have been obeyed in Rome, since such decrees were typically inspired by a momentary burst of moral outrage, then promptly forgotten. But even if it was obeyed in Rome, women would have continued to perform in arenas outside the city limits.

As with male gladiators, the women could be freeborn or slaves, and, if slaves, could earn their freedom by serving three to five years in the arena. Training included rigorous bodily exercise. One of Juvenal's passages has this to say of Roman matrons training with weights: "At night she goes to the baths and sweats amidst the noise and hubbub. When her arms fall to her sides, wearied by the heavy weights, the skilled masseur presses his fingers to her muscles and makes her buttocks resound with a smack."

Roman matrons and courtesans were both apt to participate in the glad-iatorial ring, and, Juvenal tells us, they usually owned their own weapons and armor, of the finest crafting, and were long in training for what was, to these women, a serious and important event. He wrote,

Who hasn't seen the wounds on the practice pole which she hollows out with continual strokes of her practice sword and challenges with her shield, and goes through all the forms? This matron is worthy of the trumpets of Flo-ralia. . . . What modesty can helmeted women display? How beautiful if there'd been an auction of your wife's things: swordbelt and armguards and helmet-plumes and left leg shin-protector—or, if she's going in for a different style of combat (you lucky man!) a pair of greaves the girl is selling. Look with what grunting she delivers the demonstrated strokes, with what a weight of helmet she's bent, what a ponderous density of wrappings covers her calves—and laugh when, weapons laid aside, she picks up the pot. Tell me, you daughters of Lepidus and blind Metellus of Fabius Gurgis, what showgirl would ever put on this get-up? When would Asylus' wife grunt at the practice post?

The Floralia was a festival of courtesans, which included athletic dis-plays such as women's chariot races and gladiatorial fights. From Juvenal's description, participation was by no means limited to courtesans, but involved wives and matrons and daughters of upstanding citizens, such being common enough that they owned their own equipment and trained in advance with quite serious intent, even if, as for women wrestlers in our own day, satiric delight or criticism was inescapable.

Glaphyra: Priestess of the War-goddess **Bellona** at the temple in Cappadocia. She allied herself to the cause of Marc Antony, supporting his traitorous wars. [Hale]

Glar, Martha: At the battle of Frauenbrun against the French on March 3, 1798, this "daughter of William Tell" led her family and 280 women into battle and martyrdom. Martha was sixty-four years old. Including herself, 160 women perished, among them her two daughters and her three granddaughters (the youngest was ten). The men of her family also fell. The women who survived the ill-fated battle "were carried wounded or mutilated from the field." [Starling]

Glauce: "The Owl." From evidence on Greek black-figure vases, there was an alternate and probably older version of Heracles' ninth labor that regarded not **Hippolyte** or her war girdle, but some lost episode set in a period when **Andromache** was queen of the Amazons. Glauce, or Glauke, one of the chief braves, killed Lykos, and was slain by Telamon. Evidence suggests that the triad of Amazons ruling at the time of Heracles' invasion were Andromache, Glauce, and **Iphito.** [Tyrrell]

Gloriana: Spenser's warrior-queen who represents Queen **Elizabeth I** in the same idealized condition as she viewed herself.

Gnor: One of the **Valkyries.**

Goll: "Shrieker," a **Valkyrie.**

Gondul: "Staff-Carrier." A leader among **Valkyries.** She and her battle maidens were of particularly noble aspect, leaning casually on spears and shields, or as mounted Valkyries leading dead kings and heroes to Valhalla. In Danish and Icelandic hero tales, they assisted young princes on the mortal plain and became their brides. Gondul commonly rode with **Hild** and **Gunn.** Perhaps Emily Brontë had heard of Gondul when she invented the Queen of Gondal, **Augusta Geraldine Almeda.** [Davidson]

Gonges, Olympe de: (d. A.D. 1792) Heroine and martyr of the French Revolution. In response to Rousseau's Declaration of the Rights of Man, Olympe gave her Declaration of the Rights of Woman. "Woman has the right to mount the scaffold; she must have the right to mount the platform of the orator." Robespierre gave her the scaffold.

gorgoneum: A Gorgon mask that came to be associated with **Athena,** who assisted Perseus in the slaying of the Gorgon **Medusa,** although in Tegea the story was told without Perseus' inclusion, Athena personally slaying Medusa. However, the legend of Medusa's murder occurred late (no earlier than the fifth century B.C.), invented to explain the mask, the real significance having already been forgotten, and Medusa being originally a dark manifestation of Athena herself. [Farnell]

Gorgons: "The Grim Ones," three sisters, Stheino ("Strength"), Euryale ("Wide-Roaming"), and the best known, **Medusa** ("the Cunning One"), having claws of bronze and writhing serpents for hair, said to be able to turn men to stone by a stare. Their names are titles of the Moon-goddess, hence the moon is called the Gorgon's head by the Orphics. They were guarded by the **Graeae,** or Gray Maids, who were born **hags** and shared but one eye among themselves, though other stories portray them as beautiful, but born with white hair. The Graeae may themselves be corrupt remembrances of a far more ancient Amazon race, as their names are Perphredo the horrifier (or the wasp), **Enyo** the warlike (or shaker), and Deino the terrifier. Their original role as war hags is further bolstered by the mere fact of their being appointed guards of the even more overtly warlike Gorgons. That the Gorgons and Graeae each went in threes hints again at their connection with the Moon-goddess trinity and with the Amazon governmental system of three warlike queens. Some ancient authors place the Gorgons among the Hesperides, the same original homeland of the Libyan Amazons also called Gorgons; and Boccaccio avoids the legend of their horrible visages that turn men to stone, in favor of a wistful sentiment regarding Medusa, "If she looked kindly at someone, he remained almost motionless and beside himself."

Legends of beautiful maidens who become predatory hags are common throughout the world, symbolic of a time when peaceful matriarchal societies became warlike because pressed by roving patriarchal tribes. It was only rational that older women, beyond child-bearing age, would elect to be the warriors, hence the common myth of killer hags from Celtic Ireland and Scandinavia all the way to Japan. The Gorgons are but one extreme example.

Gorgons: Also called **Hesperians,** the Libyan Amazons, among whom **Myrene** was their greatest warrior. Names like **Medusa** are Greek translations from the Libyan, so it is very likely that the myth of the three snake-haired Gorgons is a corrupt remembrance of fierce Libyan conquerors. They may have originated on an island off Africa, called **Tritonia** or Hesperia, which has since sunk beneath the waves.

Perseus and Bellerophon led raids against the Libyan Amazons, much as Theseus and Heracles did against the Scythian Amazons. Herodotus tells of these Libyan Gorgons surviving into the sixth century B.C., training girls from an early age for battle. Herodotus believed they worshipped **Athena,** although legends of Perseus and Bellerophon suggest Athena may have been as much the enemy of the Gorgons as she was of the **Thermodontines.** [Sobol, Graves, Kanter]

Graeae: Guardians of the snake-haired **Gorgons.**

The Grave of the Unknown Woman Soldier: From the Vienna newspaper *Der Tag:*

> In the cemetery of Falze di Piava in the province of Treviso there is the grave of a woman who participated in the Italian defensive in November, 1918, and who died in the Italian hospital of injuries sustained in this campaign. She wore the uniform of an Austrian officer and fought in the first ranks of the Austrians, participating in the conflict with the Arditi Italiani at Isola dei Morti. She was found dying by the Arditi. Captive Austrian soldiers were unable to identify her. Today her grave is marked by a stone with the inscription: *"An Unknown Woman who cannot be better identified than with the words, Clothed as an Austrian Officer."* [Hirshfeld]

Grendel's mother: *Beowulf* is a medieval Christianization of a Germanic folktale about a fellow called Bear's Son who slays an ogre and as a result must face a more powerful foe: the ogre's vengeful mother. In an Icelandic legend, Brusi's mother is similarly more powerful than the son. In *Beowulf,* this woman is called "Grendel's mother, a terrible monster-princess," though her monstrousness might well mean only that to the men of the tale, *any* woman that strong was *ipso facto* ugliness incarnate, i.e., "the horror she inspired was only less to the point that the strength of a woman is [supposed to be] less, the horror inspired by a woman in a fight, compared to that of armed men." Her motivation is poignant to extreme, "the mother ravening and with a grievance on her mind, bent on carrying out a course of action full of grief to avenge the death of her son."

She is also called "the mighty woman of the lake" and might have some connection with Merlin's Lady of the Lake, who was also a sword keeper. Scholars have shown that several of the figures in the legend were historic.

But the historical origin of the nameless mother of Grendel, and her unnamed country, can never be known. The mighty lady of the lake was doubtless an actual fighting woman, one who could only be slain but by her own sword, because hers alone was the sword of victory.

Groa: Bravest among the viking women who followed **Alfhild.** This group of Saxon, Goth, and Swedish women pirated the coast of several nations, but mostly terrorized their common foe, the Danes. "They offered war, not kisses, and went about the business of arms, not amours. They devoted those hands to the lance, not loom. They assailed men with spears. They thought of death, not dalliance." [Saxo]

Guanhumara: Better known as **Guinevere.** Norma Lorre Goodrich, the discoverer of King Arthur's castles, called Guanhumara "the British Battle Queen."

Gudr or **Gudur:** One of the **Valkyries** who dispense victory and take the slain into Valhalla. She was simultaneously one of the **Asynjor,** attendants of **Freya.** [Davidson]

Gudrun: In her youth, Gudrun had gone a-viking with her brothers and Sigurd. Although her nature changes in the *Volsung Saga,* in the Elder Edda *Greenland Saga,* she is a swordswoman: "She grasped a naked sword and defended her kinsmen, showing her skill in fighting." This daughter of Giuki confronted two fighters at once, and slashed off one warrior's leg.

Guinevere: After Malory, Arthurian legend became increasingly disconnected from the original secular tradition—stolen, as it were, from the peasants, and reworked to suit the upper class. Virtually all modern novels of Camelot are derived not from England but from French interpretation. Is the "powerful woman as villain" (Morgan le Fay) and the "passive woman as heroine" (Guinevere) *really* at the heart of Arthurian tradition? It seems to be a late invention. Jean Markale in *Women of the Celts* suggests that "Guinevere symbolizes true sovereignty according to the Celts," while Arthur is merely a "mocked and cuckolded king," it being the true sovereign's prerogative to take what lovers she desires, as did **Medb** of Ireland and the historical warrior queen **Aethelflaed.**

According to Katherine Briggs in *The Fairies in Tradition and Literature,* the legendary couple of Arthur and Guinevere was "supposed to have sat on two great rocks at Sewing Shields, and Guinevere said something that annoyed her husband so that he threw a stone at her, which she caught on her comb." The rock, weighing several tons, still exists for viewing. The giantess who caught boulders on her comb has been reduced in literature to a frail heroine whose sexuality causes misfortune. It may be closer to the truth that Guinevere was an Amazon and Arthur's equal.

Guirande de Lavaur: In A.D. 1211, she defended the castle of Lavaur against the bishops of Toulouse, Lisieux, and Bayeux and against the famed warrior Simon de Montfort. Simon was so frustrated by her excellent defense that, when finally she surrendered, he unmanfully placed her in a well and had it filled with stones. [Gribble]

Gullveig: "Madness of Gold." A Scandinavian sorceress-spy and warrior whose flesh was made of gold. She has no counterparts elsewhere in mythology, unless with **Parvati,** "the Black One" whose flesh turned golden through meditation. Gullveig may be a symbol of insanity, conquering like Dionysus by altering morality in subtle or sinister patterns. Or she may only symbolize greed. She inspired women to theft and adultery. She was pierced with spears in the house of her enemy, but would not die. She was consigned three times to death by fire, and three times survived. [Dumézil]

Gunn: In *Njals Saga,* Gunn, **Hild,** and **Gondul** were guardians of princes, allotting victories and changing the destinies of kings. Gunn was keeper of war birds—eagles and ravens. Her name is derived from *Gunnr,* "war," as are many other **Valkyrie** names and names of active Nordic heroines. [Davidson]

Gunner: One of the **Valkyries.** Her name is a poet's term for "battle." [Davidson]

Gunvara: In Saxo's *History of the Danes,* Gunvara was Erik's lover, described in terms of a classical *skaldmeyjar,* or shield maiden. When they were attacked in their bed, Erik called the name of his mother Kraka as a protective charm, causing his shield to fall from the wall and cover his naked body before a spear could pierce him. Gunvara simultaneously rose from the bed and with great vigor ran a spear through her attacker, "matching a man's spirit with her woman's body."

Guth: "War," one of the **Valkyries** of *Volsunga.* She appears also in *Gylfaginning,* in the company of **Rota** and **Skuld.** Valkyries often manifest themselves as a trinity, as do the Celtic Battle-goddesses.

Gwenllian: In A.D. 1136, with the Welsh princes successfully striking against the Normans, who had long encroached on Welsh territory, a southern prince Gruffyd ap Rhys joined his brothers-in-law from the north in their uprising. His wife Gwenllian fought for her brothers as well, at the head of an army of her own, in battles farther south, at Cydweli. She ultimately fell in battle and is still commemorated for her patriotism, for the ancient battlefield is now called Maes Gwenllian.

Gwiddonot: Celtic Amazons; singular is Gwiddon. See the **Nine Witches of Gloucester.**

Gwyneda and **Siara:** Henry Treece's names, in his 1958 novel *Red Queen, White Queen,* for the daughters of **Boudicca.** He portrays all three badly. See **Voada.**

◆◈◆◈◆◈◆◈◆◈◆◈◆◈◆◈◆

Haas, Elena: Czech Resistance fighter, well known to the Gestapo for her successful sabotage missions. In 1944, armed with submachine gun, she helped French agents take and demolish a vital bridge, killing many Nazis and destroying their supplies. She died in January of 1945, leading a guerrilla raid against strong German forces. The survivors of her unit said that as she collapsed from the fatal wound, she continued to fire her Sten into the enemy ranks. [Truby]

Haec Vir: A butch, aggressive roaring girl treated allegorically for polemical purposes in moralistic pamphlets published in England in 1620. Haec Vir is vilely ridiculed as an immoral man-woman and the female equivalent of a fop. Yet the portrait inevitably reflects attitudes toward the female "rufflers" and bravas, who were violent, androgynous women of the coffeehouses and theaters, hinting that they were despised chiefly because so many people found them admirable.

hags: The deadly mother is a separate branch of the same fertility-and-violence goddesses that produced the warrior-mother. She is generally of a less noble aspect and fights with tooth and nail rather than ax or bow. She is much closer to nature and less civilized than the Amazon. Her daughters were cannibal witches.

Hag legends occur everywhere from Ireland to Japan. In the names, places, and legends of these legions of cannibal ogresses (whose names could produce an encyclopedia larger than the present one) can be found many echoes of ancient tutelary deities, even though they have degenerated in most places into mere bogeys used to keep children out of the woods.

These deadly women, because of their lack of weapons skills, and their feral nature, have not been included in the present compilation as Amazons per se. But there are certain hag types that seem intentionally to hint of the continuing physical prowess of Amazons in old age. These include in Greek mythology numerous haglike beings who stand outside the rule of the Olympians and are of inconceivable power, notably the **Furies** and the **Moirae,** or Fates. A large number of trinity-goddesses of major and minor importance are of the hag type, and clearly related to the Amazons, including **Medusa** and her two immortal sisters; the **Graeae,** who were guardians of the Gorgons; and the **Harpies,** who were winged hags. There is **Hecate,** the hag portion of **Cybele's** trinity, which also includes **Artemis** and **Phoebe,** which is similar to the Celtic **Babd,** hag portion of the **Morrigu** trinity that includes **Macha** and **Nemain.**

Baba Yaga is the typical cannibal hag who can slay heroes, but can transform herself into Vasilisa the Wise, a beautiful maiden. These types of goddess-hag represent the aging process and death, but also regeneration, for none of them are *invariably* hags, but are occasionally portrayed as beautiful maidens. Such regenerative myth is seen in the Irish tradition of hags representing national sovereignty. Such a hag comes before a hero destined to kingship, and, upon his appointment, the hag is transformed into a beautiful maiden.

Halasi, Janos: Freedom fighter in the mountains of Hungary, she became a legend among her people. "A tiny woman who lugged around a .303 British Enfield almost as long as herself," she took over command of her unit in August 1944 upon the death of her husband. [Truby]

Haletchko, Sophie: The dramatist Franz Molnar recorded a long conversation with one of the women of the Ukrainian volunteer battalion of World War I, when she was twenty-four. She wore a medal for bravery. She had already been promoted to the rank of sergeant major of cavalry. Molnar remarked on her beauty and delicate appearance, but she had been in the war since the beginning, with only nine days of bad health. She had interrupted her studies for a doctorate in order to distinguish herself among the army of the Ukrainians. [Hirshfeld]

Hancock, Mary: She fought in the American Civil War in an Illinois regiment. She was a schoolteacher motivated by a dislike of slavery. [Laffin]

Hangaku: Hangaku-jo was an especially famed Amazon in the battle between Yoshinaka (**Tomoe Gozen's** lover) and the Taira in northern Echizen province. When Moritsuna's stockade was attacked in 1201, his dutiful daughter held one gate single-handedly against a horde, fully armored and armed with swords. She was a noted archer, able to hit a target one hundred times in succession, exceeding in skill both her brother and father. She hurried atop the stockade from whence she fired arrows at the attacking army, piercing their heads and chests and killing their horses.

An enemy archer wounded her, but she stood alone at the main gate defending her father's house with a **naginata.** Eventually, she collapsed from loss of blood and was taken prisoner of war. When she was summoned before the shogun, he was impressed to find her both fearless and beautiful. One of his retainers wanted Hangaku for his wife, but the shogun laughed, saying, "That woman is beautiful but has no woman's heart, hence she has no attraction for men!" [Beard]

Hannahanna: Hittite Mother-goddess worshipped in Anatolia, noted for her fury. The stinging bee was her emissary.

Harmonia: Or Harmony. Originally a cult title of the Theban **Aphrodite.** In the *Iliad,* Aphrodite as a War-goddess is seen aiding Ares after he is injured by **Hera,** and in the *Odyssey* she is caught by Hephaestus in Ares' bed. The marriage of love and war echoes many Battle-goddesses throughout the world and confirms the cult origins of the erotic aspect to the Amazons.

According to Pherecydes (475 B.C.), the nymph Harmonia was the mother of the Amazon race, by Ares. This nymph is generally thought to have been the embodiment of peacefulness, but no irony should be found in her mothering so violent a race. The Amazons were considered guardians of harmony in matristic culture. That they were relentlessly warlike and barbaric was an unfavorable Greek characterization, not wholly justified. Harmonia was believed to have taken the form of a dragon in Thebes and Illyria.

Harmothoë: "Sharp Nail," one of **Penthesilea's** twelve companions.

Harpalyce: "Ravening She-Wolf." A Thracian princess similar to **Atalanta.** A warrior and huntress, not to be confused with the Harpalyce who cooked her infant and fed it to her rapist. The huntress Harpalyce lived as a robber in the forests and was able to outrun a mare. [Virgil, Graves]

Harpies: "Snatchers." Winged women with the faces of beautiful virgins and the claws of lions. The Harpies were Cretan Death-goddesses who snatched away the dead, but were also manifestations of the **Artemis** trinity in her most destructive form. Homer considered them personifications of storms at sea. They were sometimes in the service of the **Furies,** bringing them evildoers for punishment. The Sirens similarly are shown to be half-human birds of prey, representing death angels as well as storms. Aeneas and the Trojans battled the Harpies and discovered their bronze feathers to be stronger than armor. They fled the land of the Harpies without victory. The Harpies' association with bronze perhaps links them to the Bronze Age nation of Amazonia.

Hart, Nancy: (A.D. 1755?–1840?) When her cabin along the Wahatehe ("War Woman Creek," named for a woman who had previously lived at the mouth of the river) in Georgia was attacked by Loyalists during the American Revolution, six-foot-tall Nancy killed two and held the rest at gunpoint until help arrived. During the Civil War, the town of LaGrange, Georgia, had the only female militia of the Confederacy, calling themselves the Nancy Harts. [Evans, Meyer, Schmidt, Ellet]

Hart, Nancy: A Confederate scout from West Virginia, she was probably named for the American patriot of the Revolution, whom she resembled in height, being six feet tall. In 1861, she was captured in Summersville and tormented by a guard. As the town burned, she escaped from the attic in which she had been imprisoned, kidnapping her rude guard. She put him in a dress, tethered him, and marched him for hours behind her horse. [Blashfield]

Hart, Pearl: (b. A.D. 1872?) Planned but ineptly executed the last stage-coach robbery in America. When captured, she was asked to sign autographs for little old ladies. [Horan, Aikman]

Harthgrepa: A Scandinavian Lust- and War-goddess; a giantess identified as one of the **Valkyries,** but one that more commonly advocates peace. She was a shield maiden to Hadingus, subsequently torn to pieces for performing witchcraft in his service. [Dumézil]

Haru-jo or **Oharu:** In a famous story and play, Haru was a fencer who served as a maid to Onoé, a peasant's daughter, who, for her great beauty, became a warlord's wife. Because of Onoé's low birth, Iwafuji, another of the daimyo's wives, humiliated her many times, finally striking her with a sandal. Onoé in consequence committed suicide. Haru took the offending sandal to return to Iwafuji, and challenged her to a duel with swords. In the ensuing duel, Iwafuji was defeated, but her life was spared, although she was thereafter unable to wield power over castle women. [Bacon]

Hasselaar, Kenau and **Amaron:** Sisters who in A.D. 1568 donned swords and harness to defend the little city of Haarlem near Amsterdam from the Spanish. "They fought in the ramparts and even outside in the thick of the fight." They organized and led a battalion of three hundred women. Kenau was in later life a successful businesswoman. [Schmidt, Gribble]

Hate Woman: A Blackfoot Indian. When she married Weasel Tail, she loved him so much she refused to let him go to battle without her, so that they would never die apart. She went on five raids armed with a six-shooter. On one raid, she stole a saddle, ammunition bag, and war club. After another raid with her husband and one other man, they returned with fourteen good horses. Hate Woman was asked to tell her adventures at the Sun Dance celebration, an unusual honor. [Hungry Wolf]

Hathor: The Eye of Ra, a bloodthirsty goddess who was simultaneously a Cow-goddess of fecundity. She was Baalat to the Canaanites, female counterpart to Baal, related to **Anath,** the Warrior-goddess of Ugarit on the Syrian coast.

Whenever there was warfare, Ra sent Hathor forth, and she would not return until rebellion was quelled. On one occasion, she was ordered to destroy humanity entirely. She killed half the world's population and was about to set forth to kill the other half, when Ra, with a change of heart, tried to stop her. He could not restrain her except by tricking her into drinking red beer, which she had mistook for blood, and she drank so much she could no longer see where to attack humankind. There would appear to be some association with the Indo-European **Maenads** and their violent wine cult. [Kramer]

Hatshepsut: (d. 1479? B.C.) Egypt's great female Pharaoh. She "fought at the head of her troops and laid claim to masculine power and prerogative." She was worshipped for eight hundred years after her death. [Miles]

Hatsu-jo, and the Japanese swordswomen avengers: Hatsu-jo (or Ohatsu) was a female avenger immortalized in the Tokugawa period kabuki play *Onoye Iwafuji*. She killed Tsubone Iwafuji. Another such was Tora Gozen of Oiso, a swordswoman who helped the Soga brothers in their attempt at revenge in the late 1100s. Miyagino, whose name means "dutiful daughter," was yet another swordswoman, who, with her younger sister Shinobu, avenged their father Yomosaku against an official who killed him unjustly. Such avengers were common in medieval Japan, where the tents of *kataki-uchi,* or honorable revenge seeking, were followed almost as a religion, and their bloody actions were among the most popular themes for plays, stories, and present-day cinema.

Hatzler, Elizabeth: A French dragoon who fought in the losing battle against the Cossacks in 1812. It was common for wives to accompany husbands in the role of *cantinère,* and many such women were in the retreat from Moscow. Elizabeth, however, wore the dragoon uniform, and delivered more than water to the soldiers; she delivered death to the enemy. Her husband was wounded and she carried him on the long retreat. [Gribble]

Haye, Nicolaa de la: (A.D. 1160?–1218) Heiress of the de la Haye barony and hereditary castellan of Lincoln, she lived during the reign of Richard I. She had several military encounters. During the rebellion prior to Magna Carta, Nicolaa was besieged in Lincoln Castle and successfully defended it against rebels. In 1216, she was made sheriff of Lincolnshire.

Hays, Mary: See **Molly Pitcher.**

Hazrat Mahal: The Begum of Oudhad, an Indian Muslim queen-regent of the mid-1800s. She defended Lucknow against the British. She was described by John Low of the East India Company as "one of the tigress women more virile than their husbands." Sir William H. Russell, the leading war correspondent of his day, called her a **Penthesilea.** [Fraser]

Hecate: Goddess of the dark of the moon, and of the underworld, she "shatters every stubborn thing." A Death-goddess, beloved of sorceresses, the darkest aspect of the usual moon trinity representing birth in the sky (**Phoebe**), life on the earth (**Artemis**), and death below ground, or, agriculturally, planting, harvesting, and fallowness of winter. She is also Persephone, the dark aspect of **Aphrodite.**

Hedea: At the Isthmian Games in A.D. 45, she won a race in full armor, and won also the chariot race. At the Nemean Games, she won the single-course race. She was also a musician, winning honors for her lyre performance. Her equally athletic sisters were **Dionysia** and **Tryphosa.** [Lefkowitz]

Hé-é-é: A warrior-girl told of by the Hopi Indians. She did one side of her hair like a woman and the other like a man. [Niethammer]

Heid: She and **Wisna** were the king's standard-bearers at the Battle of Bravalla. Heid led a hundred of her own champions as well as a company of berserkers. [Saxo]

Hell Cat Maggie: In the gang warfare of Old New York, the best-remembered gang, the Bowery Boys, came against the Plug Uglies, the Shirt Tails, and the Chirchesters, who allied themselves under the emblem of the Dead Rabbits. These gang battles sometimes raged continuously for two or three days, streets barricaded with carts, muskets and pistols flashing in the dark. Whenever there was a break in the defense, women scurried forward with armloads of ammunition, and were always willing to enter the fray. Some fought regularly in the ranks. "During the Draft Riots it was the women who inflicted the most fiendish tortures upon Negroes, soldiers, and policemen captured by the mob, slicing their flesh with butcher knives, ripping out eyes and tongues, and applying the torch after the victims had been sprayed with oil and hanged from trees."

During the 1840s, the Dead Rabbits "commanded the allegiance of the most noted of the female battlers, an angular vixen known as Hell-Cat Maggie, who fought alongside the gang chieftains in many of the great battles with the Bowery gangs." She filed her front teeth to points and wore long artificial nails constructed of brass. When she gave her battle cry and ran biting and clawing into the fight, "the stoutest gangsters took flight." [Asbury]

Hepatu: Warrior-wife of the Hittite god of weather. She rides a panther, much as the Great Mother **Cybele,** to whom she is related, rides a lioness.

Hera: Originally the Great Goddess of Argos, with the same warlike aspects as **Cybele** and **Artemis.** Later, she became the wife of Zeus, but continued even into late myths to war against patriarchal standards. She was the enemy of Dionysus, inveterate usurper of the mysteries of Mother-goddesses, and of Heracles, against whom she stirred the Amazons when it appeared there might not be a war for **Hippolyte's** girdle. In Rome, she was called **Juno.**

Heraclea: The female Heracles, called also Palaemona. As Heracles' name means "Glory of Hera," it is strange that throughout his adventures, **Hera** is his most devout enemy. Such a penultimate patriarchal hero could not have existed in the earlier eras of goddess worship. The penultimate matri-archal heroine was Heraclea, whose cycle Bernard Evslin reconstructs in the excellent *Heraclea: A Legend of Warrior Women.* The cities that she founded were only much later centers of Zeus and Heracles worship. Evslin observes, "The mother-goddess raged and rutted her way through the infant civilization of the Mediterranean, and legends attended her," and, "The myth of Heracles in its entirety is a corruption of a more ancient body of legends pivoting upon the exploits of the gigantic young woman Heraclea."

Heraean: A women's sports event founded by Queen **Hippodameia.** The Heraean occurred every four years and was, centuries later, the model for the Olympics, and continued until suppressed in the Christian era for its pagan associations. Foot races were the first and central event, but there is evidence as well that the event included chariot races, javelin toss, and nude wrestling.

Herfjioturr: "War-fetter." One of the **Valkyries.** [Davidson]

Herland: Charlotte Perkins Gilman's feminist utopia in a novel of the same name. James Tiptree, Jr. (pseudonym Alice Sheldon), did it far better in "Houston, Houston, Do You Read?" (1976). Gilman avoids the image of the Amazon for the most part, giving a diluted Amazonia. The book fails as satire or as fiction, but is satisfying if one is in the mood for a political tract. When Ellador, to prove that only men are violent, asks, "Did the Norse women raid the coasts of England and France? Did the Spanish women cross the ocean and torture the poor Aztecs?," it is clear that Charlotte never heard of **Gudrun, Alfhild,** or **Rusla, the Red Maiden** (among vikings), or Marie **d'Estrada** and Inez **Suárez** (among conquistadoras).

Hermangarde: Great-granddaughter of Charlemagne, she flourished in the eleventh century, a contemporary of Philip I. She defended the town of Vienne for two years against Comte d'Autun. [Gribble]

Hermione of Argos: Victrix of the chariot races at Olympia in 197 B.C., 189 B.C., and 182 B.C. She was the daughter of Polycrates of Argos and **Zeuxo** and had several equally athletic sisters.

Hervor the Allwise: A **Valkyrie,** sister of **Hlathguth the Swanwhite.**

Hesperians: The Libyan Amazons, or **Gorgons.** Hesperia (or **Tritonia**) was an Atlantic island destroyed by cataclysm (the Canary Islands are all that remain of it), so that Libya became the second homeland of the Hesperians. Diodorus gives the economy of the Hesperian Gorgons as based on orchard agriculture and flocks of goats and sheep, but no grains whatever, indicating that they were barbaric and meat eating, the Atheneans preferring bread. They began to conquer all surrounding islands and the coast of Africa, hence their naval fame that separates them from the **Thermodontines.**

Hesperides: "The Western Maids." In Greek myth, daughters of Night, or of Atlas and Hesperia, progenitrix of the Libyan Amazons. The Hesperides, together with a hundred-headed dragon born of **Echidna** and presented to them by **Hera,** were guardians of the Golden Apples of the Sun.

Hessel, Phoebe: Her famous gravestone in Brighton churchyard, Sussex, reads:

In Memory of Phoebe Hessel, who was born at Stepney, in the Year 1713. She served for many Years as a private Soldier in the 5th Reg't of foot in different parts of Europe and in the Year 1745 fought under the command of the Duke of Cumberland at the Battle of Fontenoy where she received a Bayonet wound in her Arm. Her long life which commenced in the time of Queen Anne extended to the reign of George IV, by whose munificence she received comfort and support in her latter Years. She died at Brighton where she had long resided, December 12th, 1821, Aged 108 Years.

Hetep-Sekhus: One of the Egyptian Cobra-goddesses (see also **Serket, Renenutet,** and **Meretseger**). She was an Underworld-goddess who used crocodiles as soldiers. She annihilated the souls of Osiris' enemies. [Hart]

Hetha: A sea captain from the town of Sle who brought her ship to the Battle of Bravalla. "Graceful in battle-gear," she had a private guard of "very active men," each a famed champion, and a company of one hundred soldiers. Two other women captains, **Wisna** and **Webiorg,** had brought their ships as well, and arrived together to storm the beaches with their numerous small body shields rattling and their breasts exposed so that the enemy Swedes would know they were killed by women. Hetha afterward became queen of Zealand. [Saxo]

Hida: A woman samurai best remembered for saving the Minamoto banner in the thick of battle, as recorded in *Heike Monogatori* (*Tales of the Heike Clan*).

Hidr: One of the **Valkyries.** Her name is a poetic word for "battle."

Hi'i-aka: Hawaiian Forest-goddess, a huntress, and sister of **Pele.** When Pele dreamed of a distant lover, she asked Hi'i-aka to find him. Hi'i-aka traveled through fierce storms, battled the Lizard-goddess, found Pele's lover dead, and revived him with her magic. In Hi'i-aka's absence, Pele wickedly conquered her sister's land, setting fire to the forests, and war between the sisters resulted. [Sinclair]

Hild: Her name means "Combat," from the same root word *hildur* or *hilda* found in such names as **Brynhild, Kriemhilde,** or Clothilda. Hild was a Norse **Valkyrie,** guardian of princes. She brought war between King Hagni and Hethin in the Battle of the Hjathnings. Like **Skuld,** she had the power to raise the dead and set them fighting anew, but without the power of speech. [Davidson, Saxo]

Hild: Saxo Grammaticus tells also of Hild, elder sister of Asmund, king of Vik, who usurped her brother, but was later crushed by Harold so that Asmund could be restored.

Hind al-Hunud: (seventh century A.D.) A devotee of the Cult of the Lady of Victory. Her Quaraish people had been in power at Mecca when Muhammad arrived. "The Hind" and her family engaged in battle in A.D. 624, resulting in the death of her brother and father. In battles to follow, she led other aristocratic women in war chants and wild dances, surrounded by her foes. After victories, Hind al-Hunud stood atop heaps of enemy corpses "flaunting her personal revenge in spontaneous satirical verses." [Beard, Miles]

Hippo: Queen of the Amazons concurrently with **Marpesia** and **Lampedo,** when, by some accounts, the nation was divided into three main tribes, each with a separate queen. More than likely, there were innumerable "queens" more akin to military mayors or high priestesses of roving camps and cities. As the original horse-riding race, many Amazons have derivations of the word "hippos," meaning horse, as part of their names.

An expedition of conquest led by Marpesia and Hippo crossed Asia Minor as far as the Aegean Sea. They founded numerous cities, including Ephesus, Smyrna, Cyrene, and Myrine. At Ephesus, Hippo raised an image of **Artemis,** around which Amazon braves performed a wild shield dance with "full-throated howls of ecstasy." The temple later built for this statue was unrivaled and included among the Seven Wonders of the World. During this same expedition, the Amazons conquered Troy, which a generation later **Penthesilea** would temporarily free from siege during the Trojan War. When Marpesia was slain by barbarians while quelling an uprising, it was Hippo who avenged her by leading her soldiers willy-nilly over the land, murdering innocent and guilty alike. [Sobol, Graves]

Hippodameia: "Horse Trainer." Queen of the matrilinear tribes of the Peloponessus. She was an incarnation of **Hera** and herself sometimes designated a Moon-goddess. She arranged the athletic **Heraean** games in which women of various ages participated every fourth year. The earliest record of these games places Hippodameia as active before 1,000 B.C., well before the founding of the Olympics, but the Heraean continued until Christianized Romans suppressed it as pagan. The victrix of this feminist Olympics was allowed to raise a statue in honor of herself. The first victrix was **Chloris.**

Hippolyte: Queen of the Amazons, daughter of **Otrera** and Ares, her name means "Of the Stampeding Horse," or "She Who Unleashes the Horses." Heracles' ninth labor was to secure Hippolyte's war girdle, a gift of Ares, and deliver it to the War-priestess **Admete,** whom he served as he had served **Omphale.** Hippolyte was impressed by his strength and awarded him the girdle willingly, but her Amazons attacked Heracles fearing an abduction, and Hippolyte was slain. Another version recounts how she refused Heracles the girdle, who waged war as a result. When Hippolyte's horse threw her, Heracles hovered over her with his war club, ready to bash in her head. He offered mercy, but she would rather die than give in. Her girdle was shown in classical times in the temple of **Hera** in Argos.

In other tales, she survives the encounter only to be won by Theseus in a later war and give birth to a son, Hippolytus, named for herself, although the Amazon who was courted by Theseus is more properly identified as **Antiope.** In yet another tale, Hippolyte was still a queen among the Amazons when the Argonauts passed the shores of Amazonia many years later, or at least the Argonauts believed so. One tradition places her tomb, instead of that of **Orithia,** at Megara. See also **Melanippe.** [Graves, Evans, duBois]

Hippolyte II: The sister of **Penthesilea,** a full generation after the incidents involving the Queen Hippolyte of the war with Heracles. Penthesilea accidentally killed this later Hippolyte while they were on a hunt together. In expiation, Penthesilea left the capital of the Amazons and went to war.

Hippomache: "Mare Warrior." One of the cavalry braves of the Attic War. [Bothmer]

Hippothoë: "Imperious Mare." One of the elite corps of Amazons with **Penthesilea** at Troy.

Hlathguth the Swanwhite: A **Valkyrie** and daughter of King Hothver. She befriended the young hero Ragnar and gave him a sword. She traveled at the head of a group of warrior maidens. Her sister Valkyrie was **Hervor the Allwise.** [Davidson]

Hlokk: "Battle," a **Valkyrie** of *Grimulsmal.*

Honchi: In A.D. 515, Regent Honchi came to rule Wei due to her husband's ineffectiveness as king. She waged war against the Chinese Empire, winning some battles, losing others. One tactical failure led to her overthrow and imprisonment. Yet she managed to return to power as sovereign for one more assault on China. At the height of her career, a treasonous general disposed of her violently. Her death was avenged, and the general gained nothing for his treason.

Hon-cho Lo: After her husband's death Madame Hon-cho Lo took charge of her husband's pirate band in the early 1920s. See also Madame **Ching** and Madame **Lai Choi San.**

Hor Lhamo: In northern Tibet's Thridung county in 1918, a peasant army was rallied by a woman named Hor Lhamo to fight an ancient feudal government.

horse-godmother: Old British derogatory term meaning "coarse Amazon," interesting in part because various War-goddesses were Horse-goddesses, and sometimes depicted with a mare's head.

Ho Te Que: "Spectacular in her combat gear and with a .45 revolver at her hip," this mother of seven was known as Tiger Lady. She led Vietnamese soldiers against the Viet Cong. In the jungles, rumor spread that she was a devil and not human at all. She was killed in action in 1965. Three thousand women served officially as combatants in the South Vietnam Women's Army in 1966.

Hotot, Agnes, and the Medieval Tourney: The coat of arms of the House of Dudley shows a woman in war helmet, disheveled hair hanging out, and her breasts exposed, commemorating a female champion.

In the fourteenth century A.D., Agnes Hotot's father, of the House of Dudley, quarreled with another man and agreed to a lance fight to settle the affair. Upon the appointed hour, Agnes's father was seriously ill. Agnes put on a helmet and disguised her sex, mounted her father's horse, and set out for the tourney grounds. "After a stubborn encounter," Agnes dismounted her father's foe. When he lay on the ground, "she loosened the stay of her helmet, let down her hair, and disclosed her bosom," so that he would know he had been conquered by a woman.

It can never be known how commonly women fought in the tournaments we are all so familiar with from tales of knights and damsels. One thing is certain, the damsels *were* sometimes the knights, and Agnes was not the lonesome example. Tourney exercise would seem to have been essential or women such as Adelaide **Ponthiey** could never have gained the required expertise for her successes in the Crusades (see under the **Virgin Mary**). Hunting with hound or hawk and equestrian arts were encouraged in the aristocratic lady of the Middle Ages; it is not a far leap from there into the tourneys.

A 1348 British chronicle tells of women "free from matrimonial restraints" whose behavior startled the public:

> When the tournaments were held, in every place a company of ladies appeared in the diverse and marvelous dress of a man, to the number sometimes of about forty, sometimes fifty, ladies from the more handsome and the more beautiful, but not the better ones, of the entire kingdom; in divided tunics, with small hoods, even having across their stomachs, below the middle, knives which they vulgarly called daggers placed in pouches from above. Thus they came on excellent chargers or other horses splendidly adorned, to the place of the tournament. And in such manner they spent and wasted their riches and injured their bodies with abuses with ludicrous wantonness. [Rickert, Starling]

Hringerth: A Norse giantess and battle demon who set out to avenge her father's death, similar to the avenging **Grendel's mother.** [Damico]

Hrist: "Spear-Brandisher." One of the **Valkyries** in the Elder Edda's *Grimulsmal.* The others were **Mist,** Skeggjoild, **Skogul, Hild,** Thrúth, Hlokk, Herfjioturr, Goll, Geironul, Randgrith, Ranthgrith, and Reginleif. Only two overlap the list given in Volsunga: Skuld, Skogul, **Guth,** Hild, **Gondul,** and Geirskogul. [Davidson]

Hsiao Ch'iung: A warring goddess of China, protector of the House of Shang (or Chou, an early people who came into conflict with aboriginal tribes). Among her enemies was the philosopher Lao Tzu, who destroyed her "flying scaly-dragon scissors," but she returned to battle with a pair of magic two-edged swords. One of Lao Tzu's lieutenants fought her with the philosopher's jade scepter, jade being symbolic of purity, and the goddess was slain. Her sister **Hsiao Pi** attempted to avenge her. [Werner]

Hsiao Pi: Legendary warrior, sister of **Hsiao Ch'iung,** defenders of the House of Shang. When Ch'iung was killed in battle, Pi rushed to avenge her, but was captured in a magic box. When it was opened, she had melted into blood and water. [Werner]

Hsien, Lady: In the early Ch'ing period, a work called *Wu-shuang P'u* was published, consisting of decorative wood-block prints of famous historical figures, each accompanied by a poem. Included is Lady Hsien, wife of Feng Pao, prefect of Kao-liang in the sixth century. As she was known for military skill, she is depicted with spear in hand, sword sheathed at side, wearing long frontal bamboo armor. A jade pendant of the Tzu-kang style, carved in the K'ang-hsi period, in the Bei Shan Tang Collection, shows Lady Hsien in relief, in a similar pose but with larger spear.

Women such as Lady Hsien inspired literature as well as art, a most extravagant fantasy being Li Ju-chen's 1825 utopian novel in which one hundred fairy-women take over the posts of mandarins and instigate a new Amazonia in which men are as vengefully treated as they have treated women, including having their feet bound. [Rowbothan]

Hsi Wang Mu: Mother of the Great Tortoise that holds the earth upon its shell, Hsi Wang Mu ruled a mythical continent or Chinese fairyland, and led a troop of mountain genii. Other warring Chinese goddesses include **Nu Kua Shih, Kuan Yin, Miao Shan, Hsiao Ch'iung,** and **Tou Mu.** [Werner]

Hua Mu Lan: See **Mu Lan.**

Huang Pemei: Nicknamed Madame Two-Revolvers, she was a Chinese pirate who preyed on fishing boats and merchant vessels. Her activities supported Chiang Kai-shek, and she was rumored to be a U.S. Secret Service operative. She personally commanded seventy vessels. [Croix]

Hueca, La Niña de la: In the late 1500s and early 1600s, several Hispanic women became notorious swordmasters in Central and South America. La Niña of Chancay Valley in Peru is one such, living in a time of easy violence and cruelty. She stood six feet tall and was muscular. An expert with pistol and lance, she was never reluctant to fight bare fisted.

La Niña de la Huaca's occupation was with the **encapado,** a sort of mounted police who ranged the Peruvian mountains and forests capturing highway robbers and runaway slaves. It is said that de la Huaca was never merrier than when beating some poor slave or criminal near to death. She captained four men, a feared company of **encapados** ranging from Lima to Caluma.

Hui Po Yung: She led a troop of Min Top peasant women soldiers (see **Dho Minde** and **Ding Le Tunn**) against the Viet Cong in the 1960s. She had been a physical education teacher in Saigon. [Laffin]

Hyale: "Woodswoman," an archer nymph of **Diana.** See **Crocale.** [Bulfinch]

Hyld: "Battle." A **Valkyrie** given by Saxo as the mother of the hero Rani who fought at Bravalla.

Hypsicratea: She ruled with King Mithridates a confederacy of states with twenty-four different languages. She rode with him into battle to suppress rebellions and to defend the confederation against the empire of Rome. Since women's costumes were unsuited to battle, Hypsicratea had her blonde hair shorn short, and dressed as befitted a warrior, with helmet "under which her face was often covered with sweat and dust," and coat of mail. She fought with ax, lance, sword, and bow and arrow.

When at last their luck turned against them, Hypsicratia accompanied her husband into exile, and made every effort to be a consolation to him. Boccaccio, and Christine de Pizan after him, fancied that she transformed herself into a rugged knight solely for love of her husband, i.e., "What can love not achieve?" Rather, what can woman not achieve!

Hypsipyle: "Of the High Gate," suggesting leadership, and referring to the moon at its high point. She was a Lemnian princess who saved her father's life by secretly setting him adrift on a raft without oars during the women's revolt on the Isle of **Lemnos.** When the Argonauts visited Lemnos a few years later, they were confronted by a host of armoured women intent on continuing their habit of slaying men. Hypsipyle was a member of the counsel and suggested that the Argonauts merely be denied access to the capital city of **Myrene,** named for a Libyan Amazon conqueror who established gynocratic rule on Lemnos. Polyxo, another counselwoman, whose name is a sexual pun ("Itchy"), argued to let the Argonauts into the city so that the Lemnosians could mate with them, for otherwise their race would die out. Her argument won out and the Argonauts were not slaughtered after all, and Jason became Princess Hypsipyle's paramour.

After the Argonauts were gone, it became known that Hypsipyle had treacherously saved her father's life during the revolt, so she was sold into slavery. Another account, however, suggests she was captured during a battle with Thracian pirates.

Another Hypsipyle (or the same in her far-traveling youth) was one of **Andromache's** braves in her battle with Heracles, and mentioned by Sobol as a brave in one of the successful skirmishes against Heracles' captains during the reign of **Hippolyte.** [Pomeroy, Graves, Bothmer]

I

Igrat: Lust- and Warrior-demoness, identified by the kabalists as a princess of Granada. On Sabbaths and Wednesdays she sets out with her attendants to battle humanity and rival camps of demons. She is the sister of **Naamah.** [Patai]

Ike Gozen: Pronounced "EE-KEH." Twelfth-century martial nun of Japan, of the Zen sect that appealed to many samurai, and a Fujiwara clanswoman. She was skilled with **naginata** and saved Yoritomo's life on a battlefield early in his career.

Ildico: (fl. A.D. 453) "The Song of Daghar" praises her thus:

> Woman of woe, Ildico, the mighty maid,
> Avenged with awe the race of men.

She was a Teutonic princess promised to Attila the Hun as bride. She hated him as the conqueror of her people, but had no fear of him, and he was cowed in her presence. He tried to win her over by promising that their son would rule the world, but she replied, "I will crush the head of any child of Attila that tries to escape my loins." Upon their wedding night, she killed the Hun, strangling him with her golden hair. [Shoenfeld]

Inanna: The "Awesome Lady, First Daughter of the Moon," Sumerian goddess of human and agricultural fecundity (love and plenty), and of war, equivalent to **Ishtar.** She was called "ambitious and aggressive, with power to destroy the indestructible and perish the imperishable." **Enheduanna,** the world's first named poet, and a priestess of Inanna, wrote a hymn praising her as a wonderful, destroying dragon.

Inanna declared war on her older sister **Ereskigal,** goddess of death, because of the death of Inanna's shepherd-lover, and because she wanted to extend her reign even into the land of death. She passed through the seven gates of the netherworld and came to Queen Ereskigal's palace of lapis lazuli. Her battle was unsuccessful for, stripped and humiliated, she was tortured and killed, her corpse hung on a stake. But confederates reached her, as she had planned, with the food of life and the water of life, reviving both Inanna and her lover. She returned to the land of the living accompanied by an army of demons, whom Ereskigal would not restore to the netherworld except in the company of a deity to replace Inanna.

Inanna restrained the demons from killing any god who swore vassalage to her cause. Her husband meanwhile had failed to praise Inanna, but declared himself "no longer a mortal, but the husband of a goddess," and lived riotously. Inanna was so annoyed that she allowed the demon army to have him.

In another myth, she battled gods and sea monsters for possession of the boat of heaven, returning to the city of Erech with its treasures. Inanna was to Erech what **Athena** was to Athens. [Kramer, Friedrich, Wolstein]

Ino: "She Who Makes Sinewy." With **Autonoë,** sister-generals to **Agave.** They led Theban **Maenads** into mountain retreats when King Pentheus, Agave's son, declared himself the enemy of the cult. The story of the suppression of three "mad" huntresses parallels that of **Iphianassa, Iphinoë,** and **Lysippe,** madwomen-sisters who waylaid travelers in the mountain passes. [Tyrell]

Iphianassa: "Mighty Queen." Sometimes called Cyrianassa, "Queen of the Chieftains." Divinely afflicted madwoman who, with her sisters **Iphinoë** and **Lysippe,** waylaid travelers along mountain passes. She may have married Eudymion after being "cured" of (or retiring from) her rowdiness. She may instead have married Bias, who had helped Melampus hunt down the madwomen. They would seem to have been guerrilla fighters whose mischief ended in marriage alliances.

Iphigenia: "Mother of a Strong Race." Saved by **Artemis** from human sacrifice, Iphigenia became the battle-priestess "of the cruel goddess" of the Tauric Chersonese (today Crimea), an Amazon stronghold. The Tauri immolated all shipwrecked sailors to Artemis. Iphigenia consecrated these hapless victims for the slaughter.

Iphigenia was also an appellation or cult name for Artemis herself, especially in regard to the worship of **Tauropolos.** Although most of the surviving myths of Iphigenia have been diluted in power, in Euripides' *Iphigenia in Taurus* her fiercer traits are suggested.

Iphinoë: "Mighty Intelligence." Sometimes called Hipponoë, "Horse Wisdom." With **Lysippe** and **Iphianassa,** divinely afflicted madwomen who waylaid travelers through their mountain region. Iphinoë died in retreat when Melampus and his followers hunted the madwomen down. Probably mythologized remembrances of guerrilla fighters.

Iphito: "Shield Strength," an Amazon brave during the reign of Queen **Hippolyte.** She followed **Pantariste** onto the beach where Heracles' captains were defeated.

In an alternative myth of the ninth labor, as evidenced by a black-figure vase dated at 575 B.C., Hippolyte and her girdle are not evidenced, and **Andromache** is queen of the Amazons. This is the oldest version to be found in art, but no written record of the episode survives, so it is somewhat mysterious. On the same vase, Iphito is shown killing a nameless Greek. [Tyrrell, Sobol]

Irnan: A warrior-sorceress who fought the Fenians (or Fianna) of the Celtic heroic age. She and her two sisters were called "the **hags** of Conaran." Irnan was the mightiest of the three, and was able to transform herself into a monster. She met Goll, also of a monstrous race, in single combat, and was killed. See also Goll's wife, **Lot.** [Ellis]

Irpa: Warrior-maid of *Flateyarbók,* a Scandinavian saga. She and her sister **Thorgerd** assisted Jarl Hakon in the forefront of battle.

Isabella I: (A.D. 1451–1504) This famous queen of Spain is best known for her liberality in supporting sciences and exploration and her attitudes against slavery. It is less well known that during her life she was considered a great military genius. She led troops in the early war of succession that settled her and Ferdinand on the throne. She had herself formally crowned queen even before Ferdinand was king, and revived an ancient custom so as to be the first female monarch in Spain for whom the unsheathed sword of justice was carried at the coronation ceremony.

She had been deprived of a monarch's education during her childhood, and so set out, as an adult, to learn the language of diplomacy, which was

Latin, and to study knightly fighting arts. In her wars against **Juana la Beltraneja,** after the death of the king of Castile, can be found the reason for her early history of miscarriages, for she was constantly riding across the countryside and undergoing the hardships of the field. One such miscarriage occurred during her siege of Toledo in the summer of 1475.

Even when her corule was established, Isabella scarcely relaxed. She had sworn to re-Christianize Aragon and attended the sieges of Moorish towns, clad in mail armor, "mounted on a spirited Andalusian horse with a flowing mane." A famous quote from Isabella indicates a bisexual propensity not often admitted in so saintly a heroic woman, but she was not as sexless as some have painted her, for she held, "There is no sight in the world as fine as a fighting-man on the field, unless it were a beautiful woman in her bed." [Walsh, Fraser, Beaumont]

Isabella Clara Eugenia: Governor of the Spanish Netherlands, until its sale to Brussels in 1643. The Infanta's skill in archery was celebrated in poems and paintings, and she was compared to **Tomyris, Semiramis, Penthesilea,** and **Camilla.** A Spanish poem praises her thus:

> With her own supernatural powers [she]
> Fulfills, by making war, her royal destiny.

And from the French:

> Her Highness has taken from us
> With the bow and arrow all the glory.

In 1615,

> the Guild of the Great Company of the Crossbow in Brussels, oldest and most influential of the city's military guilds, invited Archduke Albert and Archduchess Isabella to participate in the "Shooting of the Popinjay," an annual festival event witnessed by the townspeople. The target of the shoot was a wooden bird placed on a long pole atop the spire of Notre Dame du Sablon; the weapon used was the crossbow. Albert did not participate; Isabella, however, shot down the popinjay at the first attempt, to the wild delight of the throng. She was declared "Queen of the Great Company," a title she retained for the rest of her life. [Berger]

Isabella de Lorraine: (A.D. 1410?–1453) Mother of the warlike **Margaret of Anjou** and a contemporary of **Joan of Arc.** She "became equally renowned in arts and arms, to found colleges and win battles." In 1429, her husband, René, duke of Anjou, was imprisoned by the duke of Burgundy. Isabella at once placed her children under the protection of nobles of Lorraine and set out with an army and was soon her husband's liberator. In 1435, she fought for René's recognition as sovereign of Sicily. [Hale, Gribble]

Isabelle of England: (A.D. 1285?–1313?) Daughter of Philippe le Bel of France, wife of Edward II of England. She took up arms against her husband and his supporters. When Edward III came to the throne, he forced Isabelle to flee to Scotland, where, during the ensuing war, she traveled with a defending troop of like-spirited women, including two sisters of Nigel and Robert Bruce (see **Christian, Lady Bruce**), and **Isobel, Countess of Buchan.** Against this troop of noblewomen, Edward issued a formal proscription. He did capture several, and imprisoned them. Isabelle he forced to retire to a convent lest she try for further conquests. [Gribble, Fittis]

Ishijo: See **Hatsu-jo.**

Ishtar: In Syria, she was **Anath,** the Lady of Battle, characterized as especially bloodthirsty and vengeful. In Arabia, she was Atar; in Greece, **Astarte;** in Egypt, **Isis.** An Inanna-Ishtar Violence-goddess called **Hanna-hanna** was at the center of Hittite religion as well. Canaanite and Babylonian Ishtar, the Supreme Creatrix, overlaps Summerian **Innana,** just as the cultures overlap in territories and time. Semitic Ishtar diverges in some respects and may have a different origin, just as **Tauropolos** (Artemis Taurica) and **Artemis of Ephesus** are derived from the violent **Cybele** and **Rhea,** distinct from the Olympian huntress **Artemis.**

Ishtar was the enemy of Gilgamesh, much as **Hera** was the enemy of Heracles. Like the Hindu Mother-goddess **Devi** and the majority of these ancient goddesses, she had two aspects—one merciful and nurturing, the other exceedingly dark. In the latter capacity, she was "clad in terror." The martial Assyrians "delighted in their great ally in battle, as did the Philistines, who hung up Saul's armor as a trophy in her temple." A portrait on a cylinder seal in the British Museum shows her standing with bow and arrow, one foot resting on a lion. The seven hundred wives and three hundred concubines presented to King Solomon by the Phoenicians were Ishtar virgins, i.e., warlike priestesses, sent into his vassalage as his defenders more than for romantic purposes. [Edwardes, Friedrich]

Isis: "Throne." The Egyptian Mother-goddess associated by the Greeks with **Athena.** Like **Devi** of India and **Ishtar** of Babylon, Isis had a dark aspect. Venomous serpents could spring from her slaverings. In one of her chief legends, she challenges the great god Ra and takes from him the supreme godhead. The Ptolemaic creed of Isis states, "I am the Goddess of War, Queen of Lightning. I stir the sea and calm it. I am the rays of the Sun." Her worship was widespread in the ancient world, including Greece, Rome, and Britain, and **Cleopatra** donned the mantel of Isis in her capacity as a warrior-queen. In the service of her son Horus, Isis once speared the god Seth when he had taken the form of a hippopotamus. She spared Seth's life and Horus was so angered that he decapitated his own mother, but her head was later restored in the form of a cow, suggesting a link to **Hathor** and **Nut.** [Kramer]

Isobel, Countess of Buchan: (A.D. 1296–1358) Isobel MacDuff left her husband, the earl of Buchan (taking the finest warhorses with her), to fight for the Bruce, a cause of which her husband did not approve. The earl went so far as to issue a warrant for her death. Captured by Edward and taken to England, the countess of Buchan was imprisoned in a small cage for four years. She afterward retired to convent life. See also **Isabelle of England.** [Crawford, Fittis]

Isoltsev, Apollovna: A Russian volunteer in a regiment commanded by her father in World War I. "In the midst of battle Apollovna dashed through the flames, discovered her father's body, and carried it, under storm of shot and shell, back into Russian lines." [Gribble]

Itagaki: Led a charge of three thousand warriors of the Taira clan against ten thousand of the Heike in A.D. 1199. "She rode her warhorse expertly, guiding it skillfully with her knees, and at the same time wielding her razor-sharp naginata with amazing speed." She had resolved to die boldly and was respected even by her enemies for her courageous action and skill.

Throughout Japanese history, all women of samurai caste were expected to master certain weapons, especially the **naginata** and the tanto (knife), as well as to be capable of rigorously exercising warhorses. Ihara Saikaku told of the wife of Takebashi Jinkuro, an ex-samurai turned farmer. In 1570, she was surrounded by soldiers but "drew her sword. Her gallantry would have put a man to shame for she fought bravely." The wife of the seventh-century samurai Kamitsuken Katana trained castle women in archery and led them into battle. Tomotori's mistress, a naginata fighter among the Taira, defended the young Emperor Antoku in 1185, and, when things became hopeless, she drowned herself with the child and her husband rather than be captured. In the Kamakura period, warfare was so acute that women commonly took to the battlefields, using their skills for more than defense of homes, Itagaki being among the many extraordinary examples. [Ribner]

Ivanovna, Liza: In 1941, the studious existence of this young woman of Runa on the Volga was shattered by Hitler. "I shall become a soldier," she wrote a friend; "that's my ambition." In August, she took a group of sixty-eight volunteers, many of them virtual children, and joined the guerrillas in the forests. After a year of action, she was betrayed to the Germans, refused to talk under torture, and faced the firing squad. On the first volley, she shouted the guerrilla oath, "Death to German Invaders!," but they had intentionally missed her, thinking it would make her talk. When she remained uncowed, they fired a second volley, and though her body was ripped by bullets, she shouted, "I am dying of victory!" They fired a third volley and she called her last, "For our people!" She was bloodily avenged. [Laffin]

Izanami: Mother of Gods and primeival ancestress of the Japanese. She birthed also the elements of the universe, including fire, which caused her death and transformation, so that afterward she was a Demon-queen in the underworld, akin to **Lilith** or **Hecate.** When her consort Izanagi tried to regain her in Orpheus-like fashion, he was alarmed at her new appearance, and fled in fear and disgust. She pursued him with an army of storm-demons, forcing him out of her world, never to return.

J

◇◇◇◇◇◇◇◇◇◇◇◇◇◇

Jacqueline of Bavaria, Countess of Holland: (A.D. 1402–1437) Daughter of Count William of Hainault, one of the foremost knights of his era. He called Jacqueline "Dame Jacob" because of her boyish ways. The family crest was the lion, for which reason a pride of three lions was kept in the castle as living emblems of William's clan. Jacqueline played with them as though they were enormous, playful dogs. When little more than a child, she was already an expert falconer and daring horsewoman.

On May 13, 1417, Count William died, and Jacqueline inherited the title, making her countess of Hainault, Holland, and Zealand. The lord of Arkell, who had once suffered the indignity of being defeated in battle by his own mother for possession of their family castle, despised women's rule, and therefore staged a revolt. He lay siege to the fortified town of Gorkum, and Jacqueline responded to their cry for aid. She set forth with three hundred ships and six thousand knights, sailing up the Maas. In December, the battle was engaged. At first, it seemed likely the lord of Arkell might prevail, until Jacqueline personally entered the fray. At the head of her reserve troops, she charged the towered fortress gate, and gained access to the city. The foe was pursued throughout Gorkum, and cut down. Her victory was absolute. [Brooks]

Jael: "Wild Goat." A biblical heroine who in 1285 B.C. killed the Canaanite invaders' leader Sisera. There are two versions of this Kenite chieftainess's story, the most popular being that she seduced Sisera into her tent and, when he slept, took a tent peg and nailed it through his forehead. But her contemporary **Deborah** sings of Jael's act as soldierly, like Deborah's own, making it clear that Sisera was not sleeping when Jael slew him:

> She put her hand to the tent peg
> And her right hand to the workman's mallet.
> She struck Sisera a blow
> She crushed his head.
> She shattered and pierced his temple.
> He sank, he fell, he lay still at her feet
> At her feet he sank, he fell.
> Where he sank, he died.

Another Jael, symbolizing feminist rage, is encountered in Joanna Russ's classic science-fiction novel *The Female Man* (1975). She is a man-killing warrior from an alternative future.

Jagiello, Appolonia: (b. A.D. 1825) Polish-Lithuanian heroine. While still a teenager, she participated in Poland's war of liberation from Austria. In Krakow, she was to be seen on horseback, "in the picturesque costume of a Polish soldier, in the midst of the patriots who first planted the white eagle and flag of freedom on the castles of her nation's ancient capital, and was one of the handful of heroes who fought the battle near Podgorze, against a tenfold enemy."

She went to Vienna "in time to take heroic part in the engagement at the foubourg Widen." On August 15, 1848, after a grueling journey across the countryside, including the crossing of two rivers, swimming with her horse, she reached the Hungarian camp near Eneszy, and took part in her first large battle with the Austrians. She was soon promoted to lieutenant, participating in many battles and, between engagements, working in the hospitals. [Hale, Schmidt]

Jane, Countess of Montfort: (fl. A.D. 1342) Of her, it was said she was "a formidable and worthy rival, both in the cabinet and the field." In the fourteenth century, at the time of Edward III, her husband's inheritance was seized by rival claimants. The countess drew together a small retinue and went from duchy to duchy gathering supporters. Lola Montez said she could do "a better business of defending her Duchy, with sword in hand, than any man of her day."

The pretender for the duchy of Bretagne was Charles of Bois, who, believing a war conducted by a woman would go quickly in his favor, proceeded to Hennebonne, where Jane's forces were preparing. She "performed prodigies of valor; clad in complete armor, she stood foremost in the breach, sustained the most violent assaults, and displayed skill that would have done honor to the most experienced general." Her boldest tactic was to lead five hundred men from the fort and set fire to the besieging camp. Finding her route back into the city cut off, she galloped to Auray to regroup. Five days later, she returned with her little army, cut her way through Charles's camp, and reentered the town in triumph. English supporters arrived soon after, and Jane's cause was certain.

She later fought a sea battle off the coast of Guernsey. Froissart, who said she had a lion's heart, described her "with a very sharp sword to hand, fighting with great courage." The historian Roujoux called her "a new **Penthesilea,** with all the grandeur of a noble character." Among her antagonists was **Jeanne de Penthièrre.** [Starling, Hale, Gribble, King]

Janine-Marie de Foix: Between A.D. 1377 and 1380, she served as a cavalry fighter with Charles V and Marshal Bertrand du Guesclin. [Edwards]

Jeanne de Belleville: Lola Montez described her as "one of the handsomest women in Europe, who, with a sword in one hand and a torch in the other, directed all the horrors of war." Upon the execution of her husband Oliver III, lord of Clisson, who was beheaded in A.D. 1343, Jeanne de Belleville became leader of a band of loyal knights. "She traveled far and wide. Towns trustingly allowed her to enter their gates. Then she massacred every notable who had espoused the cause of Charles of Bois. Her bloody task accomplished, she would depart, escaping the troops sent in pursuit." She continued for some while to persecute the followers of King Philip VI. When too many of the king's forces were after her, she obtained three ships from Edward III of England, with which to harry and sink French ships. She became a legend in her own life, credited with innumerable atrocities in her unslaked passion for vengeance, keeping with her at sea her two children, with whom she shared all acts of revenge for their father. In time, this mother lioness retired comfortably and remarried. [Croix, Gribble]

Jeanne de Montfort: See **Jane, Countess of Montfort.**

Jeanne de Penthièrre: During the wars of Brittainy, in which the most famous warrior was **Jane, Countess of Montfort,** another bold woman stormed the battlefield. When Jeanne de Penthièrre's husband, Charles de Blois, was taken prisoner by the English, she took to the field in his behalf. [Gribble]

Jeanne des Armoises: In A.D. 1438 and 1439, she fought for France in the marches on Poitou and Guienne. Through her appeals, Spain sent a fleet of warships. The Maréchal de Rais placed her at the head of a large body of soldiers, in part because memory of that other Jeanne, **Joan of Arc,** loomed so large over soldiers' sentiments.

She was married and had two children. This caused her to be contrasted harshly to the virgin Maid of Orleans, but Jeanne maintained, "My value is not dependent on virginity." The provincial population supported her, but the clergy that dragged down Joan also despised Jeanne des Armoises. When the king reoccupied Paris in 1440, Jeanne was arrested and forced to declare herself a Joan imposter (there were several such, including **Pierrone** and **Joan the Maid of Sarmaize**). As punishment for her excellence, she was placed on public display on a cold slab of marble to be preached at by the repulsive clergy. She then vanishes from history, virtually unheralded.

Jeanne Hachette: (b. A.D. 1454) Women have inevitably fought atop the walls of besieged fortresses and fortified cities, and one such was Jeanne Laisné (or possibly Forquet), who in 1472 captained a group of women in the defense of the French city of Beauvais, attacked by Charles the Bold. As soldiers came over the battlements, one of the attacking Burgundians planted Charles's flag. But the teenaged Jeanne gave him a shove into the moat and proceeded to chop down the flag with a hatchet (by other accounts, "a battle ax," conjuring the image of the **labrys** of the ancient Amazons). Her boldness lifted the spirits of the citizens, who turned the tide of battle and won the day. Louis XI organized a procession honoring Jeanne, which continued to be held annually in Beauvais until the late nineteenth century. During the festival parade, women strode in the front and men followed behind. [Hale, C. Morris, Gribble]

Jeanne La Férone, the Maid of Le Mans: One of many fifteenth-century impersonators of **Joan of Arc** (see **Pierrone** and **Jeanne des Armoises**). She purported to be able to heal ulcers and to prophesize. She had been a **camp follower** and, after a brief fame as the new Joan, her warrior credentials came under suspicion when it was known her claim to maidenhood was false. She was arrested and sentenced to wear a fool's cap in various towns, where the same repulsive clergy that dragged down Joan of Arc preached at her in public squares. [Gribble]

Jeanne of Navarre: (A.D. 1271–1304) Married Philip the Fair of France. "When the Count de Bar attacked Champagne, Jeanne placed herself at the head of a small army, forced him to surrender, and kept him a long time in prison." Philip never used the marriage to claim authority over Navarre, Brie, or Champagne, admitting Jeanne's full authority. [Hale]

Jeh: The ancient Iranian version of **Lilith.** She was the first woman, called also "the primeval whore," later appointed queen of demons, who were her soldiers in defiling humanity. She was older than her husband, Gayomart, the first man. Jeh's reduction from All-mother, to an Evelike figure, and finally a demon-queen, echoes the similar downfall of innumerable goddesses in the transition from matristic to patriarchal attitudes. [Kramer]

Jehlweiser, Olga: A Russian who served in the Manchurian War under General Rennenkampf, participating in many important battles. In the 1930s, she was still active in battles around Grodno. [Hershfeld]

Jezebel: (d. 884 B.C.) This biblically maligned queen "slew the prophets of the Lord" during their violent, patriarchal uprisings. She was a priestess of **Anath** and Baal, deities roughly equivalent to **Artemis** and Apollo, whose worshippers according to the Second Book of Kings "cried aloud, and cut themselves as was their custom, with swords and lances, until blood gushed out upon them," a ritual practiced not only for Anath but for **Ishtar, Inanna,** and **Astarte.** The new patriarchal god inspired his own votaries to "avenge the blood of all the servants of the Lord against Jezebel. And the dogs shall eat Jezebel and none will bury her." As a warrior-queen, her cause was just, but doomed, and her enemy historians have transformed her into a villain. See also Jezebel's daughter, **Athaliah.** [Patai]

Jinga: See **Nzingha.**

Jingo Kogo: Martial empress of Japan, skilled with sword, bow, and **naginata.** She conquered Korea in A.D. 201. She is also called Okinaga Tarashi. Because she was pregnant at the beginning of her campaigns, she used a magic stone to delay the development of her infant. She instructed her navy, "Do not rape or plunder. Do not fear many or despise few. Give mercy to all who yield but no quarter to the stubborn. Victors will be rewarded; deserters will be slain." Among the tributes she brought back to Japan was her nation's first written language.

Jingo governed for seventy years and was succeeded by her son Emperor Ojin, deified after his death as the War-god Hachiman, hence Jingo is considered the Mother of War. [Seth, Bacon]

Jirel of Joiry: This powerful, flame-haired lady-knight was the protagonist in a series of short heroic fantasy tales by Catherine L. Moore, one of the few successful women to write for the science-fiction pulp magazines of the 1930s and 1940s. These heroic fantasy stories were eventually reprinted in a handsomely illustrated volume as *Black God's Kiss* and in paperback as *Jirel of Joiry*. Ms. Moore was a major influence on later women writers of fantasy and science fiction.

Joan Beaufort, Queen of Scotland: (A.D. 1405?–1445) She violently avenged the murder of James I and later wed James Stewart the Black Knight. She and her second husband unsuccessfully defended the castle of Stirling. [Crawford]

Joan of Arc: (A.D. 1412–1431) French Catholic national heroine. Joan was a peasant girl who, believing herself guided by the voices of saints, set forth to liberate France from the English. Though wielding banner in lieu of sword, Joan at least led French soldiers against the English, drew the battle plans, and took wounds. In recompense for her valor, the French burned her at the stake.

Joan the Maid of Sarmaize: In the wake of **Joan of Arc's** rise and destruction, many "false maids" came temporarily to prominence. No one knows the actual identity of the Maid of Sarmaize. She appeared as from nowhere, claiming to be the Maid restored, dressing in male clothing, and traveling about attempting to be accepted by Joan's relatives and comrades. Some of them housed her with mild amusement. In Anjou, she inspired a small religious following and earned food and lodging by her imposture.

A document survives, dated February 3, 1456, giving Joan of Sarmaize permission to return to Saumer if she would cease to wear men's clothing and live respectably. [Gribble]

Jowanowitsch, Sophie: A young Serbian of World War I who received permission from King Peter to fight in the army wearing the uniform of a common soldier. [Hershfeld]

Juana la Betraneja: (A.D. 1462–1530) Rival of **Isabella** for the Castilian throne. She allied herself, through marriage, with Portugal, and played a military game of tug-of-war with Isabella to make Castile Portuguese. After her failure, she retired to a convent. [Fraser]

Judith: When Holofernes held Bethulia siege, Judith, a wealthy and influential widow, chastised the city council and said that she would go forth and, trusting in God, deliver the city from danger. Taking with her her waiting maid and a large basket of figs, wine, and bread, she strode boldly beyond the city gates to Holofernes's camp. Such was her beauty that she

was taken to his tent. Adah Isaacs **Menken** wrote a poem for Judith that
goes in part,

> Stand back!
> I am no Magdalene waiting to kiss the hem of your garment.
> I am Judith!
> I wait for the head of Holofernes!
> Oh, what wild passionate kisses will I draw from that bleeding mouth!

Filling Holofernes with wine, and putting off his advances by means of
flattering discourse, she in essence "drank him under the table." While he
was in a stupor, she grabbed him by the hair and, drawing forth his own
sword, lopped off his head, handing it to her maid to place in the basket.
They then strode as boldly back into the city and, come dawn, Holofernes's
head greeted the Assyrian troops from atop the walls of Bethulia. The
enemy was soon defeated. Holofernes's tent and spoils were awarded to
Judith. She took them to Jerusalem and placed them in a temple as an
offering. She lived to the age of 105.

Judith: Queen of the Falash, or Black Jews. She attacked Axum, sacred
capital of Ethiopia, in A.D. 937. She spared no one, killing even the
descendants of Solomon and the Queen of Sheba. [Taylor, Loth]

Juliana: Christian warrior-saint of Anglo-Saxon epic poetry who "became
bold in battle beyond all races of women." She confronted a demon,
grasped him, bound him in fetters, and refused to release him until he told
her his true identity, and acknowledged her as "wise in spirit." [Damico]

Juliana: (A.D. 1658–1733) Born in Bengal, of Portuguese descent. After a
shipwreck, she was taken into the Mogul court of Aurengzebe of Hindustan, becoming harem-queen to Aurengzebe's son, Behadur Shah, who
succeeded to the crown in 1707. During battles to defend her husband's
authority, Juliana rode upon a war elephant alongside Behadur. Shah Au-
lum said, "If Juliana were a man, she would be my vizier." [Hale]

Julianna of Breteuil: Or Julienne, daughter of Henry I of England, wife of
Eustache de Breteuil. "She fought for her husband against her father,
withstood siege," and formed an unsuccessful plot to capture Henry in
A.D. 1119. [Hale, Gribble]

Julienne du Guesdin: A **martial nun** of Pontersay in Brittainy who in
A.D. 1370 defended her convent against the English Captain Felton. She

scurried along the walls of the convent snatching Englishmen from their scaling ladders, tossing three of them to their deaths. Her brother arrived the following day to take the defeated Felton prisoner. [Gribble]

Juliette: Sade's antiheroine, a beautiful sadist, symbol of absolute vice, contrasted with Justine, absolute purity. Juliette seems to have been based on a respectable Dame of Grenable. Sade's excellent villain is stated to have been the product of the Panthémont convent. This convent actually existed in Paris, a retreat for wealthy and aristocratic women of the most pleasantly depraved character. A member of this convent, Mademoiselle d'Abert, wrote a notorious book, *Escapades of a Jolly Girl.* From police records of the eighteenth century, it is clear that the Marquis de Sade rarely exaggerated his portraits. It was Sade's genius to pretend allegory in what was essentially a historical chronicle padded with cynical philosophy. See also **Wanda von Dunayer** and **Samois.**

Juno: Roman name for **Hera.** In modern texts on mythology, Juno is commonly described as the trod-upon, hearth-bound, jealous, and not very impressive consort of Jove/Zeus/Jupiter. One must bear in mind that Zeus was a comparatively minor deity at least until the fall of Troy, and was originally a vegetation spirit of Crete. Tales older than the Trojan War, which in revisions give Zeus prominence, almost certainly did not include him in their original versions. Juno held a much more important position than wife in those most ancient times. So we shouldn't be surprised to see the colossal statue of Juno in the Vatican Museum, depicting her with shield and spear, the spear held for attack. She was, in part, a War-goddess, worshipped by the Amazons, appearing in their midst to encourage them to attack the archetypal patriarchal hero Heracles.

Juno's strength was such that she was able to hold violent **Artemis** stationary, snatch the quiver from her back, and slap the huntress on the cheeks with her own quiver, scattering arrows through the halls of Olympus.

junoesque: Because the word "Amazon" has meant, too often, in the vernacular of the last hundred years, "a mannish woman," a separate word was needed for strong, tall women upon whom no insult was intended. Until about the 1940s, "junoesque" filled the need. It described a woman who was large, stately, and imposing. The social changes wrought by two world wars were in great part responsible for the tightening oppression of women, and a change in people's attitudes causing even tall, stately women to be considered mannish, since a properly feminine woman would not have the audacity to be more than five foot six and utterly submissive. So, "junoesque" has fallen from use, and should be revived at every opportunity.

Juturna: In the *Anaid* of Vergil, Juturna is a bodyguard and charioteer. She accompanies her brother Turnus into battle.

K

◆◇◆◇◆◇◆◇◆◇◆◇◆

Kaahumanu: In A.D. 1819, upon the death of her husband, King Kamehameha I of Hawaii, Queen Kaahumanu donned "the feather cloak and helmet reserved for chiefs and warriors. Thus attired, she waited to greet the heir to the throne, son of the dead king." She demanded corule, and received it.

Women "could and did sometimes fight at the side of men in battle. One of the most glorious heroic battles of the chiefesses was the battle of Nuuanu Valley. There, the chiefesses took up arms against the overwhelming forces of King Kamehameha I, and fought to the death." [Mrantz]

Kaipkire: Warrior of the Herero people of southwest Africa in the eighteenth century. She led resistance forces against British slave traders. She was not unusual among her people. Herero fighting women faced German soldiers as late as A.D. 1919. [Sertima]

Kali: Protohistoric India was a center of goddess monotheism, and we may safely assume many of the avatars of this Great Goddess had once been actual persons whose exploits became heavily mythologized. In post-Aryan India, male deities became of increasing importance, and many War-goddesses were rationalized as the feminine aspects of male gods; others were said to be overcome by male gods, marriage after combat being typical. Kali, however, was born fully armed from the brow of her mother, and represents the goddess in one of her earliest aspects, before fathering was recognized.

The original Mother-goddess or **Devi** had multitudes of incarnations divisible into roughly two kinds: domestic and warlike. Of the latter is undefeated Kali, the Dark One, in greater antiquity called **Uma,** with tusks, three eyes, four arms, claws wielding swords and spears, a necklace of human heads, and girdle of severed hands. In one tale, she defeats the monster Raktavira by holding him above her head, piercing him underneath, and sucking out his blood. Her victory dance was so vigorous that she nearly destroyed the earth, and even trampled Shiva underfoot.

Cretan representations of the **Gorgons,** with thickly coiled hair rather than snakes, bear striking resemblance to Kali because of the lolling tongue. Other connections between India and antique Europe are to be found in the bacchic rites of the **Maenads,** the cult of which was introduced from Thrace and Asia Minor and was probably of earlier Indic origin. The murderous rages of the drunken Maenads, faces stained with wine, resemble, in ancient art, the blood-stained face of tongue-lolling Kali. Such interconnections and exchanges have suggested to some scholars a time of worldwide goddess monotheism, the various cults in occasional contact with one another. The far-ranging Amazons of the Thermodon and of North Africa each conquered lands from northern Europe to Asia Minor, leaving, perhaps, this widespread legacy of Warrior-goddesses and deified tongue-lolling cannibals. [Mookerjee, Ions, Sen]

Kallipateira: In 440 B.C., when the Olympics still forbade women's participation or attendance (as men could not attend the far older **Heraean** games), Kallipateira elected to disobey the rule. She had been an athlete in her youth, a widow of a boxer, and became her son's trainer. When her son entered the Olympics, his coach had no intention of not seeing him compete. Disguised in voluminous robe, she entered the spectator's box and, when her boy won, leaped onto the field to embrace him. [Blue]

Kane-jo or **Okane:** A Japanese peasant woman of Omi province, where strongwomen were common (see **Oiko**). One day, Okane was carrying a load of laundry down the road when she saw an enormous stallion that had escaped from a temple. Its grooms were unable to capture it without being trampled. It ran near Okane and, as her arms were full of laundry, she stomped on the reins that were dragging on the ground. The fierce animal screamed and tried to kick her with its hoofs, but she held it firm with just her foot.

Kang Ke-ching: (b. A.D. 1912) Or K'ang K'o-ch'ing, wife of Zou Enlai. She was "toughest of the small band of women who survived" the year-long, six-thousand-mile "Long Walk" of Mao Tse-tung's revolutionaries. She took her own weapons with her and twice carried wounded soldiers over her knapsack as the marchers continued along their route, fighting nationalist armies, provincial warlords, and bandits. She first took command in 1934, when: "By chance we met the enemy and grabbed our guns to fight. I was temporarily elected commander of three hundred men. We fought two hours and the enemy retreated. I must say this was a happy day for me." [Rowbothan, Miles]

Kannagi: A heroine of the *Silappadikaram* (*Lay of the Ankle Bracelet*) who ripped off her breast in fury over the unjust murder of her husband and used its blood and milk, acidified with rage, to burn the city of Madurai. The goddess of the city transformed Kannagi into a deity. She was worshipped thereafter as Patlini Devi, the "Wife Who Became a Goddess," or the "Goddess of One Breast." [Berkson, Narayan]

Kara: A **Valkyrie.** She had been **Sigrun** in her previous life, and **Svava** before then. She was accidentally slain by Helgi when she had taken the form of a swan. [Davidson, Dumézil]

Karnavati, Rani: A heroine of medieval Rajasthan, defender of Chitor for several months. Clad in armor, she strode the walls and exposed herself to every danger. When Chitor was falling, she had a great funeral pyre made from all variety of combustibles, then walked into the flames, followed by Rajaput noblewomen who had assisted in the lost defense. [Tod, Masud-al-Hasan]

Kascha: A Bohemian Medea and one of Queen **Libussa's** ministers in the establishment of a northern Amazonia. See also **Tetka.**

Kaumari: A War-goddess of India's elaborate pantheon. She fought with javelin. See **Parvati.** [Berkson]

Keith, Anne: The Restoration brought woe to Scotland in more than one way, the wars against the Covenanters but one of them. Anne Keith, Lady Methven, who preferred the riggings of a battleship to the threads of a spinning wheel, survived wounds taken in fighting for her country, and later defended the estates of her husband. When in 1678 she was left to rule the parish of Methven, she took advantage of her husband's absence to wage wars against the Covenanters, who had the audacity to have their field meetings in sight of her castle, keeping by them several soldiers of defense.

Anne rallied her soldiers, not all of whom agreed with her policy, so that she had to watch her back as well. Sometimes she was able to break up meetings by threats alone, other times skirmishes resulted, and the defenders of the Covenanters were killed. She received "a hearty reprobation from the Archbishop Sharp," and the Covenanters soon gave Methven parish wide birth for fear of Anne Keith. [Fittis]

Keith, Margaret: In A.D. 1395, Margaret, Lady Lindsay, defended the Scottish castle of Fyrie in the district of Buchan against her nephew. The castle's great age made it difficult to defend, but Margaret defied Robert Keith, showing the same boldness as **Black Agnes** of Dunbar. [Fittis]

Khawlah Bint al-Azwar al-Kindiyyah: (seventh century A.D.) Sometimes given simply as Khaula, sister of Derar. At the Battle of Yermonks in the seventh century, this Arab woman warrior, together with other female captains, drove off the attacking Greeks. She was "a tall knight muffled in black and fighting with ferocious courage," credited with turning the tide against the Byzantines.

Captured at Sabhura near Damascus, she felt that she was rudely treated, so she rallied the women to revolt against their captors. As they had been deprived of weapons, they used their tent poles to fight (see **Afra' Bint, Oserrah,** and **Wafeira**). She was afterward wed to Caliph Ali. [Hale, Miles]

Kikunoyo: Swordswoman of kabuki drama. She was pursued by Danjuro, who wanted to steal her heirloom sword. They fought in the forest by night and she disarmed him.

Kleoptoleme: Amazon brave in the war of Heracles and Telemon against Queen **Andromache.** [Bothmer]

Klothod: A female war-jinn who, in *The Testament of Solomon,* could be overcome only by Marmarath, one of the seven planetary angels. Another of the female war-jinns was named Powers. There were seven in all, summoned by Solomon, each defeated by angels. They were apparently daughters of **Lilith.** [Davidson]

The Knight of Naples: Petrarch tells of a young woman of Naples he met in A.D. 1340 and again in 1343 who "from the flower of her age chose to dwell in camps and adopt military habits and a military dress." She appeared as a hardy soldier of prodigious strength, scarred all over, a clever strategist, and slept in full armor.

Koesem: (late 1800s A.D.) A Greek who became the harem-queen of the Turkish Sultan Murad III. In Turkish history, harem-queens very often became queens of state, as the Venetian Baffa ruled over Achmed I and the Russian Roxelane ruled through Suleiman. Biblically, **Vashti** was cast down from power for fear of her fomenting a harem revolt, and the Jewess Esther was appointed harem-queen in her stead. Esther had power enough over Xerxes to improve the condition of Jews in Persia. Koesem was the most aggressive of the type, raising her own armies and waging war to achieve her political aims. She ruled as regent for fifty years.

Kokovtseva, Olga: Russian women's military exploits date from earliest history with the case of Queen **Olga.** In World War I, the Cossack regiments always included a few fighting women. Many served in Serbia with the sixth regiment of Ural Cossacks, who had for their captain a woman named Olga Kokovtseva. She was twice wounded and received the St. George Cross. [Hirshfeld, Gribble]

Kolzany, Marja: A soldier in the ranks of Kurt Strod's Czech Resistance fighters. She saved Strod's life in March 1940, when the two of them rigged a bridge with explosives. The Germans shot Strod several times. "Marja calmly shot back, using a 'liberated' machine-gun," killing three Nazis and dragging Strod to safety. Other fighters against the Nazis include Alma **Allen,** Tania **Chernova,** Polina **Gelman,** Elena **Haas, Mira,** Elaine **Mordeaux,** and Hannah **Senesh.** [Truby]

Koman: A twelfth-century woman samurai and **naginata** practitioner, Koman made her place in history by saving the Minamoto banner from the Taira. As the Taira barge approached the ship upon Lake Biwa, she took the banner in her teeth and swam ashore, arrows whisking into the water on all sides.

Koman: Mary Ritter Beard tells of another Koman, who lived at the end of the 1600s. She was in the service of a Settsu feudal lord's wife as bodyguard. After political intrigues, Koman was forced to arrange a clever escape for her ward and two children, taking back roads to Kyoto. Waylaid by a band of highwaymen, they were threatened with robbery and rape, and the children with captivity. Koman's ward yelled, "Accompany me to death!" as she drew her short sword and attacked the bandits. Both women fought valiantly, skill in fencing arts being "customary among women of the military and aristocratic classes." The mother killed four men but was herself fatally wounded. Koman killed six and escaped injury.

The Koniag Huntress: Among Eskimo hero tales are many regarding fierce, independent women. A legend from Kodiak, Alaska, tells of a girl who, on achieving puberty, left her parents so they would have enough to eat. She grew weak on a diet of seaweed, until receiving the gift of strength from a spirit. She then made her own arrows and killed seals. She traveled by kayak, which she made herself. She defeated her jealous brothers in feats of hunting. When she matured, many men sought her in marriage, because she was so handsome. When she selected a husband, they fought together, and she continued to travel to many places. [Lantis]

Kornilov, Ludmilla and **Volkensteii:** Sister members of the Russian women's Battalion of Death in World War I. This battalion was noted for its ferocity and suffered many casualties at the front. Battalion members each carried a dose of cyanide in the event of being taken prisoner.

Korravai: Goddess of victory in southern India. She fights with spear and is portrayed standing on the neck of the buffalo she has slain. She is an aspect of **Durga** and is called by many names: Kumari, Kavuri, Samarj, Shalini, Laksmi, Mahishasuramardani, Saraswati, and others. [Berkson]

Kosanjo Ichijosei: Also called Goodwife Hu, the Chinese warrior-daughter of General Kotaiko, in the thirteenth-century Japanese novel *Suikoden*. She was skilled in yadome-jutsu (arrow-deflecting art) and with her two swords.

Krasilnikov, Olga: In 1915, this nineteen-year-old soldier, disguised as a youth, participated in nineteen battles in Poland before sustaining a leg wound and being returned to Moscow. She received the St. George Cross. [Hirshfeld]

Kreousa: Amazon brave in the Attic War, slain by Phylakos in single combat. [Bothmer]

Kriemhilde: In the first part of the epic *Nibelungenlied*, Kriemhilde is a conventional woman of her day, but in the second part she becomes an avenging devil. Although to some extent the development of the story plays into the misogynist idea that too much power in a woman leads to the victimization of men, it is sometimes difficult to tell if she is really a tragic villain or justifiably avenging herself against the sniveling Gunther, who cheats to win his wife; ruthless Hagen, who betrays Siegried by using friendship as a weapon; Rudegar, who, though in some ways is the only heroically appealing figure, is indecisive and afraid; and Geselher, inconsistent to the point of being a traitor, at least in his treatment of Kriemhilde.

Kriemhilde, by her very obsession, is no weak adversary. There are wonderful images of her in the end of Fritz Lang's silent epic (scripted by Thea von Harbou, who was married to Lang) where Kriemhilde, not a merely passive avenger turning men against themselves, takes up sword and slays her greatest enemy with her own hand. See **Brunhilde.**

Kruger, Augusta: Lieutenant in the 9th Prussian Regiment, fought the French in the War of Liberation. She received the Iron Cross and the Russian Order of St. George. On retiring in 1816, she wed a fellow officer. [Laffin]

Krylova, Vera: Tall, pigtailed, and by all accounts stunningly attractive, Vera joined the medical corp in 1941. She was already a markswoman and equestrian and took every opportunity to practice with machine guns and pistols, awaiting the chance to become a combatant in World War II. When Nazis marched toward Moscow, she found herself commanding an impromptu guerrilla army, gathering an increasing number of refugees, infecting them with valor when previously they had felt only terror. One of their skirmishes lasted twenty-three hours before the Germans were routed. They passed through a village where only a seven-year-old child had survived, and buried the dead. Breaking through enemy lines at last, sentries refused to let the de facto officer see General Zakharkin, but Vera caused such a scene that the general finally came forth, at first scoffing the horsewoman. She dismounted, limped toward him with steady gaze, and demanded supplies for her company. Her ragtag guerrillas marched in parade for the general's inspection. Krylova was awarded the Order of the Red Banner. She was later in action with a battalion of ski troops. She was several times wounded. [Laffin]

Kuan Yin: Chinese goddess of mercy, sometimes interchangeable with **Tou Mu,** Kwannon to the Japanese. She had innumerable arms, similar to **Durga,** and carried many precious objects, including a sword, bow and arrow, and dragon's head. Also akin to Durga, Kuan Yin is essentially benevolent, one of the few dieties who is never feared, but only loved, for her warlike aspect is devoted to the destruction of the demons, dragons, and fears that prey upon humankind. She is often portrayed riding a fierce dragon whose life she spared, for even monsters can obtain her mercy.

In one of her dragon-slaying legends, she defeats the Old Woman of the Sea, Shui-mu Niang-niang, a Sea- and Chaos-goddess resembling **Tiamat.** The Sea-goddess destroyed the ancient city of Ssu-chou by sinking it into Lake Hung-tse in A.D. 1574. Shui-mu Niang-niang then set out afoot to destroy other cities, hopelessly pursued by armies. Kuan Yin, disguised as a noodle vendor, tricked the Sea-goddess into eating iron chains by convincing her they were noodles, then sank the Old Woman of the Sea in her dragon form to the bottom of a deep well at the foot of a mountain. One of her demon-quelling avatars was **Miao Shan.** [Werner]

Kuveni: Warrior-witch and princess of the Yakhas (demon worshippers) of pre-Aryan Sri Lanka. She lured Vijaya to near doom. Although she was unable to destroy him due to Vishnu's magic charm, she nonetheless flung him and his men into a deep chasm. See also **Sugala** and **Pattini.** [Seneviratne]

Kuz, Jarema: A soldier in the volunteer Uhlan squadron of the Ukraine in World War I, "whose pale energetic little face reminded people of the early pictures of Napoleon." [Hirshfeld]

Kydoime: Amazon brave in the war between Heracles and **Andromache.** [Bothmer]

L

◆◇◆◇◆◇◆◇◆◇◆◇◆◇◆◇◆

Labé, Louise: (A.D. 1526–1566) In her youth, this daughter of a Lyons ropemaker was fond of music, hunting, and military exercise, and regularly participated in tourneys. Before she was sixteen, and during the reign of François I, she went to Perpignan and distinguished herself in the ranks of the Dauphin during the siege of that city, earning the title "La Capitaine Louise." She later wrote "Débat de Folie et d'Amour," which is today better known in a rhymed adaptation by La Fontaine, "L'Amour et la Folie." In 1555, she published love poems and, though married, confessed to amorous feelings for women. [Hale, Taylor, Gribble]

labrys: A weapon favored by the ancient Amazons, including **Hippolyte** and **Camilla.** This double-headed ax served as scepter to the Cretan Earth-mother. Because the sword is less commonly associated with the Amazons than is the ax, the inference is that the Amazons originate from a far greater antiquity than is commonly supposed, from no later than the earliest days of the Bronze Age when the design of stone and copper tools still influenced weapons design, and probably from the Mesolithic period, when such weapons were the norm. The labrys is designed to be tied with rawhide to a wooden handle. Such a Stone Age relic would have been retained by Amazons because of its symbolism of the moon and the horned beast, similar to their crescent-shaped shields and arrows. The labrys is today a common symbol in lesbian culture. [Wolf]

147

Lacombe, Rose: (b. A.D. 1768) "One of the terrible heroines, or rather furies, of the French Revolution," a leader of a women's brigade of the 1790s, consisting of market women who fashioned their own uniforms and went armed with cutlass and pike. Her mob of ferocious women attacked the Hotel-de-Ville, obliging the king to leave Versailles. These women were called the *tricoteuses de Robespierre,* the *flagellenses,* and the *furies de guillotine.*

As did Théroigne de **Mericourt,** Lacombe founded a militant women's club, gave rousing orations at political gatherings, and joined the attack on the Tuileries, presenting herself so boldly that the city presented her with a civic crown. Reckless and beautiful, she fell into disfavor because of a romantic attachment to an aristocrat whose life she attempted to save. She nonetheless survived the Reign of Terror unscathed, afterward operating a small business. [Rothery, Hale]

Laena: (fl. 505 B.C.) An Athenian athlete and courtesan, she was arrested for her part in a conspiracy but would not break under torture. She bit off her own tongue and spat it in the face of her tormentor. In consequence, she was deified and the Athenians raised a statue to her, in the form of a tongueless lioness. [Hale]

Lagareva, Alexandra Ephimowna: An officer of the Don Cossacks in World War I.

Lai Choi San: From A.D. 1920 until at least 1937, Madame Lai Choi San was active as a pirate near Macao, and was an owner of several gambling dens as well. She was a small, slender beauty exquisitely attired in white silks with jade buttons, though in battle she wore a simple blouse and trousers. She inherited her father's pirate business and commanded a fourteen-junk fleet from a thronelike chair on deck of the flagship. On the wall of her private cabin, as reported by American journalist Aleko Lilius, who spent several weeks with her, there was a painting of Ah Ma, goddess of the sea. Although it was rumored that the Japanese had killed her in 1937, she was briefly active again in 1938, and imprisoned in 1939, but she escaped and was not heard from again. [Croix, Snow]

Lakshmi Bai, the Rani of Jhansi: National heroine of India. A British general who saw her in the midst of battle said that he had never seen a greater hero. Raised in a household full of boys, she excelled at equestrian arts and managed her horse with the reins in her teeth, wielding two swords in her hands. Dark-eyed and intense, "fair and handsome, with noble presence, a dignified and resolute, indeed stern, expression," she came immediately out of purdah after the death of the Rani's husband, and began meeting her people and establishing her regency through her son. She became the key military adviser for the Jhansi army, having "an undoubted instinct for war," and became the leading figure of the Indian Mutiny (1857–1858). When Jhansi was besieged by the British, the rani called together all the noblewomen and encouraged them, too, to defy the old rules of purdah and help in the effort against the British. She died heroically at the age of twenty-two upon the battlefield. [Smyth, Tahmankar, Lebra-Chapman, Sinha]

Lakwena, Alice: Leader of the popular uprisings in Uganda in 1987, a self-styled priestess of magic. [Fraser]

Lamashtu: A demoness of Mesopotamia, kin to **Lilith.** [Lacks]

Lambrun, Margaret: A Scottish attendant of Mary, Queen of Scots. Clad in male costume and armed with pistol, she set out to assassinate Elizabeth and avenge Mary. She bungled her attempt and was captured. Elizabeth so admired her gumption that Margaret was pardoned. [Crawford]

Lamia: Her name, "Devourer," implies simultaneously an act of destruction and of sexuality, a Love- and Battle-goddess interchangeable with the Libyan **Net** but later reduced to a vampiric bogey. She took Zeus as a consort, but the children of their union were slain by **Hera** out of jealousy. In revenge, Lamia became a killer of mortal children, akin to **Lilith.** Her daughter was **Scylla.** The Lamiae, or succubi, were her vampire daughters with claws and cloven hooves. They were the swiftest of all human animals, capable also of taking the form of mermaids who delighted in sinking ships. Lamia became Great Queen of the Sirens in later fairy lore. See also the **Empusae.** [Graves]

Lampedo: "Burning Torch," referring to torchlit processions in honor of Mother-goddesses. Lampedo coruled the **Thermodontines** with **Marpesia.** [Justinus, Boccaccio]

L'Angevine: Mme. de Larochejaquelein, secretary and aide-de-camp to her husband in the royalist guerrilla wars of the eighteenth century, left an excellent memoir, recounting among so much else her observations of various women at the front of battles. "In the army of M. de Bouchamp a young woman became a dragoon to avenge the death of her father. She performed prodigies of valor during the whole war, and called herself L'Angevine." Her real name was Joanne Bordereau, but it was as L'Angevine that she would win the hearts of the French. Mme. de Larochejaquelein also saw "a young woman tall and strong with pistols and sabre hung at her girdle, accompanied by two other women, armed with pikes." She wrote of a young woman at Thouars who, when wounded through the hand, shouted, "This is nothing!" and was animated to greater courage in the thickest part of battle, where she perished. [Gribble, Kavanagh]

La Niña: See La Niña de la **Hueca.**

Laodice I: (fl. c. 353 B.C.) Syrian queen and sister-wife of Antiochus II, whom she murdered. She waged war against Ptolemy III Euergetes. She contrived the assassination of **Berenice of Cyrene,** mistress of Euergetes, for which Euergetes invaded Egypt seeking revenge.

Laodice's military strongholds were at Sardis and Ephesus. She was of very severe character and badly treated her subjects. She declared her son king of Syria and was returning to Antioch in arms when an Egyptian fleet appeared. A sea battle resulted, and her career ended. [Mahaffy]

Laodoke: Amazon brave in the Attic War. [Bothmer]

Larina: Italian Amazon, one of **Camilla's** hand-chosen companions-at-arms in the *Aeneid,* including also **Tullia, Tarpeia,** and **Acca.** "They were like Thracian Amazons when they make the waters of the **Thermodon** tremble, and make war with their ornate arms, either around **Hippolyte,** or when warlike **Penthesilea** returns in her chariot and the female armies exult, with a great ringing cry and the clashing of crescent-shaped shields."

Lathgertha: In *Hálfdanar Saga,* she is named Hladgerd, queen of a nation allied to the cause of Hálfdanar, providing him with twenty of her ships and complete crews. Saxo Grammaticus tells a more elaborate tale of Lathgertha's early career: A group of noblewomen were ordered into the houses of prostitution by a conquering Norwegian king. When Regner of Sweden heard of it, he set out to avenge this indignity. At the border he was met by the noblewomen themselves, who had escaped and armed themselves as soldiers, eager to join Regner and exact revenge with swords of their own. Lathgertha was the most famed of this group, having "a man's temper in a woman's body. With locks flowing loose under her helm, she fought in the forefront of the battle, the most valiant of warriors. Everyone marvelled at her matchless feats." Regner confessed that their victory was due chiefly to Lathgertha.

In times of peace, she is said to have kept a bear and a hound as pets to protect her as she slept, much as **Alfhild** kept two large serpents that she had raised from hatchlings.

Laval, Gabrielle and **Claire de:** Sister warriors who in A.D. 1524 defended Marseille, fictionalized in Mlle. de Grandpré's *Une héroïne,* along with **Améliane du Puget.** The Laval sisters led all-female contingents.

Laverna: Roman Thief-goddess.

Lemnos: A gynocratic island best known because of the Argonauts' landing there, discovering that all the men had been slain. Its capital was named for the Amazon conqueror **Myrene** of Libya. See **Hypsipyle, Bendis,** and **Marulla.**

Leubevére: Falsely accused of impious crimes by **Chrodielde,** Leubevére, abbess of St. Radegunde convent, repulsed her rival and afterward waged war against Chrodielde's army of thieves, outcasts, and disenfranchised peasants. The convents and monasteries of A.D. 590 tended to be little more than the estates of wealthy landholders with forces to defend their rights and to manage troublesome serfs. The bishops called upon the king of France to quell these warrior-nuns. King Childebert sent forces that were hard put to suppress Chrodielde. Leubevére was later found innocent of Chrodielde's charges, but was nonetheless dragged in the streets by her hair, then imprisoned, for leading nuns to battle. [Hale, King]

Leucippe: "White Mare." The **Maenads,** as with the Amazons, were often named in honor of horses or a horse-headed goddess. Leucippe sacrificed her son to Dionysus, aided by her sisters **Alcithoë** and **Arsippe.** They were afterward changed into bats.

Leucippe: Name for one of the mare-headed aspects of Demeter, the White Mare, Epona in Britain. She cohabits with **Melanippe,** the Black Mare. They symbolize life and death.

Leucippides: "White Mare Maidens." A cult in Sparta similar to that of the **Maenads.** They worshipped especially Demeter, Dionysus, and Apollo. They could be married only by men swift enough to overtake them. Ancestral Leucippides, swift-running goddesses, were worshipped in Corinth.

Leviathan: According to the kabalists, Leviathan the Slant Serpent was Samael (Satan), while Leviathan the Tortuous Serpent was **Lilith.** As Samael was originally only a goddess-consort, akin to the Greek daemons, out of whose petty ranks even great Zeus originated, Samael can be done away with as the ruling aspect of Leviathan, rendering the biblical monster definitively female, indistinguishable from **Tiamat** or similar Dragon-goddesses (see **Eurynome**). Thus, Lilith is called "the Serpent, Woman of Harlotry," suggesting the most ancient Serpent-goddesses in a form villainized by the patriarchs.

Further evidence of the unimportance of the male aspect of the destroying Leviathan comes from a 1648 kabalistic treatise by Naftali Herz Bacharach stating that Lilith's husband was a castrate, as was typical of the subservient lovers of many **Cybele**like goddesses. One of her lovers was Tanin'iver, or "Blind-Dragon," the crippled form of Samael. The thirteenth-century *Zohar* further states that Lilith was dual sexed, Samael embodied within her, and the female portion of the serpent was "adorned like a despicable harlot." Eve's lesbian liaison with dual-sexed Lilith produced Cain. [Patai]

Libussa: Aeneas Silvius in *Historia Boëmii* tells that the visionary Libussa succeeded her father King Crocus in the rule of Bohemia. With the support of her sisters **Kascha** and **Tetka,** Libussa remained in power from A.D. 700 to 738. She appointed only women to high offices and "trained her sex assiduously in military exercise before leading them on many victories." Her leading general, **Valasca,** effected a coup, continuing Libussa's policies but with greater tyranny. [Rothery]

Li Chen, Major General: A leader in Mao Tse-tung's campaigns as early as 1927. She stayed with the six-thousand-mile Long Walk. She engaged in battle even during pregnancy.

Mao's "women hold up half the sky" slogan and the heightened status of women did not come wholly from the importation of communism. Women's "secret societies" flourished in the late nineteenth and early twentieth centuries, the Blue Lanterns and the Green Lanterns being affiliated with the Boxers. Women held high rank in other secret societies and met with men on equal status. Their function was often to shield robbers.

Women, excluded from orthodox religious and political activity, formed the secret societies in their own behalf, and were sworn never to tell even their husbands of their membership. Their activities were typically criminal and frequently martial. Mao was able to tap into this existing reservoir. He afforded the disenfranchised of China, including women, places in the larger context of communist society. [Macksey, F. Davis]

Lieouchi: In Wei in A.D. 515, a famous battle occurred at Tsetong, where a woman general named Lieouchi was in command. When Imperial troops attempted to take Tsetong, she successfully held out against siege. As with **Mongchi** at Chanyang a decade earlier, the woman general's patriotic lectures spurred her soldiers to grim perseverance. When the enemy cut off her city's water supply, she initiated a water-conservation campaign and saw that rainfall was collected into vases through water-catching devices made from linen. Baffled Imperial forces eventually abandoned the siege.

Lilidtha: "Little Lilith." In kabalistic thought, there were two Liliths: Grandmother Lilith, the Queen of Night, and Lilith the Maid. Lilidtha was a beautiful maiden from her head to her belly button; from the navel down, she was a brightly burning flame. She led 480 demonic legions and warred against Grandmother Lilith, sometimes in concert with **Makhlath.** [Patai]

Lilith: In Hebrew legend, she was created concurrently with Adam and therefore was man's equal, unlike Eve. Due to her vitality and symbolic importance for women, she has been exceedingly villified in the millennia since as a vampire, child eater, and killer of men. Her only crime was refusal to be subservient to Adam. She was called "the Northerner," and may have some forgotten connection to the **Valkyries.** The *Zohar* supplement identifies her with **Bat Zuge,** one of the ten divinities that flanked the left side of God's throne; thus she was among the fallen angels.

Kabalists identify her as a princess of Damascus, of the House of Rimmon, or as queen of Zemargad. The Book of Isaiah calls her "the night hag." Her emblems include the jackal, hyena, ostrich (suggesting the Egg-mother), owl and carrion-eating kite. Her demon-lovers were satyrs. She was believed sometimes to be accepted by God as his consort, displacing the rightful queen of heaven, Matronit, who ruled the heavenly hosts as Lilith ruled demons. During these recurring periods of God's fascination, Israel becomes the lowest of all nations and is not restored until Matronit (or Shekinah) returns to her throne.

The thirteenth-century *Zohar* (*Book of Splendor*) describes her with "frightful eyes, a drawn sword in her hand." Just as with **Artemis,** she was credited with causing stillbirths, though originally was a protector of pregnant mothers and newborn babes. She was the dark face of **Ishtar,** also said to have been the wife of Samael (identified with Satan) before she was Adam's wife. This tells us that she existed even before the creation of Adam (see **Jeh**). As a Serpent-goddess (see **Leviathan** and **Eurynome**), she has been identified as the serpent of Eden, a harlot-temptress. A kabalistic treatise of 1648 by Naftali Herz Bacharach states that Lilith's husband was a castrate, associating her with **Cybele,** and a further indication that Samael was originally a goddess-consort (daemon), and that Lilith led the War in Heaven.

Various lists have been compiled of Lilith's other names, which are many, but it is interesting that one of the most recurrent alternative names is **Kali.** According to legend, the prophet Elijah encountered Lilith and compelled her to reveal the names she used in various guises: Abeko, Abito, Amizo, Batna, Eilo, Ita, Izorpo, Kea, Kokos, Odam, Partasah, Patrota, Podo, Satrina, and Talto. Rivals and daughters of Lilith include Hurmiz, **Meyalleleth, Lilidtha, Igrat, Nega, Naamah, Makhlath,** and **Agrath.** [Rappaport, Patai]

Lillake: The Sumerian **Lilith,** identified from a tablet dating to 2000 B.C. [Graves]

Lilliard of Ancrum: (fl. c. A.D. 1540) After the destruction of the hamlet of Maxton, the orphaned maid Lilliard donned plumed helmet, borrowed a set of armor, and set off for battle in the service of the Red Douglas. Among the heroines of Scotland was the maid Lilliard, unquestionably the most grotesquely heroic. Cut down twice, she continued to fight with great horrid wounds. Her once-famous gravestone read:

> Fair Maiden Lilliard lies under this stane,
> Little was her stature, but great was her fame;
> Upon the English loons she laid mony thumps,
> And when her legs were cutted off,
> she fought upon her stumps.

Lillibridge, Anny: In the American Civil War, she fought with the Union's 21st Regiment, rather than be separated from her lover. [Macksey]

Limareva, Maria: Russian peasant who fought Austrians in World War I until wounded. [Gribble]

Lithben: Celtic woman warrior, sister of **Bec.**

Liu Chin Ting: A mountain girl of the Tartars, she grew up with many brothers, learning their games of mock warfare. She dreamed of liberating her people from the Sung Empire of China and from harassment by rival clans of nearby mountains. At the age of sixteen, she was already clan leader and defended her mountain from raiders so well that rival clans began to fear she was a War-goddess, and learned to leave her people in peace.

A Sung general, Kao Chun Pao, learned of this woman soldier, and set out to punish her, along with other Northern clans that had ceased to recognize China's imperial authority. His battle was a disaster, for she captured him at once, and sentenced him to death. But so filled with admiration was he, and so handsome as well, that he was able to win her heart.

When the emperor learned his most able general had married rather than defeated a rebel, he was ordered arrested and put to death, but Chin Ting protected him. She agreed to conquer the city of Yang Chow for the emperor, in exchange for her husband's amnesty. After her success, she was awarded a general's commission, her husband becoming her second in command. For thirty years, she led troops and recovered territory for the emperor. [Russell]

Livak, Lydia: One of several military women pilots in the Russian air force. She had twelve victories before she was killed in action in 1943. [Macksey]

Llewei: Daughter of Seitwed. She was one of the three Amazons of the Island of Britain mentioned in the *Red Book of Hergest* (about A.D. 1400). Her name means "Devour." The other two Amazons of the triad were **Rorei** and **Mederei Badellfawr.**

Llinga: A Congo warrior-queen who fought the Portuguese in A.D. 1640. She clad herself in animal skins, carried ax, bow, arrows, and a sword. She was able to strike off a man's head with one swipe of her sword. There have been many reports of Amazons of the Congo. Eduardo Lopez in 1580 described the confederacy of Monomotapa, which had standing armies of women. [Rothery]

Longabarba, Bona: A warrior of Lombardy in the fifteenth century, she accompanied her husband Brunorius Pamensis on all their warring expeditions. "In the hottest battles, her bravery and power of managing her troops were quite remarkable." In the Milanese war, Brunorius was captured and drawn into a castle. Bona rallied fresh forces, inspired them with her orative powers, and led them in an assault of the castle that ended swiftly in her enemies' defeat and Brunorius' liberation. [Hale, Starling]

Long Meg: Heroine of a seventeenth-century jest-biography, the quintessential "roaring girl." Scholars have fought over the possibility of Long Meg having actually existed. Chances are good that she was an actual woman about whom tales were inevitable, and certainly women like Long Meg were typical of rough and fashionable sections of London. She was of great height and strong armed, innocent and kindly toward others who were poor. Any man who thought her simple and tried to fool her was apt to be cuffed alongside the head. In a typical chapter of her life, she is found at St. James Corner, a dangerous part of London, attacked by thieves. With dagger and buckler, she soon had the lot of them on their knees begging not to be killed. Before setting them free, she extracted from them an oath never to rob or bother women, children, poor or impotent men, nor any other innocents, but to waylay the wealthy at every opportunity. They bound themselves to the oath by kissing the hem of her smock. When the thieves wished to know who it was that "so lustily beswinged us," she replied:

> If any ask you, who curried your bones,
> Say, Long Meg of Westminster met with you once.

Loretta, Countess of Sponheim: A semilegendary heroine from Rhineland tradition, accurately reflecting the lives of medieval castle women. The countess's husband fell in the Crusades, leaving her and her children's inheritance in disarray and open to challenge. Numerous battles were fought in defense of her castle and lands near the village of Starkenburg on the Mosel River in Rhineland. When she captured her chief foe, the pope intervened, threatening excommunication if she wouldn't let the enemy go. She refused, and would not set him free until she had received a large ransom, his signature promising to ally himself with her against all other enemies of her cause, and possession of his castle at Birkenfeld. [Antz]

Lot: In the Celtic heroic age, she was a monstrous warrior, and the wife of Goll (see **Irnan**). She was stronger than any man in her command. She led troops against Partholón, a mythical invader of Ireland. [Ellis]

Lotis: A huntress-nymph sworn to **Artemis,** transformed into a lotus when pursued by a would-be rapist. The lotus symbolized virginity and represented the altar of Minoan priestesses. [Goodrich]

Louise, Queen of Prussia: (A.D. 1776–1810) If her ploy to bolster her soldiers' spirits had won the day, she would be remembered as the Amazon of Prussia, for even Napoleon believed her to be her nation's best minister of war. As her boldness led nowhere, she seems misguidedly playful for her appearance at the Battle of Jena near Weimar in ceremonial armor of silver and gold, polished steel helmet with magnificent plume, with a tunic of silver brocade, red boots, golden spurs, riding a valiant steed. Her soldiers cheered on seeing this **Camilla** in their midst. Though her actions struck courage in their hearts, the failing ranks could not turn the tide, and the queen was ultimately a marvelous promise of trophy for the prevailing

French. A whooping detachment of the enemy raced her to the city gates, barely missing their prize. [Starling, Hale, Schmidt, Fraser]

Lozen: (nineteenth century A.D.) This Apache woman became one of the two best warriors of her tribe, generally fighting alongside her equally famous brother Victorio. She was usually invited to sit at council fire to help decide strategy in war. [Niethammer]

Lumchuan: (A.D. 1928?–1985) A Thai Buddhist nun raised in a monastery with other girls and boys, all tonsured and not exposed to gender distinctions. In her teens, she left the temple, and, her hair still quite short, signed on as a merchant marine and sailed the world. She was involved in bar brawls from Manila to Denmark and had many startling adventures. After seven years, she had lost much of her androgynous appearance, and it had become more difficult to disguise her figure. A captain's wife, visiting the ship, saw instantly what her mates had never guessed. Lumchuan cursed the captain for firing her. "Haven't I been a good sailor? You know it! To hell with you!"

The next phase of her career took her to the opposite extreme, when, as a traditional Thai dancer, she embodied all that has been considered classically feminine. She danced for the royal family, amassed a small fortune, and married above her class. Unfortunately, her husband died two years later in a boating accident, and his upper-class parents cast out the farmer's daughter, refusing her her only child.

Soon Lumchuan, better known by her androgynous name of Lek, was operating a restaurant on the piers of Bangkok, serving meals to navy and merchant men, some of whom she had previously sailed with. Here she met an American merchant marine and, after a romantic courtship, they were married in a Buddhist temple and later, in America, in a Christian church, pleasing both families. As a stepmother, she became a beloved role model for the author of *The Encyclopedia of Amazons.*

An Amazon to the end, Lek was killed in her midfifties in a fight in Thailand, having it out with a fellow who had earned the name of One-Arm because he'd had the other arm cut off by family avengers after a previous killing. His luck was to be even worse for his newest victory. Lek's family took One-Arm and his bicycle on the then-new Thai freeway and threw them off the back of a pickup truck traveling eighty miles an hour, so that it would look like he was run over on his bike.

Lykopis: "She-Wolf." Amazon archer who engaged Heracles in single combat and died, in the lost epic of Heracles' war against **Andromache.** [Bothmer]

Lynch, Eliza: This Irish-born Parisian demimondaine became "Her Excellencia" in the mid-1800s as mistress of Francisco López, dictator of Paraguay, and rode with him into battle. She served as a colonel in his army and for five years waged wars on her lover's behalf. Without her guidance, the erratic López would have fallen much sooner. [Barrett]

Lysippe: "She Who Lets Loose the Horses." Queen of the Amazons during the period of their early settlements. The Amazons had previously lived somewhat traditional lives with men of Scythia, except that the women were trained for battle, as were the men. In a war that destroyed much of the nation, Lysippe's troops fought their way to freedom, and she led her fighting women to a new land along the Black Sea. She established the policies by which the Amazons lived and conquered for centuries to follow, including the regulation that male children be crippled at birth and only women participate in war and agriculture. Her women were the first soldiers in the world to fight astride horses. "Since her valor and fame increased, she made war upon people after people of neighboring lands, and as her fortune continued to be favorable, she was filled with pride. This queen was remarkable for her intelligence and ability as a general, and she founded Themiscrya at the mouth of the Thermodon River, and built there a famous palace." She spread the boundaries of **Amazonia,** built numerous temples to Ares and **Artemis,** and after many valorous accomplishments died heroically in battle, which Diodorus said was brilliantly planned and—the queen's death notwithstanding—successfully carried out.

After her death, her daughter ruled even more valiantly, extending the influence of Amazonia as far as Thrace and Syria. The dynasty continued many generations before the Greeks began sending heroes against them. This was their age of expansion. In this long period, the empire founded by Lysippe and ruled from Themiscrya grew and flourished. The empires of Cyrus, Charlemagne, Alexander, and Napoleon combined did not last as long. See **Tanais.** [Sobol, Graves, Diodorus, Pizan]

Lysippe: One of the three daughters born to Poetus and Stheneboea. The three were afflicted with divine madness, living in the mountains "in a disorderly manner" and assaulting travelers. Melampus hunted them, resulting in the death of one sister, **Iphinoë,** but he married Lysippe after she was "cured" of her wildness. The three sisters would seem to have been guerrilla fighters whose rebellion ended with marriage alliances. The divinity of their madness associates them with the **Maenads.** See also **Iphianassa.** [Graves]

M

◆◇◆◇◆◇◆◇◆◇◆◇◆

Ma: A War-goddess, whose name requires no translation, an aspect of **Artemis** worshipped especially in Caria and Cappadocia. Strabo, struck by the violent characteristics of Ma, assumed her to be an aspect of **Enyo.** Ma's worship overlapped that of **Tauropolos.** Her main symbols were the lion and the serpent, which were also the symbols of **Cybele, Rhea,** Agdestis, and the Horse-goddess Hipta of Lydia. In later Persian lore, she presided over the phases of the moon. See **Uma.**

Maat or **Mut:** "Mother." Lion-headed goddess of law and revenge. She was the original Eye of Heaven, displaced in a later age by **Hathor.** She was the Egyptian All-mother in the third millennium B.C., believed to be of Theban origin, associated with **Cybele** or even the Indic **Uma.** She was worshipped in later ages in the lesser role of daughter of Ra or of Atum. See **Sekhmet** and **Isis.** [Hart]

MacDonald, Flora: (A.D. 1722–1790) Scottish heroine of the Jacobite rebellion of 1745. In 1776, she was in North Carolina, where she accompanied her husband when he went to join the army. "According to tradition she was often to be seen fighting midst the soldiers" in the Highlander Uprising. During her return voyage to Scotland, there was a high-seas encounter with a French war vessel. "Flora ascended the quarter-deck in the fiercest of the battle and, nothing daunted by a wound received," a broken arm by another account, she helped beat back the enemy. [Ellet, Crawford]

159

Macha: Celtic goddess of the battle, part of a warring trinity that includes **Nemain** and **Morrigane.** They are given as the tripartite of **Bobd,** stronger than all three, though elsewhere Nemain is not mentioned and Bobd is but one of the trinity. More often, Morrigane is sometimes said to be the total of the other three; in one epic, it is said that Macha slaughters indiscriminantly, but that Morrigane is stronger.

Her name means "crow" or "raven," an animal associated with many Scandinavian and Celtic Battle-goddesses. She was associated with horses, as is the case with most Sorcery-goddesses and many Warrior-goddesses. She came once to live among mortals as a fleet-footed heroine, forced by her prideful husband into a footrace just as her labor pains were beginning. Against her wishes, she ran the race and won it, but gave birth at the finish line. She then cursed the men of east Ireland to four months of labor pains, and left her stricken husband forever. [Goodrich, Markale]

Macha Moup Guadh: "Macha of the Red Tresses." Warrior daughter of Aedh Ruadh, seventy-sixth monarch of Ireland, reigning in 377 B.C. Kingship was decided through women, and it fell upon Macha to elect her father's successor. Her decision to rule personally brought war between her and her two brothers (in another version, her cousins). She killed one, capturing five of his powerful sons, forcing them to build the fortress of Emain Macha. She married her other brother so that peace was made, but continued to rule Ireland herself. She was noted for justice and strength, and established the nation's first hospital, which was in use until A.D. 22. [Ellis]

MacMurrough, Eva: Called "Red Eva" or "Roe Eva," a medieval Irish Amazon. She was the wife of Strongbow, earl of Pembroke, and conducted battles in the field in his behalf.

Macouda: Highest ranking officer of the **Dahomey Amazons.** She kept numerous husbands, who were faithful under penalty of death.

Madame Sans-Gêne: See **Thérèsa Figuer of Lyon.**

Madeleine de Saint-Nectaire, Comtesse de Miremont: Distinguished herself in the French civil wars. "From her château at Miremont, in the Limousin, she was accustomed to make excursions, with sixty Hugenot cavaliers, against the Catholic armies in her neighborhood." In A.D. 1575, the governor of the province resolved to crush the Protestant heroine and laid siege to her château, with fifteen thousand footsoldiers and fifty horse. Instead of bracing herself against a long siege, Madeleine rode out with her smaller force and trounced the governor at once. Finding, however, that her enemy retreated into her own fortress, she galloped to neighboring Turenne, raised supporters, and returned to Miremont to vanquish her foe. In 1584, Madeleine led sorties that prompted Henry IV, although her enemy, to quip, "If I were not King, I would like to be Mlle. de Saint-Nectaire!" [Hale, Gribble]

Mad Meg: A popular fantasy heroine in the time of Peter Bruegel, a Dutch master who depicted her adventure in a famous, macabre portrait. Meg and her army of housewives donned kitchen pots as helmets, and took up cooking utensils, staves, and rusty old swords, in order to march into hell and fight the devil and plunder his fortune. Meg struck him in the eye with her sword, and they all escaped wealthy and unscathed.

Maenads: "Madwomen." Called bacchantes by the Romans. Dionysus' worship is tied closely to his role as the god of wine. Although as Bacchus he is sometimes corpulent and jolly, in his purest form he is a horned, heroic, effeminate youth, with great beauty and many macabre and sinister aspects. He is the god of madness.

His history is bound with that of the Amazons. Like Bellerophon, who fought the Libyan Amazons, Theseus' numerous wars with the **Thermo-dontines,** and Priam's defense when the Amazons invaded Phrygia, Diony-sus battled the Amazons on more than one occasion; more uniquely, he allied himself with them in order to defeat the Titans. He traveled the world with an army of satyrs and wildwomen called Maenads, who rode war-trained bulls and fought with swords, serpents, and an unusual staff twined with ivy and tipped with pine cones. With their aid, Dionysus was able to "spread joy and terror," his women's orgies invariably ending in the ripping apart of some fellow. He inspired the Argive women to eat their children raw.

Although a wine cult is at the heart of Dionysus' worship, this is insuffi-cient to explain him as chiefly a violent and woman-oriented god. He appears to have been a transitional deity, a bridge between goddess-worshipping societies and later patriarchal culture, hence his effeminacy. Like Adonis, he was a maiden among men and a youth among women. The roles of his grandmother **Rhea** (the Earth) and mother **Semele** (the Moon) as his protectors and chief sources of power, and **Hera** as his greatest foe (she had him torn to pieces as an infant, but Rhea reconstituted him), show that he was once subservient to goddesses, a phallic personification who stood at goddess shrines.

The Maenads predate Dionysus' use of them as soldiers. Earlier, they were lovers of Pan, suggesting an ancient origin for medieval witches who had orgiastic liaisons with a goat-demon. The Maenads worshipped sundry goddesses of moon and forest, of fertility and the hunt, such as **Daphoene** and Semele. Their revelries always climaxed in a grotesque sacrifice. Pan's mother, the orgiastic Mountain-goddess Penelope, indicates once again the link to ancient fertility cults and to goddess worship. Much as the Amazons valued virginity (on the symbolic level of eschewing marriage), the Maenads valued promiscuity, and both groups strove in their own ways for women's liberty and religiopolitical power, explaining why the Maenads are repeatedly portrayed as slayers of kings, occasionally shown in war paint.

Hellanicus (fifth century B.C.) described the Amazons as "a golden-shielded, silver axed, male-loving, male-infant-killing host," male loving contradicting most authorities, suggesting instead a Maenad cult, and male infant killing suggesting rites relating to Dionysus having been ripped apart in infancy at the instigation of Hera. Strabo tells of an island of women called Samnetai. The Samnetai worshipped Dionysus and allowed no men on their island, à la the Amazons, but were married, and crossed to the mainland to couple. In many instances, the Maenads and Amazons appear as only marginally different elements of related cults.

They originally used hallucinogenic bay laurel in their mystic rites, and sacrificed bulls or men. Their madness and revelry was tied also to opium and other drugs and herbs and such fermented beverages as spruce beer, laced with ivy and sweetened with mead-honey. They were thus very easily adaptable to the wine cult; and, because the newborn Dionysus had been pulled apart and boiled for Hera, his cult preserved aspects of those earlier days when a reigning queen or Moon-priestess sacrificed the sacred king. Thus did the Maenads take up arms to slay their husbands in the temple of Apollo and rend the high priest Orpheus limb from limb and carry off his head. See **Agave.** [Tyrrell, Graves, Tiffany, Bennett, Detienne]

Maeotides: Amazons of the colony near Lake Maeotis and the **Tanais** River. An early stronghold before the founding of Themiscrya, it was reinhabited by the Amazons in the days of the Greek incursions of **Amazonia** (see **Lysippe** and **Melanippe**). The Ixomatae were a Sarmatian people of this region; in the Hellenic age, they were still famous for warlike women (see, for example, **Tirgato**). [Bennett]

Maeve or **Madb:** See **Medb.**

Mafdet: Egyptian Panther-goddess noted, like the Lion-goddesses **Maat, Ubastet,** and **Sekhmet,** for her ferocity. She decapitates enemies in the underworld with her claws. Her warriors are scorpions and snakes. [Hart]

Ma Feng-i: Daughter-in-law of **Ch'in Liang-yü.** She led royalist troops toward the end of the Ming Dynasty. Records show that rebels, too, counted many martial nuns and other women in their ranks, and that women were common in the violent White Lotus secret society. [Wolf]

Mahuika: Goddess of fire in New Zealand Mauri religion. See **Pele.**

The Maid: See **Joan of Arc.**

The Maid of Saragossa: See **Augustina.**

Maillard: Actresses and opera singers were, in the Paris of the revolutionary period and before, among the most notorious of French Amazons. Lesbians of the day dressed as chevaliers, habitually with sword at hip, as was the case with Louise **Labé,** d'Aubigny **Maupin,** and La Maillard.

La Maillard was an opera singer of the early days of the Revolution, when so many women dared believe that the new citizen government included women. She portrayed the goddess of freedom at the feast of reason, "receiving homage from the frenzied people." Offstage, she donned male attire and fought numerous duels. Assisted by similarly attired women, she attempted to convert Parisian maids and matrons to her code and style. These separatists were capable of wrongful as well as heroic acts. They once decided their rival termagant Théroigne de **Mericourt** had committed the inexcusable misdeed of having an affair with an aristocrat. Dragging her to the Terrace of the Tuileries and hastily judging her guilty, they stripped her naked and whipped her in public.

Men may rape and loot and burn and yet be taken for average, but the sometimes foolish and excessive activities of La Maillard convinced the Committee of Public Safety to outlaw women's clubs, brigades, and participation in the new government. [Rothery, Beaumont, Hale]

Máire ó Ciaragáin: In the fifteenth century A.D., she led Irish clans against the English. She showed no mercy to men overthrown in battle. [Ellis]

Mai Taie: A palace Amazon under the king of Siam about A.D. 1866. There were women before her who carried this traditional name, which means "Mother of Death." She was the king's torturer and executioner. [Leonowens]

Makhlath, Mahalath, or **Mahlet:** "The Dancer," referring to her **Kali**like qualities. Daughter of Ishmael and queen of the night, warring with **Lilith** for sovereignty in the world of demons. She might reasonably be identified with Masket, one of Samael's four demon-wives (with Lilith, **Naamah,** and

Igrat) identified by the kabalists as a princess of Malta. She is sometimes called Iggereth, and is sometimes interchangeable with her daughter **Agrath.** Agrath (sometimes **Lilidtha**) together with Mahalath each led armies of 478 screeching legions of destroying angels against Lilith's 480 hosts. Their battles occur chiefly on Yom Kippur (the Day of Atonement). The War-goddesses **Inanna** and Death-goddess **Ereskigal** provide a parallel war for rule of the night. As Meshullahel ("Messenger of God"), she is a daughter of Lilith in God's service, with qualities similar to **Nemesis,** commanding a legion of destroying angels. These sinister Night-goddesses are aspects of **Ishtar.** [Graves, Rappaport, Patai]

Malatesta: The Italian Bishop Bandello of Agen, in the time of Henry II, reported that between 1504 and 1515 "there dwelt at Lyons a courtesan named Malatesta who went to her midnight assignations armed with sword and rotella, which she knew how to use in a bold and dexterous fashion." [Beaumont]

Malatesta, Parisina: She has been called the Phaedra of the Renaissance and "supplied the genius of Byron with a congenial theme." She raised Barbary horses and was a devotee of falconry and the chase, but was fond also of music and medieval romantic literature. Her elderly husband, the marquis of Este, had her put to death at the age of twenty for falling in love with someone nearer her own age. She is said to have gone calmly, after her lover. [Boulting]

Mamaea: Third-generation priestess of Tanit, a Semitic goddess introduced into Rome as Caelestis Dea. She was mother of the Roman Emperor Alexander and ruled as his regent. Gibbon credits her with "manly ambition." She accompanied her son into war in Germany in A.D. 234.

Mami or **Mama:** Her name requires no translation, and is the first word taught to babies even to the present day. She was the warlike Mother-goddess of Akka, called **Ninmah** or Nintu in Sumer, and related to the Indic **Uma.** She fashioned humanity from dirt mixed with blood from the slain god Kingu. [Kramer]

Manasa: A Bengalese War-goddess capable of taking on the shape of a venomous snake. Various Pestilence-goddesses of India may also be considered warriors, whose weapons leave the mark of pox on human flesh. There is **Shitala** the Pox Mother; Ujali the White Lady; Pox-goddesses Mahamai and Chhotimai; Kanti, who causes swelling in the neck; and the Hindu demoness Mataji, "a protective mother to those who prostrate themselves before her." In Sri Lanka, there is **Pattini,** a defeminized goddess "who desires to be a man in a future life." Such goddesses rank second in ferocity, beneath those goddesses associated with **Kali.** [Preston]

Mandana: Queen of the Amazons in the 1671 play *The Women's Conquest* by Edward Howard. Similar Amazons of Restoration plays include **Clara, Rosella,** and **Zelmane.**

Mandana allied herself with Parisatis, a Moorish warrior-queen. Her commander in chief was Daranthe; her ambassadors Cydane and Renone. Typical of the Amazon plays of the time, the valorous queen is undone by love. The high point of the play may well be an execrable song "The Amazons' Martial Ode," which her women sing when she commands, "Let's hear a Martial Ode, the Harmony our Women's ears delight!"

> To arms, to arms, the warlike fare,
> As our heroick charms,
> With martial echo's fill the air,
> Inviting unto arms.
> We challenge Diane and her host
> Of nymph-like archers all,
> Who from the quivers glory boast,
> Our proud Acteons fall;
> If ever their bright eyes beheld
> A chorus like to ours;
> Or saw themselves so far excelled
> By women's more heroick powers.

Manditsch, Milena: A seventeen-year-old student of Belgrade who joined the Serbian army in World War I. [Hirshfeld]

Mann, Pamela: (d. A.D. 1840) Pamela loaned General Sam Houston her oxen. When he failed to return them as he promised, she armed herself with pistol and reclaimed them by force. She was later involved in various crimes, but Texas was at the time lawless enough that even a roguish woman charged from time to time with assault with intent to kill, or forgery, could remain a respected citizen, which Pamela was.

Mantatisi: A formidable warrior-queen of the baTlokwa, one of the clans displaced in the early 1800s by the wars of Shaka Zulu and Matiwane. "Mantatisi rampaged across the land with a ferocity that matched Matiwane's. She scotched one threat that appeared while her men were off foraging by lining up all the women and children in a military formation and trotting the unarmed mob straight at her erstwhile attackers, who promptly fled." When she died, her son became ruler and the baTlokwa "remained a major nuisance until Mahweshwe, by then a power in the land, finally finished them off in 1852." [D. Morris]

Marfisa: A warrior in Boiardo's *Orlando Innamorato* (1484) and Ariosto's *Orlando Furioso* (1516), featuring, as well, an entire nation of malignant Amazons. Marfisa is the twin sister of Rogero and, like **Bradamante** of the same epic, skilled in battle.

> She bathed her blade in blood up to the hilt
> And with the same their bodies were mangled.

She was raised by an Arab chieftain, trained to ride horses and use weapons in the Arab cause. She set off for Europe intending to capture three Christian kings, including Charlemagne, but when she was reunited with her brother, she learned they were children of Christians, separated by Moorish perfidy. She vowed to become a Christian and avenge her parents.

Margaret Maultasch, Countess of Tirol: (A.D. 1318–1369) In 1342, she warred against her husband, the son of the king of Bohemia, and, upon his successful expulsion from Tirol, she married Louis, son of Emperor Louis IV. She fought at his side in the suppression of rebellious nobles. Legends malign her as malevolent, but she was merely typical of the rulers of her age, male or female, warlike and clever.

Margaret of Anjou: (A.D. 1430–1482) "In the chivalrous ages, women not only attacked and defended fortifications, but commanded armies and obtained victories." Margaret, by her own example, taught her impuissant husband, Henry VI, how to conquer, winning twelve decisive battles during the Wars of the Roses. She was the leading enemy of the Yorkists and a committed Lancastrian. In 1461, she defeated the earl of Warwick, as she had earlier defeated the duke of York himself, who died in the war against her. She had his head cut off and, crowned with a paper cap, displayed to the public. Shakespeare in *Henry VI* has the duke of York declare her to be "an Amazonian trull."

In 1471, she landed at Weymouth in Dorset and marched north, expecting to join Jasper Tudor. She was turned aside at the Severn, and forced into an engagement at Tewkesbury, where Prince Edward fell in battle. Sustaining her only defeat, she fled on foot into the forests, carrying her infant son.

Encountering a robber, she approached him unafraid and said, "Here, my friend! I commit to you the safety of the king's son!" Delighted by this unexpected confidence, he helped Queen Margaret and her son reach Flanders.

Eventually, the Yorkists captured her and allowed her to be ransomed by Louis XI, under oath to war no more. [Starling, Hale, Erlanger, Montez, King]

Margaret of Antioch: (third century? A.D.) Christian saint, called also Margaret the Dragon Slayer. Margaret fought off the advances of a local governor and was thrown into a dungeon with a dragon "which she subdued with a crucifix." In art, the crucifix is actually a spear or long sword, the hilt forming the cross, and she battles the dragon in the same manner as St. George. After defeating the dragon, Satan appeared to her, and she wrestled him to the ground. It was St. Margaret who along with St. **Catherine** appeared to **Joan of Arc** and encouraged her to go to war for France. In her capacity as protector of women in childbirth, she assumes the role of **Artemis.**

Margaret of Attenduli: (b. A.D. 1375) Sister of the founder of the fifteenth-century Italian house of Sforza. When her brother was taken prisoner by a prince of Naples, Margaret was with her troops at Tricarico, and responded by immediately taking the castle siege. The price of lifting the siege, she maintained, was her brother's freedom. Ambassadors arrived promising, instead, that her brother would be killed if she persisted, so she took the ambassadors hostage and soon had her way. [Hale]

Margaret of Denmark: (A.D. 1353–1411) Called "the **Semiramis** of the North," she came to power at a time when Denmark, Sweden, and Norway were at war. She began at once to expel rival armies from their strongholds and take control of key cities. In time, she forged the Calmar Union out of the three nations and became the most powerful ruler Scandinavia had ever seen. [Morris]

Margaret of Provence: See **Marguerite de Provence, Queen of France.**

Margaret of Valois: (A.D. 1553–1615) Queen of Navarre, daughter of Henry II and Catherine de' Medici. Estranged from both her father and husband, King Henry IV of France, she took up arms and seized Agen in 1586. Captured a year later, she was confined to Usson Castle, but charmed her turnkey and ruled the castle, encouraging the arts, later establishing a literary salon in Paris.

Margheritona: The sixteenth-century Italian Bishop Bandello reported that the courtesan Margheritona "served for pay as a trooper in the squadron of the Count de Gaiazzo." [Beaumont]

Marguerite de Bressieux: In the mid–fifteenth century, her father's castle was stormed by Louis de Châlons, prince of Orange. Marguerite and other maidens were brutalized by the soldiery. "When the royal troops, under Raoul de Gancourt, Governor of Dauphiné, were marching against Louise de Châlons, twelve strange and mysterious cavaliers, attired in black, wearing scarfs of crape, and carrying a banner of an orange transfixed with a lance and the motto *Ainsi tu seras,* greeted the general." These twelve women in black joined Raoul's ranks and "proved their worth in battle." Whenever they met one of the men who had raped them, they uncovered their faces so that each man would know who killed him, and why. The battle was won, but Marguerite, the leader of the troop of twelve, was badly wounded. She died by sunset and was buried with military honors, attended by her surviving companions. [Gribble]

Marguerite de Provence, Queen of France: (A.D. 1221–1295) Daughter of Raymond Berenger, she married Louis IX in 1254. She accompanied him on the Crusade and was in Damietta with him during a siege. At the height of the battle, she elicited a vow from an officer to behead her if the Moslems breached the walls. She behaved "with heroic entrepidity" when the king was captured.

There were many such women of the Crusades. They were "animated by the double enthusiasm of religion and valor," and they "often performed the most incredible exploits on the field of battle, and died with arms in their hands at the side of their lovers." [Montez, Gribble, Hale]

Maria: Regent of Aetolia in Persia in the early 400s B.C. "She commanded her troops in person and preserved the strictest discipline in her army." She was assassinated by her son-in-law. [Hale]

Maria de Molina, Queen of Castile: (d. A.D. 1321) Cousin and wife of Sancho IV. From 1295 to 1301, she was regent to her son, Ferdinand IV, successfully suppressing various pretenders to the throne, who at various times elicited military aid from France, Aragon, Portugal, Navarre, and Granada—all to no avail. Her influence was felt also during the early reign of her grandson, Alfonso XI.

Maria Eleanora: (d. A.D. 1655) Queen of Sweden, wife of Gustavus Adolphus, mother of Queen **Christina.** Christina's often dishonest and manipulative autobiography has been too easily accepted as the chief authority on Maria Eleanora, and Christina did not like her exceedingly beautiful mother, nor did Maria Eleanora seem to care much for her ugly-duckling daughter. Christina knew nothing of her mother's youth, however, when she had a more winning personality. She accompanied Adolphus on the campaigns against Germany, and helped him spread Protestantism, by force, through Catholic-dominated nations.

Maria Leonza: Venezuelan goddess of love and death. She "rides a tapir and brandishes a human pelvis, turning men into stone." [Lederer]

Maria Theresa: (A.D. 1717–1780) Queen of Hungary and Bohemia. She fought in the Silesian War but was defeated by the Prussians. In spite of many long and unsuccessful wars during her reign, she managed to improve the lot of the poor. Many consider her to have been the greatest of the Hapsburg rulers.

Marie-Christine, Princess of Espinoy: (A.D. 1545–1582) Christine de le Laing of the Netherlands organized the resistance against Spain when her town was held siege in 1581. "Dressed in cuirass and with battle-ax in hand, she took part in the battles on the ramparts. Although wounded in the arm she continued to sustain by her example the courage of the defenders. The women and children worked without stopping to fill the gaps made by the attackers." After two months, twenty-three battles, and twelve sorties beyond the city walls, the city of Tournai at last surrendered. "The Princess d'Espinoy came out of Tournai on her horse at the head of the armed garrison, flag flying," and her foe honored her with cheers, as though she were a victor. [Schmidt]

Marie de Brabançon: In the late 1500s, with fifty men in her command in the castle of Bénégon, Marie defended herself from two thousand foe. When she was captured and held for ransom by one Montaré, Charles IX, having admired her greatly, sent Montaré strict orders to withdraw his demand for ransom and to "escort the great-hearted lady, with full honor, back to her castle, and give her liberty." This contrasts drastically with the actions of **Guirande de Lavaur's** foe. [Gribble]

Marie Fourré de Poix: In 1535, Marie Fourré captained the women of the town of Saint-Riquier, which had only one hundred men within its walls when the Count of Nassau elected to lay siege with two thousand Flemish warriors. The women handled the majority of the defense, and the count called them "courageous and formidable." He raised his siege to retire *sans* his standard, captured by Marie Fourré. [Gribble]

Mariotti, Sylvia: A private in the 11th Battalion of Italian Bersaglieri, serving from 1866 to 1879. She fought the Austrians in the Battle of Custozza. [Laffin]

Markievicz, Constance: (A.D. 1876–1927) "The Rebel Countess" of Ireland. As a young woman, she was "a great and gloriously attractive tomboy" and "a ferocious rider." At forty, she was a militant suffragist and became active in Irish nationalism, founding, in 1909, a paramilitary order called the Fianna Eireann, in which she taught lads marksmanship and prepared them to fight for Ireland. As a leader of the Citizens Army, she took radical stances and believed anyone unwilling to die for Ireland was a traitor and that those Irish who fought to aid England in World War I were deluded fools. Chain-smoking and forever cleaning her pistols, clad generally in uniform, she presented a scruffy but soldierly appearance. She was a captain in the Easter Uprising of 1916, fighting in the trenches a full week before her capture and arrest. For days on end, she listened, from her cell, to the executions of her fellows outside her jailhouse window, but her own death sentence was commuted to penal servitude due only to her sex.

She would undoubtedly have applauded the 1973 founding of Ireland's Cummann na mBann, an all-female terrorist combat unit with the IRA. [Marreco, Van Voris, Mitchell, Fox]

Marpe: An Amazon brave slain by Heracles during the suicidal series of challenges after the murder of Queen **Hippolyte.**

Marpesia: "The Snatcher." Queen of the Scythian Amazons, ruling concurrently with **Lampedo.** The two queens divided their troops into two bodies and warred on different frontiers. Marpesia was one of the greatest of **Amazonia**'s empire builders, spreading Amazonia's influence throughout Europe, Arabia, and Asia Minor, in an era well before the repeated Greek invasions.

For centuries, the Caucasus Mountains bore her name, "the Marpesians." Virgil refers to the "Marpesian Cliff" near the Caspian Gates upon which was one of the chief cities of Amazonia, built by Marpesia. Alexander later built a fortress there, and the Romans counted it as an important outpost. Marpesia was killed by barbarians during an Asian campaign, and her daughter **Synoppe** ruled after her. [Boccaccio]

martial nuns of Europe and the Crusades: Medieval nuns were often members of wandering sects and traveled armed for self-defensive reasons. Others were adjunct to famous sects of fighting monks and accompanied them on the Crusades. Still others learned to fight for the protection of their lands and convents in a tumultuous age, as was the case with Philothéy **Benizélos** of Greece and **Julienne du Guesdin** of Brittainy. At the siege of Seville by Espartero, an anticleric, the nuns of Seville rose against him, so that his siege was repelled. There can be no question but that nuns and abbesses have had a great propensity for violence, as witness the stories of **Chrodielde** and **Leubevére** warring in the sixth century for control of an abbey, or **Renée de Bourbon** in the late 1400s in armed struggle for reforms. In the monk wars of early Christian Ireland, women were reported fighting amidst the clergy, undoubtedly nuns.

An eleventh-century nun's marginalia in an illuminated manuscript shows a nun jousting with a monk on horseback and defeating him. This piece can be seen reproduced in Karen Peterson and J. J. Wilson's *Women Artists* (1976). Some would say the artist was being satiric, but the reality of her age better upholds the conclusion that she was depicting actual military exercises practiced by monks and nuns. The ill-fated First Crusade led by Peter the Hermit was most assuredly made up of men, women, and children. Misson in *Voyage d'Italie* (1688) reported his personal inspection of an arsenal of the Palazzo-Real, which included cuirasses and helmets for women, which he was told were worn by Genoese ladies who fought Turks in 1301. Searching for confirmation, he uncovered three letters in the archives of Genoa, written by Pope Boniface VIII, discussing in detail the "warlike infatuation" of Genoese ladies who were Crusaders in 1383. As they are referred to as "ladies" rather than courtesans, and known to the pope, it is probable that they took vows before leaving for the East, in the manner of the monk-knights. If these women had not taken such vows, their troop would almost certainly have been referred to in a manner similar to that of the twelve hundred women-at-arms accompanying the duke of Alva in Flanders in the late 1500s, who were considered harlots for not taking vows.

An account survives, written by the sister of a monk (perhaps "sister" is not literal but a reference to her status as a nun), describing her experience during Saladin's siege of Jerusalem: "I wore a helmet or at any rate walked on the ramparts wearing on my head a metal dish which did as well as a helmet. Woman though I was I had the appearance of a warrior. I slung stones at the enemy. I concealed my fears. It was hot and there was never a moment's rest. Once a catapulted stone fell near me and I was injured by the fragments."

Crusading women were romanticized in literature, plays, and songs, so that even **Eleanor of Aquitaine** was inspired to a women's crusade and had armor made for her ladies-in-waiting. Among the queens of Europe whose valor in the Crusades is certain, we must count **Florine of Denmark, Marguerite de Provence** and **Berengaria of Navarre.** Additional indicators include the "troop of Amazons" that accompanied Emperor Conrad to Syria, and the women Crusaders in the ranks of William, Count of Poitiers, as reported by Guibert de Nogent in *Gesta Dei per Francos* (*God's Deeds of the Franks*), book VII.

Of later periods, there are clear records regarding the unconventional activity of nuns. Le Lusca in *Introduzione al Nouvellare* was amused by the women of the Alpine convents who on certain days "were permitted to dress up as gentlemen, with velvet caps on their heads, tight-fitting hose, and having sword at side," and come out of holy seclusion to partake, as gallants, in carnival society. Antonio Francesco Grazzini reports also of nuns who arrived at carnivals clad as cavaliers, swords at side, acting as gallants. Until reforms started by the Council of Trent, Italian convents were places of considerable liberty, with young patricians sporting in the gardens with the nuns, or, even more notoriously, the nuns "converting" maidens and widows by spending nights in their beds and taking them afterward to their convents. Novelists may seem to have exaggerated these propensities, yet the records show that in 1329 the nuns of Montefalco were excommunicated for such behavior; in 1447, several nuns were "reformed" by means of life imprisonment; and, in 1472, a Franciscan commissioner reported on the "irreligious and unbridled lives" of nuns. A 1403 law prohibited citizens of Bologna from any longer hanging about the convents or to converse and play music with the nuns.

Le President de Brosses, in *Lettres familière écrites d'Italie,* volume 1, was equally amused by Italian nuns, who as a rule carried stilettoes. These *Lettres* include an account of the abbess of Pomponne who fought a duel with a lady who wished to take over the abbey. Various popes found it necessary to declare the heretical nature of fighting women, in an attempt to minimize their participation. The centuries-old ban on women wearing armor would be the technicality upon which **Joan of Arc** was condemned to burn. [Beaumont, Hyde, Powers, Hale, Gribble, Boulting]

Marulla: (fl. A.D. 1460s) In the time of Muhammad II, the Turks attacked Lemnos, and the women defended their island alongside their men. Marulla's father was slain and she was wounded, yet she descended the city wall to engage the foe directly, "with all the vigor that enthusiasm and despair could inspire." Her boldness encouraged the garrison to leap down as well, so that by the time an allied Venetian admiral arrived with his fleet, the Lemnosians were already celebrating their victory. [Starling]

Mary, Countess of Falconberg: (A.D. 1636–1712) Spirited daughter of Oliver Cromwell, said to be of a more commanding nature than her brother Richard. She fought to restore Charles II. [Crawford]

Mary, Lady Bankes: (d. A.D. 1661) Defender of impregnable Corfe Castle. Refusing to surrender, and promised no quarter for the children and women that made up much of her army, her walls were assailed by more than five hundred men on June 23, 1643. Lady Bankes herself defended the upper ward with only five soldiers, but a great many maidservants as well as her own daughters, as men strove to scale the castle walls on ladders. [Fraser]

Mary of Guelders, Queen of Scotland: (A.D. 1433–1463) Upon the death of James II, Mary continued the war with England, and oversaw the successful siege of Roxburgh. She was supported in her campaigns by additional troops provided by **Margaret of Anjou.** In 1461, she demanded and received the surrender of Berwick. [Crawford]

Mary of Hungary: (A.D. 1505–1558) For her military prowess, she was called "Mother of the Camp," and for her Amazonian love of field sports she was called "the Diana." She governed the Netherlands and conducted several wars in the mid-1500s "with glory and success, frequently mingling on horseback with the troops," greatly troubling Henry II of France. In one sweep of Picardy, she burned over seven hundred villages and the royal palace of Folembrai. [Hale]

Marzia: Lady Marzia of the house of Uldani was wife of Francesco d'Ordelaffi, the only prince of Romania to maintain independence against the tyranny of the papacy. Francesco, Lord of Forli, entrusted the defense of the town of Cesena to Marzia. In A.D. 1357, she "donned the casque and the cuirass" and stationed herself with two hundred knights to await the onslaught of ten times as many foe.

After a bold stand, her forces closed themselves within the city, prepared for siege. Clad in her armor day and night, Marzia directed skirmishes at every breach, until her own father entreated his heroic daughter to surrender. She refused, having received no such order from Francesco, and being ready to die for her husband's cause. When at last the city fell, Marzia, along with her children, were imprisoned. [Starling]

Masaki Hojo: (twelfth century A.D.) When the first Minamoto shogun was conquering his way to the control of Japan, beside him in battle was Masaki Hojo, his wife and most trusted general. She was typical of the female elite of the time: Yoshitsune's mistress **Shizuka** and Yoshinaka's mistress **Tomoe** were also distinguished warriors. From the Kamakura period and earlier, right to the close of the Tokugawa period, every woman of samurai caste was expected to have mastered the **naginata** before her eighteenth birthday. Thirteenth-century women occasionally held the title of *jito,* making them land stewards and local police officials. They appointed their family members, without regard to gender, as *jittodai,* or deputy police officers. Throughout the Kamakura period, the jito was the single most important local official, answerable to the military government, or *bakufu.* Such was the background against which an exceptional woman like Masaki Hojo might rise.

When her husband died, she appointed her very young son to be the second shogun, and ruled in his name. She became known as "Ama-Shogun," or nun-general, for she shaved her head after her husband's death and became the only woman in history who was neither empress nor empress dowager to rule Japan. She established the Hojo regency so that her line, and not her husband's, were the real rulers of Japan for several generations. As she knew no defeat in battle, so she was exceptional in matters of state.

The Massachusetts Queen: Early in the 1600s, a female sachem the Pilgrims called "The Massachusetts Queen" lived through a time of frightful transition for her peoples. This woman's confederacy crumbled due to the changing values, the indirect conquest of the whites. The resultant wars went against her. It is hard to call her a failure in her campaigns, since she ruled for some forty years. But eventually her nation was reduced to a single tribe, the Nipnets. They offered themselves to British rule in exchange for protection from enemy tribes.

Many female chiefs were similarly reported by the earliest Europeans in America. De Soto captured a woman chief who'd been unfortunate enough to welcome him cordially. The Jesuit Father Lafitau wrote in *Moers des Sauvages Ameriquaines, comparées aux de premiers temps* (Paris, 1724) of the prevalence of warlike women and Amazons in the Americas.

Matilda Augustus of England: (A.D. 1102–1167) Also called Empress Maud. She was the daughter of Henry I and his chosen heir, but she had been many years in France with a Norman husband when Henry died. His self-serving ministers conspired to place Stephen, Henry's cousin, upon the daughter's throne. In 1139, Maud arrived in England and, supported by the church, waged war on Stephen. She escaped his siege of Arundel Castle and rampaged across the English countryside, challenging those barons aligned with Stephen, inspiring others to her cause. Maud bowed out in 1148, after nine years of violence.

Matilda of Boulogne: (A.D. 1103?–1152) Wife of Stephen of Blois who, in their mutual war against the Empress Maud (called also **Matilda Augusta**), led battles separately from Stephen in support of his cause. In 1136, she received the surrender of Derby. When Stephen was captured by Maud, his Queen Matilda moved to capture Maud's chief ally, with which to make an exchange for Stephen's freedom. Without his queen's militancy, Stephen's success, which came only after nine years of anarchy, would have been impossible. [Fraser]

Matilda of Ramsbury: Mistress of Bishop Roger of Salisbury and mother of his children. Early in the eleventh century, she effectively defended the bishop's castle of Derizes. [Fell]

Matilda of Tuscany: (A.D. 1046–1115) Called "the Great Countess." "With rare heroism she made and sustained sieges, maneuvered troops, and when victorious enlarged her dominions and exalted her fame." Matilda defended the papacy against Emperor Henry IV, proving herself a first-ranking tactician, defeating him several times. When Henry attacked her in 1093, she not only won the day, but captured his flag. She became the model for Tasso's **Clorinda.** The story of Clorinda burning the siege tower at Jerusalem was based on the actions of Matilda's troops when Henry held her siege at Mantua. Even at the age of sixty-five, she was active enough to punish some of her rebellious subjects by storming their city. At forty-three, she married her second husband, a Bulgarian teenager named Welfo, who lasted long enough to start issuing documents in his own name, until she sent him packing back to Este. Much speculation has been made as to why Matilda would have made this politically unimpressive marriage alliance, historians overlooking the simple likelihood of lust for the young whelp.

Arduino della Paluda reportedly taught the young Matilda to "ride like a lancer, spear in hand, to bear a pike like a footsoldier and to wield both battleax and sword." Vedriani wrote, in 1666, that Matilda's armor was sold forty-four years earlier in the Reggio market. Antonia Fraser, conservatively interpreting a wealth of metaphorical allusion to Matilda's warrior exploits, states that it is impossible to establish definitely that she led battles, as opposed to commanding from a distance. Yet, given the commonplace activities of medieval women at war, it seems unlikely that the most famed of these warriors, about whom so much legend accumulated even during her lifetime, should be the one uniquely to have avoided the actual risk of battle. The tradition of such women grew up in great part because power easily transferred to generals if the ruler failed to lead personally. It is at least certain that the Countess Matilda had long studied the arts of war. Matilda's first tomb, constructed upon her death in 1115, refers to her as a **Penthesilea,** and is upheld by four powerful female figures. [Huddy, Duff, Geis, Hale, Fraser]

matriarchy: Literally, mother rule. Since Hesiod's day, the romantic belief in a golden age of women's rule—an age of milk and honey—has appealed to philosopher-historians. Neolithic goddess figurines, found throughout the world, are certainly proof that goddess worship predates god worship, but in reality tell us nothing of early social and jural systems. It is presently unfashionable to believe in prehistoric matriarchies, and only a handful of respected thinkers are seriously enamored of the notion of women once having ruled the world. But any open-minded analysis will find "belief" and "disbelief" to be products of fashion and prejudice, more than balanced reasoning. The evidence of mythology, and a few appealing archaeological indicators, leaves open the possibility that matristic order of varying degrees was once fundamental to human society. The Amazons were but one faction of those pre- and protohistorical norms.

Maud, Empress: See **Matilda Augustus.**

Maupin, Aubigny: (A.D. 1673?–1701) The famed Mlle. de Maupin, immortalized in literature by Théophile Gautier, was not only a famous opera star and beauty of her age, but a feared swashbuckler of the violent quarters of Paris. As one of La Maupin's several biographers put it, "La Maupin was a Sappho, if not in wit, at any rate in habits, and she had the effrontery to be proud of it."

She had low beginnings. Her earliest public debut as a performing duelist so astonished audiences with the perfection of her ability that, once, a heckler jeered that the audience was duped and it was no woman dressed as a cavalier, but a young man who was some cavalier's exceptional pupil. In reply, La Maupin angrily cast down her foil and tore open her shirt so that the audience could judge for themselves.

It was not long before her talents took her to the French Opéra, wherein she played such characters as **Dido,** founder of Carthage, and the War-goddess **Minerva.** She sang contralto. Offstage, she continued to dress as a cavalier. Her behavior was such that once she was condemned to death by fire, a punishment happily not carried out. The crime was one of passion, mutual it must be noted, with a nun of Avignon. It was three months before the ravished novice returned to her convent somewhat sheepishly and La Maupin returned to Paris, daring the tribunal to see true their notice of condemnation.

Her most famous duel came as a result of her amorous inclinations. Attending one of King Louis's fabulous balls, she proceeded once more to act the role of the cavalier and to monopolize the attentions of a certain beauty. After several dances that won whispers and speculations from the guests, La Maupin suggested a secret rendezvous and, upon the dance floor before all, kissed the woman passionately.

Three of the woman's male suitors intervened. "At your service, gentlemen," said La Maupin, agreeing to the duel. In the darkness outside, she proceeded to injure and disarm her three opponents (in other tellings, she killed them). On returning to the ball, she was approached by Louis, who said, "You are the jade La Maupin? I have heard of your handiwork! Need I remind you of my decree against duels in Paris?" The next day she awaited arrest, but Louis had been amused by the incident and, while he was speculating that his law governed only men and La Maupin was free to duel at will, she was given the opportunity to flee to Brussels until the dust settled. She left the stage in 1701 and died two years later, in her early thirties. [Rogers, Beaumont]

Mavia: Also Mania or Mawia, queen of the Sarecans about A.D. 375. She led troops into Phoenicia, Palestine, and Egypt in revolt against Rome. "This war was by no means a contemptible one, although conducted by a woman. The Romans considered it so arduous and perilous that the general of the Phoenician troops applied for assistance to the general of the entire cavalry and infantry of the East." The Romans were routed and they sued for peace. Socrates Scholasticus in *The Ecclesiastic History* states that Mavia finally agreed to truce due to her belief in the teachings of a Christian hermit.

Mayer, Hélène: (b. A.D. 1910) Of the many twentieth-century Olympics heroines, Hélène Mayer found herself in the most anomalous position. Half Jewish, she nonetheless represented the Nazis in the 1936 Berlin Games. She left the safety of California in order to compete in her homeland. She may have felt the best way to weaken German anti-Semitism was to represent Germany and prove the physical excellence of a German Jew, but it is more likely that she believed it possible for an athlete to be apolitical. She was, of course, very wrong, and her token participation was a propagandistic tool.

She had studied the fence since childhood. Stocky, swift, serious in demeanor, with a long and powerful lunge, she took many awards on her rise to the Olympics. Her fans called her "Die blonde Hé," but, while studying in California, she had been dropped in absentia from the German fencing club due to her Jewish blood. In the Berlin games, she defeated all her Aryan opponents. But the small, swift Ilona Elek, a Hungarian Jew, won gold. [Blue]

Ma Ying Taphan: (fl. A.D. 1860) Chief of the palace Amazons of the king of Siam. Her name means "Great Mother of War." Her women were the best trained soldiers of old Thailand, into whose hands was entrusted the life of the king, as well as his wives and family. During civil revolts, if the regular army was failing, the palace Amazons were sent forth, and were never in their history defeated. Ma Ying Taphan's women were also addicted to dueling. Whenever her permission could be obtained, two women would meet in a ferocious sword fight. The loser received a splendid state burial, and her family received many gifts. The winner was proclaimed a hero and sent on a holy pilgrimage to purify herself. [Leonowens, Laffin]

McCormick, Patricia: After the inroads made by Conchita **Cintrón,** women became less scarce in the bullring. Patricia McCormick was born in Texas, studied bullfighting in Mexico, and rose in fame in the 1950s as the American *torera*. She was often awarded ears and tails for her performance, and also suffered gorings. "The basic thing is spiritual. I make no apology for linking bullfighting with religion, whatever theologians may think." She said, "I am not afraid of death. It is a mystery and perhaps the greatest adventure of all." [McCormick]

Meda: (fourth century B.C.) Most of the wives of Philip II—and there were at least seven wed as part of his treaty arrangements with conquered nations—were not native Macedonians, but "were brought from non-Greek territories where they learned to ride horses and use weapons." What is believed to be Philip's tomb, discovered in 1977 by Manolis Andronikos, includes a chamber for one of his warrior-wives. There were no earrings, bracelets, or mirrors among her grave goods, but arrowheads, bronze greaves, and various emblems of a warrior. This warrior-wife is believed to have been Meda, Princess of Getae, a Thracian. Women of Thrace commonly warred and ruled, for it was a center of goddess worship. See also **Olympias, Roxana,** and **Eurydice.** [Pomeroy]

Medb: To the Celts, major warfare sometimes began with cattle raids, as when Queen Maeve (Mève, Méadhbh, Medb, or Madb) carried off a bull owned by the king of Ulster. Her exploits included the war against Cú

Chulainn; and among her fallen foes were fifty women warriors of noble birth. This bloody war resulting from the theft of the bull, recounted in the saga *Táin Bó Cúailuge,* includes an intriguing supernatural interlude when Queen Maeve in her chariot sees a woman "with sword of bright bronze" ride up alongside her. This is **Féithlinn,** a fairy-prophetess. Whenever Maeve inquired as to the outcome of the pending battle she was to lead, the warrior/fairy/seer repeatedly replied, "I see crimson, I see red." [Hyde, Markale, Goodrich]

Mederei Badellfawr: "Mederei" means "skillful." She is one of a triad of Welsh Amazons mentioned in the *Red Book of Hergest* (about A.D. 1400), the other two being **Rorei** and **Llewei.**

Medusa: One of the three snake-haired **Gorgons,** perhaps originally Moon-priestesses who wore hideous masks during secret ceremonies. That Medusa birthed the winged horse Pegasus shows a connection between the Amazon horse cults and violent Moon-goddess trinities. Serpents were associated with ancient Earth-goddesses and were part of the array of exotic weaponry used by the **Maenads.** Diodorus associates her with the Libyan Amazons, who similarly were called Gorgons (or **Hesperians**) and who predated the Amazons of the **Thermodon.** Robert Graves identifies Medusa with Neith (**Net**), goddess of Hesperian Amazons. Medusa was also associated with the healing arts, the blood from her left side raising the dead, blood from the right being poisonous.

Pausanias tells the most "mortal" version of Medusa's career, doing away with the monstrous aspects altogether. She was the beautiful daughter of Phorcys and led the Libyans of Lake Tritonis into battle against Perseus. Perseus effected her assassination under cover of darkness, cutting off her head as she slept. In honor of the event, he named his daughter Gorgophone, "Gorgon's Death."

Megaera: "The Jealous One" or "The Grudge," smallest but fiercest of the three **Furies.**

Melanippe: "Black Mare." Sister of Queen **Antiope.** While the majority of the Amazon forces were upon a foreign campaign led by **Orithia,** the combined forces of Heracles and Theseus invaded the Amazon capital. Melanippe and **Hippolyte** charged upon Heracles and Theseus and "each maiden struck down her knight, horse and all, in one heap." The ancient authorities, themselves astounded, made the excuse for Heracles that it was his horse's fault. "The maidens then attacked with swords and for a long time carried out the battle, but at length—and this is the marvel, for never before had there been such a pair—they were captured." Melanippe was taken by Heracles, and Hippolyte by Theseus. It was said that Heracles defeated Melanippe "more by guile than valor." In other versions of the story, she is the sister of the slain Queen Hippolyte, and is released back to the Amazons in exchange for Hippolyte's girdle, or else slain by Telamon.

But if it was true that Melanippe remained Heracles' prisoner after the fight for Hippolyte's girdle, then Melanippe would have to have been the nameless leader who plotted a successful mutiny to free herself and other captive Amazons on one of Heracles' ships. Working loose their bonds, the captive Amazons unexpectedly attacked the Greeks, killing them and throwing the bodies overboard, taking over the ship. Being a horse-riding race, the Amazons were ignorant of sailing methods, and were at the mercy of the winds. They were driven ashore in a far part of Scythia, where the Amazons were unknown, and, stealing horses, became ferocious marauders along the coast and the foothills inland. They eventually arranged treaties and resettled an area north of Lake Maeotis, previously the site of the first Amazon settlements founded by Queen **Lysippe.** They became the progenitors of the Sarmatians, ancestors of the Poles (see **Minythya**). [Sobol, Pizan]

Melanippe: A nymph of **Artemis** and mother of Melampus who cured the daughters of Proetus of madness at a shrine of **Artemis.** These daughters were mountain wildwomen, of a cult similar to the **Maenads.**

Melic nymphs: They sprang from the blood of Ouraurs (Father Heaven) when Cronus murdered him. They were armed with spears of ashwood. The **Furies** were born of the same incident.

Melousa: Amazon brave of the Attic War. [Bothmer]

Menken, Adah Isaacs: (A.D. 1835?–1868) An Amazon of the early Victorian stage. Her most famous role was as Byron's heroic Mazeppa, played from San Francisco and New York to Paris and London. In the climax, she rode across stage strapped to "a fiery steed," wearing a body-sock giving the illusion of nudity. She was all but universally praised for her stout, powerful beauty, but one theater critic had so annoyed her that when she spied him again in her audience, she leaped from her horse and pursued the man through the aisles, bearing her riding crop. Later in her career, she received additional notoriety as Swinburne's sadistic lover. Her early poetry is Sapphic in content and she was one of Madame George Sand's lovers. [Falk]

menstrual cycle: The prevalent sentiment that exercise and sports injure women's reproductive organs or interfere with menstrual flow turns out to be mere propagandistic superstition to keep women weak and unready. New York gynecologist Mona Shangoid studied 394 women who had run in the 1979 New York Marathon. Her statistics found that ninety-three percent of the women with regular menstrual cycles retained their regularity after they became runners. Other studies have confirmed that athletic women are far healthier than women enfeebled by the fear that exercise is harmful.

In antiquity, the association between women and the moon became the most observable evidence of women's cosmic connection, which, joined with women's mystic capacity to perpetuate the race, gave rise to the sentiment that women were mortal manifestations of the Earth-mother and the Moon-goddess, but that men were not. Women of a given village tend to menstruate simultaneously when no contradicting influence, such as artificial lighting, alters the moon's regulating ability.

At the heart of every religion since the dawn of human reflection is the worship of the female as mortal and as goddess—from **Gaia** the Great Earth Mother to the **Virgin Mary**—through women's implied, assumed, or real authority over nature and creation. The spilling of blood, through menstruation (for women) and human sacrifice (for men), promised greater fecundity for the very land the people lived upon. In patriarchal society, menstruation is "the curse," but previously it was proof of a holy and supernatural connection between the earth and the sky exclusively through the auspices of the female.

Mercader, Caridad: Communist mother of five who led the rebellion that kept Franco's Nationalists out of Barcelona. She later laid the plans for Trotsky's assassination.

Mercilla: A maiden queen in Spenser's *The Faerie Queene* who wins a duel with **Duessa.**

Meretseger: Cobra-goddess of the underworld, similar to **Renenutet** and **Hetep-Sekhus.** She was a dangerous but merciful deity "whose anger is a raging lion." [Hart]

Mericourt, Théroigne de: (A.D. 1759?–1817) "The Amazon of Liège," a notorious actress and singer who had studied in London and Naples. As a successful courtesan she amassed considerable wealth. Like Rose **Lacombe** and La **Maillard,** she was fired with enthusiasm for the French Revolution. In 1789, she led an unruly mob of market women, prostitutes, and fishwives, as well as well-dressed women of the bourgeoisie, who pulled her astraddle a cannon toward the empty Bastille, where cannonballs were fired upon the tower and it was set afire. These impromptu warriors were "half friendly, half ferocious, and wholly demented."

Later that year, on October 5, Théroigne led the mob on the march to Versailles, during which the women were joined by all manner of outcasts, including homosexuals and transvestites. The march erupted into a bread riot as they swept upon Versailles, pillaging shops and taverns and storming the assembly. They rioted through the night in a raging downpour; come dawn they attacked the palace, "tearing the guards to pieces," searching the royal suites for the queen, intent on spilling "every drop of her Austrian blood," not knowing the royal family had fled under cover of storm and darkness.

In July of 1790, a band of prostitutes armed with pistols captured and robbed the royal cavalry, forcing the soldiers to chant "Death to the King!" and promising "We're all yours if you join the Revolution!" while dancing before their captives and lifting up their skirts, bringing to mind the manner by which the Xanthian women routed Bellerophon. Then, in 1792, the municipality of Paris decreed all citizens should go armed with pikes, and women responded immediately, insisting they came under the law as much as men. Théroigne formed her women into brigades, identifiable by their skirts of red, blue, and white and their red Phrygian caps that were symbolic of the Revolution, each armed with a cutlass in addition to "the democratic pike." They took it upon themselves to guard prisoners on the way to the guillotine.

An estimated eight thousand women were involved in these brigades, taking to the furthest reach Madame Rolland's sentiment, "Peace will set us back. We can be regenerated only in blood." Théroigne's crew participated in bloody rioting at La Force and at Bicêtre. She distinguished herself sufficiently that she was placed in command of the third corps of the army of the Faubourg. She went everywhere armed with a sword presented to her in honor of her unwavering service.

At the 1792 assault on the Tuileries, she encouraged her mob of women to have "a journalist who had lampooned her in the press lynched before her eyes." After the rioting at the abbey, she is purported to have found among the prisoners a Fleming nobleman with whom she had once had an affair when still veritably a child and who had abandoned her to disgrace in her village. He, daring to believe he would be fondly remembered, and hoping for reprieve, was, instead, swiftly decapitated by the vengeful Amazon, after which she "fell into a maniacal ecstasy, singing a revolutionary ballad," while dancing about his head and through the pools of blood.

An affair with the aristocrat Brissot, whom she tried to save from the guillotine, destroyed her reputation, inspiring La Maillard and her brigade to seize and whip her in public. This miserable turning is said to have deranged "the proud amazon, who was thereafter confined to the Salpêtriére, a mental asylum, where she lived until 1817, still preserving her great beauty, although most of the time a raving maniac, her ferocity surviving her intellect."

Her madness may indeed have been the response to the Terror or her own fall from grace, or it may have been syphilitic dementia, common enough among the libertines of the day. But we can't overlook the manner by which asylums have long been used as repositories for eccentrics, and few of the women who have languished in them were ever truly mad, all things being relative. [Miles, Rothery, Hale]

Merkus, Jenny: (fl. A.D. 1876) Called "the Amazon of Herzegovina," a Dutch social reformer who became a Serbian soldier, "a feminine figure in a man's cap" who rode horseback into battle. She fought in the Bosnian uprising against Turkish rule.

Messene: Pausanias tells that the Greek city of Andania was founded by Messene, who together with her husband, Polykaon, conquered the established peoples of a nation thereafter called Messene. The city of Messenia was also named for her. She established the worship of the Great Goddess of Eleusis.

Meyalleleth: "The Howling One." A name for **Lilith,** queen of night, a Hebrew version of **Hecate.** Meyalleleth was accompanied by an army of 480 hosts of destroying angels. Her rivals were **Makhalath** and **Agrath.** [Rappaport]

Miao Shan: A semilegendary Chinese princess who renounced wealth and devoted her life to Buddhist philosophy, canonized as an aspect of **Kuan Yin,** the dragon-slaying goddess of mercy. Convents and monasteries of ancient and medieval China as a rule taught, among much else, martial arts. When her convent of five hundred women was surrounded by ten times as many soldiers intent on setting the convent aflame, Miao Shan was helped by the goddess **Tou Mu** and the Sea-dragoness Shui-mu Niang-niang. By pricking the roof of her mouth, she spit blood that conjured storms, putting out the enemies' firebrands and sinking them in mud. After her victory over the five thousand soldiers, she submitted to arrest and was forced to walk in chains to the place of her execution. A sword, intended to behead her, broke against her neck, so she was garreted instead. Her soul went eagerly to hell, where she warred successfully against demons, freed many captive human souls, and established a new paradise in the infernal regions. She returned to the earth, where, disguised as a young priest, she spread the tenets of Buddhism. She was ultimately transformed into a Buddha and is still worshipped as Kuan Yin P'u-sa, portrayed riding a white elephant. [Werner]

Michel, Clémence Louise: (A.D. 1830–1905) She was a rebel during the Prussian siege of Paris in 1870 and a leading figure of the Paris Commune. "Revenge is the Revolution," she wrote in her prison memoirs. In 1883, under the black flag of anarchy, she led a mob of rioters and looters across Paris. She led the rebellion that prevented General Franco's Nationalists from taking over the city.

The environment in which she flourished provided ample opportunity for women to prove their valor. In the Paris Commune, a group of militant women were inspired by the French Revolution and the peasant market women who instigated the first riots under the leadership of Théroigne de **Mericourt,** and by the women's brigades formed in 1792. On April 5, 1871, the Commune women banded together, armed themselves as best they could, and marched to join the fighting men. As in many peoples' armies and peasant revolts, the women formed the front ranks, with the vain hope of government soldiers being slower to shoot them, and in the face of tragedy to "prove" the government's morally inferior position when so many of the dead are mothers.

Paul Verlaine called Louise Michel "nearly **Joan of Arc.**" She said of herself, "Barbarian that I am, I love cannon, the smell of powder, machine-gun bullets in the air," and, "The horrors of battle become poetry." She has been immortalized as "the Red Virgin." [Macksey, Rowbothan]

Mills, Ann: A British dragoon, she saw action on the frigate *Maidstone* in A.D. 1740. A famous print shows her with a sword in one hand, a Frenchman's head in the other. She divided her shore leave pretty equally between bedding young women and beating up young men. [Macksey]

Mimnousa: Amazon brave in the war led by **Orithia.** [Bothmer]

Minerva: Originally a War-goddess, she became more of a Crafts- and Distaff-goddess as Rome grew staid. To the Greeks, she was the warrior Pallas **Athena.**

During the siege of Pellene carried on by the Aetollians, there was a festival of Minerva in progress, and the priestess thereof was "the tallest and handsomest virgin that could be picked out, according to annual custom, in a full suit of elegant armor and a three-plumed helmet." The priestess led the festival procession into actual combat against the Aetollians, who, mistaking the elegant warrior for the actual War-goddess Minerva, raised the siege and fled, the Pellenesians in hot pursuit. [Polyaenus]

Minythyia: Warrior-queen of Albania in the days of Alexander the Great, sometimes said to have been queen of **Amazonia**. At the far earlier time of the collapse of Amazonia, ragged troops of Amazons were driven to the Albanian and Caucasian mountains, where they settled and preserved their culture. They may well have been the ancestresses of Minythyia.

Minythyia may have been only a horse-riding warrior-princess of the region, offered to Alexander in the process of treaty and marriage-alliance used also by his much-married father, Philip, who had at least six warrior-wives, including **Olympias**. Atropates, Satrap of Media, sent Alexander one hundred armed and horse-riding women, saying they were of the Amazon race. Alexander refused their service, but sent them home with a message to their queen that he would soon visit her. From this grew the legend of Alexander's visit to Amazonia and his excellent treatment in the court of the queen of the Amazons, sometimes confused with the separate legend of **Thalestris,** Queen of Bactria, meeting him at Hyrcania. [Tarn, Savill]

Mira: Yugoslavian markswoman of World War II, the fiercest of many female Partizans against the Nazis. She was tough and stocky, in her middle twenties. "She was totally dedicated to killing Germans," said a friend. Milica was also a guerrilla fighter who fought many actions, killed hundreds of Nazis, and was eventually killed in an ambush. Another woman soldier of Tito's forces was Vera Kriuzman; there were hundreds more, unheralded. "The women were feared by the Nazis. Once, two of them did a tap dance, in jack boots, on the stomach and genitals of a spread-eagle German officer. Another woman shot off the fingers of a Nazi soldier, castrated him, and made him choke on his own genitals." [Truby]

Miss Fury: A heroine of the "funny pages" of the 1940s and 1950s. By day, she was Marla Drake, society damsel. Her alter ego, clad in black tights and cat-eared cowl, battled crime and espionage. She had no special superpowers, only athletic ability and extreme bravery. She was the influential creation of Ms. Tarpe Mills, the first woman to conceive, write, and draw a female superhero.

Mist: A **Valkyrie** of *Grimulsmal*. See **Hrist** for a list of the full complement of Valkyrie companions.

Mitylenê: Sister of Queen **Myrene** of the Libyan Amazons and her most important general. She planned and executed the conquest of Atlantis, beginning with the city of Cernê, wherein all the men were executed and the buildings reduced to rubble, in a great display of barbarity. The rest of Atlantis fell into her hands without further resistance. A new city was built upon the ashes of the one destroyed, and bore her name thereafter. This island was not actually Atlantis, of course, but has been identified as Fedallah near Fez, Santa Cruz near Cape Ghir, or Arguin south of Cabo Blanco, this last having been in ancient times a center of trade with West Africa.

A city on Lesbos was founded in Mitylenê's name after the Amazons subdued all the islands of the Aegean. In a later age, **Sappho** was raised in the city of Mitylenê. She founded two other cities in Asia Minor named for herself.

The association with Atlantis was a late addition to the Gorgon cycle. The Gorgons actually originated on **Tritonia,** of which only the Canary Islands survive today. The volcanic catastrophes that destroyed the Hesperian Gorgons' first homeland gave rise to the belief that they conquered Atlantis. [Sobol, Graves, Bennett]

Miyagino: See **Hatsu-jo.**

Modthryth: A Germanic princess active about A.D. 520 who became a figure in *Beowulf.* She was "a good folk-queen who in her youth did dreadful deeds. None among her retainers, except only her father, dared set his eyes upon her in light of day, or her sword must settle it. Such is not a queenly custom for woman to practice, even so, she is peerless." The indication is that as a young woman of royal blood, Modthryth had soldierly adventures, and that, in the great hall of her father, any man who looked on her with desire (or, perhaps, sought her for marriage, as in the case of the Swedish **Torborg**) was challenged by her sword, and slain.

Moiraea: The three Fates. They are often portrayed as **hags** weaving the destinies of humankind, clipping the threads of their lives: Clotho ("Spinner"), who selected the thread; Lachesis ("Disposer"), who attached the threads to individual lives; and Atropos ("Who Cannot Be Turned Aside"), who clipped the threads. They are Birth, Life, and Death. The Goddess **Nemesis** was in their service. They were outside the authority of Zeus. Such trinity goddesses are typical of Greek, Celtic, and Norse mythology.

Molione: Little survives of her history, but her name means "Warrior Queen," which says a great deal. Molione's children were called the

Molionides, "sons of the warrior queen." They routed the army of Heracles, but he later ambushed and killed them, and Queen Molione sought revenge. She is also the Elean Moon-goddess, patroness of athletic games. [Graves]

Moll Cutpurse: See Mary **Frith.**

Molly Pitcher: (A.D. 1760–1843) Mary Hays became a lasting symbol of the American Revolution, serving for seven years alongside her husband in the Pennsylvania State Regiment of Artillery. Under fire, she swabbed cannon bores and helped load shot. In a June 1778 battle, a cannonball passed directly between her legs, carrying away part of her petticoat. She gazed at the rent with apparent unconcern and remarked it was a good thing it hadn't gone any higher. When her husband fell wounded, she continued to operate the cannon alone.

She received a war pension of forty dollars a year for life, but in old age lived penuriously, looked after by the military wives of West Point. She was entitled to a whiskey ration but was denied access by the commissary, who despised issuing liquor to women. She fought this injustice until higher brass intervened and allowed her to "walk out of the building carrying all the bottles forbidden her for months." Toward the end, she was often to be seen fishing on the waterfront, clad in an old artillery coat. Her grave is at West Point. [Meyer, Evans]

Molly Whupple: A female Jack the Giant Killer. In English fairy lore, she outwits a Spanish giant on three occasions, steals his sword, and saves her sisters' lives.

Molpadia: An Amazon among **Orithia's** troops during their attack of Athens. Her name means "Death Song." It was her arrow that slew **Antiope,** who had been the Amazons' queen, but now fought beside Theseus as his wife. In the next instant, Theseus' spear pierced Molpadia. She and Antiope were buried near each other by the Temple of **Gaia,** the Great Earth Mother. [Sobol]

Mongchi: In the year A.D. 503, a long war between the princes of Wei and the emperor of China began. A Wei general named Ginching was away from the walled city of Chanyang when Imperial soldiers marched upon the stronghold. Mongchi, the wife of the absent general, commanded the resistance and led the Chanyang troops to victory. Mongchi was not unusual for her day. Even the lowliest scullery maids of important households were trained to fight if necessary. When Ginching returned from his own campaign, he learned of his wife's valor, and was pleased.

Monterrosso de Lavelleja, Ana: Wife of a Uruguay army commander. She was chief of the "Thirty-three Orientales," patriots who in 1825 fought against Spain. [Schmidt]

Montpensier, Anne Marie Louise d'Orleans: (A.D. 1627–1693) French Patriot of the Fronde, Mlle. d'Orleans Montpensier was with the campaigns of the royal army of Orleans. She was the niece of Anne of Austria, cousin of Louis XIV, and had been a well-known athlete even before she gained further fame for martial feats. She led citizen soldiers of Paris to rescue the patriot Condé from the Bastille, in which she was herself later to be imprisoned. Her memoirs were published posthumously in 1729. [Starling, Gribble]

Moore, Madelaine: "The Lady Lieutenant" of an 1867 novel, Madelaine went with her lover into the American Civil War. During a battle, she took a fallen officer's uniform, and later talked her way into a formal commission. She led troops into battles in Virginia. [Truby]

Mordeaux, Elaine: French Resistance commander in World War II. Her unit attacked the 101st Panzers. Two hundred guerrillas killed three thousand Germans in one hour, crippling, as well, almost one hundred trucks and tanks. The handful of survivors said Elaine continued fighting to the last. "She was throwing dynamite at the Germans. Her Sten was empty; she tried to get ammunition from the bodies piled around her. A German sniper got her." [Truby]

Morgan, "La Belle": Heroine of the American Civil War, fought with a Michigan unit. [Laffin]

Morrigane or **Morrigu:** War-goddess of the Irish Celts, delighted in battles and often attended them in the form of a raven. Her name means "Queen of Nightmares." She told Cû Chulainn, "I am the gray she-wolf." She was able to appear as a beautiful maiden or a terrible hag. [Edwardes, Markale, Campbell]

Mother Ross: See Kit **Cavanaugh.**

Mu Guiying: A woman general who became commander in chief of the Sung Dynasty court. Her mother was a general, and her granddaughter was the famous general **Yang Paifeng.**

Muizeck, Marina: Sixteenth-century Russian empress. Her husband, Demetrius, was slain during a peasant revolt. Marina clad herself as a soldier and, at the head of her army, set out to quell the rebellion. She was defeated. Her captors carved a hole in the river's ice and cast her into the water.

Mujaji: About A.D. 350, the city of Meroe, last stronghold of the oldest of the great African nations, collapsed under Roman assault. The last Kushites fled, a race lost but certainly not forgotten. H. Rider Haggard attempted to resolve this riddle in his classic "lost race" novel *She*. The original "She," on whom Haggard based his romance, was the actual first queen of the Lovedu. Her name was Mujaji and she was said to be immortal. She led her warriors with shield and spear. [Vlahos]

Mukaya: A *mwanana* (princess) of the Luba people of central Africa in the late nineteenth century. She warred against rival factions and enemy tribes to support her family's rule, i.e., her own matrilineal line of descent. She fought alongside her brother Kasongo Kalambo, who fell in battle. This nation stretched along the fringe of the rain forests of Zaire all the way to northern Zambia. [Reefe]

Mu Lan: Han Dynasty folk heroine. Mu Lan was an unusually skillful swordswoman who went to war in lieu of her sickly father who, having no son, had trained her in martial arts from earliest childhood. [Kuo]

Mussasa: (fl. seventeenth century A.D.) African warrior-queen whose nation was on the Cunene River in the Congo. "She often led her soldiers to battle and victory, and extended the bounds of her empire." Her daughter **Tembandumba** ruled after her. [Rothery, Hale]

Myrene or **Myrina** or **Merina:** "Swiftly Bounding," an Amazon queen among the North African matriarchal tribes known as the **Gorgons.** She conquered Syria, Egypt, Phrygia, and the lands of the Mediterranean. The **Thermodontines,** or Scythian Amazons, reconquered much the same areas centuries later, but Myrene's conquests were vaster, including also the islands of Samos, Lesbos, Pathmos, and Samothrace, founding a city in her own name in Aeolis. Myrene was also the name of a Sea-goddess, who protected sailors from storm. The Gorgon Myrene's luck at sea and her conquest of islands show a link between the mortal and immortal Myrene.

  She may have been named for a great Moon-goddess, related to **Artemis of Ephesus,** who was known in Asia Minor as Myrene, Marian, Ay-Mari, Mariamne, or Marienna. The **Virgin Mary** in her medieval "stellar" aspect is this same widely worshipped goddess. The city of Smyrna was also named for her (Myrna preceded by the definitive article).

Myrene founded temples in Samothrace. Cities that she founded survived for centuries, and there was an additional city of Myrene, and a **Mitylene** (the name of Myrene's sister), along the borders of the Aegean, evidence of Myrene's exertion of Gorgon control over Mysia, Caria, and Lycia—areas of Asia Minor noted for women warriors even into historical times. Lycia is where Bellerophon fought the Amazons, as did the Lydians and Magnesians.

In one North African battle, Myrene led thirty thousand Libyan horsewomen against a rival tribe of Gorgons, taking so many prisoners that it nearly proved her undoing. She also founded a city, named for herself, on the isle of **Lemnos.** The Lemnians had gynocratic rule and evidence of a female revolution is found in the Argonauts' adventure at Lemnos, where they found no living men. Eventually, combined forces of Thracians and Scythians defeated Myrene's conquering horde in one of the Gorgons' colonial areas. Upon her death, the women gave up their extensive empire and returned to North Africa.

Myrene was buried near Troy, at a spot of assembly for Trojan soldiers. Later Greeks made her a Trojan ancestress, although originally she had probably been a foe. Myrene's somewhat mysterious connection with Troy may partly explain the allied cause of **Penthesilea** centuries later. [Diner, Sobol, Graves]

Myrtales: The name of **Olympias** in her youth.

N

❖❖❖❖❖❖❖❖❖❖❖❖❖

Naamah: A princess of Tyre, a land near Israel. She has also been identified as the mother of King Rehoboam and the founder of a city in Palestine, as well as the sister and/or wife of Tubal-Cain, who was originally a Smithy-god like limping Haephaestus.

To the kabalists, Naamah was a demoness, a ruler of night, and mother of Asmodeus. She took lovers at will even after her marriage to Tubal-Cain, and was adept at corrupting the angels of God. The *Zohar Hadash* of the Safed kabalists makes her one of Adam's two demon wives (the other was **Lilith**), with whom he lived after the murder of Abel and his divorce from Eve. For 130 years, the daughters of Adam by these two wives were noted for their extreme beauty but their corruption (i.e., they were Mother-goddess worshippers rather than Father-god worshippers; Naamah is a patriarchal Hebrew corruption of the oriental All-mother **Ma**). She is sometimes cited as a wife of Samael (Satan) together with Lilith, Eisheth Zenumim, and **Agrath.**

When Naamah married Tubal-Cain, she took him to her abode in the sea. She sent her children to Grandmother Lilith to be reared and educated. The Venetian Jew Meir Arama in a 1590 commentary on the Book of Psalms agrees that the children of Naamah, born of her liaisons with mortal men (whom she seduced in the form of a succubus), were raised by Lilith, who loved and cherished them. These legends clash somewhat with others that make Lilith a child killer, but remind us that Lilith was originally a protectress of unwed mothers, pregnant women generally, and newborn children, very similar to **Artemis.**

Most of the ancient Hebrew demon-queens were rivals of Lilith, and constantly at war with her. Naamah seems to have been a cherished daughter, or sister, and an actual ally in the wars against rival queens, much as Agrath aided her mother **Makhlath.** [Patai]

naginata: A Japanese weapon used predominantly by women. From the ancient Empress **Jingo Kogo** onward, Japanese women have been noted for warrior valor. Samurai wives remained vital to defense and offense right through Japan's protracted medieval era, ending, perhaps, with the Satsuma Rebellion, when Kyushu women formed battalions to fight government cavalry. Throughout, the naginata was women's weapon of choice for close combat. It consists of a sword blade inserted into a long pole, resembling a halberd. Today's All-Japan Naginata Society, a women's martial arts organization, has thousands of members, chiefly descendants of the samurai class. Some famous naginata practitioners of medieval Japan include **Fujinoye, Hangaku, Ike Gozen, Ishijo, Itagaki, Koman, Masaki Hojo, Sasaraye, Shizuka Gozen, Sono-jo, Tachibana Hime, Tamaori Hime, Tenji-no-tsubone,** and **Tomoe Gozen.** [Bacon]

Nandi: Warrior mother of the great African hero and patriot, Shaka Zulu. She battled slave traders and set an example for her son. When Shaka became king, he established an all-female regiment "which very ably defended their land against colonists." [Sertima, Qunta]

Nanny: There is a mountain range in midwestern Jamaica where for four hundred years there has lived a group of people called Maroons. One of their two main communities is descended from the most warlike tribes of western Africa, brought to Jamaica originally as slaves, but too powerful to hold or recapture. The other community is descended from the equally independent Moor and Berber soldiers of fortune who were with Diego Columbus in A.D. 1509.

This second community was founded by a ferocious woman named Nanny. Nannyville is a village near Nanny's Cauldron, a huge waterfall from which the much-legended founder tossed many a would-be slaver to his death. It is said that when British slavers fired cannonballs into the Maroon communities, Nanny caught the cannonballs between the moons of her buttocks, firing them back at the British.

In the late 1800s, Maroon people claimed that Nanny still lived, a witch to whom tribal kings were married. She remained the inspiration of their long battle against slavery throughout their bold history. [C. Morris]

Nausica: Very little is known of individual women among the **Dahomey Amazons,** though much is known of them as a group. Nausica is one of the handful of remembered names. She was the Dahomey king's favorite warrior and she danced at the court of the French Ambassador Bayol in A.D. 1889. The following year she died fighting the French, falling beside a cannon she had commandeered. Other names that are preserved include **Adadimo** and **Macouda.**

From Cudjo Lewis (African name: Kossola-O-Lo-Loo-Ay), who "arrived on the last load of slaves run to the United States and was the only Negro alive that came over on a slave ship," folklorist Zora Neale Hurston collected the following tale of his capture and the slaughter of most of his nation, the Takkoi.

> The attack came at dawn as the Takkoi were getting out of bed to go to their fields outside the city. A whooping horde of the famed Dahoman women warriors burst through the main gate, seized people as they fled from their houses, and beheaded victims with one stroke of their big swords. "Oh, oh! I runnee this way to that gate, but they there. I runnee to another, but they there, too. All eight gates they there. Them women, they very strong. I nineteen years old, but they too strong for me. They take me and tie me. I don't know where my people at. I never see them no more." He described the awful slaughter as the amazons sacked the city. The clusters of human heads at their belts.

When the king of Takkoi refused to be taken to Dahomey, "two Dahoman warriors held each of his hands and an amazon struck off his head."

Audre Lorde has written a remarkable poem "The Women of Dan Dance with Swords in Their Hands to Mark the Time When They Were Warriors," which may be found in *The Black Unicorn* (1978). She explains that Dan is "an ancient name for the kingdom of Dahomey (Danhomee)." In Dahomey today, the women maintain a tradition of martial readiness, in their sword dance.

Nega: A warlike demoness, daughter of **Lilith.** Her behavior was similar to that of **Naamah.** As a Death-goddess, she carried plague. [Patai]

Nehanda: (A.D. 1862?–1898) Originally a religious leader of the MaShona nation of Zimbabwe, Nehanda became also a military leader when the British invaded her country. Her forces struck from impregnable mountain fastnesses and were successful for quite some while. But the British had access to ever-increasing numbers of arms, and eventually Nehanda was captured, tried, and sentenced to die. A priest tried to win her conversion before she was executed, but Nehanda was defiant to the last, and true to her African faith. [Qunta]

Neith: See **Net.**

Neith-hetep: (fl. 3400 B.C.) Her name means "The War-goddess Is at Peace." She was queen-regent of Kemet, or Black Egypt, wife of Aha-menes, first king of the First Dynasty. "It is of particular importance to us that this most significant period of Kemetic history boasts a woman re-gent." Her name is always surmounted by the shield and crossed arrows of the War-goddess Neith (**Net**), so that the only definite information regarding her rule was that it was marked by warrior capacity. [Sertima]

Nemain or **Nemen:** "Venomous" or "Frenzy." A War-goddess of the Irish Celts, one-third of the tripartite of **Morrigane,** along with **Bodb** and **Macha.** Her presence when battles were in preparation was said to create such berserker rages that men began dying even before the battle was engaged. Her consort was the War-god Neit, but she is sometimes identi-fied, like **Fea** and **Macha,** as the wife of Nuada. These sister Battle-goddesses probably have the same root origin as the **Valkyries,** as there is a body of very ancient Irish myth associating the settlement of Ireland with Scythia, homeland of the original Amazons. [Davidson, Ellis]

Nemesis: "Righteous Anger," goddess of retribution, visited on wicked mortals by the Olympians and the **Moiraea** (Fates), who challenged espe-cially the proud and the insolent. In Homer, she is a concept and not a personal figure, but, in a fragment of the *Cypria,* she is a vivid personality. As Nemesis of Rhamnus, worshipped also in Smyrna, she was a shape changer who flew over land and sea, with traits similar to **Dictynna.** There is reason to suppose Nemesis an aspect of **Artemis** (see **Upis**).

Nephele: Cloud-goddess, an eidolon of **Hera** (i.e., her ephemeral double) who begat Centauros, the original centaur. Centauros fathered the centaurs by a mare. The centaurs are thereby grandchildren of Hera. The centaurs were the male counterparts to the Amazons. To the ancient world, the horse's tail was phallic, hence the Amazons achieved a large measure of their strength (in Greek mythological terms) from being the original horse-riding race. In Greek art, men who lust after the **Maenads** wear horse tails.

Some have speculated that the centaurs were once female, originating in the idea that the Amazons were the first to war astride horses, and mistaken for composite monsters. Others counter that this is impossible, because the Greeks imagined female centaurs largely as an afterthought. However, the **Empusaë,** daughters of **Hecate,** of Indic derivation, could take many forms, including half horse, half woman; so, avoiding the Eurocentric desire to credit everything to the Greeks, we see that by an Indic connection the female centaur may well predate the male.

Nephele may have been originally a mortal warrior queen whose exploits caused her to be identified as the double or avatar of Hera. A queen by that name ruled Boeotia until King Aeolian cast her aside for the Maenad **Ino.** What survives of her history parallels that of **Olympias,** similarly cast off by Philip in favor of **Cleopatra,** and who waged wars as a result. Both sought to defend the rights of their children to inherit rule. One of Nephele's daughters, Helle, gave her name to the strait called the Hellespont. Nephele leaves mythology as an archer-nymph in the service of **Artemis** (see **Crocale**). [duBois, Bulfinch]

Neptunis: A cult title for **Artemis,** and an alternative name for **Hippolyte.** [Graves]

Ness or **Nessa:** Leader of a band of Celtic soldiers. She "sowed terror everywhere and it was only when she met the Druid Cathbad that she renounced her life as a warrior" and married him, since her own future was now well secured. She remained politically active, her son becoming King Concobar. [Markale, Ellis]

Nestan-Daredian: A queen beloved of *The Knight in the Tiger Skin* in the epic poem by Shot'ha Rust'hveli. She is treated as an incarnated Sun-goddess. "She rose as fearless as if she were a tiger or a hero; joy no longer seemed joy nor did woe seem woe to her." She was served and sensuously admired by Princess P'hatman and by Princess T'hinat'hin (or Tinatin), this latter based on Queen **Tamar** of Georgia, to whom the epic was dedicated and whom Rust'hveli admired as "the jet-haired and ruby-cheeked." As with Tamar, Tinatin was to rule after her father the king, for "A lion's cubs are also lions, male and female alike."

Net or **Neith:** "That Which Is" or "The Terrifying." Her most ancient symbol is the shield and crossed bows. Believed to be of Libyan origin, "belonging to an era when fatherhood was not recognized," and perhaps worshipped by the original **Gorgons.** Net was a War-goddess to the Egyptians, a self-begotten virgin armed with bow, arrows, and distaff, identified in later myths with **Isis.** "Virgin priestesses of Neith participated annually in armed combat, the victor becoming high priestess."

The Greeks believed she was the same as their **Athena,** which later scholars have thought an error on the part of Greek commentators, brought about by mere surface similarities between these goddesses. But the Greeks may have known more about it than survives for our judgment. Athena's origin is not really known. Her name is definitely not Greek. She certainly didn't leap from the brow of Zeus as is stated in the popular but very late-occurring myth, for she was an important deity back when Zeus was still only a localized vegetation spirit in Crete. It is conceivable that she was derived from Net or another exceedingly ancient goddess of Ethiopia or Syria, dispersed by the sea trade between North Africa and Crete, thence finally to Greece. [Edwardes, Graves, Hart]

Ng Miu or **Ng Nui:** Wu Shu, a martial art that has become the national sport of communist China, was developed by a woman warrior in the Ming Dynasty who was "an expert fighter with the long pole. Her teacher was a white crane who snapped her pole in two with an easy graceful turning wing the first time they met." Another such was a martial nun of A.D. 1600s, Ng Miu. She taught Shaolin temple boxing. Her most remarkable pupil was **Yim Ving Tsun,** who went on to develop new kung fu systems that are popular even today.

Women warriors of China have been shown to Westerners through Hong Kong movies, photos of Beijing Opera, paper silhouettes, fans, vases, literature, puppets and, occasionally, historical information, as well as porcelains of such armed goddesses as **Tou Mu.** Many Westerners have come to associate the idea of the "woman warrior" with China, although swordswomen were just as common in Europe.

Nhongo, Teurai Ropa: Also called Joyce Nhongo. Teurai Ropa means "the Blood Spiller." She was a Zimbabwe guerrilla fighter in the 1970s, commander of the Women's Detachment during the liberation wars. She fought off one Rhodesian attack only two days before the birth of her daughter. After the wars, she was appointed Minister of Community Development and Women's Affairs. [Qunta, Miles]

Nicaea: A huntress who, when seen passing by Hymnus the shepherd, captured his attention so thoroughly that he became a nuisance and she killed him. Dionysus avenged Hymnus by getting Nicaea drunk and raping her in her sleep. [Tyrrell]

Nike: An aspect of the War-goddess **Athena.** Nike was the daughter of the

River Styx and a personification of victory in sports or battle. The Romans called her Victoria.

The Nine Witches of Glaucester: In Arthurian romance, the Nine Witches are women warriors who rampage and kill. One of them trained Peredur in the martial arts, even as **Scáthach** and **Aife** trained Cû Chulainn. The Nine Witches later defeated and killed Peredur's uncle and cousin; his revenge required Arthur's aid to succeed.

Such women were known as *gwiddonot* and fought in helm and armor, unlike the typical Celtic **hag,** who fought with nails and teeth. In another legend, Arthur battles one of the *gwiddon* in á hand-to-hand contest. Before the law of Adamuán in the ninth century, women warriors were typical among the Celts. Some scholars believe such fighters as the Nine Witches are evidence of women-run military academies. Nine women companions-at-arms recur in Icelandic legend, and in other mythologies of the world. In some **Maenad** rites, the sacrificial animal or man was cut into nine pieces. The number nine was sacred because of the nine moons of gestation. The nine labors of Heracles indicate his usurpation of women's mysteries and his patriarchal war against the goddess. [Chadwick]

Ninmah: Also called Nintu and Ninhursag. She was **Aruru** in Akkad; Ninlil in Babylonia; Innin to the Sumerians. She is related less directly to **Inanna** and **Ishtar.**

Ninmah was the Earth-goddess of Mesopotamia. She created six preliminary forms of mankind. Aiding her son Ninurta in his heroic deeds, she "was not afraid to enter the inimical land, because she had no fear of the terror of battle." [Kramer]

Nitocris: (fl. seventh century B.C.) Warrior-queen of Assyria about two centuries after **Semiramis.** "She distinguished herself by her conquests over the neighboring nations, and left behind her many stupendous edifices." Herodotus thought her wiser than Semiramis and nearly as bold.

Nitocris: (fl. 2275 B.C.) Daughter of Pepi I, Nitocris became queen-regent of Upper and Lower Egypt, and reigned, according to varying authority, either seven or twelve years. Many other powerful women carried the dynastic name of Nitocris and they were all, by tradition, worshippers of the War-goddess **Net,** and skilled in battle arts. [Sertima]

Nu Kua Shih: Legendary empress, virtuous progenitrix of the Chinese race. Her history survives in an eighth-century chronicle by Ssu-ma Cheng. In one form, she had the body of a snake and the head of a beautiful woman with the horns of an ox. Toward the end of her reign, believed to be about 2800 B.C., she was embroiled in wars with princes, and with an aboriginal chief of a confederacy of tribes. She killed this latter's generals and pursued him with her armies until he, finding no refuge, angrily destroyed one of the pillars of heaven, unleashing a flood upon the world. Kua Shih gathered stones of five colors and repaired the tears in heaven, halting the flood, for which act she gained the title Restorer of Heaven. [Werner]

Nur Jehan: (d. A.D. 1645) Empress of Hindustan in the seventeenth century. Her name means "Light of the Harem," but she was subsequently called "Light of the World." It was for Nur Jehan's niece, Mumtaza Zemani, that the Taj Mahal was built to house her tomb.

For twenty years, Nur Jehan ruled Hindustan over the head of Sultan Jehangir, "with a power as absolute as **Cleopatra** or **Semiramis.**" When the great General Mohabat Khan rose in power and threatened the empire, Nur Jehan came out of seclusion, clad herself as a soldier, and set out to save Sultan Jehangir. She rode to the fore of her troops "on the howdah of a high elephant, with a bow and four quivers of arrows." Her elephant forded a difficult river and arrived, ahead of her forces, with only her brother and a few principal officers at her side. "Not a moment did she waver." While balls and arrows fell about her, she "poured the content of her quivers upon her foes." Her power was felt thereafter "in every corner of the vast Indian Empire." [Pool]

Nut: Egyptian Sky-goddess, mother of **Isis.** Because she ate her own children, her brother Geb declared war against her. She later gave birth to the devoured children, a typical myth of the goddess as a warlike destroyer and fecund life giver. [Kramer]

Nzingha Mbande: (A.D. 1582–1663) Also given as Jinga, Zinga, and other spellings. She was the sister of the king of Ngola, today Angola. In 1621, she was a peace negotiator arranging treaties with Portugal to preserve Ngola's independence. During one negotiating session, the Portuguese intentionally did not provide Nzingha with a chair. One of her servants went directly to his hands and knees, and she negotiated while sitting on his back. In 1624, with her brother's death, she became queen of her nation. She appointed women to all the highest offices. The Portuguese broke their treaty and sent armed forces. Queen Nzingha's armies, in great part female, made fierce retaliations. She was described as clad in animal skins, a sword slung from her neck, an ax at her girdle, and bow and arrows in her hands. Her sisters Kifunji, killed by the Portuguese, and Mukumbu, whom Nzingha ransomed from Portuguese captivity, were also warriors.

Nzingha renounced her previous conversion to Christianity and adopted ritual cannibalism. Until 1635, she fought against the invaders, while at the same time conquering other African kingdoms in the effort to build a confederacy extensive enough to counter her European foes. She lived to the age of eighty-one. She is still remembered today, for, immediately after Angolan independence in 1975, a street in Luanda was named for her. [C. Williams, Blashfield, Fraser, Loth]

❖❖❖❖❖❖❖❖❖❖❖❖❖

Oakley, Annie: (A.D. 1860–1926) The darling of Wild West Show enthusiasts around the world, Annie Oakley was typical of a type of woman common in her day. Most such women gained their skills as ordinary ranch hands; the ones who are remembered represent a fraction of the total number of cowpunching, hard-riding ranchwomen from Oklahoma to Oregon. Physical beauty was often a prerequisite for such a woman to graduate from ranch hand to rodeo queen or Wild West Show performer, thence, often enough, to silent film star, leaving us the odd impression that Wild West Amazons were extraordinarily feminine—and indeed Annie was very beautiful in her youth. After working briefly for Sells Brothers Circus, she joined Buffalo Bill's Wild West Show in 1885, touring the United States, Canada, and Europe. In Germany, Annie shot a cigarette out of Kaiser Wilhelm II's mouth.

Obizuth: A snake-haired demoness of Hebrew myth, related to **Medusa** and who, like **Lilith,** killed children. She warred against King Solomon, whom she told, "I am a fierce spirit of myriad names and many shapes."

Octavia: (d. 12 B.C.) Wife of Marc Antony, her second husband, and sister of Emperor Augustus. She accompanied Antony in the war against the Parthians about 41 B.C. Supplanted by **Cleopatra VII** in his affections, she returned to Italy in sadness. She later was to raise Antony's children by his first wife, **Fulvia,** as well as those by Cleopatra.

Ocypetc: "Swift Wing," one of the **Harpies** battled by the Argonauts.

Oigme: An obscure Amazon brave known from a single **Amazono-machy's** inscription. Her name is of Oriental derivation.

Oiko: A strongwoman of medieval Japan. Oiko was a farm daughter of Tashima, Omi province. She used her strength to help peasants, as when she dammed a river with a huge boulder in order to irrigate the rice paddies. A story tells how she was walking down the road one day with a large basin of water balanced on her head, when a warrior sought to molest her, but she grabbed him by the wrist. Without losing a single drop of water, she continued walking, dragging him along, refusing to let go or even speak to him until he begged her politely and promised never to molest women again.

In later versions, a sumo wrestler thought it would be a good joke to tickle her under the arm and make her drop the water, and got his hand stuck in her armpit. Omi has always been famous for strongwomen (see **Kane-jo**), some of them becoming popular sumo wrestlers in the military capital of Edo of the Tokugawa period. One promoter arranged sumo wrestling between strongwomen and blind men, such exhibition becoming hilarious and lewd. By 1872, the sport had degenerated to such a degree that wrestling between men and women was prohibited, though professional sumo women continued to participate against one another.

Okuni, Izumo no: The founder of kabuki theater could never have predicted that one day women would be outlawed from the art a woman created. Izumo no Okuni, "with two swords at her belt, one long and short, and dressed like the ruffians who roamed the streets of Kyoto," was famous for onstage warrior impersonations, erotic to the homosexually inclined samurai class. Some of the legends about her suggest that she was a sword fighter offstage as well. [Higuchi, Beard]

Okyale: An archer who fought under **Orithia** in the Attic War, she engaged Astyochos in single combat. [Bothmer]

Okypous: A brave in the war of Heracles and Telamon against Queen **Andromache.** [Bothmer]

Old-Lady-Grieves-the-Enemy: (fl. nineteenth century A.D.) An old Pawnee warrior who gained her name at the age of fifty when her village was attacked by the Poncas and Sioux. The men tried to run away, but she grabbed a war club and took out after the enemy, shaming the Pawnee men into action. [Niethammer]

Olga: About the ninth century A.D., according to the *Chronicles of Nestor,* the oldest authority on the age, King Igor of ancient Kiev (present-day Ukraine) was slain by the Drevlians while on a mission to exact heavy tribute. When his conquering days ended, those of his fierce wife began. Queen Olga set out to avenge her husband of his many enemies, who still conspired against her country through emissaries sent to convince her to marry a prince of their land. The first group of emissaries was buried alive; the second group was boiled in their baths. She visited her husband's tomb in the enemy nation and, before returning to Kiev, set her guards upon the remaining foes, cutting them to pieces. Unplacated by these vengeances, she intended to see the entire nation brought to rein. The next time she rode out from her country, it was at the head of a conquering army. She lay siege to Korosten, capital of the despised Drevlians. The city held against the siege too long, so that Olga's impatience birthed a clever strategem.

"I have slain the enemies of Igor!" she told the city, striding before its walls. "My vengeance is satisfied! Why are you afraid of me?" Heartened, the Drevlians offered tribute of meat, honey, and furs. Olga, feigning generosity, refused heavy tribute, asking a token instead: She would accept a living pigeon and three sparrows from each household. The Drevlians hastened to collect birds from their rooftops, delivering them in cages. That night, Olga set the birds free, small lighted brands dangling from their legs. All the roofs of Korosten were quickly set aflame. As the people fled their burning capital, the invaders cut them down. Thereafter, Olga's rule was unquestioned in those lands that would one day be called Russia, and her reign was marked by such public services that she was loved by all the peasants. [C. Morris]

Olof: A mighty, fierce warrior-queen of Danish legend. In Icelandic legend, she is Queen **Thora.** [Damico]

Olrun the Wise: A **Valkyrie,** daughter of King Kiar.

Olympias: (fourth century B.C.) A descendant of Achilles, militant priestess, and princess of Epirus. She became the first of Philip II's warrior-wives, and mother of Alexander the Great, born 355 B.C. on the same night that the **Artemisium** at Ephesus burned. Olympias conducted battles in the costume of a **Maenad.** When widowed, she conquered and imprisoned **Eurydice, Queen of Macedonia,** and later executed her to ensure the royal line passed through her children rather than through the children of another of Philip's militant wives, **Eurydice**-Audata.

Olympias, to whom "moderation was unknown," was far more influential in shaping the character of Alexander than was his father, or any other individual except his tutor Socrates. But for the militancy of Olympias in establishing her line for the rule of Macedonia, Alexander should never have been known as "Great," but only as one more in a long list of Philip's children by numerous wives.

Of Philip's wives, most were taken as part of political alliances, and had no legal status in Macedonia. But Olympias, as his first wife, and mother of his first son, had a higher standing even in Macedonia. Yet she was herself a foreigner, and therefore Philip's marriage to the native Cleopatra, niece of Philip's general Attalus, threatened the position of Olympias and her child. She left Macedonia to raise an army, resulting, ultimately, in the execution of Cleopatra (who, like Eurydice, was forced to hang herself) together with her child.

As a devotee of "the orgiastic worships of Thrace," she had selected Philip during a **Maenad** celebration. This was the only one of seven marriages that was not motivated by Philip's ambition, and in which he was not the instigator. There is irony in the fact that, many years later, when Philip neglected Olympias, her intrigues resulted in his murder. Her religion of "strange and barbaric vagaries" has been given as the reason for her soldierly magnificence.

This Epirote princess kept pet serpents to wear as garlands (a Maenad habit) and gave them to travelers as gifts. We may imagine just how exciting this strong, sensual, eccentric princess was to Philip when she first introduced him to the mysteries of Dionysus in Samothrace. But it was purportedly this same religion that stopped Philip from coming to her bed, shared as it was with her pet snakes.

In the year 315 B.C., though nominally retired, she commanded the defense of Pynda. When two hundred soldiers reached her with strict orders to kill her, they were so menaced by her appearance that they fled in terror. Her long career, which outlasted that of Alexander, ended in 314 B.C., when she was stoned by family survivors of men she had killed. [Hale, Pomeroy, Robinson, Tarn]

O'Malley, Grace: Or Grainne Mhaol (A.D. 1530?–1600?) An Elizabethan Irish princess and warrior whose naval activities were directed against the English invasion. Her base of operation was Clare Island. She first appears in history as a fierce fighter among a pirate crew, but is later to be found in command of her own fleet, the terror of the sea. Only once was she arrested, but her political connections were excellent. She was quickly released, having evaded conviction and even official charges.

The world over, piracy has been caught up in the politics of each age, and for Grace it was no different. Her second husband was knighted by the viceroy of Ireland in 1576. Grace was in the interesting position to seriously offer the viceroy three of her galleys and two hundred of her crew members as auxiliary navy men.

In 1586, she was still upon the sea, though she must have been well into her fifties. The business of piracy had grown riskier by then, and O'Malley had fallen into financial distress upon her husband's death, a widow receiving none of her husband's estate, all holdings passing to the sons. Her response to her crisis was to make a personal trip to England in 1583 to ask Queen **Elizabeth I** for amnesty and a stipend. She received both and retired comfortably. [Course]

Omatsu: Her story was first preserved by Tokugawa period street performers of Edo, who based their tales on popular events. Her husband was a samurai who had lost his sight and hence his position. To support herself and her husband, Omatsu opened a fencing school and taught sword fighting. By night, she was a bandit and highway robber. By the time her story crystallized into a kabuki drama, she had been transformed into something of a villain, though the rudiments still suggested the original Omatsu must have been tragically heroic. On one night of banditry, her victim turned out to be her husband's brother. Her blind husband sought to track the slayer and achieve revenge, so on an especially black night, he lay in wait for the mysterious bandit. They met, fought on equal terms in absolute darkness, and Omatsu was killed. Her blood restored her husband's sight.

Omphale: Queen of Lydia, she wore Heracles' lion skin as symbol of her mightiness, and fought with his wooden club. Heracles became her subservient lover. In some versions, he is her slave, in expiation for a murder, and must spend three years dressed as a maid. When Heracles returned from the battle with the Amazons, he had many spoils, including **Hippolyte's** two-edged ax, the **labrys.** This he presented to Queen Omphale, and it was afterward a sacred treasure to the Lydian kings. She has also been identified as an avatar of the **Devi,** Great Goddess of Asia Minor. [Stone, Evans, Graves]

Opis: "Awe." A warrior-nymph in the service of **Diana,** sent to avenge the death of **Camilla.** Diana gave the warrior-nymph her own arrows so that the goddess herself would be the punisher of Arruns, the man destined to kill Camilla. After his victory, he fled in terror of Camilla's women lieutenants, but Opis waylaid him. [Virgil]

Ordynska, Stanislawa: More than two hundred women fought in the Polish legion in 1916. One such, Stanislawa Ordynska, married young and, refusing to be separated from her husband, went to battle with him. [Hirshfeld]

Oreades: Mountain nymphs, huntress attendants of Our Lady of Wild Things, probably indicating extremely ancient colleges of priestesses devoted to **Artemis.**

Orithia or **Oreithyia:** "Woman Raging in the Mountains." After the death of Queen **Marpesia** at the hands of barbarians during an Asian campaign, her daughter, Orithia, named for the Libyan goddess of creation (and a cult name for **Eurynome**), succeeded her in rule and completed the subjugation of numerous Asian cities. She achieved an alliance with Sagillus, King of Scythia, who sent his son, Pansagoras, with cavalry to aid in the revenge of Marpesia's death. By this, we can see that the Amazons were able to fight with men in their ranks.

According to Justinus, Scythian Amazons ruled in pairs, one queen organizing offenses outside **Amazonia,** the other ruling at home. Orithia's sister **Antiope** ruled before or concurrently with her; her daughters **Penthesilea** and **Hippolyte II** ruled after her. **Melanippe** and **Hippolyte** were her most outstanding generals, although other accounts give Melanippe as the queen of the home front and Orithia as the queen on the expanding frontier. Other ancient authorities suggest the Amazon nation was divided into three great tribes, each with its own queen, and Orithia ruled concurrently with Hippolyte and Antiope.

When Orithia, still at the frontier, received word that Heracles and Theseus had invaded the Amazon capital and taken its leaders captive, she marched on Athens, occupied the Areopagus, and besieged the Acropolis. It was the only time Athens was thus attacked, and while many authorities have called this revenge raid a failure, the specifics of the encounter suggest otherwise. After four months of warfare, and with the accidental death of Antiope (or Hippolyte) who fought for Theseus, Orithia gave up the battle and signed treaties with the Atheneans. Other sources say that Antiope merely intervened, having as she did divided loyalties, and brought about a mutually acceptable treaty. Graves survive into modern times bearing the names of the victims of Orithia's revenge raid, and the **Amazoneum** commemorated the treaty. This is hardly the routing some authors have made of it.

Orithia died in retirement in Megara, for she was ashamed to return to

Themiscrya without clear victory over Athens. At Megara, a tomb was built for her in the shape of an Amazon's shield. [Diner, Justinus, Graves, Kanter, Pizan, Boccaccio]

Orithia: A nymph of the cult of Boreas and the triple-headed Horse-goddess. The orgiastic cult taught that the North Wind inseminated mares. In Libya she was the goddess of creation, derived from the Egg-mother **Eurynome.** [Graves]

Ornias: A beautiful, violent, vampiric demoness against which King Solomon battled. She has been identified with **Lilith.** [Lacks]

Ornoskelis: A Hebraic wind-spirit who manifests as a fair-skinned woman who seduces, then strangles men. She lived in crevices, caves, and high upon precipices. She waged war against King Solomon.

Oroku: "Even snakes were afraid of Oroku" goes the saying. She was a figure of drama dating to Tokugawa period theater in Japan, and undoubtedly indicative of a type of woman encountered in the cities and along the roads. Oroku is always portrayed as a hard-drinking brawler.

Orthia: "Severe." Spartan Warrior-goddess, usually identified as an aspect of **Artemis.** Boys were taken to her altar and tortured annually. Although her temple did not date to the Bronze Age, the types of votive offering she received were Minoan-Mycenaean, showing her to have been of ancient origin and perhaps known to the Amazons. [Seltman, Nilsson]

Orthosia: A cult title for the War-goddess **Artemis** and an alternative name for **Antiope,** queen of the Amazons.

Orthryth, Queen of Mercia: (fl. late seventh century A.D.) Daughter of King Oswiu of Northumbria, she defended the Fladbury monastery in Worcerstershire from her father's people. She was brilliant at statecraft, always striving to end the wars between the countries. But Southumbrian nobles believed her policies aided Northumbria more than Mercia, and so set upon her in large numbers, and killed her. [Crawford]

Oserrah: (seventh century A.D.) Moslem woman warrior and friend of **Khawlah;** they fought together against the Greeks.

Otrera: "The Nimble." Consort of the War-god Ares, elsewhere said to be the Amazon daughter of Ares and **Harmonia.** She built a temple and bird sanctuary upon a flat island in the Black Sea when the Amazons first settled the coast. It was here the Amazons retreated to worship and sacrifice horses before their major battles. She is sometimes cited, in lieu of **Orithia,** as the mother of **Penthesilea,** although their generations do not overlap, and this would have to have been a later Orithia. [Evans, Bennett]

Oya: Goddess of tornadoes and floods of the Niger region of Africa. She shakes and uproots trees, dresses in blood red, and lightning is her sword.

P

❖❖❖❖❖❖❖❖❖❖❖❖❖

Padilla, Maria Pacheco: Spanish patriot of the sixteenth century. When her husband, a noted general, fell in battle, she assumed command of the troops and successfully defended Toledo.

Padmini: Wife of Rama of Chitor in fourteenth-century Rajptana. Her fame of beauty reached the tyrant Mogul emperor who ruled from Delhi. She "fought valiantly against the Mohammedan conquerer," during his many invasions. The Fort of Chitor was finally held siege and Padmini's husband was captured in a skirmish. The Mogul offered her an exchange: her concubinage for her husband's freedom. Instead, she attacked the emperor's camp with fifty of her fiercest warriors, killing him and liberating her husband. [Schmidt, Pool]

Pakhet: "Tearer" or "She Who Snatches." **Sekhmet**like Egyptian Lion-goddess. She was a huntress like **Ubastet** and resembles in many ways the Greek **Artemis.** [Hart]

Palaeologina, Helen: A Greek woman of exceptional character, daughter of Theodore Palaeologus, despot of Moroe. She wed John II of Cyprus, an irresolute man, and became de facto ruler of the island in A.D. 1442. She liberated the Orthodox Church from Latin tyranny, conquered Constantinople in 1453, and passed rule to her daughter, Carolotta, who unfortunately was overthrown in a battle against the Turks in 1470.

Pantariste: A young Scythian Amazon who participated in the battle against Heracles after he murdered Queen **Hippolyte.** Her shield's device was a white sphinx. Three of Heracles' famous captains—Telamon, Theseus, and Tiamides—fled the battlefield, but Pantariste pursued them along the beach. Two Greek footsoldiers rushed to face her and keep her from their captains. The first she grabbed by the hair, pulled to the ground, and impaled with her spear. Unable to free her spear quickly enough, she grabbed the next Greek attacker by the throat, shook the sword from his hand, and held him stationary until he suffocated. She then reclaimed her spear and threw it at Tiamides with such ferocity that, although he deflected it with his shield, he was thrown to the ground. Pantariste then drew forth her **labrys** and beheaded Tiamides. [Sobol]

Paraminta, Rani: Queen of an Amazon nation of protohistoric India. She was said to have been of the rhackshasis, those demonic females of India and Sri Lanka who made love to men, then devoured them. The **Maenads** are linked to the rhackshasis, as the cult of Dionysus may well have begun in India.

Paraminta kept her lovers for one month and if they failed to leave her at that time, she killed them. The Vedic hero Arjuna, like Heracles and Theseus of Greece, wished to conquer the rani's nation, but he knew "the women are of great strength. We shall find it hard to stand against them." She met him with her army and war elephants, challenging him boldly, and they exchanged insults. She defeated him and wished to take him as her lover, but Arjuna, understanding that Paraminta's paramours were ultimately killed, elected instead to pay heavy tribute, which the victor carried away on her elephants.

Contrary to the Greek legends, in which trouncing women is a sign of manliness, the Brahman legend is moralistic and the hero needs only to avoid lustful entrapment. [Rothery]

Parthenia: Huntress of Phineas Fletcher's Spenserian poem *Purple Islands* (1633), modeled on Spenser's **Belphoebe.**

Parvati: "The Black One." There is no evidence that the god Shiva was known during the Harappa civilization of the Indus Valley in the third millennium B.C., but there is inarguable evidence that his wife, Parvati, was already well known as the Great Mother, for whom horses were sacrificed. Pottery figurines show her pregnant and correspond in time and appearance with Great Mothers of Egypt, Cyprus, Crete, the Balkans, and elsewhere, indicators of goddess monotheism throughout the world well into the

Bronze Age. She was later known by many names, including **Uma, Ambika, Bhairavi, Durga, Koravai, Chamunda, Chandika, Salini, Seri,** Gauri, and Minakshi. Worship of the Indian All-mother survives in various parts of India, particularly in the south, as Shakti or **Devi,** most especially among low-casted and non-Brahmanic people, indicating her pre-Aryan roots.

Parvati was originally black. Taunted by Shiva for her skin color, she withdrew into a period of austerity, and became golden. **Kali,** too, was black, and a cultural connection between India and North Africa, even before the Bronze Age, may account for the black goddesses, who were originally conquering women from ancient Meroë. Africanist scholars have convincingly argued that such goddesses are derived from Ethiopian invasions of Asia Minor, and that Africa is the origin of all civilization. These are fascinating possibilities in light of the myths of the Libyan Amazons called **Gorgons,** and the proliferation of black goddesses in Europe and Asia, surviving in the West in the form of **Black Mary.** [Kramer]

Pattini: A ferocious goddess of disease and drought in Sri Lanka. She is highly defeminized, planning as she does to be a man in a future existence. But she is an aspect of the feminine **Kannagi** and, like her, destroyed a city by setting it on fire with her left breast, symbolizing her refusal to milk or nurture humanity. [Preston]

Peirson, Mrs.: The Scotswoman whose name is known only as "Mrs. Peirson" was the daughter of the Earl of Carnwath. She obtained a commission from the Earl of Newcastle in A.D. 1644. She raised a troop of horse and joined Montrose on the march across the border to Dumfries. But the expedition was a failure, and Mrs. Peirson is not heard of again. [Fittis]

Pele: Hawaiian War-goddess, presides over a Valhallalike paradise for warriors. Pele destroyed her foes with fire and lava. Her worship survives into the twentieth century, as evidenced by the many natives who admit to having seen her wandering near her volcanic home. Her sister was the Lady of Wild Things, **Hi'i-aka,** with whom she once warred.

Penthasilée: Amazon princess, daughter of Queen **Calpendre.** She fought twenty thousand warrior-maids, each mounted on a unicorn. A figure from medieval romance, named for **Penthesilea.** [Kleinbaum]

Penthesilea: "Compelling Men to Mourn." Daughter of **Orithia,** and coruler of **Amazonia** with her sister, the second **Hippolyte.** Elsewhere given as queen of the Amazons of Alope in Pontus, and having Thracian lineage. Although the long-lasting and widespread empire established by the Amazons had dwindled and collapsed in the wake of repeated Greek incursions during Penthesilea's mother's reign, the nation of Amazonia itself continued to thrive in peace, its soldiers still regarded the finest of the ancient world. The Argonauts passed the shores of Amazonia and pondered a new Greek campaign, then thought the better of it, seeing that the country lived in tranquillity.

Penthesilea was esteemed for her bravery, skills in weapons, and also for her wisdom, but as it was no longer an age of conquest, her strength was expended chiefly upon the hunt. During one such hunt, her own spear tragically killed her sister. Grief stricken and ashamed, she chose in expiation to set out upon what was to be the last important battle of the Amazons.

The ancient verse *Aethiopis* survives only in fragments. It tells how this Amazon queen temporarily liberated Troy. Quintus Smyrnus quotes Penthesilea saying, "Not in strength are we inferior to men; the same our eyes, our limbs the same; one common light we see, one air we breathe; nor different is the food we eat. What then denied to us hath heaven on man bestowed? O let us hasten to the glorious war!"

The aid of Penthesilea's Amazon nation may have been elicited by Hecuba, Queen of Troy, who, contrary to Homeric and Euripedian retellings long after the historic defeat, was the powerful ruler of Troy. (See **Myrene** and **Egee** for earlier connections between Troy and the Amazons of Africa. The African connection to Troy was far more important than any European connection, and Homer possibly copied the greater part of his double epic from the twelfth-century Egyptian poetess Phantasia, adapting it to Greek appetites.)

Achilles' retaking of the city marked the demise of the last stronghold of the Great Goddess that had been extant among the nations of Asia Minor and the Mediterranean since the days of the Mesopotamian settlements. It may also have marked the downfall of the last great societies governed and defended by women. Diodorus Siculus maintained that Penthesilea was the last queen of the Amazons, "a brave-spirited woman, after whom the nation grew weaker and weaker and at length wholly extinct, causing these later ages to look upon the old stories concerning the valiant acts of the Amazons to be mere fables." Pliny believed Penthesilea invented the battle ax, but, if so, it must have been of a form other than the already ancient **labrys.**

Penthesilea, daughter of Ares, killed many heroes outside the walls of Troy, including Machaon and Achilles himself. But Zeus brought Achilles back to life, and Penthesilea had to fight him again. When she was at last defeated by him, his grief was so great that he killed several of his own allies who had mutilated her dying body by gouging out her eyes, and chided Achilles' emotionalism. In a macabre version, he was so overcome by lust on seeing the beautiful Amazon dead at his feet that he raped her corpse.

Philippa of Hainault: (A.D. 1314?–1369) Queen of Edward III. In 1346, she led twelve thousand soldiers against invading Scots, capturing their king, David Bruce. She was a patroness of Chaucer and founded Queen's College. [Taylor, Hale, King]

Philippis: "Woman Who Loves Horses." Amazon brave slain by Heracles. It was the custom of the Amazons to attack a foe one-on-one. Even understanding that Heracles was little short of a god and utterly invulnerable, the braves set up a macabre rhythm of attack and die, attack and die. Philippis followed **Aëllo** and was second to die; **Prothoë** came next, then **Eriobea, Deianeira, Asteria, Marpe, Tecmessa,** and **Alcippe.** [Sobol]

Phoebe: Amazon spearwoman, named for the Titan Moon-goddess. She lived during the reign of **Hippolyte.** She fought shoulder to shoulder with two other spearwomen, **Celaeno** and **Eurybe.** They died together at the hands of Heracles.

Phoolan Devi: In the 1970s, a notorious bandit queen of central India terrorized the Chambal Valley. Phoolan Devi was believed responsible for more than sixty murders, yet she became a folk hero. At age twenty-six, she turned herself over to authorities with a formal surrender ceremony attended by five thousand cheering people who were delighted to find that Phoolan was a short, slender woman with long dark hair, flashing black eyes, a red shawl and headband, and police uniform. She was beautiful even when she was scowling and snarling at her admirers, strong looking even as she laid down her rifle and knelt to kiss the chief minister's feet in feudal obeisance.

Phung Thi Chinh: A supporter of the **Trung** sisters in the Vietnamese revolt against China in A.D. 39. Although advanced in pregnancy, Phung Thi Chinh unhesitantly joined the fray. When labor began, and her child was born, she paused long enough to strap the newborn to her back, and continued fighting. [Fraser]

Phyla: A Graecean athletic beauty of great height. She accompanied Pisistratus to Athens when he was seeking to reestablish his authority. She went in a war chariot, clad as **Athena.**

Physcoa: Heroine of ancient Elis. She was a priestess of the War-goddess **Orthia** and introduced the worship of Dionysus at Elis. She was honored during the **Heraean** (the women's Olympics) in the fifth century B.C.

Pierronne: The maid Pierronne fought in the ranks for the king of France, contemporary with **Joan of Arc,** who had inspired many such women to boldness. Like Joan, she felt herself to have been guided by voices, in this case by God himself, who appeared to her in robes of purple and white. And like Joan, the disapproving clergy saw to her downfall, and she was burned at the stake.

Pisto: A brave in the war of Heracles and Telamon against Queen **Andromache.** [Bothmer]

Pitana: Possibly named for a goddess of the pines, worshipped by the **Maenads.** Pitana was commander of ten thousand footsoldiers and one thousand cavalry, which was one-third of a larger army that set out successfully to expand the empire of the **Gorgons** during the reign of "swift-bounding **Myrene.**" The host descended upon cities "like wolves" and spread their empire into Egypt and Asia Minor and numerous islands of the Aegean. [Sobol]

Plater, Emilja: (A.D. 1806–1831) Emilja held **Joan of Arc** as her ideal while seeking independence for Poland. Daughter of Count Ksawery and Countess Anna Plater, she was singular in her desire to move amidst peasants and learn their ways and needs. In 1830, at the age of twenty-five, she organized her first detachment and led a series of successful battles against Russia. [Schmidt]

Podarge: "Speed," a **Harpie** of Greek myth.

Poena: Greek mythological goddess of punishment, attendant of **Nemesis.**

Pohaha: A Tewa Indian warrior of North America, "ha ha" because she laughed in battle, "Po" because she was so excited in battle it made her wet between the legs. In battle, she lifted her skirt up repeatedly to make sure the enemy knew a woman was killing them. [Niethammer]

Poker Alice: (A.D. 1851–1930) Cigar-chomping Wild West Amazon, Alice Ivers became the queen of the gamblers, eventually ran her own casino, and was not afraid to use her six-shooter.

Early in her career, she was gambling in Pecos with a dealer who repeatedly took cards from the bottom of the deck. She watched him and waited until there was enough money on the table to make trouble worthwhile. Then she wrapped one arm around the pot, drew her Colt revolver with the other hand, and said, "I don't mind a cheat, it's a *clumsy* cheat I can't stand." She took the five thousand dollars and had a week-long spending spree. [Richards, Horan]

Polemusa: One of **Penthesilea's** companions-at-arms.

Polly Ann: See **Connie Ann.**

Polyanitza: The Polyanitzi were Slavic Amazons remembered in folklore as the equals of or superior to men in all manner of heroic deeds, defeatable only by trickery and treachery. See also the Serbian **Veela.**

Poncet, Ducaud Laborde: At the Battle of Eylau, on February 8, 1807, she slew the Russian captain with her sword. At the Battle of Friedland, on June 14 of the same year, she received a deep saber wound at the thigh, and a bullet in the armpit. She bound her own wounds hastily and carried on, taking six prisoners. Napoleon is said to have taken off his own medal of the Legion of Honor and pinned it to her bosom. She dressed masculinely but was considered very beautiful. [Laffin]

Ponthiey, Adelaide: During the Crusades in the time of St. Louis, Adelaide was a famous adventurer who fought in the Holy Wars, becoming the subject of opera and epic romance.

Priénê: Commander of one thousand cavalry and ten thousand footsoldiers of the Libyan Amazons, one-third of a larger army over whom **Mitylenê** was general under Queen **Myrene.** They established a vast but short-lived empire. [Sobol]

Procris: "Preference," a consummate huntress who received from **Artemis** a hound that could outrun any prey, and a javelin that could never miss its mark. She gave them to Cephalus as dowry when they were wed. He was kidnapped by the Dawn-goddess **Eos,** who lusted after him because of his beauty, but he remained faithful to Procris, so that Eos freed him with her curse, and planted in Procris' heart the unjust fear that Cephalus was unfaithful. Procris tracked her husband in secret when he was alone hunting and he, perceiving movement in the brush and thinking it a rabbit, threw the magic javelin, killing her.

In a variant, Cephalus is unfaithful and Procris turns to King Minos for comfort, receiving from him the hound and javelin of Artemis. Afterward, she disguised herself as a handsome boy and traveled widely as a hunter. She later made up with her husband and gave these treasures to him.

Artemis, annoyed that her hound and spear so blithely changed hands, allowed the javelin to kill Procris. [Bulfinch, Graves]

Prothoë: "First in Might," an Amazon of **Hippolyte's** reign, slain by Heracles. She was also one of Kleist's Amazons in *Penthesilea*.

Pyrgomache: "Fiery Warrior." Amazon brave of the Attic War, known from an inscription on an **Amazonomachy.** [Bothmer]

Pythodoris: (fl. 50 B.C.) Daughter of Pythodorus of Tralles and warrior-wife of Polemon of Armenia. She reigned equally with Polemon and, after his death, ruled Armenia alone. She lived to old age and was a contemporary of Strabo of the Geographies. Strabo takes for granted that she was in some way related to the Amazons who still lingered in localized areas of Armenia. She conquered and ruled Colchis. Her capital for a time was Diospolis, which she had adorned and renamed Sebastê (Augusta) because Diospolis inappropriately referred to Zeus.

❖❖❖❖❖❖❖❖❖❖❖❖❖

Qáqon: See **Bowdash.**

Qedeshet or **Qadesh:** "Holy." Syrian War-goddess, an aspect of **Anath** or **Astarte.** She was also the Eye of Ra, and Mother of All Gods. She was associated with serpents and, like **Cybele,** with the lion. She is aggressively sexual, like **Eos.** [Hart]

Qin Jin: Or **Ch'iu Chin** (A.D. 1875–1907). The Heroine of Lake Chien, she was beheaded in 1907 after leading an antidynastic rising in Chekiang province.

Ch'iu Chin was a romantic who believed in the glamor of heroism as a revolutionary triggering device. Well aware of her country's long history of swordswomen, Ch'iu patterned her personal image upon an ancient heroic ethic. She was an equestrian. She wielded a sword, even into company that was not apt to appreciate oddity. She prided herself on a large wine-holding capacity. Part of her education was gained in Japan, where Marxism was popular among radical students. She participated in the Lower Yangtze revolutionary movement and various risings, and joined progressive, then revolutionary, organizations and secret societies and the Reconstruction Army.

Born to a somewhat influential family, her genius was quickly realized, for she was spoiled and indulged and given a pristine education. From readings in Chinese classics, history, and poetry, she quickly identified herself with the *yu-hsia,* or knights errant. Later, she would add to her self-image elements of Western tragic heroes such as the guillotined Madame Roland, Polish revolutionaries, the Russian populist Sophia Perovskaya, and, rather strangely, Napoleon.

She was a poet who saw herself in a tumultuous world of dragons, tigers, clouds, and raging seas, "where only the brave might prevail." The Chinese heroic tradition forever in mind, she took the personal title "Heroine of Lake Chin." She published radical treatises and led open rebellions. She was also cursed, or blessed, with a kind of madness, a sense of displacement in time. She was an egoist with messianic tendencies, melancholy and impatient in outlook.

Chin knowingly allowed herself to be captured by officials rankled by their repeated military losses to revolutionary societies. Her hasty execution did not entirely end her career. Public sentiment was in her favor; her bid for martyrdom was successful. Her death was no boon for the government.

Her house was restored for public viewing in 1979, having been severely damaged by the Red Guard during the Cultural Revolution. It is today part of a temple and museum complex in Shaoxing. [Rankin, Wolf]

R

◆◇◆◇◆◇◆◇◆◇◆◇◆◇◆

Radigunde: Amazon of Edmund Spenser's *The Faerie Queene.* The famous knights she defeated were sworn to subservience in her court, where they spun and carded and performed other feminine chores.

Rahab: "Violence." Semitic Dragon-goddess, known also as **Tiamat** and **Leviathan.** In William Blake's *Jerusalem* she is transformed into a Trinity-goddess and the Great Whore. She is frequently an angel of death.

Ralphson, Mary: Called "Trooper Mary," a Scotswoman of the 3rd Dragoons who fought at Fontenoy in A.D. 1745, beside her husband. She had five fingers and a thumb and lived to the age of 110. [Laffin]

Randalin: See **Aslog.**

Randgrith: "Shield-fierce," a **Valkyrie.**

Rangda: "Widow" or "Witch." Balinese goddess of death and destruction, with tangled black hair, long fingernails, pendulous breasts, hairy legs, long tongue, terrible fangs, and protruding eyes. With masks, dancers act out her myths at shrines throughout Bali. [Preston]

Rani of Jhansi: See **Lakshmi Bai.**

Ranthgrith: "Fierce Counsel," a **Valkyrie.**

Raven: Lesbian swordswoman of Samel R. Delaney's *Tales of Neveryon*

(1979), one of the very few swordswomen in heroic fantasy novels who genuinely seems to come from a matriarchal nation significantly different from our own patriarchal world. She expresses a worldview radically opposed to the, for her, alien attitudes she encounters in the male-dominated countries of her travels. She fights with a two-bladed sword.

Raviyoyla: One of the **Veela,** Serbian combinations of Greek huntress-nymph and Scandinavian **Valkyrie.** Veela were armed with bows and arrows and selected which heroes were to die.

The Veela Raviyoyla was the shield maiden or sister-god of Marko, Serbia's national folk hero. Whenever he was in a tight fix, so long as he did not war on Sundays, he could call upon Raviyoyla to appear and help him win his battles. But in her role as the chooser of the dead, she used her arrow to kill Marko's brother, and Marko leaped upon his fantastic steed to hunt Raviyoyla through the mountains and through the sky.

Raviyoyla could "leap the height of three spears and bound the length of four lances." But Marko threw his mallet and knocked her from the sky. Threatening her life, he forced her to restore his brother. This ability to restore life, as well as take it, shows the connection between the Veela and the ancient Earth- and Moon-goddesses of death *and* fecundity.

When Marko's last hour approached, it was his sister-god's duty to inform him of his selection. Marko was not ready to die and cursed her with his last breath. Sad but undaunted, she led his soul away. [Petrovitch]

Razia, Sultana: "Not one of my self-fulfilling sons is fit to rule this land," complained Sultan Iltutmish, second of the slave-monarchs of Delhi in the thirteenth century. "When I am dead, there is only my daughter to guide the state."

After her father's death in A.D. 1236, Razia inherited the throne of Delhi and quickly proved herself a benefactor to her country. She saw that highways and universities were built, wells dug, trade encouraged, and unjust taxes abolished, and she insisted that laws be applied equally to all faiths. This latter decree won her as many enemies as friends, so that she had to betimes ride out at the head of armies to quell religious rioting. For nearly four years, she knew only victory.

In a battle to hold the throne in October of 1240, Sultana Razia, the Moslem Warrior Queen, blazed across a gory field, slaying. Suddenly there was an arrow in her breast and she reined her horse aside. For Delhi's warrior-queen, the fighting was done. [Zakaria, Pool]

Read, Mary: (A.D. 1692?–1721) As a youth, Mary Read served as a page to a French lady in Bristol, England, having already spent her earliest childhood raised as a boy. When the French lady died, Mary fought as a mercenary for the duke of Marlborough in Flanders, first in the infantry, later in a regiment of horse, where she became an expert duelist. She married a comrade, and they operated an inn in Flanders called The Three Horse Shoes. Upon her husband's sudden death, Mary reverted to her old ways, shipping from Holland to the West Indies, where the ship was captured by Anne **Bonney's** pirates, whom Mary eagerly joined. Mary may have continued to pass as a young man for some while, though the stories are unreliable in this regard, and she does not really seem to have called herself "Mark" as some report it, but only Pirate Read. She once picked a quarrel with a man twice her size in order to save a naive "actor" cum navigator from being killed by the brute. First dueling with cutlass, she nimbly inflicted several wounds but received none. They then drew pistols and, in a smoky explosion, the giant was killed.

Pirate Read and Anne Bonney, together with Calico Jack Rackam and his "mate" Pierre the Pansy Pirate, attempted to retire to a peaceful home life, but fate wouldn't allow it. They returned to the sea at a time when most pirates were accepting amnesty and it was impossible to hold a competent crew.

They were eventually captured near Jamaica, where they were tried and sentenced to be hanged. Anne and Mary claimed to be pregnant in order to stall the hanging, and a doctor whom they had saved from the rack on a prison ship the year before returned the favor when called in to see if it was really possible they were pregnant, a life-saving lie that far too many reporters have since failed to see through. Mary died within the year in prison, but Anne may have survived. [Carlova, Myron, Croix]

The Red Maiden: A viking who, inspired by legends of the **Valkyries,** led raiders against the northern coast of Ireland. She is believed to have been the same **Rusla** mentioned in the Danish histories. [Saxo, Lederer]

Red Peony: A gangster-princess of cinema, comics, and fiction. Japanese gangster movies, or "yakuza-eiga," flourished in the 1960s, offering romantic portraits of society's outcasts, gamblers living by an older code in a world with fewer and fewer places for such remnants of an earlier Japan. The "good" gangster is often one who lives as a gambler and troubles only those people who are in his world and deserve to be troubled, otherwise keeping humbly to the shadows and self-effacingly steering clear of "decent" people. The "bad" gangster is a pimp or businessman using strong-arm tactics to rob and harm innocent people. The morality of the films is obviously suspicious, but, in the wake of the Pacific War, when Japan lost its "innocence" by losing its belief in the emperor as God, it was easy to romanticize the gangster world as a bastion of samurai ethos, devoted to custom, obeisance, and ritual.

One of the more winning clichés of the genre is that of the gambling princess, living as devoutly as any male counterpart by an ancient code of duty, humanity, and honor. She has her origin in part with the earlier dramatic figure of **Oroku** and the woman avengers of the Tokugawa period who were so highly romanticized in kabuki plays (see under **Hatsu-jo**). Many such heroines have fought across the screen with flashes of steel and streaks of blood, including the Dragon-Tattooed Lass, the blind swords-woman "Crimson Bat," Lady Snow Blood, Tiger Lily, Quick-Draw Okatsu, and the most popular of the type, the Red Peony Gambler played by Fuji Junko.

She took her name from the peony blossoms tattooed on her back. She was invincible in a sword fight, the choreography of which, in the final reel of each episode, embodies some of the most exciting action sequences ever filmed. Women who live as chivalrous gamblers are said to have "given up woman's happiness," i.e., marriage; hence, over and over again, Red Peony and other characters of her type walk alone into the moonset, toward the next adventure. But in the last Red Peony movie in 1972, Junko and her best-loved costar, Takakura Ken, are finally able to survive the ultimate battle and retire from the yakuza underworld. Red Peony gazes from the screen directly at the audience to say her good-byes and to thank all of us very, very much.

Red Sonja: Created by author Robert E. Howard in the pages of the 1930s pulp magazine *Weird Tales,* Red Sonja was one of a series of interesting swordswomen among Conan the Barbarian's sidekicks. The clichés of pulp fiction demanded that most "good" girls were passive and had blonde hair; most aggressive girls were whorish villains and had black hair; and most powerful girls had red hair but no freckles and carried swords. Pulp heroines **Jirel of Joiry** and the Red Peri adhered to this typical pattern. Robert Howard broke the stereotype with **Belêt,** a dark-haired Jewess pirate at whose feet Conan became a fawning admirer. Red Sonja remains his best known Amazon. She rose to fame long after Howard's death, when, in the 1970s and 1980s, she found her way into comic books, daily funnies, and cinema.

The Red Virgin: See Clémence Louise **Michel.**

Reginleif: "Strength-maiden," a **Valkyrie.**

Renée de Bourbon, the Pearl of Fontevrault: In A.D. 1477, she set out to complete the reform of a number of convents and monasteries. The reform of Fontevrault was the most difficult. After twelve years of struggle, Renée repaired to Paris and returned at the head of an army. The monks and nuns were soon scattered. Any who wished to return swore oaths of obedience to the abbess. Her admirable achievement is typical of many similar stories, as entrenched powers, even in "seclusion," do not often change their systems easily or peacefully. [J. Morris]

Renenutet: One of the Egyptian Cobra-goddesses (see **Hetep-Sekhus** and **Meretseger**). She defends pharaohs. The invincible flame leaps from her mouth. Her gaze vanquishes foes. But she is beneficial to crops and aids childbirth. [Hart]

Retz, Madame de: A noblewoman of seventeenth-century France who led an army against her own son.

Rhea: Earth-goddess of Crete, nearly interchangeable with the Phrygian **Cybele.** [Farnell]

Rhiannon: "Queen of the Demons," a Welsh Mare-goddess akin to **Macha, Hecate,** or **Freya.**

Rhodogune: (second century B.C.) Word of revolt came to Rhodogune, queen of ancient Parthia, while she was coming from her bath. She vowed that her hair would not be dressed until the revolt was put down. She went directly for her horse and rode to the head of her army. She directed a long, tedious war, not bathing or brushing her hair until she had won. For this exploit, she was thereafter depicted with disheveled hair.

Since ancient times ablusions were connected with numerous superstitions, beliefs, and religious activities. We must wonder at the possible original meaning of both **Semiramis** and Rhodogune going to battle straight from their baths, and wonder, too, if there is any possible connection between the myth of the **Medusa** and her snaky hair, and women warriors like Rhodogune who fought with hair disheveled. [Polyaenus]

Richilde: Wife of Bandonin VI of eleventh-century Flanders. She allied herself with Philip I of France and warred against her husband. [Gribble]

Rizpah: "Hot Stone." Widowed concubine of Saul. In 1021 B.C., King David turned over her sons to the Gibeonites to be hanged. Rizpah became the symbol of valorous motherhood by standing day and night beside the dangling corpses, armed with a branch, doing battle with vultures and hyenas, until David took pity and had the bodies buried with that of his dead friend and lover Jonathon.

Rochefoucalt, Mademoiselle de la: "She never missed an opportunity to be foremost in battle, and the last to retreat. As terrible during the contest, as generous and humane when it was over." She was the Amazon of the Vendeans, fighting against the Republicans after the murder of Louis XVI, while she was yet a teenager. "Sometimes repulsed, often conquering, Mademoiselle La Rochefoucault always fought undaunted." Her eloquent speeches carried her followers through unfortunate moments: "Follow me! Before the end of the day we either sing our victory on earth, or hymns with the saints in heaven!"

The day before she fell in battle, she had had a presentiment, and wrote to a woman friend in Paris: "God knows that I do not fear death. But I hear the trumpet sounding alarm, and I must bid my tender friend a long, I fear too long, adieu." [Starling]

Rodiani, Onorata: This fifteenth-century A.D. mural painter was painting the Tyrant of Cremona when she was interrupted by an "importunate nobleman." To save or to redeem her honor, Onorata drew forth her dagger and killed him. She then went underground, where she became captain of a band of professional soldiers, or *condotieri*. She died defending her birthplace of Castelleone in 1472. [Petersen]

Rodríquez, Dolores: A corporal in the 1st Regiment of Peruvian Sappers who at the age of eighteen fought against Spain. [Laffin]

Rorei: Daughter of Usber, one of the three Amazons of the Island of Britain, mentioned along with **Mederei Badellfawr** and **Llewei** in a manuscript dating to about A.D. 1400, the *Red Book of Hergest.*

Rosella: Queen of the Amazons in John Fletcher's *The Sea Voyage* (A.D. 1622), a poor variant of the tale of the Argonauts' landing at **Lemnos.** As in most such Restoration plays the women begin aggressively enough but become timid in the face of love.

Rose of Cimmaron: Oklahoma heroine, rode with the Doolin gang and participated in the last great gun battle between Doolin's outlaws and U.S. marshals. [Horan]

Rota: One of the Icelandic **Valkyries** who dispense victory and take the slain into Valhalla. She was also an **Asynjor,** attendant of **Freya.** In

Gylfaginning, she is said to ride with **Guth** and **Skuld.** Saxo Grammaticus, in his *History of the Danes,* calls her Rothi, *skaldmeyjar* or shield maiden to King Ingel. Ingel at one point is counseled, "Be sensible, king, and escape your barbarous wife, lest the she-wolf bear a litter like herself." [Davidson]

Rous, Lady: When Mary the First, eldest daughter of Henry VIII, became queen of England, she appointed numerous women to highly placed positions. One such was the Lady Rous. She was made a judge in Suffolk, and went girt with sword. [Hale]

Roxana: (d. 311 B.C.) Bactrian warrior-princess captured in battle by Alexander the Great in the war against Darius III. She and her sister **Statira** became his wives by treaty, a merely political arrangement that Roxana took rather seriously, as she later assassinated her sister. After the death of Alexander, she and her son, Alexander's only child, were imprisoned and ultimately put to death by Cassander.

Roxana: An earlier Roxana was one of the at least seven wives of Philip II, king of Macedonia, father of Alexander the Great. She, too, was a Bactrian princess, and with **Euridyce** (also called Audata) traveled with Philip when they joined Perdiccas on an expedition into Egypt, having with them "a force that could not be resisted in the open field." They were called "the three kings."

Running Eagle: A Blackfoot Indian girl named Brown Weasel begged her father to give her bow and arrows and let her hunt with her brothers. Against his wives' wishes, he even permitted Brown Weasel to accompany him on the honored buffalo hunts. It was on one such hunt that they were attacked by an enemy war party, and Brown Weasel's father had his horse shot out from under him. Braving enemy fire, Brown Weasel rode back to save her father. It was her first act of valor, but not her last.

Some members of the tribe doubted a woman should go to war, but those who rode beside her were less and less hesitant. On her first raid, she captured many horses and killed one enemy; a warrior who had ridden with her gave her the gift of a rawhide shield to show his respect. On her second raid, that shield stopped two arrows that would have taken her through the chest. During that raid, six hundred horses were taken, many Crow Indians were killed, and only one of their own party was lost.

At a medicine lodge meeting, Brown Weasel joined the other warriors in telling of their deeds. Women had told their war tales before, but Brown Weasel's exploits were especially bold and the people applauded, whooped, and beat their drums when she was finished speaking. Then the chief of the tribe did a rare thing. He rewarded the woman warrior with a new name. Thenceforth, she would be called Running Eagle, a special name reserved for the greatest warriors of the tribe's oral history.

It was a big responsibility to live up to that name. Running Eagle swore herself to the Sun-god and never married. Eventually, she became the leader of war parties. Many years later, on a revenge raid against the Flathead, a very large and messy battle was to mark the end of her career. After the fighting was done, Running Eagle's body was found lying between two slain enemies who had attacked in tandem and died for their success. Running Eagle's exploits are still told among the Blackfoot people. [Hungry Wolf]

Rusla or **Rusila:** "Red." A Danish battle-maiden, she staged a coup to capture the throne of Norway from her brother Thrond, and gained sovereignty. Saxo Grammaticus reports that as a viking with several famous captains under her command, Rusla terrorized the Irish coast. The Irish remember her as Ingean Ruadh, **"The Red Maiden,"** described in *The War of the Gaedhil with the Gaill.* Her constant companion was the shield maiden **Stikla.** Such shield maidens exist throughout Scandinavian history and folklore, usually as the companions of men, and have been mythologized as **Valkyries.** They were inevitably comrade-lovers. **Alfhild** similarly went a-viking with her shield maiden **Groa.**

For a time, Rusla ruled the people of Telemark, whom she had conquered. She warred against Iceland and also sought sovereignty over the Danes. "Seized with overweening hopes," she waged a losing sea battle against the king of Denmark. Escaping with very few ships, she encountered the deposed King Thrond, and routed him anew, but was later killed by her brother's champion, Harold, who had also slain **Hild,** being, apparently, one of the few men capable of defeating such women. Her rovers in Ireland returned to try for her revenge.

Saxo, who tells of a great many Norse and Danish fighting women, says of them, "There were once women among the Danes who dressed as men and devoted every waking moment to the pursuit of war. Those who had force of character or were tall and comely were especially apt to enter into such a life."

Ruta: A **Valkyrie** who attended the last battle of King Hrolf Kraki and his warriors. [Davidson]

Ruz, Helen: A member of the Voluntary Ukraine Legion in World War I.

The legion fought at the front, and Corporal Ruz went through the worst of it in the Carpathian Mountains and the whole of the Galician campaigns. She saw her father, two brothers, and fiancé fall in battle. She won two medals but after being transferred to the Uhlans had two ribs broken by a piece of shrapnel. She was nineteen years old. [Gribble]

S

❖◇❖◇❖◇❖◇❖◇❖◇❖◇❖

Sadie the Goat: To the roll call of such famous pirates Anne **Bonney,** Madame **Ching,** and Grace **O'Malley** should be added that of Sadie the Goat, a gangland Amazon of old New York. A group of Hudson River bandits, with only a couple leaky rowboats, were doing rather poorly until the spring of A.D. 1869, when Sadie arrived on the scene. She earned her name from the habit of unexpectedly butting strangers in the stomach, whereupon her male companion slugged the victim unconscious and they robbed him at their leisure. She was a favorite of the Fourth Ward gangs until she was badly defeated in an encounter with **Gallus Mag.** Mag enjoyed biting off the ear of her victims, and Sadie was unable to face her old friends while one of her own ears was in a pickle jar behind the counter of the old Hole-in-the-Wall tavern.

Under her leadership, the Hudson Bay pirates stole an excellent sailing sloop, hoisted a Jolly Roger, and roared up and down the Harlem and Hudson rivers to Poughkeepsie and beyond, robbing farmhouses and riverside mansions, Sadie proudly pacing the deck. They were not above holding men, women, or children for ransom. Any gang member who disobeyed her edicts Sadie made walk the plank.

They were doing rather excellently, fencing all manner of goods in the pawnshops of the slums of New York, until one too many murders caused the farmers to unite. Too often the pirates were greeted with musket and pistol fire and, by the end of their first summer, they were forced to abandon

228 JESSICA AMANDA SALMONSON

their by then well-known sloop. Sadie the Goat returned with her loot to the Fourth Ward, the acknowledged "queen of the waterfront," and even Gallus Mag dipped into the pickle jar to return the only female ear in her collection. Sadie had her ear enclosed in a locket and wore it on a chain. [Asbury]

Sagana: (first century A.D.) A priestess of **Hecate** in a violent Roman cult of lesbian sorceresses maligned by Horace for their ritual maiming of youths. Her most famous follower was **Candidia.** Horace also thinks ill of the violent bacchante **Chloris,** requesting that she cease to "sport among damsels," but **Evoë,** an equally violent bacchante who dominates men, Horace praises.

Saint-Balmont, Madame de: She "was never without a sword at her side, and was reputed to have taken or killed more than four hundred men," according to Barbe de Ernecourt (born A.D. 1608) in *Memoires de l'abbe Arnauld* (Michaud et Pougoulat Collection). The same author mentions Mlle. Liance, who, insulted by one Benserade, delivered "a great blow to the chest with her fist," then drew her sword to evict him from her home, threatening to "run my poniard into you." [Beaumont]

Salani: A mortal avatar of the Indian Mother-goddess "born in the family of the Maravar who ever had bows in their hands," a heroine of the *Lay of the Ankle Bracelet.* See also **Kannagi.** [Berkson]

Salaym Bint Malhan: A war leader who "with an armoury of swords and daggers strapped round her pregnant belly fought in the ranks of Muhammad and his followers." [Miles]

Samois, Mme. de: Tallemant des Réaux in *Historiette 460: Femmes vaillantes* states that Mme. de Samois "was fain to fight a duel in every field corner." In *The Story of O,* her name is given to a lesbian **dominatrix,** who in turn gave her name to a San Francisco organization of lesbian sado-masochists, whose best-known spokeswoman was Pat Califia, who took her name from the black Amazon of Spanish medieval romance. See **Juliette.**

Sampson, Deborah: (A.D. 1760–1799) Under the assumed name of Robert Shurheff, she served the 4th Massachusetts Regiment during the American Revolution, fighting British Tories and Indians. She was twice wounded, by saber in a skirmish near Tarrytown, New York, and a few weeks later by musketball in a fight near East Chester, which she privately excised from her groin since she dared not let a surgeon look at her. After the war, patriot Paul Revere intervened in her behalf, assuring her a reasonable war pension.

On April 10, 1944, a World War II liberty ship was christened *Deborah Sampson Gannett* in her honor. [Meyer, Evans, Wright]

Samsi: Possibly the successor of **Zabibi**. Samsi flourished as an Arabian warrior-queen about 720 B.C. [Fraser]

Sandes, Flora: (A.D. 1876–1956) An Englishwoman of Irish descent who in her forties fought in the trenches with the Serbian Army in World War I. Colonel Militch made her a soldier, since she wished it, and he felt she would be "as effective a soldier as the Serbian peasant women" already in the ranks. Despite weeks of endless rain, freezing nights, typhus, and marginal provisions, not to mention the murderous Bulgarians harrying the army from hill to hill, Flora felt a great romance for camp life. She became known as "Nashi Engleskinja" ("Our Englishwoman"), loved first as a sort of mascot, then as a respected comrade. In the midst of action, armed with pistol and rifle, she noted, "Bullets came singing round one's head directly one stood up, but they did not seem awfully good shots." In quieter moments, she played a battered violin for the Serbs.

She rose to the rank of corporal in charge of a platoon. In August 1916, she was severely injured by a grenade. Her right arm and leg smashed, she was blinded by near unconsciousness. She knew her platoon was in retreat. "I felt a tail of an overcoat sweep across my face," she said in a letter. "Instinctively I clutched it with my left hand, and was dragged two or three yards. The Lieutenant who wore it told me later that he felt every button tear off, but had not the least idea what was dragging behind him."

Hospitalized in Solinka (with a peasant woman called Milunka, a Serbian sergeant who had also taken wounds), she received from an aide to the prince regent the Kara George Star—pinned to her pajamas. It was the most coveted decoration of the Serbs and with it came promotion to the rank of sergeant major. After convalescing, Flora was able to return to the front. [Mitchell, Macksey, Sandes, Hirshfeld, Burgess]

Sappho: (fl. 600 B.C.) The great poetess was also an athlete and wrote poetry for women who were athletes, physical sports being an important aspect of the lives of her colony of women:

> I taught poetry to Hero
> a girl athlete
> from the Island of Gyra.

She was reared in the city of Mitylene, named for a warrior-queen of the **Gorgons.** Sappho was a conspirator against the Tyrants of Lesbos, resulting in her exile to Sicily. [Weigall]

Sarka: An ancient Czech Amazon who led a company of Teutonic knights. A district in present-day Czechoslovakia is named for her. She is celebrated, along with **Libussa,** in Smetana's tone poem "Ma Vlast," as they are in the operas *Libussa* and *Sarka.*

Sasaraye: (twelfth century A.D.) Mochimitsu's mistress, who accompanied him in battle. She is sometimes portrayed in Japanese block prints as fighting with **naginata** on a sinking ship in the Taira wars.

Scanagatti, Louisa: Prussian infantry lieutenant in the Napoleonic Wars. [Laffin]

Scáthach: A Celtic Amazon contemporary with **Aife** and **Medb,** "the greatest warrior and teacher of warriors." Scáthach operated a military school on Skye, south of the Isle of Ornsay, whereon rose her Dunscaith Castle, an impregnable fortress, the gate of which was guarded by her daughter **Uathach.** There, she trained the most famous heroes of the Celtic heroic age. Among her specialties were pole vaulting (so that only her graduates could effectively assault forts), underwater fighting, and combat with a barbed harpoon, the *gáe bolg,* invented by herself and which was thrown with the foot. She is also described as a prophet, sage, and poet; works survive that are attributed to her. Her name means "Shadow," suggesting some connection with the underworld, à la **Hecate** and the **Valkyries.** Some scholars believe her legend to be evidence of women's military academies having once existed among the Celts. [Chadwick, Hyde, Goodrich, Markale, Davidson]

Scenmed: In the Celtic heroic age, she was sister of Forgall, who was slain by Fionn Mac Cumhail. Scenmed raised an army and pursued the Ulster champion to avenge her brother, but was slain in the ensuing battle. [Ellis]

Schellinck, Marie: (A.D. 1771–1859) Heroine of the Napoleonic Wars. Belgian by birth, she fought for France in no less than twelve campaigns. She was wounded at Jemmappes, Austerlitz, and Jena, and received the red ribbon of the French Legion of Honor. She retired to her native Ghent, on pension, in 1808. Other Legion of Honor Amazons include Virginie **Ghesquière** and Angélique **Brûlon.**

Scholtz-Klink, Gertrud: (b. A.D. 1902) Nazi leader. Toward the end of World War II, with so many German youths dead, Scholtz-Klink began to form battalions of women to carry on the final defense of the crumbling Reich.

Scyleia: Amazon brave in the war of Heracles and Telamon against Queen **Andromache.** [Bothmer]

Scylla and **Charybdis:** Destructive Sea-goddesses. Charybdis, whose name means "Sucks Down," was a personification of a whirlpool deadly to ships. Her sister was Scylla at the Straits of Messina, whom Charybdis resembled in once having been a beautiful woman. Charybdis had been thrown into the sea and transformed into a monster because of cattle rustling. Scylla, "She Who Rends," manifested herself as a giant squid, or as a serpent with many doglike heads (her name is sometimes translated "puppy," and she is related to the dog-headed **Hecate**). She snatched men from ships and ate them.

Scylla: Another of several mythological women named Scylla was a worshipper of **Galatea,** an immortal sea nymph whose votaries were akin to the huntresses of **Artemis.** Scylla fled to Galatea's grotto, pursued by a brute, and Galatea counseled her to war against ungentle men. [Graves, Bulfinch, Godophin]

Seelye, Sarah Emma: See Sarah **Edmonds.**

Seh-Dong-Hong-Beh: Warrior of the **Dahomey Amazons.** She was famous well beyond her country, serving in the time of King Gezo. In A.D. 1851, she led six thousand women against the Egba fortress of Abeokuta. Before the attack, she stepped to the front of the combined regiments, her body glistening with oil. She held up her spear and called the attack. Only 1,200 of the Amazons survived the extended battle, the Egba having European cannons. [Laffin]

Sekhmet: Egyptian goddess of destruction, personification of heat, fire, and sun, with the head of a lioness, depicted as wading in blood. In one myth, she strives with **Hathor** to annihilate humankind, while in others both goddesses are identified as one, Hathor-Sekhmet. She was worshipped also in Europe and Asia Minor, where her cults overlapped those of **Cybele,** whom she greatly resembles. Heracles' wearing of the skin of the Nemean lion—born of the sexual ogress **Echidne**—represents his war against this universal Lion-goddess. [Edwardes, Campbell]

Sela: Scandinavian woman warrior mentioned by Saxo Grammaticus as the sister of Koller and foe of Orvendil, "a warring amazon and accomplished pirate."

Selene: Moon-goddess, sister of Helios, sometimes treated as an aspect of **Artemis,** sister of Apollo. Selene of the Sky, Artemis of the Earth, and **Hecate** of the Underworld became a device of later poets, reforming the earliest goddess trinities. She was worshipped especially in Iberia, where each year holy madmen, in violent frenzies, were anointed and slain for the goddess, often by means of a mallet to the head. Where the victim fell, auguries were derived from his position. [Strabo]

Selene of Egypt: See **Cleopatra V.**

Semele: A violent Moon-goddess worshipped in Athens on the Festival of the Wild Woman, during which a bull symbolizing her son Dionysus was cut into nine pieces, the number nine being sacred to Semele. One piece was burned as offering, the rest eaten raw. Her worship survived into medieval times, when nine Moon-priestesses killed the acolyte of St. Samson of Doi, and ate him (see also the **Nine Witches of Glaucester**). Semele was the granddaughter of **Hera** and mother of the War-god Ares.

Semele is the darkest aspect of Persephone and is called also Thyone, the "Raging Queen." Significantly, she died in childbirth, and her son restored her to life—a reversal of the more common order of Mother-goddesses being the life takers, then life givers—showing Dionyses to be an intermediary deity bridging the gap between matristic and patriarchal government and worship. [Graves]

Semiramis: Popular name of Queen Sammuramat of ninth-century Assyria, about whom little has been said that rigid scholars trust, although a wealth of information survives from Greek and medieval authors. "With her great courage she feared no pain and was frightened by no danger, and so bravely exposed herself to every peril and vanquished all her enemies from the countries she had conquered," wrote Christine de Pizan in the thirteenth century. Polyaenus tells us that when she was informed of a Siracian revolt while in her bath, she didn't even wait for her sandals, but took immediately to the fields. The revolt was quickly settled. She eventually extended the boundaries of landlocked Assyria to four distant seas. She conquered Babylonia and raised a memorial to her success, the famed Hanging Gardens, one of the Seven Wonders of the World. When Alexander later repeated the long march to Babylonia, he was criticized for merely trying to outperform Semiramis, whose march began with 100,000 soldiers and ended successfully with one-fifth still standing.

An early conquest was of Bactria, which held against her husband's siege until Semiramis arrived to subjugate the country. A distinguished warrior, she conquered her neighbor, then Ethiopia, and also repulsed the armies of India. According to Ctesias, she led at a time as many as 300,000 foot-soldiers, 5,000 horses, plus cameleers and war charioteers.

Upon a pillar which once supported a bronze statue of Semiramis, armed with sword, was engraved one of her speeches:

> Nature made me a woman yet I have raised myself to rival the greatest men. I swayed the scepter of Ninos; I extended my dominions to the river Hinamemes Eastward; to the Southward to the land of Frankincense and Myrrh; Northward to Saccae and the Scythians. No Assyrian before me had seen an ocean, but I have seen four. I have built dams and fertilized the barren land with my rivers. I have built impregnable walls and roads to far places and with iron cut passages through mountains where previously even wild animals could not pass. Various as were my deeds, I have yet found leisure hours to indulge myself with friends.

She was worshipped, after death, as an avatar of **Astarte.**

Sempronia: A revolutionary and agitator of Rome in the third century B.C. She "committed many crimes that showed her to have the reckless daring of a man." Educated in Greek and Latin, a dancer, a musician, and a sensual-ist, "of ready wit and considerable charm," she was nonetheless a sus-pected murderess, a perjurer, and a participant in the conspiracy led by Catiline. [Lefkowitz, Assa]

Sena: "Army," War-goddess of antique India, worshipped by the Amazons of the Gulf of Amisenus. One of their settlements was supposed to have been called Amastris (meaning "**Uma's** women"), situated on the Black Sea. Edward Pocoke sees this as incontrovertible evidence that the Ama-zons were of Indic origin.

Senesh, Hannah: (A.D. 1921–1944) Hungarian Jew who in her late teens fought the rise of fascism in Europe. During World War II, she joined a commando unit dedicated to bringing Jews out from occupied territories.

In 1944, she parachuted into Yugoslavia and made it to Hungary, but was captured, tortured, and executed by the Nazis.

Serket or **Selkis:** Scorpion-goddess of the Egyptian underworld. She battled the dragon-snake Apophis and tied him in a knot. She is sometimes "the Divine Mother," armed with knives, having a lion's head like **Sekhmet,** but with an additional crocodile head projecting from her back. Scorpions and serpents are her soldiers. She cures sickness and negates venom, hence is patroness of physicians. [Hart]

Sforza, Caterina: (A.D. 1463–1509) Famed for her beauty and her military prowess, Caterina "relished military activity as she had once relished hunting." In 1500, she rode into battle even when she was seven months pregnant. "Cruel and tough, she hated her husband, yet fought for him and defended his city, Forlì, with fanatic courage. Though in the end she was vanquished, all Italy admired her." She was the spiritual godmother of the queen in the game of chess, which acquired its supremacy over the king late in the fifteenth century. [Marek, Breisach, Hale, Fraser]

Sforza, Christierna: (d. A.D. 1590) Wife of Francesco Sforza, duke of Milan, and daughter of Christian II, king of Denmark. She effectively defended a small state from Henry II of France.

Shakhovskaya, Princess Eugenie M.: The first woman to become a military air pilot, flying reconnaissance for the tsar in 1914. During the Russian Revolution, she was a member of the secret police and hunted down members of her own aristocracy. She was also chief executioner of Kiev. [Robertson, Macksey]

Shapsh: Canaanite Sun-goddess, **Anath's** ally in battle. [Kramer]

She: See **Mujaji.**

Sheena, Queen of the Jungle: A female Tarzan who debuted in 1938 in a comic book series that lasted until the 1950s, when the character was adapted to television and played by the strapping beauty Irish McCullough. Her success birthed many imitators until, by the late 1940s, the comic book racks had several jungle Amazons clad in skins of leopard, tiger, panther, or zebra, swinging through the trees to save wildlife or their moderately competent boyfriends, such as Sheena's milquetoast Bob. Similar jungle heroines were Princess Pantha, Zegra, Judy of the Jungle, Rulah, Tiger Girl, and Camilla, Queen of the Jungle. A come-lately entry was Rima the Jungle Girl of the 1970s.

Shen Yün-ying: (1624–1661) One of the "demonic viragos" of the Ming Dynasty. She led her dead father's troops in battles to defend her city, obtaining victory and military fame. [Wolf]

Shitala: "The Cool One." A beautiful maiden, Bengal goddess of plague, especially small pox, who "vacillates between rage and mercy." She lives independent of any god. Her companions include the triple-headed Fever-demon Jvarasura and her shadowy serving woman Raktavati ("Blood"). A supernatural tiger also serves her. She is worshipped alongside the Bengali Snake-goddess **Manasa** and the Moslem Cholera-goddess Olabibi. Shitala rides to war astride a monstrous ass. She conquered the country of Virata and became the Healing-goddess when its citizens bowed to her. [Preston]

Shizuka Gozen: (fl. A.D. 1185) A Japanese heroine contemporary to **Tomoe Gozen.** She is often portrayed in classical art in the costume of male-impersonating *shirabyoshi* dancers, complete with long sword. She was the mistress of Yoshitsune, Japan's great national hero, and accompanied him into battle armed with **naginata.** She participated in the defense of Horikawa palace in 1185. "Gozen" is a title of high respect given to many martial women.

Sichelgaita: A medieval Teutonic princess of the Lombards who lived up to her race's ancient tradition of women's mightiness (see **Gambara**). "A true **Valkyrie,** tall, imposing, and muscular," she customarily went into battle with her husband, soldier of fortune Robert Guiscard. Byzantine historian Anna Comnena described her in *The Alexiad* as "dressed in full armor, a fearsome sight." When enemy soldiers fled the sight of her, she cried out, "How far will ye flee? Stand, and quit you like men!" They would not, so, taking her long spear, she galloped after them, forcing the confrontation. Her husband died in A.D. 1085. She remained politically influential for her remaining five years. [Gies, Davidson]

Sigrdrifa: "Giver of Victory." A **Valkyrie** and holder of secret knowledge (witchcraft). She killed Hjalmgunna, though Odin intended him to live, and as a result was afterward slain in her sleep. She was reborn as **Brynhild.** [Davidson]

Sigrlinn: "Victorious." A **Valkyrie,** daughter of King Svafner, perhaps an alternate name for **Svava.**

Sigrun: A **Valkyrie** and daughter of King Hogni. Her name was a rune for victory. She was a later incarnation of **Svava.** Sigrun married Helgi the Hunding-Slayer, a later incarnation of King Helgi. [Davidson]

Sigurana, Catherine: "A patriotic virago," in A.D. 1517 she repulsed Barbarossa from the citadel of Nice. [Rothery]

Sinopa: A warrior-squaw of Blackfoot folklore. She and her brothers and sisters battled **Bearskin-woman.** [Spencer]

Skadi: In ancient regions of Norway, she was worshipped as the goddess of the chase, equivalent to **Artemis.** Her name contributed to the name of "Scandinavia," just as **Europa** and **Asia** gave their names to entire continents.

Snorri Sturleson wrote that after her father was slain, Skadi sought revenge. "She took his helmet, his coat of mail, and all his battle armor," and marched against her foe, a class of deities called Ases. They soon sued for peace, and, after Odin made Skadi laugh by tying his beard to his testicles, she agreed to a marriage-truce. She became the wife of the Sea-god Njördr, but they were not comfortable together, because Njördr feared Skadi's wolves of the mountains, while she disliked the shrill cries of his birds of the sea. They soon divorced. [Saxo, Dumézil]

Skeggjold: "Ax," a **Valkyrie** of *Grimulsmal.*

Skíalf: Queen of ancient Sweden, she was a priestess of **Freya,** wearing for her helm the image of a boar, one of the symbols of her goddess. Skíalf sacrificed her king, Agni, in a ritualistic manner to Freya.

Skogul: Although her name has sometimes been translated "Spear Point," its more likely meaning is "High-Towering" or "Lofty" from the same word for "Mountain," suggesting that she was a giantess as well as a **Valkyrie.**

The giantesses of Norse mythology are as numerous as the Valkyries but only rarely are one and the same. **Brynhild** told a giantess, on her descent to Hel, "I fought alongside heroes; of us both, I am the better, whereas your kind are uncouth to humankind." The passage suggests a degree of antipathy between the classes of beings, despite the fact that a few of the Valkyries as well as some of the **Asynjor** were giantesses, Skogul being but one example. [Davidson]

Skuld: One of the three Norns (Fates) who was also a **Valkyrie** and rode with them to battles. [Davidson]

Smirnow, Zoya: Survivor of an unmounted corp of twelve Russian girls, some of them as young as fourteen years of age. They disguised themselves as boys and set out together to join the army. They fought in Galacia and the Carpathians in World War I. When the first of their number was killed, the youngest girls cried, but they killed many of the enemy. [Hirshfeld]

Snell, Hannah: (A.D. 1723–1792) Going in search of her lost husband, she joined the Frazer Marines and embarked for the attack on Pondicherry in 1748. She was wounded eleven times in the leg and once in the groin, removing the bullet from her groin secretly so that the surgeons could not learn her sex. She later saw service on a man-of-war. "She was at Carlisle at the time of the Young Pretender's invasion, and was sent to India, where she distinguished herself in action." She afterward made enough money from her autobiography and stage appearances to open an inn, which she called The Woman Warrior. [Macksey, Miles, Gribble]

Solkalski, Annie: A captain's widow who kept thirteen hunting dogs, she could outride the average cavalryman and was a sure-shot with revolvers (one strapped to each hip) and a crack markswoman with a rifle. Annie wore wolf-skin clothing, wolves' tails dangling from her skirt hem and hat. General Sherman met her for the first time at Fort Kearney, Wyoming. When her horse galloped before him on the parade ground, he took one look at the rider and asked, "What the devil of a creature is that? Wild woman, Pawnee, Sioux, or what?" a query that incidentally reveals Sherman's knowledge of fighting women among the Pawnee and Sioux.

Sono-jo and **Kiku-jo:** Warrior daughters of Yoshioka Ichimisai, sometimes identified as his daughter and wife. In a famous story and play, they avenged Yoshioka's murder. A block print shows them with chain weapons and **naginata** in an arranged duel between them and the famous warrior Kyogoku Takumi.

Sonza, Doña Eustaquia de: A Peruvian Amazon who, together with her lover Doña Ana, had numerous adventures in the mid-1600s, recorded in the million-word *Historia de la Villa Imperial de Potosí* by Bartolomé Arzans de Orsúa y Vela, who died in 1736. He prefaced his remarkable chronicle of "The Adventures of the Warrior Maidens" with these words:

> Whoever thinks that it is not possible for a woman to succeed in whatever she attempts is mistaken, for many women surpass men in valor, in the use of arms, and in knowledge. In use of arms there have been three Corinnes, two Aspasias, a Hortensia, a Sappho, a Zenobia, a Cornelia, and a Praxilla, not to mention others such as Arete, Proba, Eudocia, Istrina, and Cassandra; and in valor a Penthasilée, an Artemisia, a Cleopatra, and the Castilian queen Isabella the Catholic, heroic among famous women and a singular miracle of strength. No one need be astonished by such excellence in women.

Arzans saw a portrait of the two women, painted in their later years, in the full dress of *caballeros,* a sight he thought exceedingly handsome and erotic. See Doña Ana Lezama de **Urinza** for a synopsis of this couple's career—then try to follow Arzans's advice not to be astonished.

South American Amazons: See **Gaboimilla.**

Squaw Sachem: See **Weetamoo.**

Stanga, Luzia: Bishop Bandello of Agen in the mid–sixteenth century reported that a very noble woman, Luzia Stanga, was a famed *cavalieressa* (lady cavalier), who "with sword in hand equals many brave men." Bandello told also of a gardener's daughter who with sword defended her unarmed father from two *shirri* (police). [Beaumont]

Stark, Cordelia: Eldest daughter of a wealthy farmer who disguised herself as a young man and set off to several years of seafaring adventure. "In my vagrant wanderings, I have become thoroughly acquainted with mankind and their various passions," she reported in her self-published memoir *The Female Wanderer; An Interesting Story, Founded on Fact* (A.D. 1824).

Starr, Belle: (A.D. 1848–1889) Belle is a much maligned figure of history, who even the greatly legended **Calamity Jane** thought of as a bad egg. Belle was shot in the back and killed after a successful career of holdups, rustling, and inevitable bloodshed. Originally Myra Belle Shirley, she was a guerrilla fighter in the Civil War. After the war, guerrilla groups were posted as outlaws and not permitted to surrender as soldiers of a defeated army. They were forced into the position of fugitives, or Belle's history might have taken a totally different road. Romantics would have us believe an affair with outlaw Cole Younger turned Belle to crime, but it was the unreasonable decision of the conquering Union Army that sent many a rebel west and not home. [Reiter, Aikman]

Statira: (d. 331 B.C.) Warrior daughter of Darius, king of Persia. She was captured in battle by Alexander the Great. He took her, along with her sister **Roxana,** as a treaty-wife, a mere formality of Alexander's empire building, as he was generally disinterested in his wives. Statira was soon after assassinated by Roxana, who hoped to prevent anyone but herself from providing Alexander with heir.

Stikla: She and **Rusla** fought the king of the Thronds and would have defeated him but that the famed warrior Olaf arrived to repulse the attack. Sticklastad on Troudheimsfjord was named for her. [Saxo]

Stratonice: (fl. 239 B.C.) Sister of Antiochus II, wife of Demetrius II of Macedon, whom she divorced. Grace Macurdy is of the opinion that she had the same character as the earliest Macedonian queens, **Olympias** and Audata-**Eurydice**, but that the times were not quite as suited to her actions. She was of Epirote stock, even as Olympias herself. When Antiochus II Theos was driven from Syria by Seleucus II, he scurried to Stratonice and begged that she avenge him. In 227 B.C., she set out for Syria and started a rebellion, forcing Seleucus out of Antioch. When he later recaptured the city, Stratonice was already on her way to Seleuceia, planning to leave Syria with her navy. But a dream encouraged her to dawdle at Seleuceia. She was captured and slain. [Cook]

Suárez, Inez: In A.D. 1537, Inez Suárez voyaged to the New World and settled in Peru. She became mistress to Pedro de Valdivia, conquistador of Chile, and rode at his side at the head of the armies that conquered the interior. Later in beleaguered Santiago, she took up weapons against the Araucanian Indians. It was typical that Spanish wives and mistresses accompanied their men to South America and many of them became fighters. But Inez Suárez stands out as exceptional of an exceptional lot, "enjoying the esteem of the conquistadors." [Shepherd]

Sugala: Twelfth-century warrior and queen of Ruhuna on the island of Sri Lanka. "At times she was the glorious victor, triumphantly riding over the flowing stream of white 'parada' laid out on the roadways in her honor." When she suffered setbacks, she and her troops withdrew into the hills of eastern Sri Lanka, where she built a series of frontier forts. For ten years, she held out against a southern king, her nephew. "She refused to submit to his power and determined to overthrow the reign he had established on the land." She became renowned as "Sugala the rebel queen fearless, undaunted, incredibly heroic, brave, willing to die gloriously for the cause she believed in." [Seneviratne]

Svanhild: "Swan-Maid Warrior." A **Valkyrie** from the Eddic poem *Völundarkvitha*. An old German romance also mentions her as the daughter of **Gudrun** and Sigurd. "On a false charge against her womanly honor, she was condemned to be trampled to death by the hoofs of wild horses. But when she looked up at them, the horses dared not tread upon her." [Shoenfeld]

Svanhvita: One of Saxo's **Valkyries.** She could take the form of a raven. [Davidson]

Svava: Fairest of the **Valkyries,** she guarded King Helgi against malignant powers, and became his wife. She said, "Swords I know. There is Praise in a hilt, Power in the blade, Awe in the edge." She was reborn as **Sigrun,** the warrior-princess who married a later Helgi. She was again reborn as **Kara.** [Davidson]

Swaminathan, Colonel Lakshmi: Led the Rani Jhansi Regiment of the Indian National Army against the British during World War II in Burma. She was from Kerala State, which has had a long history of fighting women, praised in ancient songs ("Vadakkan Pattukal: Songs from the North"), and reflected in the weapons art of Theyyam, which in Malabar is practiced by women and men alike. The matrilineal Nayars of southern India also maintained a tradition of women's martial readiness and had a small standing army of Amazons, which in their long history had never known defeat until confronted by British guns.

Synoppe: Daughter of the great conqueror **Marpesia** and queen of **Amazonia** after her. She cared only for martial enterprise and could sate her pleasure only by conquering other lands. She founded a city on the Euxine (Black Sea) named for herself. She continued **Orithia's** revenge against the barbarians who slew her mother. [Pizan, Bennett]

Syrinx: "Reed." A huntress devoted to **Artemis.** "You would have thought it was **Diana** herself in her hunting dress, only that her bow was of horn and Diana's of silver." To evade the amorous embrace of Pan, she begged the naiads save her, and was transformed into water reeds. Pan made his flute from such reeds, in honor of the huntress. In an almost identical legend, the huntress Pitys ("Fir") is transformed into a tree to escape Pan. [Bulfinch]

T

◆◇◆◇◆◇◆◇◆◇◆◇◆◇◆

Tachibana Hime: (fl. A.D. 300) Wife of Prince Yamato, she was a **naginata** practitioner who accompanied the ancient hero Yamatodate on many of his campaigns. She drowned herself to appease the waves that were destroying their boat. In an *ukiyoe* block print portraying the event, she leaps wildly onto the stormy waves with sword drawn and does battle with a dragon.

In another version, Prince Yamato insulted her by saying a woman's place was not in battle, but upon the tatami mats (i.e., at home, or in bed). Outraged, she threw mats from the ship into the sea, and leaped atop them.

Takiyasha Hime: Warrior and witch, who with sword and magic achieved revenge for her father in the tenth century A.D.

Talbot, Mary Anne: "The British Amazon," a sailor active in the late 1700s. She first accompanied her husband into battle, disguised as a drummer boy, in the 82nd regiment of infantry. Deserting her unpleasant husband (and the infantry), she joined the navy as a powder monkey and was with Lord Howe in the War with France, where she was captured and imprisoned for eighteen months. [Gribble]

Tamaori Hime: (fl. A.D. 1185) A fighting princess and wife of Atsumori, she fought along the beach in the Taira war. In one portrait, she rides astride a giant seahorse armed with **naginata.**

Tamara, Queen of Georgia: (A.D. 1160–1212) In Lermontov's *The De-mon*, the twelfth-century warrior-queen is described as a beautiful witch dwelling in a gloomy tower on a crag. She took lovers and, when they were spent, hurled them to their deaths. Shakespeare called her "beast-like and devoid of pity." Despite acts of war in keeping with those warring times, history's Queen Tamara was a benevolent monarch noted for her leniency. The monstrous portraits are unjust.

With the title "Mountain of God," she was her father's chosen successor. She was an accomplished huntress but, during her early reign, was adverse to war. Her husband, a warrior of Kiev, waged war against the Moslems, until she dismissed him from court, giving him lavish gifts to take into exile. He subsequently attempted to revolt against her, but was unsuccessful.

In 1191, when a Russian prince warred against her but was captured, her characteristically magnanimous nature led her to exile him to Byzantium rather than kill him. He rose again in 1200, leading Turks, but was repulsed by her. Internal revolts were endemic, and Tamar often personally led her soldiers. Warfare under queens might easily lead to power passing from the woman on the throne to the man leading the wars, for which reason it was typical for queens such as Tamar to appear on the battlefield. In 1205, when in her forties, she marched barefoot into battle, haranguing her men at every bend. A contemporary saying has it that, "The lioness is known by her claws, Tamara by her deeds." See also **Nestan-Daredian.** [Fraser]

Tamatori: In Japanese legend, Tamatori was an *ama* (nun) who battled a giant octopus and the Dragon Lord under the sea to recover the sacred jewel. When it became clear that Tamatori would not be able to make it back to the surface, she ripped open her stomach with her sword, and inserted the jewel inside herself. When her corpse washed ashore, the jewel was recovered.

Tanais: The warrior Tanais was compelled by **Aphrodite** to fall in love with his mother, Queen **Lysippe,** founder of **Amazonia.** Rather than betray his oath of chastity to **Artemis,** or offend his mighty mother, he drowned himself in the river that thereafter bore his name. Lysippe in grief moved her tribe of women to the Thermodon River and there established her laws of prohibition against men fighting. Thereafter, sons of Amazons were crippled by having an arm or leg pulled from the socket, and raised to the distaff.

The legend of Tanais is interesting for revealing the love Amazons felt for their male offspring, irrespective of the ferocity of their regulations. We may imagine justifications for the treatment of men that resemble the modern world's rationales for limiting women's mobility in society, and the average Amazon was no more a man hater than the average "good" husband or father today is a woman hater. The often repeated notion that the Amazons had no motherly compassion for their sons is contradicted by the evidence of Tanais.

In the history of the Goths, it is recorded that they waged a disastrous war against Scythians along the Tanais River, where warriors claimed to have been the husbands of Amazons. Perhaps they were descended of the Amazons and like Lysippe's son were exempt from the rule that men not battle. Or they may have been the consorts of Amazons during erotic festivals on the borders of Amazonia.

The Tanais was considered by the ancients to be the border between Europe and Asia. The Amazons were well situated in the region beyond the Tanais to conquer both east and west. [Jordanes, Sobol]

Tanantsi: A benevolent but warlike goddess of ancient Mexico. She triumphed over **Coatlicue,** goddess of snakes and skulls. [Preston]

Tania: After her husband's death, Tania ruled ancient Dardania with skill and might. "Drawn in a chariot, she always went to battle and, what has scarcely happened to any general except herself, she never suffered defeat." Treachery alone took her life. She was slain in her private chambers by her own son-in-law, tragically a spy. [Polyaenus]

Tania: Code name for the famous Cuban revolutionary Tamara Bunke. She was born in Argentina of German communist émigrés. In 1961, after John F. Kennedy's failed Bay of Pigs invasion, she went to Cuba, where female militia were typical. In Bolivia with Che Guevera, she became a guerrilla in jungle warfare. She was assassinated along with eight comrades. A paramilitary and technical college for women was founded in her name in Cuba. [Roja, Randall]

Tarabai of Rajasthan: Tarabai, whose name means "Starlight," became famous during the Sepoy mutiny of the 1850s. Her battle gear included a charmingly decorated tent, ornate saddle, and retinue of fighting maids. She rode into battle with a sword in each hand. "She was in her element and accomplished wonders on the battlefield," restoring usurped lands to her father and battling her treacherous father-in-law. She was eventually killed by a British soldier who, unfamiliar with Rajput codes of honorable battle, stabbed her in the back.

Traditional Indian culture has a prehistoric matriarchal base, with emphasis on veneration of the Mother-goddess and the cults of Shakti and the Warrior-goddess **Kali.** This cultural base and the strict Rajput code gave rise to a class of veiled woman warriors. They were treated as any other soldiers, facing all the dangers of the battlefield, but because of the Rajput code of honor, were in no danger of molestation from their fellow (male) soldiers. However, they knew that if they were captured by the enemy, they would be tortured and raped, so they tended to fight to the death.

The women's army attracted widows who would otherwise have been sacrificed or impoverished. When Rajput territory was threatened by Moguls or other enemies, women of every sort joined the fight. Women warriors were reputed to be warmly affectionate, family oriented, and feminine, but fiercely courageous. Many peasant women and young girls are noted in Rajput folklore for deeds of valor in defending their homes.

The Rajput army included one troop composed entirely of women, who tied their saris in a special manner, enabling them to ride horseback. Among the aristocracy, the women commonly studied martial arts and fencing. Some aristocratic women became political leaders, generals, and commanders of thousands of troops. [Tod, Chandrakant]

Tarpeia: Companion-at-arms to **Camilla.** She was especially skilled with bronze battle ax, or **labrys.**

Tauropolos: The Tauric **Artemis** worshipped by the **Thermodontines.** She was known in Crimea, Attica, and on the island of **Lemnos.** Most manifestations of Artemis are associated with forests and wild things and as such she is not actually a War-goddess, but is distinctly a huntress; War-goddesses were all but invariably city oriented. Tauropolos was of the latter category, the most overtly vicious, cruel, and warlike of all aspects of Artemis, and derived (like **Artemis of Ephesus**) from **Cybele** and **Rhea,** not the Olympian Artemis. Artemis of Brauron was another aspect most like Tauropolos, for whom young girls danced in the skins of she-bears. Brauronia's cult spread to many regions.

Evidence of coins from Laodicea and statements by Pausanias agree that the Tauric Artemis held a shield and upraised ax. She was also portrayed with a bull's head at her feet, and carrying a torch, indicative of night orgies and an association with **Hecate** and bloody sacrifices typical of her festivals and rites. See **Iphigenia.** [Farnell]

Taylor, Sarah: "The Tennessee **Joan of Arc.**" She fought in the Civil War at age eighteen, the inspiration and pride of the Tennessee regiments. [Laffin]

Tecmessa: "The Ordainer," or "She Who Judges," a Phrygian princess among **Amazonia's** hoplites. She was one of the many Amazon braves who attacked Heracles, one by one, after he murdered **Hippolyte.** Though seeing that he was genuinely invulnerable, the Amazons continued with suicidal frenzy to pursue revenge for their queen. [Sobol]

Teisipyle: Amazon brave in the war between Heracles and **Andromache.** [Bothmer]

Telepyleia: "Far Sailing." Amazon brave in the war of Heracles and Telamon against Queen **Andromache.** [Bothmer]

Telesilla: A musician by trade, she organized a woman's army after the king of Sparta defeated the men of Argive, leaving seven thousand Argive men dead upon the field of battle, in the fifth century B.C. The king thought the city walls would fall quickly, there being few men remaining, but was surprised by Telesilla's female defenders. The king of Sparta and his allies were repulsed by the Argive women. "The most signal honors were rendered to these female warriors, some of whom fell in the contest; and a statue was erected in gratitude to Telesilla." Thereafter, the monthly Festival of Numenia was celebrated with women in men's tunics and men in women's gowns. [Polyaenus, Starling, Lefkowitz]

Tembandumba: (early sixteenth century A.D.) Daughter of the African warrior-queen **Mussasa,** who raised her daughter to the same warlike pursuits. She trained a women's army and refused conventional marriage in favor of politically advantageous liaisons, "killing her lovers after brief dalliance." She rebelled against her mother, proclaiming herself queen. As her power grew, Tembandumba's vision of a women's nation became more macabre, embroiling her in constant warfare. She directed all mothers to grind their male children into magic ointment and follow her to war. Some of the mothers rebelled, so that she lightened her edict and demanded that only captured infants be used in ointment manufacture.

The fierce black warrior lost an eye in battle and was reportedly "a repulsive looking creature." In the end, she was poisoned by a lover, the instant he suspected conjugal unrest. [Rothery]

Teng Ying-ch'ao: Wife of Zou Enlai and one of the thirty-five militia women of the six-thousand-mile Long Walk of Mao Tze-tung. [Miles]

Tenji-no-tsubone: At the great sea battle of Dan-no-ura in A.D. 1185, she fought beside her lover Sagami Goro, armed with **naginata.**

Terwagne, Anne Joseph: The actual name of "The Amazon of Liberty," heroine of the French Revolution better known by her stage name, Théroigne de **Mericourt** (see that entry).

Tescon, Trinidad: At the end of the nineteenth century, she fought under various guerrilla leaders for the liberation of the Philippines. In the battle of Zaragoza, she was badly wounded but recovered and was soon fighting again. She participated in all key engagements against the Spanish after A.D. 1895 and was known as "Ina" (Mother). [Miles]

Tetka: One of Queen **Libussa's** sisters, bearer of the sword of justice. Prince Chroudoch of Czechoslovakia, despising the new Amazon government of Bohemia, waged war against the three sisters, but was defeated.

Teuta: The pirate queen of Illyria (today Albania), a nation that produced many women warriors, including **Eurydice,** a wife of Philip. Teuta was the principal wife of King Agron and ruled after his death in 231 B.C. The Illyrians were already famed pirates, akin to vikings. They habitually waylaid ships and attacked Greek coastal towns. Agron and Teuta became ambitious and not only raided but began to conquer neighboring islands and the coast, expanding Illyrian territory.

Rome became annoyed because its trade ships were captured and its citizens slain or sold into slavery. When Roman ambassadors were sent, they found Teuta personally commanding the siege of Issa, the only island still holding out against her. When the ambassadors objected, Teuta promised that her government planned no action against Rome, but that it was the custom of Illyrian rulers never to interfere with their citizens' right to make a living. The ambassadors stated clearly their outrage at this answer, promising (somewhat imprudently) that Rome would therefore step forth to alter the Illyrian custom of honoring piracy. As the ambassadors set off for home, Teuta's partisans intercepted them, and silenced them forever.

Rome sent a fleet to clear Illyrians from the Greek islands. In concert with the Greek government, they were able to force Teuta to raise the siege of Issa. She withdrew to the inland fortress of Rhizon. From this refuge, she entered into heavily one-sided negotiations with Rome, ceding her authority over the islands, and agreeing to pay an annual indemnity to Rome. In exchange, she received a warm good-bye, and history never hears from her again. [Ormerod]

Thadhellala: A Moorish **Long Meg,** who in folklore was an extremely lucky and roguish woman who stole her way to a throne. She wandered from city to city, tricking men out of their money, horses, anything she needed at the moment, sometimes things she didn't need. She is always found out but is never punished, for, when captured, she always escapes. Fate eventually brought her to a city whose sultan had just died, and, by tradition, the first individual to pass through the gate becomes ruler. Fleeing from her previous misadventure, Thadhellala hurried through the gate, was captured at once, and to her amaze and happiness was appointed sultana. [Hawthorne]

Thalestris: Queen of an Amazon nation on the Black Sea in the days of Alexander the Great.

Alexander was well acquainted with Amazons, from his militant mother **Olympias** and other of his father's warrior-wives, and his sister **Cynane** (see also **Meda, Eurydice,** and **Minythyia**). The women of Hellenic Egypt and Mesopotamia were of two types, the Graecian type, who was more the homebody, and the foreign princesses—such as Thracians, Illyrians, and Ionians—who tended to have military educations.

The meeting with Thalestris is the most celebrated of Alexander's encounters with warring women. In a tradition recorded by Diodorus, Quintus Curtius, and others, Thalestris left the bulk of her army on the borders of Hyrcania and with only two hundred retainers rode to meet Alexander in the wilderness. There they hunted lions together and enjoyed thirteen nights of lovemaking—thirteen being the number of moons in a year, a sacred number aiding fertility for moon worshippers. Thalestris had gotten it into her head to have a daughter by Alexander, believing their combined warrior ability would produce a superwoman who, like her conquering father, would one day rule the world. Unfortunately, she died soon afterward without issue.

Thalestris probably existed, but not as queen of **Amazonia.** Like Philip, Alexander finalized treaties with conquered peoples through marriage alliances. Thalestris has been identified as a nomadic warrior-princess of Bactria, circa 329 B.C., for it is known that the king of the Scyths offered Alexander his warrior daughter. W. W. Tarn speculates that her expanded legend originated with Alexander himself, who, intrigued by "the nomadic girls riding and shooting, naturally thought of the Amazons," hence the first seeds of the story of the queen of the Amazons seeking him to bed. [Pomeroy, Tyrrell, Kleinbaum]

Thalia: At Pompeii, in the gladiators' barracks, there were discovered the bones of a woman clad in expensive jewels, who archaeologists have failed to suppose was herself a gladiator. Among the graffiti of Pompeii is a reference to "Thalia the Undefeated," whose foe in the arena was **Thymele.**

Thalia was also the name of the muse of comedy, not a prepossessing name it would seem, except that gladiators, like many other performers, took "stage names," often from Greek mythology, and such mild ones as Paris and Cupid were typical even for the men. There may have been a greater element of comedy in the gladiatorial games than is now supposed. Certainly Juvenal in his *Satires* keeps his tongue firmly in cheek regarding female gladiators, whom he describes as only one of several types of women to avoid as wives. That Thalia of Pompeii took her name from the muse of comedy, and that Juvenal makes female gladiatorial events into erotic jest, suggests a burlesque quality to the women gladiators, but this aspect existed in the erotic glorification of male gladiators as well, and it does not mean that female gladiators were not deadly earnest in their displays or failed to take themselves seriously in such sport. See also **Achillia, Eppia,** and **gladiatorial women.**

Thamiris: "Enormity." She may derive only from a misunderstood variant in the story of Cyrus the Great's death. Cyrus was decapitated by **Tomyris,** the warrior-queen of the continental Celts. Tomyris spared none of Cyrus's army, not even his **camp followers** and messengers, so that none in Persia ever knew with any certainty what became of their emperor. As rumors spread through the world, the story arose that Thamiris of the **Thermodon-tines,** or Scythian Amazons, had crucified him. A Thamiris may have ruled some remnant of the Thermodontines in this era, or more likely was a nomadic warrior-queen very like Tomyris, and successfully routed Cyrus, crucifying his captains. But Cyrus did not himself fall that day. [Pizan, Boccaccio]

Thea: "The Divine," sometimes called Thetis, "the Destroyer." A prophetess and companion of **Artemis** on the chase.

Themis: Queen of heaven before **Hera's** rise, daughter of **Gaia.** During the War with the Titans, she taught honor, justice, and moderation. She later became the law giver and counsel to Zeus. Her name means "Justice" and she is still worshipped in judicial circles, where she is portrayed as blindfolded and holding scales.

Themiscrya: The capital city of **Amazonia,** invaded by Greeks seeking proof of their manhood. It was founded by **Lysippe.** Two other regional capitals were Lycastia and Chadesia. The "nation" of Amazonia may well have consisted of a series of ashrams or religious centers that served as city-states. Chinese and Indic mythologies describe such centers on the Euxine Sea, just as the Greeks remembered them. *The Cambridge Ancient History* states that the legends of the Amazons east of the Halys "are not even now extinct." There is good reason to suppose Themiscrya did once exist, a magnet for goddess-worshipping, highly athletic women of the ancient world.

Thérèsa Figueur of Lyon: Napoleonic era heroine. She was called Mademoiselle Sans-Gêne. She was the subject of an unflattering play by Sardou, popular in Paris and London theaters from the 1890s and during World War I. During the French Revolution, she served under Dugommier at the siege of Toulon. She took part in battles at Ulm and Austerlitz. She briefly served Empress Josephine, who didn't like her, and was involved in romantic intrigues. She was occasionally rumored not to be a woman at all. She ultimately married happily and France marveled than a dragoon should wed a gendarme. Although her behavior struck some as uncouth, she was admired as kind, intelligent, and spirited. [Gribble]

Thermodon River: The capital and two other cities of **Amazonia** were situated on a great plain along the River Thermodon, which sprang from the Amazonian Mountains and emptied into the Euxine (Black Sea). These Scythian Amazons were therefore known as the **Thermodontines.** See also the **Tanais.**

Thermodontines: The Indo-European Amazons, identified by the Greeks as having a Scythian racial heritage. They may actually have been Sarmatians, but also included immigrants from all key goddess-worshipping city-states. See also the **Maeotides.**

Thermodosa: One of the twelve select companions-at-arms of **Penthesilea,** liberator of Troy.

Thora: Warrior-queen of Icelandic legend, Queen Olof to the Danes. [Damico]

Thorgerd: Warrior-maid who with her sister **Irpa** assisted Jarl Hakon at the front of battle, in stories from *Flateyjarbók.* Hakon worshipped her as a deity, indicating a higher order of **Valkyries.** She was capable of shooting ten arrows at once and may originally have been of the Laplanders, who were renowned for bow skill.

Thraso: "Confidence." Companion to **Hypsipyle** during **Andromache's** war against Heracles. Her shield's device was a **gorgoneum** similar to that of **Athena.** [Bothmer]

Thrúth: "Mighty," a **Valkyrie** of *Grimulsmal.*

Thusnelda: She was the key military adviser to Hermann of Germany in the fight against Roman domination in the first two decades A.D. Eventually, she was captured and taken to Rome in chains, but the heartsick Germans were only driven to larger battles for freedom. To this day, the valor of Thusnelda is remembered in folktales. [Morris]

Thyiades: Delphic **Maenads** who, according to Pausaneus, held violent orgiastic rites on Mt. Parnassus.

Thymele: Reconstructed from evidence of graffiti at Pompeii, Thymele appears to have been a gladiator and the underdog in a match with "undefeated **Thalia,**" whom the fans preferred. Referring to Thymele in the diminutive, the graffiti appears to say, "Get out, Thy! Hooray, Thalia the Undefeated!" See **gladiatorial women.**

Thyone: See **Semele.**

Thyra, Queen of Denmark: (fl. A.D. 891) In the absence of her husband, who had gone to distant battles, Queen Thyra ruled Denmark as sole sovereign, and warred against the Germans, who made repeated incursions into Sleswick and Jutland. She raised a great wall, called the Danneverke, over a period of three years, portions of which survive today, and it was Denmark's chief point of defense for centuries to follow. [Morris]

Tiamat: Ceto in Greece, **Rahab** to the Hebrews. In one of the oldest surviving religious texts, *Enuma Elish (When on High)* of Babylonia, about the second millennium B.C., the Dragon-goddess Tiamat overthrows the assembly of gods. They afterward elect a new, young god as their hero:

> When Tiamat heard the challenge
> She became as one possessed;
> She became berserk
> She recited spells
> While the gods of battle polished their steel.
> Then joined Tiamat and Marduck, the young god.
> They strove in single combat, locked in battle.

This is essentially a myth of the overthrow of the Mother-goddess and the rise of patriarchal rule, evoking an earlier time of women's rule. In other ancient texts, including the Torah, the original Creatrix is likened to Chaos, whose voice called forth the world, and the patriarchal god wrestles her into submission in order to establish his rule of the cosmos. See **Eurynome** for a parallel goddess. [Heidel]

Timoclea: (fl. 374 B.C.) Sister of Theagenes of Thebes, she was threatened with rape by one of the soldiers of Alexander the Great, so she drowned the soldier in a well. Alexander thereafter forbade his men to attack Theban women. [Hale]

Tirgato of Ixomatae: Tirgato, whose name has been translated as "Noble Arrow Defender," married the king of a neighboring country, who later tried to rid himself of her in order to achieve a politically more potent marriage-alliance with a third and larger country. Tirgato escaped imprisonment and, hunted by men seeking her life, survived the hardships of a fugitive and made her way back to her homeland. There, she married the young king and used her position to form an alliance with other warlike peoples in an attack against her faithless first husband's country. Defeating him, she went on to ravage the larger country with which her ex-husband had wished to ally himself at her expense. The king of that country quickly sued for peace, but he had no intention of honoring the treaty. Tirgato was set upon by two assassins, but she was too strong for their swords. Under torture, they confessed the plot, and Tirgato retaliated against the treacherous king. He was slain on the battlefield, his country completely subjugated. Tirgato accepted heavy tribute from the king's heir, then returned to her country. [Polyaenus]

Tisiphone: Her name means "Avenger of Blood." She is a female demon of the underworld, one of the **Furies.** Horace implies that a Roman cult of sorceresses worshipped not only **Hecate,** but Tisiphone, without regard to the other two Furies. The frenzies of these witches appear to have combined the violence of the **Maenads** with conjurations and **hag**like behavior similar to those associated with medieval witches. The Roman cult of Tisiphone may be a link between the Greek Maenads and the witches of the Christians' witch-burning era.

Tisiphone was also a daughter of the Trojan chieftain Antimachus. She tried to convince the women of Troy to join **Penthesilea** and her war maidens on the field of honor.

Tomoe Gozen: (fl. eleventh century A.D.) The warrior aristocracy of medieval Japan produced many women warriors of note, the most famous of whom was Tomoe Gozen, mistress of the ambitious General Kiso Yoshinaka. Her name is sometimes written with three characters, the first meaning "archer," the second "wrist shield." It also translates "comma," and is a term used to describe a type of cut made with **naginata.** She and her husband operated a martial arts school for men and women wishing to master the naginata.

According to the medieval epic *Heike Monogatori,* Tomoe was "match for god or devil" and in one long battle, "when all the others had been slain, among the last seven rode Tomoe." She killed many famous warriors of the Taira clan, and even her horse was so fierce that the Taira thought a score of enemy were attacking, so much snow was tossed into the air by her charging mount. She once single-handedly held a bridge against a horde. In one block print, she is portrayed defeating a foe with a tree trunk for her weapon.

When her husband was finally trapped and intent on honorable suicide, he denied Tomoe Gozen the privilege of dying with him. Hurt by this, she decided on one final deed to prove herself. She met the Herculean warrior Uchida Ieoshi on the battlefield and fought him blade to blade, cutting off his head and placing it high upon a pole. Announcing her victory to her husband's ghost, she then threw off her armor and fled east, where she had relatives.

tom-rig: An Elizabethan tomboy or roaring girl. The quintessential tom-rig was Moll Cutpurse (Mary **Frith**). See also **Long Meg.**

Tomyris: Queen of the Celtish Massagetae, in an area now encompassed by Iran. She was a superior military tactician and founder of the city of Tomis, named for herself, on the shore of Pontus in Moesia, an area associated with **Amazonia** in greater antiquity. When her nation was attacked by Cyrus the Great, she promised him "enough blood to sate your gluttony," and the final battle was reported to be the most ferocious of any in those fierce days. Her army slaughtered 200,000 Persians, so that not even a messenger survived to return home with the news of the conquerer's doom; thus, the Persians never knew what became of him. Rumors gave rise to numerous speculations, including the story that he died at the hands of Scythian Amazons (see **Thamris**). When Cyrus lay dead, Tomyris, the victor, set up a skin filled with human blood and, tossing Cyrus' head into the macabre broth, said, "I have fulfilled my promise. You have your fill of blood." [Herodotus, Pizan]

Torborg: A Swedish princess of antiquity, daughter of King Erik of Upsala. "She cared nothing for women's work but was the equal of any man of the court in riding, fighting with sword and shield, and other athletic sports." She received a province to rule, and in this capacity liked to be called "King Torborg." Because she was beautiful, many princes came to court her, but she held them in contempt, putting out the eyes of some, cutting off the hands and feet of others, driving the rest away with sword and spear. She finally married, when defeated in combat by a powerful enough suitor. [C. Morris]

Tou Mu: Goddess of the North Star, or the Bushel Mother (akin to Demeter, the Barley Mother), worshipped in China both by Buddhists and Taoists. In India, she is called Maritchi. She is partially interchangeable with **Kuan Yin,** sharing with her a dragon-slaying, warlike component that serves to destroy the fears of humankind. In her eighteen hands are numerous precious objects, including bow and arrow, spear, sword, general's flag, dragon's head, and war chariot. She is at once a goddess of life and of death, resembling many of the nearly universal goddesses of fertility and war. [Werner]

tourneys: See Agnes **Hotot.**

Toxaris: "Archer." Amazon brave in Telamon's and Heracles' war against **Andromache.** [Bothmer]

Toxis: One of Queen **Andromache's** archers in her war against Heracles. [Bothmer]

Toxophile: An archer in the war between **Andromache** and Heracles. [Bothmer]

Triaria, Empress: (fl. A.D. 60) Wife of the Roman Emperor Lucius Vitellius. She accompanied him everywhere into battle, armed as a knight, and fought vigorously. At a battle for a city of the Voscians, "she felt neither fear nor revulsion but conducted herself bravely"; fully armed and girded with her sword, "she rushed here and there against the wretches and in the midst of blood-curdling cries, flashing weapons, blood, and the death rattles of her victims, she missed none of the atrocities of war." [Pizan, Boccaccio]

Trieu Thi Trinh: Or Trieu Au. "I will not resign myself to the lot of women, who bow their heads and become concubines," said Thieu Thi Trinh in A.D. 248. She said, "I wish to ride the tempest, tame the waves, kill the sharks. I want to drive the enemy away to save our people." By the age of twenty-one, she had led thirty battles and liberated Vietnam, for six months, from Chinese tyranny. [Eisen-Bergman]

Tritogenia: Cult name of **Athena,** goddess of wisdom and war.

Tritonia: The Libyan Amazons, or **Gorgons,** originated on the volcanic island of **Hesperia** ("Evening," for its position toward the setting sun), also called Tritonia, later destroyed by cataclysm, and of which only the Canaries survive today. Their island origin has falsely tied the Gorgons to the legend of Atlantis. Libya became their second homeland, where their chief inland body of water they called Lake Tritonia. [Diodorus]

Trivulzio, Cristina Belgiojoso: (A.D. 1808–1871) Author, adventuress, agriculturalist, revolutionary, and founder of two newspapers in Milan. This versatile woman went to Naples in 1848 to enlist a battalion that she herself led to Milan in the "Five Days Revolution." [Schmidt]

Trung Trac and **Trung Nhi:** Enraged by the atrocities of a Chinese governor who had executed her husband, Trung Trac began to organize a Vietnamese peasant revolt. She wrote her proclamation of revolution upon the skin of a previously invincible tiger that had terrorized villagers, which she had slain as evidence of her might. She was an even greater military tactician than tiger slayer; nevertheless, it was her sister, Trung Nhi, who became the more famous in battle. Together in A.D. 40, these sisters led an army of eighty thousand against the tyrant To Dinh, who shaved his head and beard to flee to China as a monk. It was the first time in a thousand years that Vietnam had been free of Chinese dominion.

The Trungs took control of sixty-five fortified towns and continued for three years to threaten the Chinese government in Vietnam. Thirty-six lesser generals, all women, were selected and trained by the famed sisters, including the Trungs' own mother. When Chinese reinforcements defeated the tactically superior Trungs by weight of numbers alone, the women escaped capture by performing suicide in its most dignified, heroic context, centuries before the Japanese had codified the procedures of hara-kiri.

In the centuries to follow, the Trungs became idealized examples of national courage. They were deified; temples were built to their honor in the twelfth century, at least one of which still stands in Hanoi, where the anniversary of their suicide is a recognized holiday. In the eighteenth century, a nationalist movement selected a native emperor who gave the two Trung generals posthumous titles of nobility as a direct counter to Chinese/ Confucian attempts to belittle the Trungs' ancient exploits.

"Trung" has become the Vietnamese word for "Amazon," connoting patriotic valor. Other "Trungs" include **Phung Thi Chinh, Trieu Thi Trinh,** and **Xuan Bui Thi.** [Eisen-Bergman]

Tryphaena: Personal name of the Ptolemy queen **Cleopatra VI.**

Tryphosa: Victrix of the girls' single-course races at the Pythian Games and again in the Isthmian Games circa A.D. 45. She was of a family of girl athletes from Caesaria, her sisters being **Hedea** and **Dionysia.** [Lefkowitz]

Tsanahale: Women with feathered backs born of virgins in Navaho myth, cruel like the **Harpies.**

Tubman, Harriet: (A.D. 1815?–1913) Operated an "underground railroad" to remove her enslaved people from the Confederacy. She served as a soldier in the northern Union Army, taking part in raids against the Confederacy. On June 2, 1863, she had three Union gunboats under her command and led a crucial mission on the Tennessee River. She destroyed a bridge, gathered vital intelligence, and rescued 756 slaves. The U.S. government, after the Civil War, unjustly refused to recognize her part, and denied her a veteran's pension. [Macksey]

Tullia: One of the Italian Amazons hand selected by **Camilla** to accompany her in battle, "an excellent helper in peace or war." Also, a daughter of Servius Tullius of Rome, assassinated at Tullia's behest. She drove her chariot back and forth upon his corpse. [Virgil, Hale]

Turfida: Shield maiden to Hereward in *Gesta Herewardi.* She provided him his mailcoat and helmet. See also **Rota.**

Turkan Kahtun: (fl. eleventh century A.D.) Daughter of Tamghaj Khan and wife of Malik Shah, ruler of Turkey. She went into battle during the civil war, appointed her four-year-old son sultan, seized the city of Ispahan, and waged war against rival claimants of the throne. Her stepson's treachery ended her regency in execution. [Beard]

Turunku, Bakwa: (fl. A.D. 1530) Queen of Zazzau, later renamed Zaire after her youngest daughter. Queen Turunku ruled the extensive empire of the Hasau, which had come into existence by A.D. 1050. The queens of this empire were by tradition and necessity warlike. Her eldest daughter, Queen **Amina,** ruled after her. [Qunta]

Tychmini, Natalie: Because so many women served in the Russian army in both world wars with official sanction, it was less necessary for women eager for combat to disguise themselves as men, but Natalie Tychmini was one of many exceptions who did fight in disguise, as did Zoya **Smirnow** and Princess **Wolonsky.** Tychmini received the St. George Cross for distinguished service fighting Austrians at Opatow in 1915. When she was wounded, her sex was discovered, and she was returned to Kiev. [Hirshfeld]

Tzavella, Moscho: She came from an illustrious family of Greek guerrilla fighters and was a respected military tactician. She led an army of peasant women against the Turks and, though armed only with staves and rocks, defeated the pasha's army.

◆◇◆◇◆◇◆◇◆◇◆◇◆◇◆

Uathach: "Specter." Daughter of **Scáthach,** guardian of the gate of her mother's castle. She and her mother and her aunt **Aife** have associations with the underworld and an unclear relationship with Scandinavia's **Valkyries.**

Ubaldini, Cia degli: In the fourteenth century A.D., Cia defended Cesane in the absence of her husband, Francesco Ordelaffi. When her own father begged her to give up the battle, she declared, "For death and all else but my duty, I care but little," and continued the defense. [Boulting]

Ubastet: Rage-goddess of Bubastos in Egypt who became a lioness when angry. She was goddess of the hunt, associated by the Greeks with **Artemis.** She is often portrayed with a cat's head, the cat as well as the lion being sacred to her. [Kramer]

Uma: "Light." An aspect of **Parvati,** still worshipped as **Durga,** who in great antiquity inspired a warrior caste of women who were called Uma-soons, or "Daughters of Uma." Edward Pocoke believes Uma's worship to be evidence of the Indic origins of the Amazons of Greek myth. In later ages she became, like **Athena,** the goddess of wisdom. See also **Sena.**

Ummu-Khubur: Queen-mother of the six thousand monsters of darkness raised by **Tiamat** in her war against Marduk. Also called Melili.

Unca: A cult name for **Hera** as worshipped in Thebes and Phoenicia.

Upis: "Watcher," the goddess of moral law, "an ancient and half-forgotten name of **Artemis**," related to **Artemis of Ephesus.** She incorporates characteristics of **Aphrodite** and **Nemesis** of Rhamnus, and is sometimes referred to as Artemis-Aphrodite.

Urinza, Doña Ana Lezama de: With Doña Eustaquia de **Sonza,** lesbian swashbucklers of Potosí, Peru, in the mid-1600s. Ana, orphaned, was raised with Eustaquia. From an early age, they were more interested in the fencing lessons of Eustaquia's brother than in needlework. Both were indulged in their fondness for weapons, especially after the death of Eustaquia's brother. By their thirteenth year, they were studying with a fencing master and learning to shoot firearms.

In the 1650s, Potosí was a booming, rowdy metropolis, but Ana and Eustaquia were raised in such seclusion that few people even knew of their existence. They knew of the bullfights, theatrical performances, balls, and fiestas only secondhand, from a servant.

The young women began to sneak away from their guardian's hacienda by night, clad as two dashing young *caballeros,* to experience the night life of their violent city. This inevitably led to street duels. In one fight, two against four, Ana was wounded and had fallen. Eustaquia stood over her, "brandishing her cutlass in all directions," until Ana came to herself and "rose to her feet like a lioness and, recognizing the man who had wounded her, said, 'Monster, now I will revenge myself!'" She ran forth and gave him such a blow with her cutlass that his shield was cleaved in two, and his hand injured. Then she rejoined Eustaquia to defeat the remaining three ruffians. Near dawn, after this encounter, they removed their armor and discovered that Ana had two wounds, both very dangerous, and Eustaquia had three, one in the back.

For five years, they traveled Peru together, experiencing numerous thrilling adventures. When Doña Eustaquia's father died and left her his estate, the two women were able to remain independent their whole lives. Doña Ana eventually died of a lingering ailment caused during a bullfight, an art she had practiced on horseback. Four months after her death, her grieving companion followed. They were remembered long after as "The Valiant Peruvian Ladies of Potosí." [Arzans]

Urraca, Queen of Aragon: (A.D. 1081–1126) Queen Urraca ruled an enormous section of Spain in the twelfth century, as her half sister Teresa ruled in Portugal. A widow in her late twenties, she ascended the throne of León-Castile, and for thirteen of her seventeen years as queen, warred against her troublesome second husband, the king of Aragon, Alfonso the

Battler. Her son succeeded her to the throne after she was defeated in battle in 1111. [Reilly]

Ursula, Saint: This German Catholic saint is typically portrayed with arrows in hand. She was killed by a rebuffed king, many such saints having presumedly died for their chastity (see Saints **Catherine** and **Barbara**), though in reality for their religious zeal and attendant authority over the common people, sharing, therefore, much in common with the pagan holocaust of martyred witches and midwives.

Ursula in many ways resembles **Artemis,** whose functions were indeed incorporated in her legend. She was the protector of virgins and founder of a college for girls, all of whom were martyred, said variously to have numbered from only five to as many as eleven thousand. The Ursalines afterward established teaching convents in the farmost reaches of the world, often in places where there were no previous European settlements. St. Caterina da Vigri, a monastic woman artist, painted St. Ursula with arrow in hand, her cape enveloping young girls. Unlike many of the armed saints, her arrow represents her own victory, and is often not in her flesh, but held pointing outward.

❖❖❖❖❖❖❖❖❖❖❖❖❖

Valasca or **Dlasta:** Ruins on Mt. Vidovole were known as Divinhrad, "The Virgin's City," believed to be the capital of the warrior-queen Valasca, who, wresting control of Bohemia from Queen **Libussa,** began her several years of tyranny. According to the fifteenth-century author Aeneas Silvius, she had the right eye and thumbs of all males removed, so that they were useless in battle, and attempted to establish a new **Amazonia,** placing women in all offices and conscripting the whole female population as soldiers. As the Slavs were descended from the Amazons of the Caucasus, we may suspect some lingering cult activity that inspired both Libussa and Valasca, and for which they and Libussa's sisters served as priestesses. Upon Valasca's death, "the business of the nation resumed its normal course." [Rothery]

Valkyries: Battle maidens and demigoddesses of Norse legend who, meeting in council in Valhalla, decided the outcome of battles. They aided in battles according to the whims of Odin, and sometimes ate the dead. After battles, they led the souls of the slain into Valhalla, a hell that is paradise for warriors. Some of their individual names were synonyms for "battle" such as **Hidr** and **Gnor.** They were very likely corrupt remembrances of actual women, priestesses of **Freya,** a goddess who shared half the dead with Odin and who in some Valkyrie legends is their commander in lieu of Odin. In "The Shield Maiden" (1928), a story by Nobel Prize author Vernor von Heidenstam, a woman warrior becomes a Valkyrie by dying in battle (for historical equivalents, see **Wisna** and **Risla**). There is in addition a class of Nordic giantesses who serve as guardians, prophetesses, and foes, such as **Gefjon, Hringerth, Skadi,** Gerda, Jord, Fenja, Gunnlod, Bestla, Rind, and a great many others. They share much in common with the Valkyries, occasionally become Valkyries or **Asynjor,** and some are corruptions of exceedingly ancient Earth-mothers.

See **Brynhild, Geiravor, Gondul, Gunn, Harthgrepa, Hlathgruth, Hrist, Rota, Ruta, Sigrdrifa, Skogul, Svava,** and **Thorgerd.** For Serbian Valkyries, see the **Veela,** and for Slavic Valkyries see the **Polyanitzi.** [Davidson, Edwardes]

Vansa, Sofie: Widow of a Russian army colonel. She joined the second Women's Battalion of Death in World War II, after her two sons were hospitalized with wounds.

Vashti: (fl. 519 B.C.) Harem queen of Xerxes, mentioned in the Book of Esther. She refused to obey Xerxes, preferring the company of women. He, fearing a harem revolt, replaced her with Esther.

Vasilisa Vasily: In a Russian folktale, she was a priest's warlike daughter. When out hunting, she was uncommonly handsome, and she was usually thought to be a young man. A king set various tests or snares for her in order that he might discern her sex. For instance, she was invited into a room with a spinning wheel and weapons, with the expectation that if "he" were not truly male, the handsome soldier would first notice the spinning wheel. Vasilisa Vasily evaded each test. In a Romanian version of the tale, she was called Fett Frunners and, after evading the tests (set, this time, by a giantess), she went on to perform great deeds in various countries, save a damsel in distress, purportedly change her sex, and marry the aforementioned damsel. In a similar German tale, she is the lady knight Katrine. She performed a similar series of tests, activities presumed impossible for women, but, unlike the Romanian example, she claimed a husband in the end. [Lang]

Veela: In Serbian myth and folklore, the Veela were demigoddesses whose nature was partly that of the **Valkyries,** and partly that of the huntress-nymphs of **Artemis.** They could either slay a hero with their arrows or become his "spiritual sister" or "god-sister" and protect him in battle. The Serbian ballad *The Building of Scadav* tells of a Veela who single-handedly razed the fortress walls, though opposed by a hundred men. Another Veela legend names Oossood as an especially **Artemis**like figure who pronounced the fate of newborn children. Only peasant mothers could hear her.

In yet another Veela story that parallels the story of Artemis and her nymphs spied upon by Actaeon, a Serban youth hid near a magic pool where Veela gathered for lustration ceremonies. When they detected the youth, they leaped upon him and tore him into four pieces.

An especially famous Veela was **Raviyoyla,** spiritual sister to the Serbian national hero Marko. [Petrovitch]

Velásquez, Loreta: A darkly beautiful Cuban who fought in male guise, complete with false mustache, in the American Civil War on the Confederate side. She fought at Bull Run, served also as a spy, and when the war was done, traveled west to try her hand at gold mining and the women's lecture circuit. [Gribble, Laffin]

Venus Victrix: Goddess of **camp followers** (see **Aphrodite**).

Vercheres, Mademoiselle Madeliene de: (A.D. 1678–1766) In the early 1690s, the Iroquois attacked the French-Canadian fort of Vercheres while the soldiers were upon a mission elsewhere. Mademoiselle de Vercheres, remembered as the Canadian **Joan of Arc,** only fourteen years of age, held off the Iroquois single-handedly, having loaded innumerable muskets, by appearing at random around the palisades so that the Iroquois never knew from where she would be shooting at them next. The story is told in Lord Kames's *Sketches of the History of Man,* and he suggests another assault of this fort when there was only one young woman, perhaps the same Madeliene, plus one soldier present. The girl appeared at random around the palisades, even changing her costume on the run, so that the Indians would believe there were more defenders. [Starling, Schmidt]

Victorina: A celebrated matron who placed herself at the head of the Roman armies and as a partisan to her sons warred against Emperor Gallienus. She was poisoned in A.D. 269. [Hale]

virago: Renaissance Italian Amazons were popularly called viragoes, a word that in those days had chiefly positive connotations, implying a woman of beauty and ladylike demeanor who, in time of necessity, and in terms of intellect, was the equal of or superior to men. Caterina **Sforza** was the ideal. Though first used to describe eager huntresses and warlike castle ladies, the term came also to indicate women who had gained some degree of independence through arts and letters. In Restoration England, it became debated, some holding that the virago was patriotic, brave, and beautiful, others that she was unacceptably, vulgarly aggressive.

virginity: In the ancient world, virginity did not invariably mean chastity; it meant unmarried, or independent, and the virgins of antiquity in several cases had numerous consorts. It connoted the unattachment of youth, and wanderlust, while in the mature woman it indicated self-sufficiency whether as wife, mother, or conqueror. Hence, the virginal Amazons met with men on the borders of **Amazonia** upon sanctified occasions of orgiastic rituals, or bedded the men of conquered nations, and **Artemis,** the virgin goddess, killed her lovers after copulating. [Pomeroy, Weigle]

Virgin Mary: Mary, Mother of God, is a modern remnant of ancient goddess monotheism. She was first declared "the Godbearer" in A.D. 431 at Ephesus, anciently the great center of goddess faith and site of the Artemisium founded by the Amazons. As "the Virgin of the Pillar" Mary was a warrior, and an inspiration to "the nun ensign" Doña Catalina de **Erauso.** In 1808 in Portugal, in accordance with a custom that appointed saints to army ranks, the Virgin of the Pillar was nominated captain of the Aragonese troops. Pillar cults were phallic in origin and Pillar-goddesses easily associated with war. As the Catholic "Queen of Angels," she is interchangeable with Pistis Sophia of the gnostics and the kabalists' Shekinah (Shakti in India), called also the Holy Ghost, the Dove, Malkuth, and Matrona, sometimes named as the rival of **Lilith** for God's affection.

Gottfried Keller, "the Swiss Shakespeare," retold the medieval legend of "The Virgin as Knight," in which a frightened young man on his way to a tourney stopped at a wayside shrine to beg for Mary's assistance. He fell into a deep sleep and she stepped down from the altar, took his armor and steed, rode to the tourney, defeated his opponent for him in a lance fight, and even courted a maiden. In this profane peasant tale can be seen the last echo of the warring Moon-goddesses of the ancient world.

Visconti, Bianca Maria: (A.D. 1423–1468) Wife of Francesco Sforza, she defended Cremona against the Venetians and headed a naval attack against them. She overthrew the Ambrosian Republic in 1447 and consolidated various territories into a new, powerful duchy in the north of Italy. [Boulting]

Voada and **Voadicia:** The sixteenth-century scholar Petroccio Ubaldini erroneously believed Voadicia to be a separate personage from **Boudicca,** queen of the Iceni. Hector Boëce in his *History of Scotland* calls her Queen Voada and assumes her to be the widow of Prasutagus and sister of King Corbrede of Scotland. Her elder daughter was also called Voada, according to a 1577 study by Ralph Holinshed, and the younger daughter is Voadicia, both characters broadly drawn in a later Restoration drama. The younger

Voadicia, after her mother's death, gathered soldiers on the Isle of Man and attacked the Romans, only to be captured by Petilus at Galloway. When she was rude in captivity, he let his soldiers kill her.

Careful investigation causes the Scottish Voadicia to vanish into the British Boudicca, but the names of her daughters might still be alotted some degree of acceptability, supposing a document (subsequently lost) or an oral tradition (since forgotten) existed in the sixteenth century. The actual names of Boudicca's daughters are unknown, but it is not entirely unreasonable to assume the confusion regarding the spelling of the queen's name stemmed in part to the similarity with the names of her daughters. It is entirely feasible that Queen Boudicca's daughters led battles in other parts of the British Isles, as when Tacitus described the Roman war against the Druids, whose ranks included "black-robed women with dishevelled hair like Furies brandishing torches." [Fraser]

Volcana and the Victorian strongwomen: Throughout the Victorian era and until World War I, when circuses still thrived, the strongwoman was a regular feature. During the popular culture era at the turn of the century, she was wed to the physical culture movement, adding nobility to her stature.

Volcana (Kate Roberts) was a British champion weight lifter and a physical culture superstar, famous in Europe and America, a Renoir beauty wrought giant. She said, with typical physical culture bombast, "Strength is the ruler of all earthly things; those who fight for Health and Right can raise the world on golden pinioned wings."

"Miss Ella" of the Sciavoni troupe in Italy carried four men around the stage, or held two men above her head. "Minerva" (Josephine Blatt of Hoboken) in the 1890s stood six foot one, 230 pounds of muscle. She harness-lifted twenty-three men weighing, with platform and chains, two and a half tons.

Katie Sandwina was also six foot one and weighed 209 pounds, "distributed over a handsome figure." She twisted steel bars in a vaudeville act as a teenager, later becoming a star of Barnum & Bailey Circus, posters calling her "Germany's Herculean Venus, the Most Perfect Female Figure, the Strongest Woman that Ever Lived." She lifted half-ton cannons and served as a bridge over which forty men and horses trotted.

Madame Montagna was an Italian circus Amazon. Her act included a 230-pound cannon held on her back, loaded, and fired. She did not budge with the recoil. [Gaines]

Wadjet: One of Egypt's Cobra-goddesses. She is usually personified as a snake rearing up to protect the pharaoh. She is a familiar symbol even in the West, without our knowing it, as many popular reproductions of Egyptian art show pharoahs wearing this protectress as a crown formed like a cobra ready to strike. Wadjet sometimes has vulture wings and overlaps the Vulture-goddess Nekhbet as a protector of shrines. She is later somewhat absorbed into **Isis.** See also **Renenutet.** [Hart]

Wafeira: Afra' Bint Ghifar al-Humayriah, given sometimes as Wafeira, was an Arab chieftainess of the seventh century A.D. At Yermonks in the war against the Greeks, she and other chieftainesses were in the forefront of battle. One of them, **Khawlah,** was knocked to the ground by a Greek soldier and would have been slain but that Wafeira's sword beheaded him. She later participated in the "tent-pole battle" of women armed only with the dismantled tent braces. [Hale, Miles]

Walker, Nancy Slaughter: "Nancy Slaughter" was a rough rider with William Clarke Quantrill in the American Civil War. After the war, the rough riders, Nancy Slaughter with them, became raiders in Indian Territory and Texas.

Wanda of Poland: Daughter of King Krak, who founded Krakow, Queen Wanda ruled after him, about A.D. 730, and rode at the head of her army into battle to repulse invaders. Romantic legend has it that her foe, Ridieger of Germany, waged war only because he sought Wanda's hand in marriage, and that she ended the recurrent incursions by leaping to her death from her castle's battlements. The recurrent notion in romance of wars waged in order to gain marriage partners merely reflects the primitive political reality of marriage-alliance.

There is a peasant folk song called "The Warrior Princess of Poland," and while this anonymous princess lived much later than Wanda, she gives added evidence to the valor of Polish women:

> When the king came to old age
> Bitterly he wept with rage
> "Though I have fair daughters three
> I've no son to fight for me."
>
> Then he called the oldest one
> "Come, my child, fight as a son."
> "No, my father, I'll not go
> Never can I fight the foe."
>
> Then he called the second one
> "Come, my child, fight as a son."
> "No, my father, I'll not go
> Never can I fight the foe."
>
> Then he called the smallest one
> Though he thought her weak and young
> "Come, my child, do you agree
> To go forth and fight for me?"
>
> "Yes, my father, I will go
> I fear neither pain nor foe
> Brave my heart and strong my hand
> I'll lay waste the foeman's land."
>
> She led soldiers to the fray
> Bravely did they fight that day
> By her mighty sword did fall
> Full three hundred Turks in all.

Wanda von Dunayer: Fictional heroine of Chevalier Leopold von Sacher-Masoch's landmark novel *Venus in Furs*. She enslaves the fortunate protagonist and allows him no pleasure without her permission. The character was based on the Chevalier's lovers, including Anna von Kottowitz, who "had no objection to knocking Leopold about pretty regularly," or cuckholding her husband for that matter, and Fanny Pistor Bogdanov, with whom the Chevalier signed a contract making himself her slave, to be punished at her will, so long as she would wear furs. In 1873, Leopold married Aurora von Rumelin; she afterward wrote a number of novels under the pseudonym Wanda von Dunayer, and her controversial memoirs appeared in 1906. See also **Juliette** and **Samois.** [Cleugh]

Ward, Nancy: (A.D. 1738?–1822) A Cherokee Indian who took command of braves after her husband was killed in a skirmish with the Creeks, she successfully routed the enemy. She later headed the Women's Council and sat on the Council of Chiefs. She married a white man in 1760 and attempted to keep peace between the races, though always putting the interests of the Cherokee first. [Macksey]

warrior-courtesans: Some 1,200 women-at-arms accompanied the duke of Alva in Flanders in the late 1500s. They are described by *Varillas in Histoire de Henry III,* volume III, as "fair and gallant as princesses and very well appointed," eight hundred afoot and four hundred "mounted courtesans." There also survives a portrait by an anonymous Italian artist of a courtesan of somewhat Chinese countenance and exceedingly serious demeanor, clad in full armor and girt with swords. An edict published in 1516 attempted to outlaw the warrior-courtesan by prohibiting women *in men's clothing* to follow after men-at-arms; the edict did not otherwise prohibit camp following.

The warrior-courtesan grew partly out of the tradition of **camp followers,** but grew as well from the aggressive choices made by independently wealthy city courtesans, singers, and actresses who may already have gained fame in such stage roles as **Dido** and **Minerva** before setting off to the Crusades or defending their own cities. Théroigne de **Mericourt,** La **Maillard, Margheritona,** and **Malatesta** are typical of a type of actress/courtesan whose fame, wealth, and personal aggression led them, in time of war, to rise as leaders in the forefront of peasant revolution.

Water-sitting Grizzly: A lesbian warrior of the Kootenay of the Pacific Northwest, also known by the name Bundash or **Bowdash.**

Weber, Hélène Marie: Feminists and suffragists per se have by and large been excluded from this survey, as have heroines of the labor movements and the temperance leaders who, with Cary Nation, for example, were capable of surprising violence, as all seemed a half degree outside the perimeters of this book; nevertheless, Hélène Weber demands exception. She was a European feminist, born in 1824, who promulgated the rights of women to retain property and civil existence after marriage, to study in universities, to vote and engage in politics, to become ministers and priests, and to hold any occupation but especially in the area of agriculture. She argued against prudery and advocated androgyny so that there would no longer be such a deep-seated alienation between men and women, symbolized, she believed, even in human dress. She lived her theory, dressing always in male attire, and cutting her hair short, so that "she appears like an elegant gentleman." [Hale]

Webiorg: A medieval Danish sea captain "inspired with warlike spirit" who fought at the tenth-century Battle of Bravalla, the greatest battle in Scandinavian history. Among Webiorg's followers were men and women of Britain and other nations besides Denmark. They "cast away all protection to their breasts and exposed their bodies to every peril, offering battle with drawn swords."

Webiorg killed a champion, Seth (or Soti), and "while she was threatening to slay more champions, was pierced through by an arrow from the bowstring of Thorkil of Tellemark," who had strung his bow taut enough to pierce armor. In another telling, she continued to fight until many bolts from Thorkil's crossbow filled her body. In both versions, the fact that she could not be killed in close combat is important. [Saxo, Damico]

Weetamoo: "King Philip" was an Indian sachem, or chief of a confederacy of tribes, who in A.D. 1675 tried to repulse the English invaders in North America. His most important ally was Weetamoo, also known as "Squaw Sachem." She led three hundred warriors against fifty-two of the ninety English settlements, annihilating twelve of them. She might have succeeded in her goal except for treachery. She and twenty-six of her warriors were surprised in a set-up English attack. Weetamoo drowned in a river during her escape attempt. Her corpse was mutilated by the British and her head put on a pole before her twenty-six captured warriors, who wept and sang their sorrows. [Josephy]

West, Sarah: A broadsheet entitled "The Sorrowful Lamentation of Miss Sarah West" published in A.D. 1782 tells of a woman onboard the man-of-war *Formidable,* commanded by the brave Rodney. Her lover was press-ganged, and Sarah disguised herself as a man so that they might serve together. In an engagement with De Grasse, Sarah was mortally wounded.

Her lover, raging and distraught, seized her corpse and leaped into the ocean, "amid the tears and lamentation of his brave companions."

Wesuriyanza: "She Who Strangles." A Hittite demon-goddess with lion's head, ass's teeth, and bird's claws. Serpents are her soldiers. She is protectress of newborn animals and is portrayed suckling dogs and pigs, but she is also vampiric, and related to **Lilith.** [Lacks]

White Snake: The title character of the Beijing opera *White Snake* is a serpent-princess who by the purity of her spirit attained immortality and took the form of a beautiful woman who fell in love with a mortal. In the course of the story, she uses her skills as a swordswoman to free her husband from captors and to win a magic herb from armored deities. Her maid Green Snake is not as far along in spiritual development and, in her utter devotion to White Snake, is more prone to violence in White Snake's defense. Together, the two snake-women battle an entire army of gods. The opera dates to the Ching Dynasty, but the legend itself is much older, a sentimentalized **Lamia** myth in which the snake-woman, for all her great power and venomous potential, is essentially trustworthy, and her husband is foolish to mistrust her simply because of her demonic origins. [Han]

Wise, Mary Ellen: In the American Civil War, she fought with the 34th Regiment Indiana Volunteers, and was wounded in action. [Laffin]

Wisna: She was "a woman filled with sternness and a skilled warrior," leader of a host of Wends who fought with long swords and bucklers. Wisna was one of three famous "she-captains" (see **Webiorg** and **Hetha**) who brought their ships and soldiers to fight at the Battle of Bravalla, where Wisna attended one assault as King Ring's standard-bearer. Starkad, leader of the Slavs, lopped off her hand to make her drop the banner, but she continued to fight.

The Battle of Bravalla was the greatest and bloodiest of the battles between the Danes and Swedes, involving 200,000 soldiers, 5,000 ships, and kings of twelve nations. The "she-captains" led their respective armies onto land and into the thick of battle, their bodies covered with small, jangling shields, fighting with extremely long swords. "They exposed their bodies to every peril, offering battle with drawn swords." Female warriors were common in Scandinavian history, **Rusla, Stikla, Heid, Irpa, Torborg, Groa,** and **Alfhild** among those whose names are remembered. For the mythic counterparts that inspired such women, see the **Valkyries.** [Saxo]

Witneg, Hannah: Irishwoman who in the 1760s served his majesty "with fortitude and valor" for six years, in male guise, as a marine. [Laffin]

Wolonsky, Princess: In World War I, this athletic twenty-one-year-old Russian aristocrat disguised herself as a man and participated in the offensive of Wolhynia as an ordinary soldier. She had joined the infantry to avenge her husband and brothers, fallen in battle. When her sex was discovered, she was sent to Kiev, but escaped and returned to the front where she again fought undetected. Wounded and shipped to a hospital in Charkov, she expressed only the desire to heal quickly and return to battle. [Hirshfeld]

Woman Chief: Edwin T. Denig wrote in 1855 a biography of the Woman Chief of the Crow. "Long before she ventured on the warpath she could rival any of the young men in all their amusements and occupations, was a capital shot with the rifle, and would spend most of her time in killing deer and bighorn, which she butchered and carried home on her back when hunting on foot." In a battle confrontation,

> Several Blackfeet came to meet her, rejoicing in the occasion of securing an easy prize. When within pistol shot, she called on them to stop, but they paid no attention. One of the enemies fired at her and the rest charged. She immediately shot down one with her gun, and shot arrows into two more without receiving a wound. The remaining two then rode back to the main body, who came at full speed to murder the woman. They fired showers of balls and pursued her as near to the fort as they could. She escaped unharmed and entered the gates amid the shouts and praises of the whites and her own people.

When councils were held, this woman ranked third in the band of 160 lodges. She had a long career of hunting and warring until, by treachery alone, her traditional enemy the Blackfeet murdered her during her attempt to secure peace.

Wonder Woman: Classic comic book character created by the psychologist William Moulton Marston. She came from an Amazon island ruled by her mother. In the patriarchal world, she had a Clark Kent–like secret identity, as Diana. She fights supercriminals and saves Steve, the moderately competent boyfriend typical of the superheroine genre, from doom. Given the male-dominated nature of the comics industry, wherein all marketing tactics are for boys and all heroines basically sex objects, Wonder Woman stands out as a notable feminist success. More typical, alas, is Supergirl, a pale feminine counterpart to Superman, or Mary Marvel, very much second string to Captain Marvel. Firehair was a Lone Ranger type of heroine from the *Ranger Comics* of the 1940s.

Wosret: "The Powerful." A very ancient Theban War-goddess. [Hart]

Wu Ching-hua: Heroine of the modern dance drama "Red Detachment of Women." She was a peasant who fought in the communist revolution, at first for revenge, ultimately out of idealism. She was not merely a romantic fabrication, for women's militias were commonplace during the revolution. The Fourth Front Army included an independent regiment of two thousand women. [Rowbothan]

Wu of Hwang Ho (fl. A.D. 635) "The Dauntless One." Her foster father was a bannerman, soldier of high station, with whom she traveled in her childhood. They were once waylaid by Tartar highwaymen and her father took a suicidal stand, shouting for the girl to flee for her life. Instead, she stood boldly against the mounted robbers. When one of them tried to snatch her from the ground, with rape and enslavement in mind, she ran underneath the horse's belly, then took off for the hills laughing. The robbers were drawn off from her father, whose life was thereby saved, and the swift girl could not be captured on the rocky hillside.

When asked, "What of all things wouldst thou like?" the young Wu replied, "To be a boy!" She prayed to her divinities that it become so. The following year, she learned her true identity as daughter of Prince Kung-ti, the imperial heir who had been assassinated by the current occupant of the throne. Wu, though only fourteen years old, swore revenge. She loved archery and, in a contest with the emperor's son, defeated him, so that he set his private guard upon the upstart maiden. She stood her ground and declared herself the true empress of China and, being recognized as Prince Kung-ti's lost daughter, set justice, and revenge, in motion.

She became known to Western authors as the **Zenobia** of China, and her reign was one of the longest of any Chinese monarch. She governed wisely, extending her nation's boundaries, and received obeisance from India, Persia, and Korea. [E. Brooks]

◆◆◆◆◆◆◆◆◆◆◆◆◆◆◆

Xanthippe: "Yellow Mare." Amazon sabrer in the Attic War led by **Orithia**. Also, the much-maligned wife of Socrates, probably not the shrew made of her. [Bothmer]

Xantho: A huntress and nymph, companion to **Cyrene**.

Xuan, Bui Thi: In the late 1700s, inspired by such national heroines as the **Trung** sisters, this Vietnamese woman became a famous general in a wave of peasant rebellions that helped establish a reformist dynasty. When the dynasty collapsed, Bui Thi Xuan continued to fight. When she was finally captured and executed, the new emperor fed her heart, arms, liver, and lungs to his troops, believing that her remains would imbue his troops with courage. Today in Hanoi, there is a street named after her.

Americans learned during the Vietnam War, as the French had learned before them, that such powerfully patriotic women were not merely the heroines of antiquity. A Vietnamese woman guerrilla, tortured to death by the French, left a poem in her cell, written in her own blood:

> A rosy-cheeked woman,
> Here I am fighting side by side with you men!
> On my shoulders weighs the hatred which is common to us.
> The prison is my school, its inmates my friends.
> The sword is my child, the gun my husband.
> [Rowbothan, Eisen-Bergman]

Yaa Asantewa: (d. A.D. 1921) An Ashanti Queen Mother in what is now Ghana, who led her people in several successful battles against the British in 1900 and 1901. [Lorde, Qunta, Sertima]

Yang Paifeng: Her story is recorded in *Generals of the Yang Family,* written during the Sung Dynasty, and dramatized in the two-hundred-year-old Beijing opera *Young Phoenix Soars to the Sky.*

Yanshao, commander of the Sung troops on the northern frontier, learned that two of his generals (his sisters) were trapped in a ravine with enemy on all sides. An urgent message was sent to the dowager general (herself a famous warrior in her youth), who recommended a servant named Yang Paifeng as the tactician most capable for the emergency. The generals of the family were not in agreement with the recommendation. Despite the fact that Yang Paifeng excelled in martial learning, she was yet of low status and therefore unsuited to captaining more than housemaids. When matters worsened, the family finally agreed to the dowager general's advice, and Yang Paifeng accepted the commission. Leading a surprise assault, she rescued the generals from the ravine, and earned a place in the family records.

The story of the Yang family generals has been the inspiration of songs, stories, theater, and art for nearly one thousand years. Many of the family generals were women, including Yang Paifeng's grandmother, **Mu Guiying.**

Yatsushiro: Japanese woman warrior, wife of Kiheiji, a retainer to Tame-tomo. She fought with **naginata** and went into battle even while pregnant. Her pet wolf Nokaze was always at her side.

Yellow Martha: A Cossack warrior of World War I, named for her yellow hair. [Hirshfeld]

Yim Ving Tsun: Or Yin Wang Chun, a Shaolin nun of the sixteenth century A.D. who studied temple boxing under another nun, **Ng Miu.** Tsun went on to develop many kung fu training aids. She also developed a new style called Ving Tsun kung fu or Wing Chun Pai ("Eternal Springtime System"), inspired by her observations of a snake and a crane. Her style is popular to this day, and she is often referred to in martial arts books published after the cinematic fame of Bruce Lee, for he was a disciple of this nun's style, upon which he patterned his own Jeet Koon Do.

Yoko, Madame: A diplomat, organizer, agriculturalist, and warrior, Madame Yoko ruled fourteen tribes constituting the Kpa Mende Confederacy of the 1800s. It was the largest chiefdom of Sierre Leone. Far from being a historic anomaly, she is fairly representative. In her day, full fifteen percent of all tribes around Sierre Leone were ruled by women. To this day, despite changing values, nine percent of the tribes have women chiefs. Although their histories have been obscured, many of the greatest warchiefs of Africa, as well as the peacemakers, have been women.

Accounts of women's armies throughout Africa are numerous. The ancient historian Diodorus Siculus discussed warlike women's nations of western Africa, and much that he recorded was confirmed by later explorers from the 1500s to the 1700s, including an East African Amazon state described by Father Alvares; Monsieur d'Arnaud's account of female guards on the Upper Nile; and Pigafetta's account of women soldiers of the Monomotapa. The French archaeologist Henri Lhote studied Sahara rock drawings in the 1930s and 1950s, finding evidence of a troop of bow-carrying women warriors, powerful evidence of Diodorus' Amazons of western Libya.

Magrizi, a medieval Arab writer, reported Amazon lancers of the Beja tribe. Eduard López saw women archers who served the ruler of Mono-motapa in central Africa. As late as 1964, an elite body of five thousand Amazons were obedient to Dr. Hastings Bando, founder and first premier of Malawi (Nyasaland). His female corps was instrumental in helping achieve independence for Malawi and of guarding the crucial boundary with Tanganika. In Henry Morton Stanley's *Through the Dark Continent* is a photograph of a troop of riflewomen in the service of King Mtesa of Uganda. The Yoruba of West Africa tell stories of female heroines and of a women's army displaced by men, and of Aderemi, female ruler of the Ilesha. [Kanter, Diner, Courlander, Loth]

Z

◆◇◆◇◆◇◆◇◆◇◆◇◆◇◆

Zabbai, Bat: Aramaic name of **Zenobia.**

Zabibi: Arabian warrior-queen who led armies circa 740 B.C. She was succeeded by **Samsi.** [Fraser]

Zahara: In medieval Spanish romance, Amazon queen of the Caucasus. She was battled by Amadis's grandson, much as Amadis had battled **Califia.**

Zainab: In Arab legends, Zainab, whose name is the Arab rendering of **Zenobia,** was one of two warrior sisters, the other being **Zebbâ,** whose castles were built on opposing banks of the Euphrates.

Zaire: (fl. sixteenth century A.D.) Youngest daughter of Queen Bakwa **Turunku** and sister of Queen **Amina** and one of her generals. The capital of their extensive West African nation was in Zazzau. It was afterward renamed for Zaire and still carries her name. [Qunta]

Zarina: Ancient warrior-queen of Scythia, from a tradition postdating the **Thermodontine** Amazons. From her name is derived the term "czar" and she was said to be very beautiful as well as warlike. She founded the city of Roxanacé and was the conqueror of Media. She slew her own husband to save a Median prince, but when she refused to take the prince as her new consort, he committed suicide. [Diner, Goodrich]

Zebbâ: Also given as al-Zabbâ or az-Zabbâ, a woman warrior of Arab legend, famous for her beauty as well as her valor. She had two fortresses on opposing banks of the Euphrates and in some versions her sister **Zainab** occupies one of them. The name could be based on that of Queen Zabel, thirteenth-century ruler of Lesser Armenia. [Fraser]

Zelmane: Warrior-queen of Sir Philip Sidney's Restoration play *Arcadia*.

Zelmura: Warred against Memphis and defeated that city in Thomas Durfey's 1676 play *Siege of Memphis; or, The Ambitious Queen:*

> The Queen did dauntless stand,
> Terrour coucht in her eye, death in her hand;
> The Heartless Crowd wondering, look up to spy
> This new Bellona ushered from the Sky.

Similar Restoration plays include *Amazon Queen; or, The Amours of Thelestris to Alexander the Great* by John Weston (1667); *Boadicea, Queen of Great Britain* by Charles Hopkins (1697); Edward Howard's *The Women's Conquest, A Tragi-Comedy* (1671), featuring **Mandana,** queen of the Amazons; the earlier *Bunduca* (1614) by John Fletcher, a misogynist retelling of **Boudicca's** history; the late-occurring *Zenobia: A Tragedy* (1768) by Arthur Murphy; and many others. The story of Zelmura is a cut above most, with pleasing turns of phrase here and there:

> And women's courage by ambition warm'd
> Dares laugh at danger, though all Hell stood arm'd.

An adequate history of women of the Restoration has yet to be written, but the recurrent characterization of the Amazon on the stage is an indicator of the depth of feminist (and antifeminist) concerns in that era.

Zenobia Septimia: An accomplished hunter of panthers and lions, Zenobia was of the same royal line as **Cleopatra.** She came to govern Syria from about A.D. 250 to 275. She wrote the history of her nation, being accomplished in letters, and during her reign was unsurpassed in courage and judgment. "When she rode out in arms, which happened frequently, she did not speak to her army unless she was in armor. She was never carried on a litter as was common among rulers, but went always on a warhorse."

Rome attempted to exert control over the rival Empire of the East, but was met with Zenobia's stern refusal. Therefore, Rome invaded Syria. Zenobia met the Romans with such ferocity that the self-proclaimed masters of the world fled back to Europe in disgrace. Zenobia was instantly heralded Mistress of Nations. Arabia, Armenia, and Persia allied themselves with her. She extended her control to the Euphrates over much of Asia Minor, claimed dominion over Egypt by right of ancestry, and purportedly used her authority to preserve a veritable libertine empire. Claudius feared her after the Syrian defeats and did not urge further military confrontation.

After the death of Claudius, it was an Illyrian peasant who rose in the military ranks to restore the Roman Empire. His reign was short, less than five years, yet rivaled the first Caesar in achievement, reclaiming lands of the Goths, Gauls, Vandals, Franks and eventually Zenobia's allied nations of Persia, Egypt, and finally Syria itself. Had Rome not been given a virtual savior in its terrible hour of need, the outcome might have been otherwise, with European history shadowed by the might of the East. When Aurelian sent messengers to her capital demanding Zenobia submit to Rome, her reply was firm: "It is only by arms that the submission you require can be achieved. You forget that Cleopatra preferred death to servitude. When you see me in war, you will repent your insolent proposition."

Aurelian by no means underestimated Zenobia. He sent the best of his legions. Long and dreadful as the campaign was for both sides, Zenobia's empire was eventually reduced to her capital city, firm-walled Palmyra. At length, the city fell, and the legions returned to their emperor with ten martial queens, including the magnificent Zenobia, in chains. In the famous procession of conquered queens, Zenobia rode in a war chariot of her own design, and was weighted down not only with chains, but also with fabulous jewels.

Aurelian was lenient, or respectful, and Zenobia was forced to retire to a rich villa at Tibur (now Tivoli) near Rome, exerting the lesser political influence of a Roman matron. Her daughters married into important families and her line was influential for almost three more centuries. [Vaughan, Pizan, Hale, Jameson]

Zephrytis: An ancient poetic name for **Arsinoë II Philadelphus,** because of her temple on the promontory of Zephryion.

Zerynthia: A Scythian Amazon.

Zeuxo of Argos: One of three sister-charioteers, the others being **Eu-**

crateia and **Hermione.** They raced their horses in the Panathenaea about 197 B.C. and in Athens in 194 B.C. and 182 B.C. [Lefkowitz, Pomeroy]

Zeuxo of Cyrene: Wife of Polycrates of Argos. Her name is a derivation of Zeuxidia, a name for **Hera,** who in Lebadeia, Boeotia, was worshipped as "the Charioteer." Zeuxo was also the name of a Sea-goddess. Like **Berenice II,** Zeuxo was from Cyrene, a city noted for equestrian arts, and named for its Amazon founder. She raised her daughters to be athletes as well. The sisters **Eucrateia, Hermione,** and **Zeuxo of Argos** followed their mother's example, racing at the Panathenaea about 197 B.C. [Pomeroy, Lefkowitz]

Ziska's Army of Women: Queen Sophia of Bohemia, widow of mad King Wenceslas, garrisoned the royal castles against Sigismund, emperor of Germany, and John Ziska, a fierce, cruel, one-eyed patriot who in the early 1400s sought control of Bohemia for himself. On at least one occasion, at the battle on the plains near Pilsen, Ziska's motley army of "reformers" consisted largely of women and some of their children. When Sophia's army rode against him, he gave the order for the women to strew the ground with their gowns and veils. The orderly attack was thrown askew by this surprise tactic, for the horses' legs were entangled in the cloth. Ziska, "the blind warrior of Bohemia," ordered the footwomen to drag the soldiers from their horses, and they responded so fiercely that Sophia's professional army was defeated. See also **Libussa.** [Morris]

Zobeida the Whipper and other Arabian Nights Amazons: About A.D. 800, Scheherazade told her tales of *The Arabian Nights* to a cruel, despairing sultan in order to keep him from murdering more women. Her tales featured an endless array of female characters, many in occupations that do not seem very traditional. Some were historical figures and contemporaries of Scheherazade, as in the case of Zobeida the Whipper, who cowed even great princes. The historic Zobeida (A.D. 765?–831) founded the city of Tauris and was of a very vigorous character. Her name is sometimes given as Zoebd-el-Khematin, "The Flower of Women."

Similar *Arabian Nights* characters include a prince-eating ogress; a magician-princess who slays a lion with her sword; the queen of El-Wak-Wak and her father's 25,000 spearwomen; Aladdin's most trusted messenger, his far-traveling mother; and a fighting princess who enslaves a magic bird and helps right an injustice against a queen.

Zosteria: "Girt" or "Armed for Battle." A name for **Hera** as worshipped in Thebes and Boeotia.

Zoulvisia: A beautiful maiden-warrior of Armenian legend. After she had slain thousands in combat, a hero came to avenge the dead, but he fell in love with her instead. He defeated her by learning her cult mysteries, rather than in combat, for otherwise she was invulnerable. As Armenia was one of the areas of Amazon activity in antiquity, Zoulvisia's gift of power given to a conquerer cum lover appears to be a late-surviving memory of the Amazons' absorption into patriarchal tribes. [Lang]

SELECT BIBLIOGRAPHY

❖❖❖❖❖❖❖❖❖❖❖❖❖

Abbott, Nabia. *Aishah: The Beloved of Mohammed*. Chicago: University of Chicago Press, 1942.

Aikman, Duncan. *Calamity Jane and the Lady Wildcats*. New York: Holt, 1927.

Antz, August. *Legends of the Rhineland*. Bonn: Wilhelm Stollfus Verlog, n.d.

Ariosto, Ludovico. *Orlando Furioso*. Middlesex: Penguin, 1976.

Arzans de Orsúa y Vela, Bartolemé. *Tales of Potosí*, tr. Frances M. López-Morillas. Providence, Rhode Island: Brown University Press, 1975.

Asbury, Herbert. *The Gangs of New York*. New York: Garden City Publishing, 1928.

Assa, Janine. *The Great Roman Ladies*, tr. Anne Hollander. New York: Grove, 1960.

Bachofen, Johann. *Myth, Religion and Mother Rite*, c. 1861, tr. George Boas. Princeton, New Jersey: Princeton University Press, 1967.

Bacon, Alice Mabel. *Japanese Girls and Women*. Boston: Houghton Mifflin, 1902.

Barrett, William E. *Woman on Horseback: The Biography of Francisco Lopez and Eliza Lynch*. London: Peter Davies, 1938.

Beard, Mary R. *The Force of Women in Japanese History*. Washington, D.C.: Public Affairs Press, 1953.

————. *On Understanding Women*. London: Longman's, 1931.

————. *Woman as a Force in History*. New York: Macmillan, 1946.

Beaumont, Edouard de. *The Sword and Womankind*. New York: Panurge Press, 1929.

Bennett, Florence Mary. *Religious Cults Associated with the Amazons*. New York: AMS Press, 1967.

Berger, Robert W. "Ruben's 'Queen Tomyris with the Head of Cyrus,' " in *Bulletin of the Museum of Fine Arts*, vol. 77 (Boston, 1979).

Berkson, Carmel. *The Amazon and the Goddess: Cognates of Artistic Form*. Bombay: Somaiya Publications, 1987.

Bethune, G. W. *The British Female Poets*. New York: Hurst, c. 1884.

Blashfield, Jean F. *Hellraisers, Heroines, and Holy Women*. New York: St. Martin's, 1981.

Bloss, C. A. *Heroines of the Crusades*. Auburn: Alden & Beardsley, 1853.

Blue, Adrianne. *Faster, Higher, Further: Women's Triumphs and Disasters at the Olympics*. London: Virago Press, 1988.

Boccaccio. *Concerning Famous Women*, tr. Guido A. Guarino. New Brunswick, New Jersey: Rutgers University Press, 1963.

Botchkareva, Maria. *Yashka: My Life as Peasant Officer and Exile*. New York: Stokes, 1919.

Bothmer, Dietrich von. *Amazons in Greek Art*. Oxford: Clarendon Press, 1957.

Boulting, William. *Woman in Italy*. London: Methuen, 1910.

Breisach, Ernst. *Catarina Sforza: A Renaissance Virago*. Chicago: University of Chicago Press, 1967.

Briggs, Katherine M. *A Dictionary of British Folk-Tales* 4 vols. Bloomington: Indiana University Press, 1971.

Brontë, Emily Jane. *Gondal's Queen*, ed. Fannie E. Ratchford. Austin: University of Texas Press, 1955.

Brooks, E. S. *Historic Girls: Stories of Girls Who Have Influenced the History of Their Times*. New York: Putnam, 1887.

Brooks, Geraldine. *Dames and Daughters of Colonial Days*. New York: Arno Press, 1974.

Brown, Dee. *The Gentle Tamers: Women of the Old Wild West*. New York: Putnam, 1958.

Bulfinch, Thomas. *Bulfinch's Mythology*. Boston: Tilton, 1881.

Burgess, A. *The Lovely Sergeant*. New York: Dutton, 1963.

Burnett, Virgil. *Towers at the Edge of the World: Tales of a Medieval Town*. New York: St. Martin's, 1980.

Campbell, Joseph. *The Masks of God: Primitive Mythology*. Middlesex: Viking Penguin, 1959; rev. 1969.

Carlova, John. *Mistress of the Sea*. New York: Citadel, 1964.

Chadwick, Nora. *The Celts*. New York: Pelican Books, 1970.

Chandrakant, Kamala. *Tarabai, The Valorous Queen of Rajasthan*. Bombay: India Book House, n.d.

Cintrón, Conchita. *Memoirs of a Bullfighter*. New York: Holt, Rinehart & Winston, 1968.

Cleugh, James. *The Marquis and the Chevalier*. New York: Duell, Sloan and Pierce, 1952.

Conrad, Barnaby. *La Fiesta Brava: The Art of the Bull Ring*. Boston: Houghton Mifflin, 1953.

Conrad, Jack Randolph. *The Horn and the Sword*. New York: Dutton, 1957.

Cook, S. A., *et al.* (eds.). *The Cambridge Ancient History*. New York: Macmillan, 1923.

Courlander, Harold. *Tales of Yoruba Gods and Heroes*. New York: Crown, 1973.

Course, A. G. *Pirates of the Western Seas*. London: Frederick Muller, 1969.

Crawford, Anne, *et al.* (eds.). *The Europa Biographical Dictionary of British Women*. Detroit: Gale Research, 1983.

Croix, Robert de la. *A History of Piracy*. New York: Manor Books, 1978.

Damico, Helen. *Beowulf's Wealtheow and the Valkyrie Tradition*. Madison: University of Wisconsin Press, 1984.

Davidson, Hilda R. Ellis. *Gods and Myths of Northern Europe*. Baltimore: Penguin, 1964.

————. *Myth and Symbol in Pagan Europe*. Manchester: Manchester University Press, 1988.

Davis, Elizabeth Gould. *The First Sex*. New York: Putnam, 1971.

Davis, Fei-Ling. *Primitive Revolutionaries in China: A Study of Secret Societies of the Late Nineteenth Century*. Honolulu: University of Hawaii Press, 1971.

Day, Lillian. *Ninon: A Courtesan of Quality*. London: Jarrolds, 1958.

Defoe, Daniel. *The Life and Adventures of Mother Ross*. London: Peter Davies, 1928.

De Quincey, Thomas. *Joan of Arc, The English Mail-Coach, and the Spanish Military Nun*, edited and with textual notes by Carol M. Newman. New York: Macmillan, 1905.

Detienne, Marcel. *Dionysos at Large*, tr. Arthur Goldhammer. Cambridge, Massachusetts: Harvard University Press, 1989.

Diner, Helen. *Mothers and Amazons: The First Feminine History of Culture*. New York: Doubleday, 1965.

Diodorus Siculus. *The History of the World*, tr. G. Turnbull. London: Birt & Dodd, 1746.

duBois, Page. *Centaurs and Amazons: Women and the Pre-History of the Great Chain of Being*. Ann Arbor: University of Michigan Press, 1982.

Duff, Nora. *Matilda of Tuscany*. London: Methuen, 1909.

Dumézil, Georges. *From Myth to Fiction: The Saga of Hadingur*, tr. D. Coultman. Chicago: University of Chicago Press, 1973.

Eberhardt, Isabelle. *The Oblivion Seekers*, translated and with a preface by Paul Bowles. San Francisco: City Lights, 1972.

Edwardes, Marian, and Lewis Spence. *A Dictionary of Non-Classical Mythology*. London: Dent, 1912.

Edwards, S. *Daughter of Gascony*. Philadelphia: MacRae Smith, 1963.

Effinger, John R. *Woman in All Ages and in All Countries*. Philadelphia: Rittenhouse, 1908.

Eisen-Bergman, Arlene. *Women of Viet Nam*. San Francisco: People's Press, 1975.

Ellet, Elizabeth F. *The Women of the American Revolution*. New York: Baker and Scribner, 1850.

Ellis, Peter Beresford. *A Dictionary of Irish Mythology*. London: Constable, 1987.

Erlanger, Philippe. *Margaret of Anjou, Queen of England*. Florida: University of Miami Press, 1971.

Etienne, Mona, and Eleanore B. Leacock (eds). *Women and Colonization*. New York: Praeger, 1980.

Eudes, Dominique. *Partisans and Civil War in Greece*. New York: Monthly Review Press, 1972.

Evans, Bergen. *Dictionary of Mythology, Mainly Classical*. New York: Dell, 1970.

Evans, Elizabeth. *Weathering the Storm: Women of the American Revolution*. New York: Scribner's, 1975.

Evslin, Bernard. *Heraclea: A Legend of Warrior Women*. New York: Four Winds, 1978.

Falk, Bernard. *The Naked Lady: A Biography of Adah Isaacs Menken*. London: Hutchinson, 1934.

Farnell, Lewis Richard. *The Cults of the Greek States*. 5 vols. New Rochelle: Caratzas Brothers, 1977.

————. *Greece and Babylon: A Comparative Sketch of Mesopotamian, Anatolian and Hellenic Religions*. Edinburgh: Clark, 1911.

Fell, Christine, Ciciley Clark, and Elizabeth Williams. *Women in Anglo-Saxon England*. London: British Museum Publications, 1984.

Fisher, Elizabeth. *Woman's Creation: Sexual Evolution and the Shaping of Society*. New York: McGraw-Hill, 1979.

Fittis, Robert Scott. *Heroines of Scotland*. London: Alexander Gardner, 1889.

Fox, R. M. *Rebel Irishwomen*. Dublin: Talbot, 1935.

Fraser, Antonia. *The Warrior Queens*. London: Weidenfeld & Nicolson, 1988.

————. *The Weaker Vessel*. New York: Knopf, 1984.

Friedrich, Paul. *The Meaning of Aphrodite*. Chicago: University of Chicago Press, 1978.

Gaines, Charles, and George Butler. *Pumping Iron II: The Unprecedented Women*. New York: Simon and Schuster, 1984.

Geis, Frances and Joseph. *Women in the Middle Ages*. New York: Crowell, 1978.

Glasspoole, Richard. *Mr. Glasspoole and the Chinese Pirates*. London: Golden Cockrell, 1935.

Godolphin, F. R. B. (ed.). *Great Classical Myths*. New York: Random House, 1964.

Goodrich, Norma Lorre. *Medieval Myths*. New York: Signet, 1977.

————. *Priestesses*. New York: Watts, 1989.

Grant, Michael. *Gladiators*. London: Weidenfield & Nicolson, 1967.

Graves, Robert. *The Greek Myths*. 2 vols. Middlesex: Penguin, 1955; rev. 1960.

————. *The White Goddess*. New York: Knopf, 1948.

————, and Raphael Patai. *Hebrew Myths*. New York: Doubleday, 1964.

Gribble, Francis. *Women in War*. New York: Dutton, 1917.

Hale, Sarah Josepha. *Woman's Record; Or, Sketches of All Distinguished Women, from "The Beginning" till A.D. 1850*. New York: Harper, 1853.

Han, Tien. *The White Snake*. Beijing: Foreign Language Press, 1957.

Harksen, Sibylle. *Women in the Middle Ages*. London: Abner Schram, 1975.

Hart, George. *A Dictionary of Egyptian Gods and Goddesses*. London: Routledge and Kegan Paul, 1986.

Hawthorne, Julian (ed). *Moorish Literature*. New York: Colonial Press, 1901.

Heidel, Alexander. *The Babylonian Genesis*. Chicago: University of Chicago Press, 1951.

Herodotus. *The Histories*, tr. Aubrey de Sélincourt. Baltimore: Penguin, 1954.

Hickok, Jane Canary. *Calamity Jane's Letters to Her Daughter*. San Lorenzo, California: Shameless Hussy, 1976.

Higuchi, Chiyoko. *Her Place in the Sun: Women Who Shaped Japan*. Tokyo: The East Publications, 1973.

Hirshfeld, Magnus. *A Sexual History of the World War*. New York: Panurge Press, 1934.

Horan, James D. *Desperate Women*. New York: Putnam, 1952.

Hosey, Timothy. "Samurai Women: Masters of Broom and Sword," in *Black Belt*, December 1980.

Huddy, Mary. *Matilda, Countess of Tuscany*. London: John Long, 1906.

Hungry Wolf, Beverly. *The Ways of My Grandmothers*. New York: Morrow, 1980.

Hurston, Zora Neale. *I Love Myself When I Am Laughing . . . And Then Again When I Am Looking Mean and Impressive*, ed. Alice Walker. New York: Feminist Press, 1979.

Hyde, Douglas. *A Literary History of Ireland*. London: Ernest Benn, 1899.

Ions, Veronica. *Indian Mythology*. London: Paul Hamlyn, 1967.

Jameson, Anna. *Memoires of Celebrated Female Sovereigns*. New York: Harper & Row, 1868.

Jay, Karla. *The Amazon and the Page*. Bloomington: Indiana University Press, 1988.

Jordanes. *Origin and Deeds of the Goths*, tr. Charles C. Mierow. New York: Barnes and Noble, 1915.

Josephy, Alvin M., Jr. *The Patriot Chiefs: A Chronicle of American Indian Resistance*. New York: Viking, 1961.

Kanter, Emanuel. *The Amazons*. Chicago: Charles H. Kerr, 1926.

Katz, Jonathon Ned. *Gay/Lesbian Almanac: A New Documentary*. New York: Harper & Row, 1983.

Kavanagh, Julia. *Women in France during the Eighteenth Century*. New York: Putnam, 1893.

Kelly, Amy. *Eleanor of Aquitaine and the Four Kings*. Cambridge, Massachusetts: Harvard University Press, 1950.

Kerényi, C. *Zeus and Hera*. Princeton, New Jersey: Princeton University Press, 1975.

King, Dorothy. *Stories of Scotland in Days of Old*. London: Jack, 1906.

King, William C. (ed). *Woman: Her Position, Influence and Achievement throughout the Civilized World*. Springfield: King-Richardson Co., 1900.

Kirk, G. S. *The Nature of Greek Myths*. Middlesex: Penguin, 1974.

Kleinbaum, Abby Wettan. *The War against the Amazons*. New York: McGraw-Hill, 1983.

Kramer, Samuel Noah (ed.). *Mythologies of the Ancient World*. New York: Doubleday, 1961.

Kuo, Louise, and Yuan Hsi. *Chinese Folk Tales*. Millbrae, California: Celestial Arts, 1976.

Lacks, Roslyn. *Women and Judaism: Myth, History, and Struggle*. New York: Doubleday, 1980.

Laffin, John. *Women in Battle*. London: Abelard-Schuman, 1967.

Lang, Andrew. The colored Fairy Books.

Lantis, Margaret. "The Mythology of Kodiak Island, Alaska," in *The Journal of American Folk-Lore*, April-June 1938.

La Rocca, Eugenio. *Amazzonomachia: le sculpture frontonali del tempio di Apollo Sosiano*. Rome: De Luca, 1985.

Lawrence, Dorothy. *Sapper Dorothy Lawrence*. London: John Lane, 1919.

Lebra-Chapman, Joyce. *The Rani of Jhansi: A Study in Female Heroism in India*. Honolulu: University of Hawaii Press, 1986.

Lederer, Wolfgang. *The Fear of Women*. New York: Harcourt Brace Jovanovich, 1968.

Lefkowitz, Mary R., and Maureen B. Fant. *Women's Life in Greece and Rome*. London: Duckworth, 1982.

Leonowens, Anna H. *Siamese Harem Life*, 1873. London: Arthur Barker, 1953.

Logan, Mary S. C. *The Part Taken by Women in American History*. Wilmington, Delaware: Perry-Nalle Publications, 1912.

Lorde, Audre. *The Black Unicorn*. New York: Norton, 1979.

Loth, Heinrich. *Woman in African Art*. Connecticut: Lawrence Hill, 1978.

Louise, Michel. *The Red Virgin: Memoir*, tr. Bullit Lowry and Elizabeth Ellington Gunter. Tuscaloosa, Alabama: University of Alabama Press, 1981.

Mackenzie, Faith Compton. *The Tale of Christina, Queen of Sweden*. London: Casell, 1931.

Macksey, Joan and Kenneth. *Book of Women's Achievements*. New York: Stein & Day, 1975.

Mackworth, Cecily. *The Destiny of Isabelle Eberhardt*. New York: Ecco, 1975.

Macurdy, Grace Harriet. *Hellenistic Queens: A Study of Woman-Power in Macedonia, Seleucia Syria, and Ptolemaic Egypt*. Baltimore: Johns Hopkins University Press, 1932.

Mahaffy, Sir John P. *The Empire of the Ptolemies*. London: Macmillan, 1895.

Marek, George R. *The Bed and the Throne: The Life of Isabella d'Este*. New York: Harper, 1976.

Markale, Jean. *Women of the Celts*. London: Gordon Cremonesi, 1975.

Marreco, Anne. *The Rebel Countess: The Life and Times of Constance Markievicz*. Philadelphia: Chilton, 1967.

Marshall, Rosalind K. *Virgins and Viragos: A History of Women in Scotland from 1080–1980*. Chicago: Academy Chicago, 1983.

Masson, Georgina. *Queen Christina*. New York: Farrar, Straus & Giroux, 1969.

Masud-ul-Hasan. *Unique Women of the World*. Pakistan: Unique Publications, n.d., c. 1980.

McCormick, Patricia. *Lady Bullfighter*. New York: Holt, 1954.

Meyer, Edith Patterson. *Petticoat Patriots of the American Revolution*. New York: Vanguard, 1976.

Miles, Rosalind. *The Women's History of the World*. London: Michael Joseph, 1988.

Mitchell, David. *Monstrous Regiment*. New York: Macmillan, 1965.

Montez, Lola. *Lectures of Lola Montez*. New York: Rudd & Carleton, 1858.

Mookerjee, Ajit. *Kali the Feminine Force*. Boulder: Inner Traditions, 1989.

Moore, Frank. *Women of the War: Their Heroism and Self-Sacrifice*. Hartford, Connecticut: Scranton, 1866.

Morris, Charles. *Historical Tales, The Romance of Reality*. Los Angeles: Angelus Press, 1908.

Morris, Donald R. *The Washing of the Spears: The Rise and Fall of the Zulu Nation*. New York: Simon & Schuster, 1986.

Morris, Joan. *The Lady Was a Bishop*. New York: Macmillan, 1973.

Mrantz, Maxine. *Women of Old Hawaii*. Honolulu: Aloha Publishing, 1975.

Muller, Herbert J. *The Loom of History*. New York: Harper, 1958.

Murphy, Yolanda and Robert F. *Women of the Forest*. New York: Columbia University Press, 1974.

Myron, Nancy, and Charlotte Bunch (eds.). *Women Remembered*. Baltimore: Diana Press, 1974.

Narayan, R. K. *Gods, Demons, and Others*. New York: Viking, 1964.

Niethammer, Carolyn. *Daughters of the Earth: The Lives and Legends of American Indian Women*. New York: Collier, 1977.

Nilsson, Martin P. *The Minoan-Myceneaen Religion*. Lund: Gleerup, 1950.

O'Hara, Albert. *The Position of Women in Early China*. Taiwan: Mei Ya Publications, 1971.

Ormerod, H. A. *Piracy in the Ancient World*. New York: Doreste, 1987.

Overman, Alfred. *Die Grosgrafin Mathilde von Tuscien*. Germany, 1895.

Patai, Raphael. *Gates to the Old City: A Book of Jewish Legends*. New York: Avon, 1980.

Patel, Toni. *Chand Bibi the Valorous Princess*. Bombay: India Book House, n.d.

Peterson, Karen, and J. J. Wilson. *Women Artists*. New York: Harper & Row, 1976.

Petrovitch, Woislav M. *Hero Tales and Legends of the Serbians*. London: Harrap, 1914.

Pizan, Christine de. *City of Women*. New York: Persea, 1982.

Pocoke, Edward. *India in Greece*. Delhi: Oriental Publishers, 1972.

Polyaenus. *Stratagems of War*, tr. R. Shepherd (1793). Chicago: Ares Publications, 1974.

Pomeroy, Sarah B. *Goddesses, Whores, Wives, and Slaves: Women in Classical Antiquity*. New York: Schocken, 1975.

_____. *Women in Hellenistic Egypt*. New York: Schocken, 1984.

Pool, John J. *Famous Women of India*. Calcutta: Susl Gupta, 1892, 1954.

Powers, Eileen. *Medieval Women*. London: Cambridge University Press, 1975.

Preston, James J. (ed.). *Mother Worship: Theme and Variation*. Chapel Hill: University of North Carolina Press, 1982.

Puhvel, Martin. *Beowulf and Celtic Tradition*. Ontario: Wilfrid Laurier University Press, 1979.

Qunta, Christine. *Women in Southern Africa*. London: Allison & Busby, 1987.

Randall, Margaret. *Cuban Women Today*. Toronto: Women's Press, 1974.

Rankin, Mary Backus. *Early Chinese Revolutionaries: Radical Intellectuals in Shanghai and Checkiang 1902–1911*. Cambridge, Massachusetts: Harvard University Press, 1971.

Rappaport, Angelo S. *Myth and Legend of Ancient Israel*. London: Gresham, 1928.

Reefe, Thomas Q. *The Rainbow of the Kings: A History of the Luba Empire to 1891*. Berkeley: University of California Press, 1981.

Reich, Emil. *Women through the Ages*. 2 vols. London: Methuen, 1908.

Reilly, Bernard F. *The Kingdom of León-Castilla under Queen Urraca 1109–1126*. Princeton, New Jersey: Princeton University Press, 1982.

Reiter, Joan Swallow. *The Women*. Time-Life "The Old West" Series. Alexandria, Virginia: Time-Life, 1978.

Reiter, Rayna R. (ed). *Toward an Anthropology of Women*. New York: Monthly Review Press, 1975.

Ribner, Susan, and Richard Chin. *The Martial Arts*. New York: Harper & Row, 1978.

Richards, Colin. *Bowler Hats and Stetsons*. New York: Crown, 1986.

Rickert, Edith. *Chaucer's World*. New York: Columbia University Press, 1948.

Robertson, B. (ed.). *Air Aces of the 1914–18 War*. Los Angeles: Aero Publications, 1964.

Robinson, Charles Alexander, Jr. *Alexander the Great*. New York: Dutton, 1948.

Rogers, Cameron. *Gallant Ladies*. New York: Harcourt Brace Jovanovich, 1928.

Roja, Marta, and Mirta Rodrígez Calderón. *Tania the Unforgettable Guerilla*. New York: Random House, 1971.

Rothery, Guy Cadogan. *The Amazons in Antiquity and Modern Times*. London: Francis Griffiths, 1910.

Rowbothan, Sheila. *Women, Resistance and Revolution*. New York: Pantheon, 1972.

Russell, Nellie N. *Gleanings from Chinese Folklore*. New York: Powell, 1915.

Sacher-Masoch, Leopold von. *Venus in Furs*. New York: private printing, 1928.

Salmonson, Jessica Amanda. "Art, History, and Amazons," in *Amazons II*. New York: DAW, 1982.

————. "Everyday Life in Amazonia" (work in progress).

————. "Our Amazon Heritage," in *Amazons!* New York: Daw, 1979.

————. *Naginata: The Women Warriors' Newsletter*. Seattle: Duck's-Foot Tree, ten issues, 1980–1983.

Sandes, Flora. *An English Woman-Sergeant in the Serbian Army*. London: Hodder & Stoughton, 1916.

Savill, Agnes. *Alexander the Great and His Time*. New York: Citadel, 1959.

Saxo Grammaticus. *The History of the Danes*, tr. Peter Fisher, ed. Hilda Ellis Davidson. Suffolk: Brewer, 1979.

Schmidt, Minna Moscherosch (ed.). *Four Hundred Outstanding Women of the World and Costumology of Their Time*. Chicago: Schmidt, 1933.

Seltman, Charles. *Women in Antiquity*. New York: St. Martin's, 1956.

Sen, Ramprasad. *Grace and Mercy in Her Wild Hair: Selected Poems to the Mother Goddess*. Boulder: Great Eastern Book Company, 1982.

Seneviratne, Maureen. *Some Women of the Mahavamsa*. Ceylon: H. W. Cave, 1969.

Sertima, Ivan Van (ed.). *Black Women in Antiquity*. New Brunswick: Transaction Books, 1984; rev. 1988.

Seth, Ronald (ed.). *Milestones in Japanese History*. Philadelphia: Chilton, 1969.

Shepherd, Don (ed.). *Women in History: Selected from Mankind Magazine*. Los Angeles: Mankind Publishing, 1973.

Shepherd, Simon. *Amazons and Warrior Women: Varieties of Feminism in Seventeenth-Century Drama*. Sussex: Harvester, 1981.

Shoenfeld, Hermann. *Women of the Teutonic Nations*. Philadelphia: Rittenhouse Press, 1907.

Shostak, Marjorie. *Nisa: The Life and Words of a !Kung Woman*. Cambridge, Massachusetts: Harvard University Press, 1981.

Sinclair, Marjorie. *The Path of the Ocean: Traditional Poetry of Polynesia*. Honolulu: University of Hawaii Press, 1982.

Sinha, Shyam Narain. *Rani Laksmi Bai of Jhansi*. New Delhi: Chugh Publications, 1980.

Smyth, Sir John. *The Rebellious Rani*. London: Muller, 1966.

Snow, Edward Rowe. *Women of the Sea*. London: Alvin Redman, 1962.

Sobol, Donald. *The Amazons of Greek Mythology*. Cranbury, New Jersey: Barnes & Noble, 1973.

Solgado, Gamini. *The Elizabethan Underworld*. London: Dent, 1977.

Spence, Lewis. *North American Indians*. London: Harrap, 1914.

Starling, Elizabeth. *Noble Deeds of Women*. Boston: Philips, 1857.

Stone, Merlin. *When God Was a Woman*. New York: Harcourt Brace Jovanovich, 1976.

Strabo. *Geography*, tr. H. L. Jones. 8 vols. London: Heinemann, 1917–1932.

Tacitus. *Complete Works*. New York: Random House, 1942.

Tahmankar, D. V. *The Ranee of Jhansi*. London: Macgibbon & Kee, 1958.

Tarn, Sir William W. *Alexander the Great*. Cambridge: Cambridge University Press, 1948.

Taylor, Ida A. *Christina of Sweden*. London: Hutchinson, 1909.

Taylor, Kathryn: *Generations of Denial: Seventy-five Short Biographies of Women in History*. New York: Times Change Press, 1971.

Tiffany, Sharon W., and Kathleen J. Adams. *The Wild Woman: An Inquiry into the Anthropology of an Idea*. Cambridge: Schenkman, 1985.

Tod, James. *Annals and Antiquities of Rajast'han*. New Delhi: KMN Publishers, 1971.

Trafzer, Clifford E., and Richard D. Scheuerman. *Renegade Tribe: The Palouse Indians and the Invasion of the Inland Pacific Northwest*. Bellingham: Washington State University Press, 1986.

Truby, J. David. *Women at War*. Boulder: Paladin, 1977.

Tyrell, Robert Yelverton. *The Bacchae of Euripides*. London: Macmillan, 1906.

Tyrrell, Wm. Blake. *Amazons: A Study in Athenian Mythmaking*. Baltimore: Johns Hopkins University Press, 1984.

Van Voris, Jacqueline. *Constance de Markievicz: In the Cause of Ireland*. Amherst: University of Massachusetts Press, 1967.

Vaughan, Agnes Carr. *Zenobia of Palmyra*. New York: Doubleday, 1967.

Vermaseren, Maarten J. *Cybele and Attis: The Myth and the Cult*. London: Thames & Hudson, 1977.

Villiers du Terrage, Marc, Baron de. *Histoire des clubs de femmes et des légions d'Amazones 1793–1848–1871*. Paris: Plon-Nourrit, 1910.

Vincent, Arthur (ed.). *Lives of Twelve Bad Women: Illustrations and Reviews of Feminine Turpitude Set Forth by Impartial Hands*. Boston: Page, 1897.

Virgil. *The Aeneid*, tr. into prose by W. F. Jackson Knight. Baltimore: Penguin, 1956.

Vlahos, Olivia. *African Beginnings*. New York: Viking, 1967.

Walsh, William Thomas. *Isabella of Spain: The Last Crusader*. New York: McBride, 1930.

Watson, Georgina. *Christina*. New York: Farrar, Straus & Giroux, 1969.

Weigall, Arthur. *Sappho of Lesbos*. New York: Stokes, 1932.

Weigle, Marta. *Spiders & Spinsters: Women and Mythology*. Albuquerque: University of New Mexico Press, 1982.

Werner, Edward T. C. *Ancient Tales and Folklore of China*. London: Harrap, 1922.

Wickes, George. *The Amazon of Letters: The Life and Loves of Natalie Barney*. New York: Putnam, 1976.

Williams, Bret. *John Henry: A Bio-Bibliography*. Connecticut: Greenwood Press, 1983.

Williams, Chancellor. *The Destruction of Black Civilization: Great Issues of a Race 4500 B.C. to 2000 A.D.* Chicago: Third World Press, 1976.

Wilson, Dick. *The Long March: The Epic of Chinese Communism's Survival*. New York: Viking, 1971.

Winderbaum, Larry. *The Martial Arts Encyclopedia*. Washington, D.C.: Inscape, 1977.

Wolf, Margery, and Roxane Witkes. *Women in Chinese Society*. Stanford, California: Stanford University Press, 1975.

Wolstein, Diane, and S. N. Kramer. *Inanna, Queen of Heaven and Earth: Her Stories and Hymns from Sumer*. New York: Harper & Row, 1983.

Wright, Richardson. *Forgotten Women*. Philadelphia: Lippincott, 1928.

Zakaria, Rafiq. *Razia: Queen of India*. Bombay: Popular Prakashan, 1966.

WRIGHT LIBRARY
1776 FAR HILLS AVE.
DAYTON, OHIO 45419
NO LONGER PROPERTY
OF WRIGHT LIBRARY